MW01245024

The Confederate Navy in Europe

The
Confederate Navy
in Europe

Warren F. Spencer

THE UNIVERSITY OF ALABAMA PRESS

Tuscaloosa and London

Copyright © 1983
The University of Alabama Press
Tuscaloosa, Alabama 35487–0380
All rights reserved
Manufactured in the United States of America

First Paperback Printing 1997

∞

The paper on which this book is printed meets the minimum
requirements of American National Standard for Information
Science-Permanence of Paper for Printed Library Materials,
ANSI Z39.48–1984.

Library of Congress Cataloging-in-Publication Data

Spencer, Warren F., 1923–
The Confederate Navy in Europe.

Bibliography: p.
Includes index.
1. United States—History—Civil War, 1861–1865—Naval
operations—Confederate States. 2. Confederate States of
America. Navy—History. 3. United States—Foreign
relations—1861–1865. 4. Great Britain—Neutrality.
5. France—Neutrality. I. Title
E596.S7   973.7'57   81-23283
ISBN 0-8173-0861-X

British Library Cataloguing-in-Publication Data available

To Lynn M. Case
teacher, scholar, colleague,
and friend

Contents

Preface

The purpose of this work is to present a comprehensive study of the Confederate navy in Europe that will tie together the individual studies available and at the same time present my own interpretations of this interesting aspect of Civil War history. It is a tale of sailors, ships, and diplomats.

Because the focus is on Confederate navy personnel, I have had to depend primarily on the only collection of Confederate Navy Department correspondence that exists, which is published in *Official Records of the Union and Confederate Navies in the War of the Rebellion (ORN)*.[1] In many instances these letters are the only record of Confederate navy plans and activities in Europe. The United States State Department Correspondence in the National Archives, Washington, is useful for certain of the activities, but I have used it mostly for the diplomatic responses of the governments of Great Britain, the United States, and France. In England I have consulted the British Foreign Office correspondence and the Russell Papers in the Public Record Office, London, and the Palmerston Papers at the Historical Manuscripts Commission, National Register of Archives, London. In France I have used the Archives de la Marine, the Archives Nationales (Marine), and the Archives du Ministère des Affaires Etrangères. Most of the American and British documents pertinent to Confederate navy activities appear in government publications. Those of the United States have been published as submitted to Congress in *Papers Relating to the Foreign Relations of the United States* (1872). Those of Great Britain are scattered throughout the multivolume set of *Hansard Parliamentary Debates* and the *Parliamentary Papers;* these recently (1971) have been republished in convenient topical collections in the Irish University Press Area Studies Series, *The United States,* volume 17, *The American Civil War.* All of the material related to the Treaty of Washington and the Geneva arbitration also is published in this series in volumes 56–59, *The Treaty of Washington.* Wherever possible I have cited the published source for any document used or quoted because it is the location most available to the reader.

Several excellent scholarly works, based on the same British and American archival material I have used, touch closely on my theme. For the benefit of readers who may find it inconvenient to seek the original documents in faraway repositories, I have cited, wherever possible, these books as sources while also at times endorsing or differing with the interpretations of their authors. Wilbur Devereux Jones in his work on *The Confederate Rams at Birkenhead* (1961) was the first to use the British law officers' correspondence extensively, and I have relied heavily upon his work. Professor Frank J. Merli in *Great Britain and the Confederate Navy* (1970) continued this kind of in-depth research by using among other sources the British Home Office and Customs and Excise papers. Although many of these are published in the Irish University Press Area Studies Series, I frequently cite Merli's work as a more handy reference. I am particularly indebted to Merli for his extensive citations of certain documents that are peripheral to my story. His use of the Charles Francis Adams and Thomas H. Dudley collections has provided me with the reactions of these United States officials in England to the activities of the Confederate navy agents there. It was not Merli's intent to focus primarily on the Confederate naval agents in England nor on their activities in other parts of Europe, and he structured his material to present various episodes in England as events in themselves. Because our approaches are different we have arrived at different interpretations and conclusions even though we have used much the same archival sources. Professor David Paul Crook of the University of Queensland, Australia, has written the most recent work that touches upon the subject. His *The North, the South, and the Great Powers* (1974) presents a sweeping evaluation of the worldwide aspects of the American Civil War and includes proper references to the impact of the Confederate navy in Europe. Again because of a different approach, I differ from him in certain important conclusions. The purely diplomatic side of the Civil War is covered in several works. Ephraim Douglas Adams's *Great Britain and the American Civil War* (2 vols., 1925) and Frank L. Owsley's *King Cotton Diplomacy* (2nd ed., 1959) still are valuable although they have been revised by more recent scholarship. Professor Norman B. Ferris's first two volumes of a projected four-volume study of William H. Seward's diplomacy, *Desperate Diplomacy* (1976) and *The Trent Affair* (1977), are excellent and refreshing diplomatic studies in detail of the first two years of the war. Brian Jenkins, by adding Canadian considerations and sources, has contributed the most recent detailed diplomatic study of the full war years in his two-volume *Britain and the War for the Union* (1974, 1980). The purely business side of Confederate navy activity in England is covered by Richard I. Lester in *Confederate Finance and Purchasing in Great Britain* (1975). His use of the papers of financial houses and shipbuilders is especially valuable.

The bibliography for France and Confederate naval activities is more modest. In *The United States and France: Civil War Diplomacy* (1970) Lynn

M. Case and I examined the issues raised between Paris and Washington by the American Civil War. That is where I first encountered the Confederate navy abroad, but the work I did in that book on the navy reflected only the diplomatic side of the story. The different approach taken in this book has led me to revise some of the conclusions reached in the earlier one.

Sources not used in any of the works mentioned above cast additional light on the subject. To supplement the *ORN* letters I have used the diary of James H. North (University of North Carolina Library) and the William Conway Whittle Papers (University of Virginia Library) for the earlier years of the war. The Matthew Fontaine Maury Papers and Diary (Library of Congress, Manuscript Division) and the Whittle Papers (Kirn Memorial Public Library, Norfolk, Virginia) have provided valuable new insights into the later years of the war. Chapter 5 is based primarily on the Maury Papers and Diary, and the Confederate navy activity in France, especially, is elucidated by the Whittle Papers. The published memoirs of the chief Confederate navy officers who served in Europe also proved to be of value. James D. Bulloch based his *Secret Service of the Confederate States in Europe* on his own wartime correspondence. This book is notable for its candor and honesty, especially as Bulloch reflected on his work and its effects. Other memoirs, such as those of Raphael Semmes and Arthur Sinclair, were useful for the C.S.S. *Alabama* story.

These sources, including the secondary works, have enabled me to view the European wartime activities of Confederate navy personnel and various government officials as a continuous and interrelated historical event. Such a whole view reveals for the first time the impact of the *Trent* affair on Confederate ironclad ship construction in Europe, Confederate disillusionment with cruiser activity, Confederate concept of fleet as opposed to individual ship construction and strategic use, and limitations of European-built Confederate ironclad ships. But perhaps the most significant value of this approach to Confederate navy activity in Europe is the new light it casts on British and French concepts and application of their neutral obligations. In France this approach was highlighted by a diplomatic incident between John Slidell and Napoleon III that revises my own previous work. And the letters of Lord John Russell, from the vantage point of Confederate naval activity beginning in 1861 when the C.S.S. *Nashville* arrived in Southampton, have led me to conclude that British concepts of neutrality were consistent throughout the war and that the neutrality was implemented finally not as the result of the battles at Antietam, Gettysburg, and Vicksburg, but rather in accordance with a principle of international law as it related to the Confederate naval activity itself. It was the same principle on which the Geneva tribunal based its decisions in 1872.

Although I have arrived at a different conclusion from other scholars on the same issue of British neutrality and have introduced new concepts concerning the Confederate navy, I consider this work to be merely in support of theirs. I remain indebted to Professor Merli of Queens College, New York, for the correspondence we exchanged at the time his book was published because that was when the idea for this study first emerged. I am also particularly indebted to Wilbur Devereux Jones, my colleague and friend, for reading the manuscript and making valuable suggestions. Any errors of concept, fact, or interpretation that may remain, however, are mine alone.

As in all such undertakings, my gratitude is greatest to my greatest helper, one whose talents, patience, and loving criticism have sustained me through the effort: my wife, Elizabeth.

Warren F. Spencer
Athens, Georgia

The Confederate Navy in Europe

Introduction

The American Civil War introduced the world to modern warfare. In the age of industrialism and nationalism it was the first war fought on a vast scale over a protracted period of time. New technologies of industrialism produced new army weapons, created new naval architecture, and forced new concepts of land and sea strategies. As battles devoured increasing numbers of men and materials, both sides sought armaments produced in Europe. They sent agents to England, Belgium, and France to buy war matériel. Purchase and shipment of war goods involved extensive maritime activities that inevitably disrupted normal international relations. European as well as American economies were affected by the battlefields. The American Civil War was a total war with worldwide economic and maritime implications.

The economics of the Civil War affected the industrial neutral nations across the Atlantic Ocean. Armaments industries prospered but luxury export industries suffered. French silk workers who produced women's gloves and bows and ribbons were put out of work by the American war, and shippers and their cargo handlers in Bordeaux suffered underemployment. But the European textile industry, Europe's largest in terms of production and number of employees, was most affected. The long-staple cotton grown along the American southern deltas fed the textile factories in England and France. The Anglo-French need for this raw product encouraged the Confederates to anticipate their diplomatic and military aid and led to the Union government's attempt to deny this to the South by naval blockades. It was a dangerous game played in Richmond and Washington, a game that might have determined the issues of the war, for if Paris and London were to seek to obtain the cotton by recognizing the South and forcing the blockades, the North's industrial advantage would have been countered; but if the Europeans were to accept the North's blockade, the South's agrarian economy would be effectively isolated. The war then would grind slowly toward a Union victory as the North mobilized its superior industrial and human resources.

The Federal government needed a navy large enough to blockade thousands of miles of southern shores. The Confederate government needed a navy powerful enough to prevent this and to allow English and

French vessels to deliver materials of war in exchange for cotton. Meanwhile, until the respective naval positions became clarified, the diplomatic agents of both sides tried to convince the governments in London and Paris of the legitimacy of their respective causes and thus gain diplomatic support. The outcome of the war rested not only on the battlefields of northern Virginia and the Peninsula, but also in the corridors of Whitehall and the Quai d'Orsay and in the shipyards of England and France. The 1861 relative naval strength between North and South in the long run played a decisive role in the outcome of the war.

The apparent Union advantage of having an existent fleet was potentially balanced by the new naval developments of the nineteenth century. In the 1850s and 1860s more changes occurred in ship construction and armaments than had taken place in hundreds of years. The innovations, long seething in the minds of imaginative designers, were brought to reality by French naval engineers. By 1859 France had the first seagoing ironclad warship, the *Gloire*. Shocked by this challenge to British sea supremacy, Queen Victoria's Admiralty soon replied with its own iron-built ship. The *Warrior*, launched in 1860, became operative only in early 1862. This challenge and response created a heated naval race between the two countries as both built additional vessels of the *Gloire* and *Warrior* classes. Despite the contributions of such outstanding individuals as Robert Fulton, Matthew C. Perry, John M. Brooke, and John A. Dahlgren, the American navy prior to 1861 had taken little note of these vast changes.

At the outbreak of war, the Union's fleet was antiquated and dispersed to distant stations. Naval personnel, because of the seniority system, were headed by old and unimaginative officers and already had lost many modern-thinking younger officers. Congress refused to appropriate funds even for the limited increases requested by the Navy Department. President Abraham Lincoln had only forty ships to implement the blockade. But this was forty ships more than President Jefferson Davis had.

Although he had no ships, Davis did have several advantages. His navy-to-be would have fewer traditions to deter innovation; many of the frustrated middle-grade and junior officers of the Union navy followed their states into the Confederacy; and Davis's secretary of the navy, Stephen Russell Mallory, was a man of much maritime experience, imagination, and resourcefulness. He early demonstrated his capabilities by rushing the conversion of the captured Federal ship *Merrimack* into the Confederate ironclad *Virginia*. This ship practically destroyed the Union blockade fleet in Hampton Roads before the hastily built ironclad *Monitor* arrived in March 1862 to engage her in their historic battle. To

Mallory the battle's greatest significance was confirmation of his thesis that a small ironclad fleet could negate the North's numerical advantage in wooden ships. The naval war, with all its ramifications, now became a contest of industrial strength: the side that could produce more ironclad ships more quickly could win control of the coastal seas and, perhaps, win the war.

Secretary Mallory was one of the first to recognize the important correlation between sea power and industrial productive factors. Although the South had an abundance of timber, it lacked sufficient metallurgical resources, transportation, skilled labor, and managerial experience to create the industrial complex needed to design and manufacture an ironclad fleet. Furthermore, time was a factor. Even had the South possessed the natural resources, the North with its industrial complex could well have won the race and gotten the new ships into service more quickly. Having analyzed the situation long before the *Virginia-Monitor* battle, Mallory had devised a plan and had requested congressional funding to execute it.

As early as May 1861 Mallory stipulated a twofold mission for the Confederate navy: to destroy Northern merchant shipping on the high seas and to force the Federal blockade of Southern ports. Destruction of the merchant ships not only would cost the Union commercially, he stipulated, but also would draw Federal naval vessels away from blockade duty. The kind of vessel best suited for this mission, he maintained, was a fast ship propelled by both steam and sail and capable of keeping to sea for an extended period of time. The sort of vessel best suited to lift the blockade was an ironclad similar in design to the *Gloire*. According to Mallory:

> The United States have a constructed Navy; we have a Navy to construct, and as we cannot hope to compete with them in the number of their ships—the results of three-quarters of a century—wisdom and policy require us to build our ships in reference to those of the enemy, and that we should, in their construction, compensate by their offensive and defensive power for the inequality of numbers. This it is confidently believed can be accomplished by building plated or ironclad ships, a class of war vessels which has attracted much attention and elicited great research in England and France within the last five years.[1]

Acting on this analysis of the Southern needs, Mallory obtained from the Confederate Congress permission to purchase or build in France or England "one or two war steamers of the most modern and improved description, with a powerful armament and fully equipped for service."[2] To carry out this mission he selected two men, both former officers of the United States Navy: James D. Bulloch, who was assigned the mission of acquiring the kind of ship best suited to cruise against Northern commerce, and James H. North, who had the duty of acquiring the iron ships.

Mallory's strategy, born from the South's inability to produce technically advanced warships, was the genesis of the Confederate navy in Europe. Bulloch and North, arriving in England during the summer of 1861, were the harbingers of the worldwide impact of the American Civil War. Their activities would entangle the two leading European governments and would require the services of over a hundred more men.

Of the 1,773 names in the *Register of Officers of the Confederate States Navy: 1861–1865,* only 104 (5.8 percent) definitely can be placed in Europe at any time during the war. Seventy-two (69 percent) of the 104 definitely received shore assignments in Europe, and over half of these (48) reached Europe only in 1863 or later.[3] The arrival of the officers was coordinated with the anticipated completion of ships under construction, especially the Laird rams in Liverpool and James North's ironclad on the Clyde River at Glasgow. When these ships were detained by the British government, the officers were assigned to various shore duties, such as inspecting purchased arms and supplies, acting as couriers, maintaining the *Rappahannock* in Calais, France; only a very few were assigned to Confederate ships that touched at European ports. Late in 1864 some of these officers were assigned to blockade-runners that were purchased in England to run supplies into the Confederacy.

The activities of so many officers—moving from country to country, buying or building ships, contracting for armaments and arms, inspecting pistols, guns, clothing—required close cooperation with Confederate diplomatic agents, finance officials, and army procurement agents, which required a clear command structure and definition of functions among the naval officers themselves. The Confederate Navy Department failed miserably in providing this structure. Slow and uncertain communications between Richmond and Europe further acerbated the situation. The officers in Europe themselves gradually developed three definite patterns of structure and function, each pattern creating a distinct phase gradually fading from one to the other.

During the first phase, from 1861 to October 1863, there was no clear-cut naval command in Europe, no distinct area of operations or clear definition of functions. Each individual received authority directly from Richmond with resultant duplication of effort, contradictory policies, and financial confusion. In October 1863 Commodore Samuel Barron arrived in Europe to assume command of a fleet of ten ships then under construction in Great Britain and France. When the neutral governments refused to release the ships, Barron settled in Paris, where he established a kind of staff and personnel headquarters. He and

Bulloch acted together to define clearly their mutual functions and duties until the fall of 1864.

Beginning early in the fall of 1864 Bulloch emerged as the dominant force in Confederate naval activity in Europe. He devoted his energies primarily to procuring small steamers to serve as blockade-runners. His Liverpool office became a veritable European branch of the Confederate Department of the Navy. Appearing to defer to Barron's higher rank, Bulloch in reality made the decisions; he used Barron as a staff personnel officer and as a contact with John Slidell and James Mason, the Confederate government agents who were then in Paris.

These variations in naval command structure inevitably related to Confederate financial policies in Europe. At first the Confederacy tried to meet the cost of overseas purchases by sending specie to England. By March 1862 some $2,816,000 had been spent. Because the South had little gold and transshipment was dangerous, the Treasury Department shifted from specie to cotton. Between August 1862 and February 1864 cotton, the South's chief natural wealth, was the principal basis for naval purchases. Various instruments of credit based on future delivery of cotton were sent to individual agents for specific projects. But this system was inefficient and wasteful. Even the appointment of James Spence, a pro-South Liverpool businessman, as business agent for the Confederacy failed to correct the situation. The chief problem with this method, however, was lack of control. At one point, for instance, two naval agents had ships under construction with the same builder and while one was behind in his payments the other had paid for his ship in cash. Such contrast did not enhance the South's credit viability.

The mechanics and personnel for the final finance method developed out of the Erlanger loan.[4] In late 1862 banker Emile Erlanger in Paris suggested to John Slidell a grand sale of cotton bonds on the major European stock exchanges. Erlanger, the young and knowledgeable Paris head of Erlanger and Company of Frankfort, favorably impressed Slidell, who fully endorsed the plan. Slidell saw potential political advantage. A successful sale would reflect public confidence in the South, which should influence the European governments' attitude toward the Confederacy. So the financial plan became also a tool in the diplomatic struggle. After approval by the Confederate Congress, cotton bonds went on sale at the exchanges in London, Paris, Frankfort, Amsterdam, and Liverpool on 19 March 1863. The time was particularly right because during the winter of 1862–63 cotton was scarce in Europe, unemployment in the textile industry was high, and the South's defensive military posture seemed sound.

At first the issue of bonds with a face value of $15,000,000 went unexpectedly well, but with Southern defeats at Gettysburg and Vicksburg the bonds fell to a low of 36 per cent of par value. Yet, despite the "setbacks and disappointments," the loan produced $8,535,486, at the 1863 exchange rate, for Confederate use in Europe. Without it Confederate naval purchases in Europe in 1863–64 would have been impossible.

To coordinate and administer the Erlanger funds the Confederate government sent General Colin J. McRae to Paris. Replacing Spence as business agent in Europe, McRae and the diplomatic commissioners determined priorities and allotted funds to the various purchasing agents. The government forced close cooperation between its Treasury and Navy Department representatives in Europe when in 1864 it decided to increase cotton deliveries to Europe by operating its own blockade-runners. McRae and Bulloch worked together effectively to make the plan a success. It was this activity that essentially established Bulloch as the dominant naval official in Europe.

The firm of Fraser, Trenholm and Company, Liverpool, served as the common bond for the Confederate naval and financial institutions in Europe. It was associated with John Fraser and Company of Charleston and Trenholm Brothers of New York City. The three companies had an interlocking management, and one of the senior partners, George A. Trenholm of Charleston, replaced C. G. Memminger as Confederate secretary of the treasury. The Liverpool office served as the depository for all Confederate funds in Europe as well as headquarters for the Confederate navy throughout the war. Bulloch and Charles K. Prioleau, the company's Liverpool manager, developed a strong mutual respect and friendship. Prioleau not only provided Bulloch with emergency funds but also gave him office space where Bulloch established a clerical staff, kept his records, and even displayed the Confederate flag. This banking firm so committed itself to the Southern cause that at war's end, along with the Confederacy, it was bankrupt.[5]

The failure of the Confederate government to establish clear operational policies and to provide clear personnel responsibilities in both the naval and financial spheres adversely affected the efficiency of its European activities. War matériel that could have reached the Confederacy did not; jealousy and antagonism among the agents increased the waste and duplications. At one point in late 1862, for instance, James Bulloch had but 4,000 pounds sterling to meet all the procurement and personnel needs of the navy.[6] This so delayed the construction of three ships that none ever entered service. The failure was not merely an act of omission. President Jefferson Davis and his cabinet acted on two premises that proved to be false. They expected the war to be short and saw no need for an elaborate organization in Europe; they also anticipated early European diplomatic or military intervention in the war.[7] The first expectation was not unusual at the time. But was there validity in the second one even in 1861?

Secretary Mallory had based half his naval strategy on that assumption. His instructions to James North reflect his thinking and his optimism concerning the role European powers would play in the American Civil War.

> In this report you will find a general outline of the French frigate *Gloire*, which made her first cruise last summer, and which is regarded as the most formidable ship afloat. The Confederate States require a few ships of this description, ships that can receive without material injury the fire of the heaviest frigates and liners at short distances and whose guns, though few in number, with shell or hot shot, will enable them to destroy the wooden navy of the enemy.
>
> The views and disposition of the French Government are understood to be favorable to our cause, the recognition of our independence at an early date is is expected, and it is thought that arrangements might be made with it for the transfer to our government either directly or through some friendly intermediary of one of the armored frigates of the class of the *Gloire*.[8]

From their very inception, then, the Confederate States's efforts to acquire a navy were closely attuned to diplomacy.

Mallory's optimism for Lieutenant North's mission reveals the Confederate government's estimate of the diplomatic power of cotton. It illustrates the increasing economic interdependence created by nineteenth-century industrialization. Statistics for a decade prior to the war showed the French and British dependence on Southern cotton. Thousands of factories, hundreds of thousands of workers, and millions of dollars were involved. Southerners reasoned that a Northern blockade of their ports would elicit an immediate intervention by European governments fearful of domestic rebellion by desperate textile workers. During the first months after secession, in face of the ineffectual blockade, they further reasoned that an embargo on exporting cotton would force European action, and from September 1861 through January 1862 this embargo reduced by almost a million and a half bales the amount of cotton available at Southern ports for export to Europe.

But King Cotton diplomacy, so infallible from the Confederate point of view, contained certain fatal weaknesses. The Southerners miscalculated when they counted the bales of cotton exported and not those used in Europe. In 1861 previously exported cotton actually filled the warehouses in Southampton and Liverpool and supplied the English and French mills until the end of 1862. Thus the embargo did not affect the workers, who remained on the job. By late 1862 and 1863, when cotton did become scarce in Europe, President Lincoln's proclamations emancipating slaves in the District of Columbia (April 1862) and announcing the forthcoming general emancipation (September 1862) clarified the issues of the war for the workers and their nations' liberal leaders—John

Bright, W. E. Forster, and Richard Cobden in England and Prince
Napoleon, Emile Ollivier, and Jules Favre in France. The workers did
not take to the streets to force their governments to intervene in the war
even when unemployed during the 1862–63 winter. King Cotton diplomacy had failed.[9]

But suppose there had been a scarcity of cotton in Europe at the outset
of the war; would Great Britain and France have entered the fray?
Would their diplomatic postures toward North America and in
mid-nineteenth-century Europe have allowed them the freedom to
intervene in the American Civil War?

During the early days of the secession crisis the two governments
began consultations to develop a common policy toward American
events. Of the great powers in Europe only Britain and France had
extensive interests in North America. Britain's Canadian and Caribbean
colonial holdings obviously would be affected by an American war and
might be endangered by it. French interests in Mexico, already extensive, could be disrupted by such a war. Both countries had large
commercial and shipping interests in American waters. These similar
interests led to a close understanding on the American question. London
and Paris were ready to make similar responses to any international
character the conflict might assume. On 17 April 1861 President Davis
announced that he would issue letters of marque for privateers to prey
on Northern shipping in accordance with "international law," and two
days later President Lincoln proclaimed a blockade of ports of the
seceded states in "pursuance . . . of the law of nations." This policy
forced the governments of Great Britain and France to act in order to
guide and protect their own subjects. With little further correspondence
they issued proclamations of neutrality in the American conflict.[10] They
maintained this cooperation, amounting in fact to a joint policy,
throughout the remainder of the war.

A proclamation of neutrality is an instrument of international law, just
as the Davis and Lincoln statements were. It informs the world at large
and the belligerents in particular that the proclaiming government will
not take sides in the war then in process. It serves also to acquaint the
belligerents with the limitations of their actions on neutral soil. In this
case, the British proclamation, issued on 14 May 1861, forbade the
belligerents to recruit British subjects, equip or arm warships on British
territory or in British territorial waters, or in any way to enhance the
war-making power of such vessels. The French proclamation, issued on
10 June 1861, included the same prohibitions and further restricted
belligerent use of ports except to make repairs resulting from "acts of
God." The proclamations also forbade their own subjects from partici-
pating in any such activities and referred them to domestic laws that
gave the governments power to enforce the neutrality.

Both governments' enforcement laws were untested during a war of extensive maritime activity. The English law was the Foreign Enlistment Act of 1819. The French government's authority was based on a series of laws dating between 1681 and 1852. Founded on tradition and practice, the two governments' prohibitory authorities restricted their subjects in almost identical ways. British and French subjects could not build, equip, fit out, or arm belligerent vessels; they could not enlist on belligerent vessels or in any way contribute to the fighting abilities of such vessels. They could contract to repair such a vessel only to render it seaworthy. There were some differences. British subjects could sell coal to a belligerent vessel only once in every three months and then only in sufficient quantity to take the ship to a home port; French subjects could sell coal to belligerents without restraint. French officials by law could allow a belligerent ship to remain in a French port for only twenty-four hours, except for necessary repairs, and they could not adjudicate a belligerent prize. England soon adopted these last two provisions.

Neither government was empowered by domestic law to interfere with ordinary trade and commerce nor did international law and practice require it. International law did require the neutral to prevent one belligerent from making war on the other directly from the neutral's soil. Thus both belligerents could purchase munitions and supplies in the neutral countries, and did so. But should a neutral subject attempt to deliver such purchases to a belligerent, he acted at his own risk; his government by law had no responsibility to protect him.

It was the duty of both belligerent and neutral governments to observe the international obligations of neutrality. The neutral governments alone had responsibility for enforcing the domestic laws. Should a belligerent subject, say James D. Bulloch, scheme within the domestic law to put a war vessel to sea, as he did the C.S.S. *Alabama,* and the neutral government had insufficient power under its domestic law to prevent this, then the neutral government was at fault under international law and would be subject to compensate the other belligerent government of any damages inflicted by the vessel. It was precisely on this basis that the Geneva Arbitration Tribunal in 1872 awarded damages to the United States.[11]

The governments of Great Britain and France, then, had similar laws to protect their neutrality. Their respective abilities to impose the law differed according to their different political and judicial systems. English society in the nineteenth century was a liberal one ruled by law. The government's right to enforce its domestic law could be tested in a court of law in each case and interpreted by judicial procedure. Should the wording of the law be subject to various interpretations, as was the Foreign Englistment Act of 1819, then the government would lose its ability to act in accordance with its international obligations. Its only remedy was to seek parliamentary revision of the law, a politically embarrassing process, or to act apart from the law. This was precisely the British government's dilemma during the American Civil War. France did not have such political and judicial traditions. When the French government found its domestic laws to be insufficient, it could and did change them by issuing additional regulations. But to do this the French ministerial cabinet had to deal with Emperor Napoleon III, and that, too, proved to be a dilemma. Both neutral governments discovered that law clearly stated is quite different from law clearly enforced.

These laws—the British Foreign Enlistment Act of 1819 and the French laws enunciated in 1852—were tested for the first time during the Civil War. The Confederate naval activities occasioned the need in both countries to enforce the domestic law. In doing so, both countries faced divided public opinion and had to act within the structure of various international crises.

In England Prime Minister Lord Palmerston and Foreign Minister Lord John Russell dominated the government.[12] Each had served over thirty years at the highest levels, each previously having been both foreign minister and prime minister. Their parliamentary majority, however, was slim and they acted cautiously in domestic and foreign affairs. Even their own supporters in Parliament were divided on the American question. In general, those who most strongly supported the North were also advocates of domestic reform, and those who supported the South represented strong industrial and commercial interests. To ask Parliament to change the Foreign Enlistment Act in order to prevent the Confederate navy from getting warships to sea would invite accusation of submitting to pressure from the United States by the one side and demands for stricter controls by the other. Palmerston was determined to avoid both. Besides, there was a strong public and press opinion throughout the nation in favor of the South. Some of this was based on family relationships, ideology, and national pride, but most of it was economic. Textile manufacturers wanted cotton and they invested in Confederate cotton certificates or bonds to get it. Once they invested their money they became committed to the Confederate cause. At the same time church organizations and abolitionist societies vociferously supported the Northern cause. Still others felt that the Confederacy was defending its independence successfully and deserved full diplomatic recognition. Even Earl Russell in August and early September 1862, prior to learning of General Robert E. Lee's defeat at Antietam (17 September), seriously considered some diplomatic act to end the war.

In France a similar divided opinion existed. The republicans who opposed the Bonapartist regime were especially favorable to the North, and the shipping and textile interests wanted peace and cotton even at the expense of recognizing the Confederacy.[13] Emperor Napoleon III's two diplomatic overtures were aimed primarily at internal conditions. By 1862–63 unemployment among the textile workers had become serious and luxury and export industries were suffering. Napoleon III had to let his people know that he tried, at least, to end the war.

On the broader European stage in the 1860s English and French self-interests, so recently united during the Crimean War (1852–55), clashed. French rapprochement with Russia, Napoleon III's intrigues in Rumania, the Polish Insurrection (1863), the Danish War (1864), and early issues of German unification strained relations between Paris and London. One of the major reasons for this was Napoleon III's active foreign policy. He tended to identify with nationalist movements at least in part to change the 1815 European settlement, which he considered to be anti-French. Palmerston tended to see the French moves as challenges to British supremacy on the seas; his Crimean ally had become a threat. Only in American affairs did the two countries cooperate successfully.

British overseas interests affected by the Civil War were neutral shipping rights and Canada's safety. The London cabinet maintained a close watch on Canadian defense capabilities. During the *Trent* crisis the British government sent military reinforcements to both the army in Canada and the North American fleet. British shipping in and around American waters led to Northern capture of some British ships as prizes and to mistreatment of British subjects captured aboard blockade-runners. English newspapers and members of Parliament demanded that their government maintain neutral rights and some advocated the use of force if necessary.[14] These North American interests combined with recurring European diplomatic crises and the naval armaments race with France to establish neutrality as the only prudent British posture. Lord Palmerston, ever sensitive to English opinion and his slim parliamentary majority, decided early that his best policy was "to give no pretext for a quarrel with either side."[15] His was a consistent voice of neutrality. From the very beginning and especially after the settlement of the *Trent* affair there was little chance of British intervention in the war. Mallory's hopes were misplaced.

There were also compelling reasons for France to avoid military involvement in American affairs. Napoleon III was pulled in two directions by the Civil War. He had developed much sympathy for the prewar United States during his short American sojourn in the 1830s. He saw the country as young, vital, democratic, and industrially vigorous. He also appreciated its pre-1861 low tariff policy. The growing power and naval strength of the United States played a role in Napoleon's grand policy as a balance to British maritime preponderance. Early in the secession crisis he expressed sincere sympathy for the preservation of the Union. But as the war dragged on, the South's strong defense against the Northern armies stimulated his sense of fair play. He began to see the South's struggle more and more as an effort at national self-determination, a principle he advocated and supported in Rumania, Italy, Savoy, Nice, Poland, and even in Germany. While he could not condone slavery, until Lincoln's 1862 preliminary proclamations he could see little difference on that issue between the two sides. By that time the war was adversely affecting the French economy. Should the South successfully defend its separation from the North, as it appeared to be doing, it would remain an agricultural and an importing area and the industrial North would still balance Great Britain. So Napoleon III could see some advantages in the prospect of two American republics.

The emperor's perception of the American war also was affected by his view of the United States and Great Britain as an Anglo-Saxon power bloc threatening Latin peoples everywhere. He already was trying to balance British Mediterranean influence by developing strong ties with the Latin countries of Rumania, Italy, and Spain. In the New World he feared the southward expansion of the United States at the expense of Latin people in Central and South America. A separation of the Northern and Southern states would cut by half the force of this southern thrust. Just as he was working in the Mediterranean against British influence, so he was involved in Mexico to balance Anglo-Saxon influence in the Americas. A French-sponsored stable Mexican Empire could be an entering wedge for a Latin sphere of influence in the New World.

As textile unemployment grew and as French soldiers marched toward Mexico City, the emperor's personal policy appeared increasingly to favor the South. When he talked with Confederate agents or their British sympathizers he left the impression of being pro-Southern. In October 1862, as he proposed a three-power mediation in the war, he at the same time quietly and unofficially initiated the trend of events that led the Confederates to transfer their shipbuilding program from Liverpool and Glasgow to Bordeaux and Nantes.

Neither of the French ministers for foreign affairs, Edouard Thouvenel and after October 1862 Edouard Drouyn de Lhuys, approved the emperor's foreign policy. When French troops occupied Mexico City and Union forces won at Gettysburg and Vicksburg, Drouyn de Lhuys gained ministerial support to refuse delivery of French-built Confederate ships and to restrict belligerent use of French ports precisely because of the threat to Napoleon III's Mexican policy. The foreign minister had instituted a neutral policy toward the American war; the emperor's personal policy had become subordinate to the minister's official policy. This was a distinction the Southerners never made and they continued to expect French aid. This misunderstanding led to greater Confederate frustration in France than in England.[16]

Various combinations of events and persons, then, acted in both France and Great Britain to thwart Confederate expectations of early European intervention. French and British neutrality in the long run prevailed. Their neutrality proclamations lifted the Confederate States to the official status of a belligerent. This status guaranteed recognition by all neutrals as a legitimate war-making state and accorded Confederate ships treatment as regularly commissioned naval vessels. This advantage was balanced, however, by the restrictions imposed by the neutral governments. As it turned out, the Confederate navy in Europe could not fulfill Secretary Mallory's plans because to do so required not neutral treatment, but favored treatment.

The United States's diplomats and consular agents played a major role in preventing Confederate navy agents from violating British and French neutrality. Minister Charles Francis Adams in London and Consul Thomas H. Dudley in Liverpool, Minister William L. Dayton and Consul General (later Minister) John Bigelow in Paris all acted with skill and perseverance to prod the host governments to enforce their neutrality.[17] They discovered Confederate naval activity, gathered evidence, and pressured the foreign offices into action. They served the Union well.

Meanwhile the Confederate diplomatic agents, on whose shoulders the naval personnel leaned so heavily, at first were optimistic about European intervention. The first team President Davis sent to Europe was less than efficient. Unlike Adams and Dayton, they represented no recognized government. They expected help from King Cotton to overcome this problem. The three Confederate "commissioners"—sent not to specific countries but to Europe as a whole—concentrated at first on Great Britain. William L. Yancey, a fiery advocate not only of slavery but of restoring the slave trade; Pierre A. Rost, French-born resident of Louisiana and a former judge; and A. Dudley Mann, a pompous, former small-time diplomat for the United States, on 4 May 1861 were received unofficially by Lord John Russell. They left Whitehall optimistically expecting early British diplomatic recognition. Rost's interview in Paris with the Count de Morny, the emperor's illegitimate half-brother, was equally encouraging. But weeks stretched into months, and even after the early Southern victory at First Manassas, after the neutrality proclamations, and with rumors of a European cotton shortage, no new diplomatic act transpired. Perplexed, the three commissioners spent their time cultivating friends in London, influencing the press both there and in Paris. Yancey became impatient with ways of diplomacy and resigned. The Confederate government, too, decided it was time to have representation in each of the important European capitals and thus dissolved the commission. Rost was assigned to Spain and Mann to Brussels. Two new appointments were announced: James M. Mason for the London post and John Slidell for the Paris one.[18]

Mason had served in the United States Senate since 1847 as an outspoken advocate of states' rights. He supported slave states' interests as the author of the Fugitive Slave Act and as a defender of Preston Brooks's attack on Charles Sumner in the Senate chamber. Mason was arrogant, opinionated, and self-assured. He was too heavy-handed for delicate diplomacy. Yet he embodied many romantic characteristics that British aristocracy attributed to Southern gentlemen and thus was a success in London high society. He contributed little to the Confederate cause and, except for occasional financial advice, nothing to the procurement of a navy. British-Confederate relations became so tense in August 1863 that Secretary of State Judah P. Benjamin terminated Mason's mission to London.

John Slidell met with more apparent success in Paris. He established contact with Napoleon III through the imperial personal secretary and with Thouvenel and Drouyn de Lhuys through a permanent undersecretary, managed several unofficial interviews with the foreign ministers and emperor, established strong personal ties with many influential members of the imperial court and government and with members of the high financial circles. He had some favorable attributes: he spoke French fluently, was shrewd and sophisticated, entertained well, and was opportunistic. In naval affairs Slidell eventually took an active and effective role. Among the Southerners he initiated the transfer of ship construction to France and insisted on the Erlanger loan which financed those ships. In the spring of 1863 he nearly accomplished what could have been an important Confederate diplomatic victory. No other Southern diplomat came so close to success. Yet, he was self-deluding, misjudged French self-interests and purposes, and failed completely to understand the political relationships existing between the emperor and the ministers.

All these factors—from the Polish Insurrection to French intervention in Mexico, from inept Southern government leadership to skillful Northern diplomats—affected Confederate navy activity in Europe. That activity in turn affected European governments and international law. Southern navy officers did not always perceive these interrelationships and they experienced high hopes and crushing disappointments. The story of these joys and sorrows is basically a story of men working against great odds in strange countries.

CHAPTER 1

Confederate Naval Activity in Europe: The First Phase, 1861

The First Purchases

The primary mission of the Confederate naval agents in Europe was to procure ships and to put them to sea fully financed, armed, manned, and equipped. The first Confederate navy official assigned to Europe was James Dunwoody Bulloch, a civilian.

Bulloch's American ancestry reached back to 1729 when the first Bulloch emigrated from Scotland to South Carolina.[1] The family prospered in the coastal South. James Bulloch's great-grandfather fought in the American Revolution and his own father, Major James Stephens Bulloch, was a wealthy landowner and businessman in Savannah, Georgia. Major Bulloch married twice. James Dunwoody, the only child by his first wife, was born on 25 June 1823. In 1839, six years before the naval academy was established, James entered the United States Navy as a midshipman. A year later his father moved his second family to piedmont Georgia to establish the city of Roswell with five other founding families. Major Bulloch's Greek Revival home still stands on the west side of Roswell Square at the end of a long driveway, just nineteen miles north of Atlanta. James Bulloch's sea life prevented his ever living in Bulloch Hall, but he visited there and became acquainted with his half-brother Irvine S. and his half-sister Martha. Irvine later joined James in England, where he served as a midshipman in the Confederate States Navy, and Martha married Theodore Roosevelt, Sr. The young couple moved to New York City, where in 1858 Martha gave birth to the future twenty-sixth president of the United States.

Meanwhile James Bulloch pursued his naval career. He saw duty with David G. Farragut and David D. Porter, who became admirals in the United States Navy during the Civil War. Bulloch's last naval command was a ship detailed by the government to carry mail to California. In 1853, still a lieutenant after fourteen years, with no prospect for promotion, and having only "the certainty of remaining in a subordinate position until age had sapped the energies and ambitions," Bulloch resigned from the navy. He joined other former lieutenants who accepted government appointment as civilian commanders of coastal mail steamers, but after a few years he left government service altogether. He became a captain for a New York shipping line, carrying passengers and cargo to various ports of call between New York and New Orleans. James Bulloch married for the second time in 1857 and made his home in New York City, where his sister also lived. He must have become acquainted with young Theodore, who in later years referred to him as "Uncle Jimmie." Friends, family ties, and financial interests centered Bulloch's life in New York; he seemed to have cut himself completely from his Georgia roots. In 1861 he was skipper of the merchant ship *Bienville.*

Bulloch was in New Orleans when he heard of the firing on Fort Sumter. He had, in his own words, "become completely identified with the shipping interests of New York" and "had no property of any kind in the South." His "personal interests were wholly . . . in the North." Yet at 10:00 A.M. the day he heard of the shot at Fort Sumter, he wrote a letter to the Confederate Provisional Government at Montgomery, Alabama, offering his services. "All doubt . . . had vanished." His "heart and . . . head were with the South."[2] Communications were slow and before he received a response Louisiana state officials tried to buy the *Bienville.* As much as he wanted to help the South, he refused to sell because he claimed a moral obligation to return the ship to the rightful owners in New York. Within a month Bulloch sailed to New York, resigned his position, wound up his business affairs, and returned by train to the South. During the trip he noticed the "feverish excitement" in anticipation of the coming conflict. His stay in Montgomery was brief. Early in the morning after his midnight arrival, on 8 May, he met Secretary of the Navy Mallory for the first time. The meeting was short and direct:

> "Mr. Secretary, here is Captain Bulloch."
> "I am glad to see you: I want you to go to Europe. When can you start?"
> "I can start as soon as you explain what I am to do."

The fact of the mission so quickly settled, Mallory explained his plan for using cruisers against Northern shipping and assigned Bulloch the mission of going to England to buy or to build ships for that function. He warned of the necessity for discretion to avoid embarrassing the Confederate government by any alleged violation of neutral law. The next day, 9 May, Bulloch began his journey without identification papers or written orders. He traveled by train to Detroit, then to Montreal, where he took passage to England. He was only thirty-eight years old as he entered upon what would become a challenging, historic five-year mission.[3]

Youth notwithstanding, Bulloch was uniquely prepared to perform the demanding duties the war would require of him. During his years in the United States Navy he had learned the proper military protocol, studied the technology of the new naval gunnery and armaments requirements, and had traveled the major sea-lanes and entered the major harbors of the Western Hemisphere. During his years in merchant shipping he had learned the business of dealing with ships' suppliers, the techniques of loading ships, the handling of money and bills of exchange. His experiences had taught him the laws of the seas and of nations. Above all he was a man of irreproachable integrity and honesty whose reputation for fairdealing was well established when he had insisted upon returning the *Bienville* to New York. Ideally suited for his tasks through knowledge, character, and temperament, James D. Bulloch served the Confederate cause better than any other agent abroad. Efficient and careful, he accomplished more under adverse conditions than could have been expected.

While Bulloch was on the high seas Great Britain issued a proclamation of neutrality (14 May) and the Confederate States capital moved to Richmond, Virginia (29 May). Bulloch arrived in Liverpool on 4 June 1861.

Liverpool must have been the busiest and most crowded city Bulloch had ever seen. By 1861 it had become an integral part of the great Midlands industrial complex of England. It was connected to Manchester by canal in the eighteenth century and by railway in 1831. Situated on the east bank of the Mersey River, Liverpool served as the overseas port for the Midlands' vast trade in cotton goods, coal, and metal goods. So great was the volume of traffic that by 1861 the port of Birkenhead had grown on the west bank of the river, across from Liverpool. Both sides of the river were lined with docks and shipyards; maritime activity flourished: oceangoing steamers and sailors, canal barges, and harbor craft plied the river, all crisscrossed by ferries uniting the two sides of the mile-wide estuary into one beehive of activity. Industrialization had increased the surrounding factory cities' population threefold within the past fifty years and Liverpool had not escaped this concentration of humanity. When Bulloch arrived, the city had the amazing average of 66,000 persons per square mile, allowing no more than seven square yards for each citizen.[4] As he observed this crowded activity and elbowed into his own seven square yards, Bulloch undoubtedly would have agreed with Alexis de Tocqueville's earlier comment about Manchester:

"From this foul drain the greatest stream of human industry flows out to fertilize the whole world. . . . Here civilization works its miracles and civilized man is turned almost into a savage." Certainly in this city, amid the milling crowds and the industrial wonders, Bulloch would experience the most exhilarating achievements and the most devastating failures of his wartime mission.

But Bulloch wasted no time in speculation. Early on the day after his arrival he called upon Fraser, Trenholm and Company.[5] Although he had no identity papers, he was well received by Charles K. Prioleau, the Liverpool manager; the two men established a warm working and personal relationship that was to last throughout the war years. Later the same day Bulloch went to London to meet with the three Confederate diplomatic commissioners and Captain (later Major) Caleb Huse, the Confederate army purchasing agent who had been in England for about a month. From these meetings within a day or two after his arrival Bulloch learned the details of the British neutrality proclamation and the techniques of discreet purchasing activity, and he established sufficient credit to take the first steps toward accomplishing his mission. Typically, he spent no time on personal comfort: he did not rest from his two-month journey or seek plush living quarters. During the next few days he inspected several shipyards, redesigned the scale drawing of a ship, and signed a contract for the first Confederate navy vessel to be built in Europe. Bulloch fit perfectly into the bustling activity of Liverpool.

He chose the firm of William C. Miller and Sons to build the wooden vessel because William Miller had much experience building the kind of ship Mallory required, having been a shipwright in the Royal Navy and a naval constructor in Her Majesty's dockyards. Bulloch adapted a Royal Navy gunboat design to fit his particular needs. He elongated the midsection to gain additional speed, and he enlarged the rigging for a better spread of canvas. Because Miller was not an engineer, Bulloch contracted with Fawcett, Preston and Company to design and build the engines. Indeed, the contract and the financial arrangements for the whole ship were made with this company. Thus, so easily and so early, Bulloch began the construction of the future C.S.S. *Florida*.

While still negotiating with Fawcett, Preston and Company over the *Florida*, Bulloch crossed the Mersey River and visited the Laird's Birkenhead ironworks.[6] Founded in 1824, the William Laird and Sons Company by 1861 had established a firm reputation for naval architectural innovation. One of the founder's sons, John, had retired from active participation in the company and had won a seat in Parliament in 1859. Bulloch then conducted his affairs with John, Jr., and another son, William. After two visits to Birkenhead, Bulloch had persuaded the Lairds to design and build a wooden vessel to Bulloch's specifications.

This would be no hand-me-down design, no variation upon a British navy gunboat; it would be a ship designed specifically to accomplish the cruiser mission Mallory had described to Bulloch in Montgomery. It would be long and narrow with two powerful engines and wide sail surface. The brass propeller, of the latest design, would have a lifting device to prevent drag when the ship was under sail. All supplies and spare engine gear for a year's cruise would be provided at her launching. Built of the finest timber, copper fastened, with the best rigging materials, she was, in Bulloch's later opinion, "as fine a vessel, and as well found, as could have been turned out in any dockyard in the kingdom, . . . superior to any vessel of her date in fitness for the purposes of a sea rover, with no home but the sea, and no reliable source for supply but the prizes she might take."[7] She was, in a word, the future C.S.S. *Alabama*.

So well had Bulloch planned that only five days after his first funds arrived in Liverpool he signed the contract for the construction of the *Alabama* (1 August 1861).

Construction time for each ship was nine months. Meanwhile Bulloch busied himself with fulfilling the first written orders he received from Secretary Mallory. Dated 9 May 1861, the day he had departed from Montgomery, the dispatch was handcarried by Lieutenant James H. North to Bulloch in Liverpool. By mid-August, Bulloch had purchased the guns for the two ships, as well as cutlasses, sea-service rifles, revolvers, ammunition, clothing, shoes, and blankets for shipment to the Confederacy. Surprised to find that the manufacturers all needed extensive preparations to fill his orders, he was pleased with the steadiness and regularity of their work once it was under way. His plan was to buy a ship and take her loaded with army and navy goods to the Confederacy.

At the same time, Secretary Mallory put into motion the action designed to fulfill the other half of his strategy. Bulloch's mission was to procure cruisers to prey on Northern shipping and to lure Federal vessels from the blockading fleet. Mallory on 17 May 1861 issued orders to Lieutenant James H. North to go to Europe and buy or build ironclad naval vessels that could clear Southern ports of the remaining blockaders. Because he thought the French government, in its need for cotton, was favorable to the Southern cause, Mallory directed North to go to France and arrange to buy the *Gloire*.[8]

Lieutenant North, a South Carolinian, resigned his commission in the United States Navy on 15 January 1861 and was appointed to the same rank in the Confederate States Navy on 26 March. He was forty-seven years old, stood just under six feet tall, had blue eyes, a Grecian nose, a round chin, brown hair, and a fair complexion.[9] The lieutenant's first assignment was a shopping trip in the North: in New York, Philadelphia, and Baltimore he sought ships that would be suitable for Confederate use, but in vain. En route north he stepped off the train in Wilson, North Carolina, for a breath of air; to his chagrin, the train pulled off without him, taking his baggage with it. "I could almost have wept," he confided in his diary. "My things all went on with the cars. A great thing for a man in a hurry."[10] On the return trip south, he stopped to visit friends and relatives in Richmond and Norfolk before reaching his home in Charleston. This knack for being left behind, this tendency to dawdle while in a hurry, the futility of his purchasing trip—all are symptomatic of James North's career in Confederate service. Of all the agents in Europe, he was to be the least effective and the most bungling.

Recalled to Montgomery by telegram on 10 May, he met with Secretary Mallory three days later. Mallory informed him of his mission to Europe and promised to fund it by an appropriation of $2 million. North noted laconically that "there is more work ahead for me." After a visit to his home in Charleston, on 21 May he went to Savannah to board the sailing yacht *Camilla.* Unfavorable winds delayed departure until 25 May and in the meantime he sent for his wife Em and his daughter Annie to join him for the trip to Europe. Just before sailing North received a telegram from Mallory that established a perfect rationale for the inactivity he displayed during the first seven months of his European mission. It read: "Appropriation not available; bill failed for present. Make all enquiries and estimates; ascertain prices of building but do not contract without further advices from us."[11]

The *Camilla,* originally named the *America,* was the famous schooner that in 1851 won the first cup race against England. Captained by Henry Decie, she was bought by the Confederate government. She ran well before the winds but rolled fiercely and almost all aboard were seasick. Among North's copassengers was Major Edward C. Anderson of the Confederate army, sent to Europe to purchase munitions and to check on Captain Huse's activities.[12] Both North and Anderson carried government dispatches for the various agents already in Europe.

James North seems never to have been excited about his mission. Perhaps he sensed its futility because in many respects it was much more difficult than Bulloch's. It was naive to expect any government simply to transfer a warship to another government; but especially was it naive to expect Napoleon III, in a naval race with Great Britain, to do so. The European international situation, which Mallory had ignored, would not permit such a transaction, and the large store of surplus cotton in Europe did not require it. Even to contract for the construction of such a ship was difficult because in 1861 the available yards and metals were devoted to government contracts in both France and England. Only by paying premium prices could Lieutenant North have persuaded a builder to schedule a ship for the Confederacy between his contracts for his own government. And North had no money.

It is difficult to visualize North succeeding even if he had had the money. He would have had to beguile government officials and contractors; he would have had to dominate the design and building of the ship; he would have had to cooperate with other Confederate agents. This would have required a strong, outgoing personality: North would have had to be willing to innovate and to deviate from his orders and from regulations. Unfortunately James H. North could not meet these requirements. He had won promotions in the United States Navy by following regulations narrowly; he was a traditional and professional naval officer. So long as problems could be solved by applying the regulations in a traditional manner, North was effective, but in any other situation he was practically helpless. He neither had that sparkle of personality that could captivate French or English officials nor possessed the social niceties that would endear him to European aristocrats. While he did reflect a quiet strength that attracted some colleagues, others found him to be quietly indolent. Furthermore, he allowed pettiness and jealousy in matters such as military rank and prestige to interfere in his relations with his colleagues. He also failed to recognize the reality of interpersonal relationships and tended to blame his own failures on others. When a situation required action, North frequently resorted to complaints and complicated excuses. It appears that in the rush to establish a new department in a new government and to create a new navy, Secretary Mallory selected exactly the wrong man for a very delicate and difficult mission.

North and his fellows arrived in Liverpool on 25 June 1861. On the same day, North and Anderson delivered the dispatches to Bulloch and Huse in Prioleau's office at Fraser, Trenholm and Company, where North also deposited almost 800 pounds sterling. The North family then sought living quarters and settled in an apartment at 6 Oxford Street, where it was "like keeping house." The next day North went to London to deliver dispatches to Confederate Diplomatic Commissioners Yancey and Mann. From then until 2 August Lieutenant North and his family waited first in Liverpool then in London to confer once again with Bulloch. During those six weeks James North did nothing but wait—wait and sightsee. In London he visited the Crystal Palace, saw the changing of the guards, heard regimental band renditions, visited the Houses of Parliament, Westminster Abbey, the Queen's Stables, Hyde Park, the tower, and even Madame Toussaud's Wax Works; but he bought no ship, he visited no shipyard.[13]

James North did do some work; he inspected two guns and on 29 July visited the British ironclad ship *Warrior* without boarding the ship, thus seeing only the exterior. He also talked with a Mr. Prichard, a shipbuilder, but did not visit his works. That is all that North did. Contrast this with Bulloch, who within a matter of days, not weeks, after his own arrival in Liverpool had contracted for the future *Florida* and designed and ordered the future *Alabama,* and who did this with no more funds than North possessed.

Toward the end of July Lieutenant North became despondent. "I have been searching around to attend to things in the line of duty, but still have done very little." His conscience still hurt a few days later, but he managed to rationalize his inactivity: "I have been so much worried at the news from America that it has almost made me sick, especially when I think how little I am doing for my poor country. The only consolation I have is that the fault is *not* mine, and I am ready and willing to do anything in the world for her."[14] Perhaps it was at this time that he wrote his first dispatch to Secretary Mallory; it was both a lament and a report: "You must not forget that I am here without one dollar to carry out your orders. . . . " He had picked up some sound information, probably from Mr. Prichard in London: " . . . if I had millions at my command I could not carry out your views, as both France and England are both anxious to get all the ironclad ships they can buy." Still, he added, if he had the means, he "would at least make the attempt." The *Warrior,* he reported, "is too large for us and will draw more water than she can carry into most of our ports"; and then another lament: "I sometimes get dreadfully sick at heart when I think how little I am doing for my poor country."[15] The realization, however, did not jolt him into action.

Wearied with waiting and sight-seeing, heavy of heart, James North accepted Captain Decie's invitation to visit the *Camilla.* The yacht was passing the time by racing in the channel, so the North family joined Decie on 4 August, remaining aboard the schooner until the seventeenth. Lieutenant North was ill the first few days but recovered in time to help in one race, which the *Camilla* lost, and to be on deck when she collided with another yacht. Did he recall his bungling and futile purchasing trip to New York, Philadelphia, and Baltimore? Did he realize that he was once again dawdling when he should have been hurrying? Probably not; the inactivity was, after all, not his fault. He had to await word from Mallory.

Major Anderson visited the *Camilla* while the Norths were aboard. To his surprise, he "found North and his family in full possession of the cabin, looking absolutely dirty and seedy. It was an outrage to impose himself on the hospitality of Decie, but he seemed to have no shame about the matter." Anderson and Huse had acquired a ship to run the blockade with munitions and needed a naval officer to give her an official character. So, as "North was a naval officer and was loafing in England without means and really without an object," Anderson proposed that the Norths return home aboard the ship. North became indignant and replied with much warmth: "I have made up my mind *not to go.*" Anderson was "surprised at his reply and still more at his willingness to sponge on Decie as he was then doing, with his wife and child along with him, and the cabin littered with their luggage."[16]

Perhaps Anderson's comments were too strong; James North noted the incident in his diary with this only: "Anderson came down on a short visit—looks very well." Could nothing arouse the man to some sort of activity? He *was* capable of sensitive feelings. While aboard the *Camilla* he learned of the Confederate victory at First Manassas and wrote in his diary: "I am thankful to Almighty God, but would to God that it may be our last fight with our brothers of the North. It is too unnatural for brothers like us to be fighting."[17]

After seven days of pleasure racing and sailing, "for want of something better to do," Decie and the Norths sailed for Cherbourg, France, to examine that nation's ironclad battleship, the *Normandie*. They visited the French navy shipyard on 16 August and "examined" the ship from afar: "I did not see half as much as I wanted. Examined externally the ironclad frigate *Normandy* and was much pleased with what I could see of her."[18] The next day the Norths left Decie and traveled to Paris. In his excitement North "left the carpet bag in the carriage"—shades of Wilson, North Carolina! But at least he had arrived in the country to which Secretary Mallory had given top priority in his hope of acquiring a Confederate ironclad navy.

Once in Paris, the Norths' top priorities were finding living quarters and sight-seeing. They visited the "Louvre Galleries" and the Palais de l'Industrie; they listened to music in the Tuileries gardens; they toured the Luxembourg Palace, the markets, Notre Dame Cathedral, the Place de la Bastille, and the cemetery of Père la Chaise. They entered Annie in a school "so she could learn to converse in French." Finally, more than two weeks after his arrival, James North visited Vincennes, "the normal school established for the army." He saw firing exhibitions of various sized guns and would have liked to have seen more "but the unfortunate want of money prevents me from doing many things which would give one so much pleasure." He met with various people from various countries: Confederate Commissioner Pierre Rost, James M. Buchanan, former United States minister to Denmark, a Mr. Sanders, and a Mr. Ravenal from Charleston. On 23 September North "had an engagement to meet Captain Portugal of the Brazilian Navy at 10:30 at Mr. Bernard's. Had a long and interesting conversation on matters and things in general and on professional matters in particular."[19]

Such is the extent of Lieutenant North's activities in Paris. If he discussed the possibilities of buying or building ironclad ships in France, he did so through adventurous intermediaries such as Bernard, or with foreign navy officers who might be on a mission similar to his own, such as the Brazilian Captain Portugal. There are no indications that North even attempted to contact a French banker or an official of the French government, or to visit any of the many French private shipyards. The man to whom Secretary Mallory had entrusted the hopes for a Confederate ironclad navy was still dawdling when he should have been hurrying. Even so, North felt confident enough on 25 September to send "a short communication to the Secretary of the Navy which I hope he may receive." It was a telegram in direct contradiction to his earlier letter to Mallory; it read: "Can do anything in the way of building if I only had the money."[20] Was he truly so misled by a French broker named Bernard and by a so-called Brazilian navy captain with the unlikely name of Portugal?

Whatever may have been North's illusions, he was abruptly shocked back to reality when he learned Bulloch and Anderson were about to return to the Confederacy. "The news I think is so *important* that I shall leave for Liverpool in the morning."[21] North knew of Bulloch's construction contracts in Liverpool; he wondered who, in Bulloch's absence, would control them. He also knew he had failed in his own initial mission; would Bulloch's successes throw light on his own failures?

Secretary Mallory, already aware of North's failures, modified his original orders. He instructed North to remain in England to ascertain "the practicability of building or buying an ironclad war sloop." He should also "attend to such affairs as may be devolved upon" him until further notice.[22] Mallory then turned to building ironclad ships in the Confederacy. North's mission had ended in failure even before he or Mallory had realized it.

Slow and uncertain communications and the lack of proper naval command structure began to create confusion. North never did receive Mallory's modified orders and he became ever more resentful of the awkward position in which he was placed. Resentment turned to frustration when in Liverpool he discussed with James Bulloch the conduct of Confederate naval affairs in Europe during Bulloch's impending absence. For the first time he learned the full details of the Anderson-Bulloch plans. This led to a direct clash between the two Confederate navy agents.

Arriving in Liverpool on 8 October, North discovered that Anderson and Bulloch had decided as early as 2 September to purchase a fast steamer in order to ship arms and supplies to the Confederacy for both the army and navy, that by 11 September Bulloch had acquired the *Fingal*, a steamer of about 800 tons, and planned to command her personally.[23] North arrived in the midst of the details of loading the vessel. To see his colleagues so active and to have known nothing of their month-old plans must have added a sense of alienation to North's frustrations.

For the civilian Bulloch to have contracted for two ships, to have purchased munitions and supplies, and, to top it all, now to command a blockade-runner back to where the action was—all this was too much for North. He demanded that Bulloch transfer to him all the contracts, plans, specifications, and money that he possessed. Bulloch refused. The next day North put his demand in writing. The transfer, he said, was necessary to carry on "the work so handsomely begun by yourself . . . in case accident or any other cause should prevent your return."[24]

Bulloch replied in as mild a tone as he could, in order, he informed North, to avoid "grating on your feelings." He reminded the lieutenant that his own mission was a civilian one, that he was personally responsible for all funds, that the ship plans were his personal property, and, the most grating of all, that "the funds necessary to carry out my instructions arrived simultaneously with yourself." He then explained that his work, which he had "immediately" set about, had prevented him from regulating his movements to accommodate North's "supposed wish to communicate." Indeed, Bulloch wrote, he could not even locate North's whereabouts and had known of his presence in Paris only ten days prior to their meeting. He had, he explained, made all arrangements with Charles K. Prioleau to handle affairs during his absence.[25]

Reminded thus of his own lethargy, North's feelings of failure, frustration, and alienation now turned to hostility. Bulloch's rebuke, North confided to his diary, was the civilian's dislike for "a naval officer to have anything to do with his duties." The rejection was "nothing more than I expected. . . . Sorry, but so much for sending a naval officer and a civilian on the same duty." Subconsciously, then, he was placing the fault for his own inactivity in the lap of Secretary Mallory; North was "utterly demoralized."[26] He returned to Paris.

This hostility between North and Bulloch later affected the *Florida* and the *Alabama*. Their efficiency in Europe was forever damaged. When Bulloch sailed out of Holyhead in the heavily laden *Fingal* on 15 October, he left behind a sullen Lieutenant North and a Confederate navy program without leadership or energy. Until Bulloch's return five months later the naval procurement program lay in dead calm.

Although the program was in shambles when Bulloch left, the *Fingal* trip was not without significance. Unlike other blockade-runners, the *Fingal*'s cargo was consigned exclusively to the Confederate government. Bulloch's success, as he arrived off Factor's Walk in Savannah on 12 November, illustrated the value of government-owned ships to maneuver through the blockade. Upon arrival Bulloch suggested that the ship be returned to England with cotton and naval stores consigned to Fraser, Trenholm and Company. This action would provide badly needed funds in Europe for the Confederate purchasing agents. The *Fingal*, with Southern coastal pilots, then could return directly to the Confederacy with munitions.[27] This system would guarantee to the government almost regular supply runs and 100 percent of the cargo space. Unfortunately, it was a system the government took three years to implement.

While the *Fingal* awaited the return cargo in Savannah, Bulloch, taking no time to visit his relatives in Georgia, consulted with Mallory in Richmond.[28] Unlike their first meeting five months earlier, this was a leisurely one extending over several days. Apparently the respect that the Secretary of the Navy felt for the civilian agent had grown into confidence and admiration. Bulloch had proven himself to be a man of accomplishment. They discussed his proposal for the *Fingal*'s future use and Mallory approved it completely. Then Bulloch asked for a naval commission and orders to command the first completed ship under construction in Liverpool. He had indicated this desire in earlier correspondence and again Mallory assented. They also must have discussed Lieutenant North's chances of acquiring ironclad warships in Europe. Bulloch undoubtedly expressed his own opinion, leaving in Mallory's mind little hope for success. At any rate, while Bulloch was still in Richmond, Mallory in effect abandoned his European ironclad program and instructed North upon completion of the second ship under construction in Liverpool to assume command and take her to sea as a raider.[29] This must have pleased North except that it was some time before he received the dispatch. Meanwhile in the South Bulloch confidently went about the business of preparing the *Fingal* for her return voyage to Europe.

Bulloch's confidence seemed well placed in November and December 1861; it was shared by Confederate officials on both sides of the Atlantic. This optimism resulted from the news of the *Trent* affair. When on 8 November Captain Charles D. Wilkes of the U.S.S. *San Jacinto* forceably removed John Slidell and James Mason, the newly appointed Confederate commissioners to France and England, off the British ship *Trent,* rumors of war between Great Britain and the United States radiated from the Bahama Straits to both coasts of the Atlantic Ocean. The threat of war was real. The British government within weeks approved reinforcement of Canadian defenses by sending 5,000 additional troops and by strengthening its North American fleet.[30] In the South, Bulloch and Mallory reacted to the prospect of a British alliance. Anticipating an early return to Liverpool to assume command of the *Florida,* which Mallory had given him, Bulloch made several sets of plans to get her safely down the Mersey River. One such plan was based on a state of war existing between Great Britain and the United States. At the same time, Mallory wrote that "the evident change of feeling and opinion in England in relation to our country induces me to believe that we may now contract for the construction and delivery" of armored and armed war vessels in that country.[31] Thus, because of the *Trent* affair, Mallory returned to his recently abandoned plans to buy or build ironclad ships in Europe. In a very real sense the decision to build the

Laird rams and the French ones, one of which became the C.S.S. *Stonewall,* resulted from the Southern optimism during the *Trent* crisis. In Southampton, England, another Confederate officer anticipated British cooperation in transforming his little dispatch vessel into a warship unless the United States should back down.[32] Indeed, the several weeks between 27 November, when news of the seizure of Slidell and Mason first reached Europe, and 8 January 1862, when news of their release reached London and Paris, were heady days when the Confederates made grandiose plans. The seizure of Slidell and Mason not only had induced the British to reinforce their military establishments in and around North America, it also had induced Secretary of the Navy Mallory to reverse his long-range naval strategy. The *Trent* crisis thus created and perpetuated diplomatic problems concerning Confederate ironclad ship construction in England and France for at least three years.

The Confederates in Europe realized before those in Richmond that an unfavorable reaction in England quickly followed the release of the two diplomats. Lieutenant North correctly noted this reaction when he warned Mallory of increased difficulties in getting ships out of England.[33] And he was not the only one. Captain Raphael Semmes, who had sailed the *Sumter* to European waters, also remarked on it, as did Henry Hotze, the South's propaganda expert in Europe, who wrote that the incident "has done us incalculable injury."[34] Although the war scare had been real enough, throughout the weeks of anxiety Lord Palmerston, with an eye to European affairs, had counted on a peaceful settlement.[35] When it came, the British government began to apply a closer surveillance over possible Southern violations of the English neutrality law.

In American waters the United States government tightened its blockading efforts. Bulloch found it impossible to take the *Fingal* out of Savannah and eventually abandoned the project. The *Fingal,* later converted to the armorclad C.S.S. *Atlanta,* remained in port until 1863 when she was captured by a Federal ironclad of the monitor class. Bulloch made his way back to England aboard a John Fraser and Company vessel out of Wilmington, North Carolina. But he did not arrive in Liverpool until 10 March 1862.[36]

During all of this time, between mid-October 1861 and early March 1862, the Confederate navy established some firsts in Europe.

The First Warfare in European Waters

One accomplishment was the arrival of the first warship bearing the Confederate flag. She was the C.S.S. *Nashville,* which arrived in Southampton on 21 November 1861. A side-wheeler, she had been used in the

New York–Charleston passenger service. Seized by the Confederates in Charleston, the *Nashville* originally was intended to take Slidell and Mason to England. The dangers of running the blockade, however, caused a change of plans that resulted in the *Trent* incident. Nonetheless, the side-wheeler under Lieutenant Robert B. Pegram's command later slipped past the Federal ships and proceeded to Europe, capturing and burning the U.S. merchant ship *Harvey Birch* en route. The arrival of the *Nashville* in Southampton was occasion for excitement, and the little ship became a temporary celebrity. Even Lord Palmerston paid an unofficial visit, according to young Lieutenant William C. Whittle, Jr. When the prince consort died on 14 December 1861, the *Nashville* half-masted her Confederate flag; this was the first time this flag had so recognized a foreign nation's mourning.[37]

The *Nashville*'s voyage decoyed three Union warships from the route actually taken by Slidell and Mason. This subterfuge could have been her chief mission. Some thought, however, that she sailed to England primarily to prove to the European powers that the Confederacy had a navy capable of taking to the high seas.[38] Such action would justify the Confederacy's status as a belligerent and contribute to demands for diplomatic recognition. The reception Southampton gave to the ship and her men seemed to justify the trip. Officers and crew members were entertained as heroes in the pubs and the hotels. Lieutenant Pegram knew, however, that the *Nashville* was not a powerful ship. Her decks were too weak to support heavy guns and her keel and side structures had been damaged during her run through the blockade. She needed repairs to make her seaworthy. Amid the excitement created by the ship's presence, Pegram quietly requested the British authorities to permit him to use the port facilities to make the repairs. Accordingly, the *Nashville* received new caulking and entered a dry dock for work on her keel.[39] This took longer than Pegram had expected, and the *Nashville* was not able to leave Southampton until 3 February 1862. Although seaworthy the side-wheeler was too small and too lightly armed to serve as a naval vessel. Upon her return to the Confederacy she was sold to private interests. Her career on the surface appears not only to have been short but also futile; she hardly awed the British as an example of Confederate naval power.

Beneath the surface, however, she had raised for the first time in the war certain serious points of diplomacy and international law and in so doing for the first time tested certain provisions of the Foreign Enlistment Act. The fact that the *Nashville* sank the *Harvey Birch* and landed her captain and crew in England prompted Charles Francis Adams to remonstrate vigorously with Lord John Russell. Adams questioned the nature of the ship and the British neutral obligations toward belligerent maritime rights to a port and use of repair facilities. He accused the ship of being a pirate and suggested she be treated as such. In the exchanges that followed, Russell stated a principle of international law that would have significant ramifications throughout the remainder of the war and would become the basic principle on which the postwar Geneva arbitration would be based.[40] Because the *Nashville*'s Southampton visit overlapped the crucial diplomacy concerning the *Trent* affair, these *Nashville* issues became blurred by the more immediate crisis. Had this overlap not occurred, it is possible that England's obligations in relation to the later Confederate ship construction in Great Britain would have been settled during the first year of the war.[41]

The appearance of the *Nashville* raised questions directly related to the queen's proclamation of neutrality, which recognized the Confederacy as a belligerent, and to the British domestic law designed to enforce that neutrality, the Foreign Enlistment Act of 1819. Its provisions pertaining to maritime affairs laid down the rules within which belligerent ships could visit British ports and could use the port repair facilities, and within British territory it forbade British subjects from enlisting in the service of such ships or from in any way enhancing the warmaking powers of such ships. All of these provisions were designed to prevent a belligerent from being able to make war on its enemy directly from British neutral territory. International custom and practice also determined the extent to which a neutral was obligated to protect its neutrality.

Even before Adams questioned Russell, these obligations, as Russell put it, caused "careful and anxious considerations" within the British government concerning the *Nashville*. Both Russell and Palmerston consulted law officers on the various issues raised. As a result Russell was able to respond to Adams with some degree of assurance. The *Nashville*, he wrote, was a regular commissioned ship of war and not a pirate. Her officers had received their commissions from a recognized belligerent power. She was entitled therefore to the use of port facilities that might be needed to make her seaworthy. She could not, however, in any way enhance her war-making power and Russell had already issued instructions to that effect. Furthermore, the British government had ascertained that the sinking of the *Harvey Birch* had occurred in international waters and therefore did not violate British neutrality. Russell assured Adams that he intended to enforce the law and maintain British neutrality. To emphasize this fact, he informed Adams on 28 November 1861 "that if, in order to maintain inviolate the neutral character which Her Majesty has assumed, Her Majesty's Government should find it necessary to adopt further measures, within the limits of public law, Her Majesty will be advised to adopt such measures."[42]

In effect Russell acknowledged to Adams that England's obligation to protect its neutrality was not limited by the Foreign Enlistment Act and that if necessary England would change that legislation in order to insure its neutrality. It was a theme to which he would return within three months and it embodied the concept of international law that in 1871 was incorporated into the Treaty of Washington, which in turn stipulated the rules for the Geneva arbitration. It was furthermore a clear statement of England's intent to treat the two belligerents in a completely neutral fashion in accordance with international practice. This statement and this intent, elicited by the *Nashville*'s visit to Southampton, strangely has been overlooked even by recent scholars. Although the United States government consistently opposed the British proclamation of neutrality because of the belligerent status it bestowed on the Confederacy, in this first test of its maritime provisions Adams seems to have accepted it with all the implications. On 2 January 1862 he informed Secretary of State Seward that in its handling of the *Nashville*'s repairs the British government "has been faithful and thorough."[43]

The *Nashville*'s presence in Southampton led to the clarification of the status of Confederate ships as regular ships of war, and it provided the first test during the Civil War for another provision of the Foreign Enlistment Act. Designed to prevent one belligerent from making war on another directly from British neutral waters, the act stipulated that if ships of both warring countries were in a harbor at the same time, the one could leave only after a twenty-four-hour delay following the departure of the other. In early January 1862 the United States warship *Tuscarora* under Commander T. Augustus Craven entered Southampton and after some jockeying tied up adjacent to the *Nashville*.[44] Tensions built between the crews of the two ships; fistfights and barroom brawls ensued. Commander Craven even placed armed men on guard over the *Nashville*. Russell complained to Adams about the conduct of the Union navy and informed him about the twenty-four-hour rule. The United States minister nevertheless was convinced that the *Tuscarora* could prevent the *Nashville* from ever leaving Southampton as a Confederate warship. He wondered if it could be sold by the Confederates and, if the British allowed the sale, if that would be a violation of neutrality.[45] Events soon answered such speculation.

The port authorities carefully had informed both ship commanders of neutral restrictions and especially of the twenty-four-hour rule. After Pegram had completed his allowed repairs and Russell was satisfied that Great Britain had fulfilled its neutral obligations, the *Nashville* was ready to sail. Pegram gave notice of his intent to leave Southampton. The Southern side-wheeler was no match for the *Tuscarora* in either firepower or speed. Pegram needed time for a head start, which would depend on how faithfully the British enforced their neutrality. How would Her Majesty's government react to this first Confederate test of the twenty-four-hour rule? No one knew, and tension grew on both sides. The *Nashville*'s safety was in the hands of the English. Pegram and his new second-in-command, Lieutenant William C. Whittle, Jr., were relieved when they saw evidence that the British intended, as Russell had said, to enforce their neutrality. The British navy frigate *Shannon* slowly moved into the harbor and anchored so as to prevent the departure of the *Tuscarora*. Under this British protection the *Nashville* safely slipped out of Southampton and with the twenty-four-hour lead time reached the Southern coast unmolested. The two commanders had learned a valid lesson: Confederate skippers could count on neutral protection; Union skippers would have to lay off in international waters to challenge a Confederate warship after she left a neutral harbor. Craven was soon to apply this lesson at Gibraltar and two and a half years later Captain John A. Winslow of the U.S.S. *Kearsarge* would do the same off Cherbourg, France.

Before leaving Southampton Lieutenant Pegram had detached Lieutenant Charles M. Fauntleroy, his second-in-command. There was a growing demand for navy officers in Europe, where only Lieutenant James North was stationed. Fauntleroy took charge of the privately owned blockade-runner *Economist* and made several trips into the Confederacy. He later served as commander of the C.S.S. *Rappahannock* in Calais, France. Three other officers of the *Nashville* later saw service aboard the C.S.S. *Alabama,* and Lieutenant Whittle and Irvine S. Bulloch, James Bulloch's half-brother, returned to European duty.

The *Nashville*'s trip, at first glance so apparently insignificant, was in fact a precedent-setting voyage. She provided needed officer personnel in Europe, she established the belligerent status of Confederate warships in face of Union protests, she proved the safety of neutral ports, and most importantly she elicited Russell's significant statement of adherence to traditional international neutral obligations regardless of domestic law. And all this was accomplished during the *Trent* crisis. The *Nashville*'s voyage was indeed a historic one.

While the *Nashville* lay in Southampton harbor, the second Confederate navy vessel arrived in European waters. She was the small steamer *Sumter,* under command of the man who would become the most famous of all the Confederate sea captains, Raphael Semmes. Semmes entered the United States Navy in 1832 and by 1861 achieved the rank of commander and was serving in Washington as secretary of the lighthouse board. During this interval he also studied law, naval and maritime subjects, and cultivated his interests in world literature. He wrote several books, including *Service Afloat and Ashore during the Mexican War,* a lively account of his experiences during that conflict. Later, after the Civil War, he would write *Memoirs of Service Afloat during the War Between the States.*[46] Born in Maryland in 1809, Semmes moved his family to Alabama in 1842 and became a strong advocate of the Southern cause. He resigned his United States commission in February 1861 and soon was appointed a commander in the Confederate States Navy. After a purchasing mission (similar to North's) to the Northern states in the spring of 1861, Semmes first served in Montgomery as head of the Lighthouse Bureau. This service was short-lived; in two weeks, on 21 April 1861, Secretary of the Navy Mallory ordered Semmes to New Orleans to take command of the *Sumter,* which was named in honor of the fort in Charleston harbor.

The *Sumter* was a small screw steamer of 437 tons with only a 184-foot length. It took Semmes two months to direct the renovations necessary to convert her into a vessel of war. He had a fine complement of officers: all were native Southerners with experience in the United States Navy and many of them later were leaders in the Confederate naval activities in Europe: Lieutenants John McIntosh Kell, Robert T. Chapman, and William E. Evans; Surgeon Francis L. Galt; Engineer William P. Brooks; and Captain's Clerk W. Breedlove Smith. The whole crew totaled ninety-two including twenty marines. Of the enlisted personnel, only about half a dozen were natives of the Confederacy; the remainder were from among the seamen of the port of New Orleans and mostly were English and Irish. This pattern of Southern-born officers and foreign seamen remained constant throughout the war for all oceangoing Confederate naval ships. It is significant that the pattern first was established by a ship completely manned from a Confederate port, because it reflects one of the South's basic naval scarcities: trained seamen. Despite her unmilitary bearing, Semmes found the *Sumter* to have easy and graceful lines with "a sort of saucy air about her." From his years at sea Semmes understood both his crew and his ship and through consistent, humane discipline and training he blended them into an effective unit, providing the South with its first commercial raider.

The *Sumter* steamed through the Federal blockade of the Mississippi River estuary on 30 June 1861 and after an exciting and close chase by the U.S.S. *Brooklyn* reached the welcomed swells of the open seas. Only three days later, off the coast of Cuba, the *Sumter* made her first capture, the United States merchant vessel *Golden Rocket.* Semmes transferred the crew and all stores he could use, then set aflame the *Golden Rocket.* Those flames, leaping from the quiet Caribbean waters, were but the beginning of Confederate destructions that virtually would drive Federal merchant shipping from the high seas, and they stimulated the Northern views that throughout the war would characterize such Confederate navy activities as piracy. Semmes thus was the first notorious Southern "pirate" and he was yet to earn an even more venomous reputation as commander of the C.S.S. *Alabama*. Thus the *Sumter* under Commander Semmes established early in the war the pattern both for destroying Northern merchant shipping and for earning the epithets so lavishly bestowed by the Northern officials and press.

Semmes was sensitive to the role he was creating. At the time in his diary and later in his memoirs he strove to establish that he was "making war on the enemy's commerce and not on her unarmed seamen." On board the *Sumter* he treated the prisoners leniently, giving them the same privileges enjoyed by his own crew. But the image of an unarmed merchant ship deliberately set aflame and burning on the high seas grated against world opinion. In the long run that opinion reacted against the Southern cause and James Bulloch soon recommended to Mallory that the South refrain from such activity.[47] Without other resources, however, this kind of warfare remained the chief naval weapon the Confederacy was able to use against the North. It was a weapon that even the Southern navy leaders did not like.

Commander Semmes as the first captain of a Confederate raider also established what might be designated as the "search and destroy" technique that later and more famous ships would use. Most cargo vessels were still sailing ships and followed sea paths laid out by the prevailing winds and currents. The flow of goods between certain markets created crossroads-at-sea for the sailing merchantmen and by laying off these known spots Semmes and his successors were able to raise many a cry of "Sail Ho!" The Confederate sea raiders, far from looking for needles in a watery haystack, enjoyed an advantage over their prey that resulted in a high degree of efficiency.

After a successful voyage, Semmes headed for European waters. On 4 January 1862 the first Confederate commerce raider arrived in Europe at Cadiz, Spain.[48] The welcome was cool. No continental government had yet faced the fact of hosting a destructive ship of the unrecognized Confederacy. Neutrality law was clear in print, but the Spanish authorities were undecided as to its application in practice. Should the rebel commander be allowed to discharge his prisoners? What was the condition of the crew's health? What was the extent of the needed repairs to the ship? Should Semmes be allowed to buy coal? Should government dry docks be made available? How long should the ship be permitted to stay in port? One harbor official passed Semmes's requests to another until the *Sumter*'s commander became dizzy. At first he was ordered out within twenty-four hours; then he was allowed to stay and to dismiss his prisoners; then the ship was permitted the needed repairs and even use of a government dry dock. But Semmes had to argue each point and he had to await telegraphic answers from Madrid. During his thirteen-day stay, a dozen of his crew jumped ship, seduced, according to Semmes, by "the agents, spies, and pimps" of the United States. Finally, low on funds, Semmes requested time to receive them from the Confederate agents in London, but the Spanish authorities would give him only twenty-four hours more. Frustrated, discouraged, and resentful, he decided to steam out of Cadiz with coal enough only for the short trip to Gibraltar.

Semmes never did appreciate fully the novelty of the situation he had created and thus he did not understand the embarrassment of the Spanish officials. Rather he blamed their attitude on their fear of the United States. But he did correctly understand that in order to enforce its neutrality a state itself must be powerful. He had learned, he wrote, "that all of the weak powers were timid, and henceforth, I rarely entered any but an English or a French port."[49] This lesson explains as well as do the maritime interests and facilities of England and France why the Confederate navy officers centered their activities in those two countries. The Netherlands, the Scandinavian countries, Italy, and Spain all had shipyards and could have built the wooden ships used as raiders, but the Confederates never once considered placing an order in any of those countries; they used only the yards of the two strongest countries in Europe, and Semmes early in the war articulated the reasons.

On her way to Gibraltar the *Sumter* took one last fling at the enemy. Sighting two Northern ships, Semmes changed course from the British harbor and gave pursuit. Observed by a large crowd on the Rock, he overhauled the bark *Neapolitan* of Kingston, Massachusetts, on her way to Boston with a cargo of fruits and fifty tons of sulfur, a contraband of war. Without hesitation, Semmes burned the New England bark in the Straits of Gibraltar within sight of two continents. After stopping another ship with a verified neutral cargo and bonding her, he turned to the Gibraltar harbor, where he arrived just after dark on 18 January 1862.[50] The *Sumter* was the first true Confederate commerce raider to enter a European port and to capture and burn a ship within sight of that port.

Nonetheless, the British unlike the Spanish received the *Sumter* with warmth and accommodation. Although the little ship would never sail out of the harbor under the Confederate flag, that was not the fault of the British. Semmes wrote of his experiences at Gibraltar in glowing terms.[51] He was received by the governor, granted a military review, conducted through the rock tunnels, feasted, and feted. His officers were entertained; his men were given provisions and recreation. And Semmes even received funds through Fraser, Trenholm and Company. He remained on the island for almost three months, thoroughly enjoying himself.

Meanwhile the *Sumter* and her crew achieved two more firsts. Her reputation had preceded her and she attracted three Federal ships that hovered off Gibraltar. She became the first Confederate ship to be blockaded in a European port by Federal warships lying in wait outside the harbor. Commander Craven, still bitter about losing the *Nashville* in Southampton, steamed the *Tuscarora* to Tangiers, joining two other ships to form the blockade. To outrun those ships, the *Sumter*'s boilers needed repair, which the British authorities permitted, and she needed a full supply of coal, which presented an unexpected problem. Private coal handlers, under pressure from the Federal consul and his agents, refused to sell coal to the *Sumter* except at double or triple the going price. Even the local British officials, by now friends of Semmes, refused to sell government coal. Stymied on both sides, Semmes sent Paymaster Henry Myers to Cadiz to buy coal. But the ship on which Myers took passage stopped at Tangiers, where the United States consul had him arrested and sent to the United States. Semmes protested but to no avail; it was another example of the dangers in dealing with a weak neutral.[52] Myers, then, was the first Confederate navy officer made prisoner in European waters.

Frustrated in his efforts to procure coal, Semmes began to realize the ship's limitations: she could store no more than eight days' supply of fuel; she was slowed under sail by the drag of her propeller; she was too small to keep to the sea over a long period of time. He decided to abandon her despite the attachment a captain has for his ship. Except for a small detail to remain aboard, he paid off the crew. The officers went to London, where James Bulloch, back in England, retained many of them and put them to work. Semmes, reluctant to leave the ship, reflected upon her cruise.[53] She had been the first ship to flex the South's maritime muscle. She had captured and burned eight Northern merchantmen and had bonded ten others. She had occupied five or six of the best Federal warships, thus weakening the North's blockading fleet. The cost of the *Sumter*'s cruise was only $28,000, about the value of one of her victims. The *Sumter* had served well, and on 19 April 1862 Semmes saluted her as he sailed out of Gibraltar en route to London.

Although her captain had left her, the little ship's story was not yet ended. A scourge to Yankee shipping during her cruise, the *Sumter*, almost as if in retaliation for her abandonment, soon became a burden to the Confederates in Europe. Semmes's hopes to reactivate the ship with coal and crew from England were frustrated by high costs and tragic events. He had detailed Lieutenant Richard F. Armstrong and Acting Master I. T. Hester with a crew of ten to maintain the ship. Armstrong left the *Sumter* in late July to rejoin Semmes, and Midshipman William Andrews replaced him. Harbor costs were high and inactivity took its toll of stores and provisions aboard the ship, most of which by early August

were not fit for use and "the rest of them spoiling very fast." Life aboard
the Sumter must have been tedious and dull; the prospects for getting
the ship back to sea must have appeared hopeless. At any rate, morale
among the ten enlisted men suffered under the leadership of the
recently arrived young midshipman. Inactivity, boredom, hopelessness
inevitably led to hot tempers. In October 1862, Hester attacked and
killed Midshipman Andrews, who thus became the first Confederate
naval fatality in Europe.[54] Arrested by the British authorities, Hester
said he acted only in the interests of his country because, he claimed,
Andrews was about to turn the ship over to Federal authorities. Hester
also claimed the right to counsel and the transfer of his custody to the
Confederate government. James Mason and James Bulloch in England
immediately sent Lieutenant Robert T. Chapman, formerly of the
Sumter and at the time on a munitions inspection assignment in Paris, to
investigate the killing and to assume command of the ship in order to sell
her. Chapman's report, based largely on the testimony of the other
enlisted men, cleared Andrews of Hester's charges and concluded that
the act was a clear case of murder. Mason and Bulloch decided under
the circumstances not to test the right of the Confederate government's
jurisdiction in the case. They provided Hester with funds for his legal
defense and left him to the mercy of British justice, which found him
guilty of murder. When Confederate Secretary of State Judah P. Benjamin objected to this, the British government finally decided to turn
Hester over to the Confederacy for punishment. The problem of
transporting the culprit into the South remained; because United States
Secretary of State Seward refused a pass for the purpose, the British
transported Hester as far as Bermuda, where they released him, and he
dropped out of sight. Hester's is a unique case during the war: he was
the only Southerner in Europe who was tried and convicted of a crime
during the whole of the war. The Sumter was accumulating more firsts,
tragic as they were. And her story was still not over.

On Mason's authority Bulloch arranged to sell the Sumter.[55] Properly,
the ship should have been sold by open auction. But Bulloch contracted
with Fraser, Trenholm and Company to buy her at appraised value. In
later November 1862, James A. K. Wilson, agent for the Liverpool
banking house, went to Gibraltar with power of attorney to act for the
Confederate government. Not surprisingly, he and Lieutenant Chapman arrived at a price, transferred certain equipment (obviously arms
and munitions) to London, and settled the matter on the spot. Fraser,
Trenholm and Company paid $19,500 for the ship and placed those
much-needed funds at the disposal of Bulloch. Later, in July 1863,
under English flag and renamed the Gibraltar, the little ship made a
blockade-running trip to the South. At the end of the war the United

States government entered claims for her but the courts upheld the validity of the sale. Ironically, years later the former *Sumter* sank in a storm off the coast of Cherbourg near the remains of the *Alabama.* So Semmes's two wartime commands lie together buried under the European waters.

Commander Semmes and Lieutenant Kell arrived in London on 20 April 1862. Semmes, promoted to the rank of captain as reward for the *Sumter* cruise, spent slightly more than a month enjoying the English spring.[56] Semmes and Kell "took rooms together in Euston Square," where their windows looked out upon the lush green lawns, the newly leafed trees, and the colorful flowers in bloom. After a six-month sea voyage it must have been refreshing to soak in the beauties of the London park. Semmes also actively consulted his Southern comrades in England. He met James Mason for the first time and found him to be "a genial Virginia gentleman, with much *bon hommie.*" As did many other Southerners, Semmes also misunderstood London society's embrace of Mason; flattered, perhaps, by the personal warmth of some members of Parliament and of various lords and ladies, Semmes confused social graciousness with government policy. He felt that Jefferson Davis could not have chosen a better person for the London post. The fact is that many of the Confederates' friends, such as the Campbells and the Lairds, were making money off the war, and others received a vicarious thrill as they chatted with the captain of the now-famous *Sumter.* Semmes was not totally absorbed in Mason's social conquests, and he devoted much time to discussions with Bulloch and North. He learned that the *Florida* already had sailed from Liverpool and that the future *Alabama* was near completion. He did not, however, sense the strong undercurrent of antagonism and rivalry existing between his two colleagues. Innocent of this, he took passage on a British steamer for Nassau in late May, fully expecting to complete his journey to the Confederacy. But the Bulloch-North dispute soon would force a change in his plans.

As the seventeenth- and eighteenth-century European wars had spread to the American continents, so now had Captain Semmes and the *Sumter* brought an American war to the shores of Europe. The global aspects of the American Civil War soon became even more manifest as the ships that Bulloch ordered in Liverpool and Birkenhead neared completion.

CHAPTER 2

The First Cruisers:
January-July 1862

James Bulloch's efficient work in planning and contracting for two cruisers during the summer of 1861 was almost negated in early 1862 as the ships neared completion. The greatest problem was not a matter of high diplomacy; it was simply a matter of personal relations between two men. In an attempt to put to sea two large warships from a neutral country, an effort requiring mutual respect and confidence, Bulloch and James North found their ability to cooperate seriously hampered by mutual resentment and suspicion. It very nearly cost the Confederacy both the *Florida* and the *Alabama*.

The dispute between the two had flared openly in October 1861 at the time Bulloch left England in the *Fingal*. During the months Bulloch was in America, North occupied himself with visits to several shipyards in the British Isles, inspections of the *Florida,* and complaints to Mallory about lack of funds.[1] He did not know of the Bulloch-Mallory discussions in Richmond and especially of the changed plans concerning purchase of ironclads and command assignments for the *Florida* and *Alabama.* The friction between North and Bulloch flared again in March 1862 with Bulloch's return to England with dispatches from Mallory. Points of dispute were the questions of naval rank, command of the two ships, and ironclad ship procurement.

Much to Lieutenant North's chagrin, he learned in March that Bulloch had been appointed to the rank of commander in the Confederate navy. Mallory had consented to giving Bulloch a commission during the discussions in Richmond and had sent the commission while Bulloch was awaiting transport back to England. Bulloch graciously acknowledged the appointment and expressed surprise at the rank because it placed him superior to other officers who, according to relative service in the United States Navy, stood higher on the promotion list. He offered to accept a lower rank rather than "be the cause of discontent in the service or of wounding the feelings" of officers already heading the list of lieutenants.[2] This sensitivity to the nature of officer rank jealousy was typical of Bulloch. It was also prophetic.

North's reaction was immediate and spontaneous: "I am not aware of anything that I have done to merit such treatment from the department. . . . " He could have done as well as Bulloch, he claimed, if only the department had sent him some money. "Rank to a military man is everything and that rank has been taken from me," he complained. He made "a most solemn protest" against Bulloch's appointment over those already holding the rank of lieutenant.[3] North had served too long in a peacetime navy and had lived too strictly according to regulations to adjust to wartime exigencies. Even his own promotion to commander on 5 May[4] did not mollify him; Bulloch's date-of-rank stuck as a thorn in North's pride and further disrupted his ability to cooperate with Bulloch.

The *Florida:* Command Confusion

It was not only rank that bothered North. He also was concerned about the matter of receiving command of a ship. The question of command assignments for the *Florida* and *Alabama* was complicated by Bulloch's trip to Richmond, Semmes's sudden availability after abandoning the *Sumter,* and North's isolation in England due to slow communications. Except for the seriousness of delay and the delicacy of circumventing the British neutrality law, the situation appears as humorous as a Gilbert and Sullivan comedy of errors.

Just before sailing on the *Fingal,* during his dispute with North, Bulloch gave instructions concerning the ships then under construction to the one person who had a detailed knowledge of their contracts and control over their funds and in whom Bulloch had great confidence— Charles K. Prioleau of Fraser, Trenholm and Company. Should the first ship (that is, the future *Florida*) be ready for sea before his return, Bulloch instructed Prioleau "to have her delivered to any commissioned officer of the Confederate States Navy . . . who may be in England at the time."[5] Later, while in the Confederacy, he changed his mind. The ease of his trip into Savannah led him to believe he could return to Liverpool in time to assume command of the first ship. So he asked Mallory to assign him to the *Florida* and North to the *Alabama.* Mallory, already having abandoned the procurement of ironclads in Europe, readily agreed. North received his new assignment in early January 1862.[6] Later Bulloch realized he would be unable to leave Savannah and asked that the assignments be reversed. Again Mallory agreed. Bulloch relaxed, thinking the problem properly solved, but James North in England never received the change of orders.[7]

While Bulloch was still searching for a route out of the Confederacy, the first ship was ready for launching and her trial runs. She needed only the final outfitting—appointments for the officer quarters and mess. Who was to handle this? Lieutenant North felt no responsibility. Bulloch, after all, had explicitly denied it to him and his most recently received orders assigned him to the second ship. As early as 9 January Prioleau asked North to inspect the ship and in late January wrote to Semmes in Gibraltar offering him the command. North planned to take temporary command of the ship and sail her to Gibraltar, where he would turn her over to Semmes. He obviously ignored the danger of the neutrality laws both in Liverpool and in Gibraltar. But Semmes, his experiences in Cadiz and Gibraltar still fresh, realized the impracticability of North's plan and telegraphed: "Do not bring her. Can come for her."[8] However, his duties toward the *Sumter* consumed too much time. Events along the Mersey River could not await Semmes's arrival.

By early February the *Florida* was afloat and Prioleau ordered W. T. Mann, the builder's agent, to engage a captain, engineers, and crew and to complete the outfitting. He suggested to North that he should meet the ship on an appointed date at Holyhead and sail on her under the command of a British captain. North immediately vetoed this plan.[9] He had his orders. Besides, North saw no need for such haste and did see the sailing of an empty ship as wanton waste. Further, he questioned whether the ship was properly fitted out and provided with the necessary charts and chronometers.

Prioleau replied indignantly that he could have nothing more to do with the ship. Certainly no cargo of arms could be taken out of England because the ship was widely known to belong to the Confederacy; she had to maintain the character, if only in fiction, of a purely mercantile ship about to be delivered empty to her foreign owners. Any other appearance, Prioleau was convinced, would result in her seizure by the British government. Washing his hands of her, yet hoping the Confederacy "in this her hour of need, will soon and safely receive what will be of so much importance to her—a good fighting ship," he enclosed Bulloch's five-month-old orders to turn her over to any available officer of the Confederate navy. North was now in a quandary: should he obey Bulloch's resurrected orders or should he obey Mallory's latest ones? Again North was overwhelmed with indecision. "I am very much at a loss to know how to act," he wrote to James Mason. "What should I do?"[10]

The two men consulted in London and North followed Mason's advice, which was no more practical than his own plan to deliver the ship to Semmes in Gibraltar. Mason suggested that North instruct Prioleau to bring the ship around to London where she could receive an arms cargo consigned to the British government by S. Isaac Campbell and Company for delivery to Nassau. Such a plan reveals Mason's incompetence, despite his brilliant social conquests, to have been as great as North's. Prioleau and the builders, from all indications, rejected this idea; Prioleau also countermanded his own orders for outfitting the ship. North confessed to Mallory that he was "at a loss to know what to do with her."[11] Such misunderstandings, indecisions, and irresponsible inaction left the vessel, for all to view, afloat in the Mersey River.

The longer she sat, the more she became the object of curiosity. The Union consul in Liverpool, Thomas H. Dudley, wasted little time. He employed private detectives; he bribed seamen for information. He became convinced the ship was built for the Confederacy as a gunboat; all he needed was time to gather legal evidence that would justify seizure by the British government.[12] North and Mason seemed intent upon giving Dudley the time he needed.

Days passed. The builders felt the pressures of Dudley's agents and by 20 February notified North that they were unwilling any longer to risk retaining possession of the *Florida*. The likelihood of being recognized by Dudley prevented North from going to Liverpool. Oddly enough he sent army purchasing agent Major Caleb Huse, who also was well known to Dudley. Huse affirmed the urgency of getting the ship to sea, and North then agreed that she should sail to Havana under a British captain. He even named the day (25 February) and wrote Mallory to send an officer to meet her in Cuba. Upset over his inability to send arms in her, however, North delayed executing the order to sail, and the *Florida* remained in port. This time North's caution was justified. All of Dudley's efforts were frustrated by the port officials' interpretation of British domestic law. They ignored the ship's warlike structure and the evidence of her intended use for warlike purposes. Following the letter of the 1819 law, they ruled that because she had no arms on board they could not recommend detention. The urgency passed and the ship sat on the Mersey River safe from seizure but still without a commander. A week later North proposed that he assume command, but when the builders rejected his suggested rendezvous he dropped the idea.[13] Two more weeks passed, then Bulloch arrived back in Liverpool and North quickly relinquished all responsibility for the ship to him.

February had been a critical month for Lieutenant James North. Bored and frustrated with his duty assignment, he yearned for sea duty, for any action duty. Afforded the opportunity to command a ship, he failed to seize it. In the process he came near to alienating the valuable assistance of Charles K. Prioleau, exposed the *Florida* to possible seizure, and antagonized the William C. Miller and Sons Company, builders of the ship. Confederate navy prestige must have sunk to a record low in the eyes of Confederate sympathizers among the British shipbuilders and financiers. North's own career was on the line.

There are two sides to the story and in fairness to North both should be told. His refusal to act was not purely negative; he had strong convictions and some reason on his side. The failure to put Captain Semmes in charge of the ship was as much the fault of Semmes as of North. Plans to load the ship with munitions flowed from North's ardent desire to further his country's interests as much as from his naiveté toward the British neutrality law, and he was, after all, right about the seizure of the ship. Finally, he did have orders from Mallory to take the second, not the first ship. He had no way of knowing those orders had been changed; he had no way of knowing where Bulloch was at the moment or when he would arrive ready to assume command in accordance with Mallory's instructions. It might well be that his complaint of "being at a loss of knowing how to act" referred less to the ship than to the whereabouts of Bulloch. North could be considered the unfortunate man caught in the middle, except for one thing: he refused to accept a proper opportunity to take command of a ship and to sail against the enemy. Even when both sides of the story are told, Lieutenant North remains a bungler whose imagination could not free him from the bonds of traditionalism, who again dawdled when he should have hurried.

Commander James D. Bulloch returned to England in March 1862. After a six-week crossing on a blockade-runner, he landed in Queens-town, Ireland, on 8 March. Crossing Saint George's Channel to Holy-head Island, he took a train running along the bank of the Mersey River to Liverpool.[14] As he neared his destination on 10 March, he must have anticipated his future in Europe with much exhilaration and some trepidation. The exhilaration would have resulted from his conviction that he had successfully fulfilled his first mission to Europe: The *Florida* should already be at sea under Lieutenant North's command and he himself would soon be roaming the sea-lanes in search of Yankee merchantmen aboard his own dream ship, the *Alabama*. Bulloch had no way of knowing of North's refusal to take the *Florida* nor could he foresee the full fury of North's jealousy over Bulloch's appointment as a commander. The trepidation would have resulted from his expected difficulties in fulfilling his second mission in Europe: the construction of ironclad ships designed to raise the Federal blockade of Southern ports.[15]

As the train approached Liverpool, Bulloch sighted the *Florida* calmly sitting amid the active ships of the busy harbor—proof that his first mission was not yet completed after all. The Confederate navy's situation in England was quite different from his expectations; there were more tasks to perform than he had anticipated. He first had to get the *Florida* to sea then he had to initiate ironclad construction, all the while pushing the *Alabama* to completion and being careful to avoid neutrality snags the *Florida* might have created. Finally, he had to accomplish all these things without sufficient funds or personnel, indeed in the face of North's hostility. That Bulloch succeeded in all these undertakings is evidence of superior competency.

For over a month the *Florida* had been the object of Federal and British surveillance. Bulloch realized at once that she must be put to sea, and within twelve days after his return to Liverpool he accomplished the task.

In his memoirs Bulloch does not mention the roles of North or Semmes in the affair. Undoubtedly he conferred with Prioleau and learned of his frustrations in dealing with North. Nevertheless Bulloch made the right gestures: on 11 March he wrote to North offering command of the *Florida* and suggesting in case of refusal that Semmes might be willing to take it. He obviously did not expect either officer to accept—North because of his previous month's procrastination and Semmes because of his duties aboard the *Sumter* at Gibraltar. Actually Bulloch also had in mind Lieutenant Pegram of the *Nashville*, who unfortunately already had left Southampton.[16] Bulloch now faced the difficult problem of sending to sea the South's first ship built specifically for military duty without a competent officer to command her. Undaunted, he devised an ingenious plan that worked without a hitch.

Bulloch used his knowledge of Confederate naval activity in American waters and the narrowly interpreted British neutrality law to accomplish his first task. To avoid seizure on the Mersey River, Bulloch hired an English merchant captain and crew, filed legitimate sailing articles, and on 22 March sent the vessel off containing no arms, munitions, or contraband of war. The *Florida* safely cleared British waters.[17]

How could the ship sit for a month in the harbor without attracting official attention? And how could Bulloch avoid suspicion when he made the necessary arrangements to send her to sea? The fact is that official attention had been given to the ship. The *Florida*, however, was the first test of the Foreign Enlistment Act concerning the construction of a ship for belligerent use. The act prohibited arming, manning, or equipping such a ship but was silent on structure and intent. The fact that the *Florida*'s structure—extended length, magazine, small hatches and cargo holes—better suited the ship for military than merchant use was outside the purview of the law. So also were the Union claims that the ship was intended for use by the Confederates. Applying the law as it was written, then, the customs officials in Liverpool cleared the *Florida* for sailing. Bulloch understood the law in the same way. He was confident that he had not violated British neutral obligations; he feared only the effect on Russell of Adams's protests.

Indeed, Adams had protested that the ship was intended for Confederate use against Northern merchant shipping. Russell's response was within the context of the law: "You have not yourself hitherto furnished me with evidence that any vessel has received a hostile or warlike equipment in British waters which has been afterwards used against the United States." Furthermore, he pointedly reminded Adams that "it is not the custom of this country to deprive any person of liberty or property without evidence of some offence." Undaunted, Adams indicated that the British government was obligated to prevent the sailing of a ship such as the *Florida* even if the Foreign Enlistment Act did not give it the power to do so. Directly responding to this, Russell wrote: "I agree with you in the statement that the duty of nations in amity with one another is not to suffer their good faith to be violated by ill-disposed persons within their borders from the inefficacy of their prohibitory policy."[18]

So far English neutrality according to the law had not been violated. But Russell had restated, as he had in the *Nashville* case, that the Foreign Enlistment Act did not limit England's neutral obligations. He was determined to apply English law to maintain neutrality and if necessary he even would recommend changes in the law. British policy was at all events to maintain a neutral posture in the American struggle.

Free of British European waters the *Florida* sailed directly to British American waters. In Nassau the Admiralty under United States pressure brought it to trial in June 1862 for violation of the Foreign Enlistment Act. The decision, which entered into the corpus of British jurisprudence, freed the *Florida* because the government failed to prove three specifics: that the ship had taken on equipment within the court's jurisdiction; that there had been intent to place the ship into Southern service; that there had been intent to use it for hostile acts against the United States.[19] This case was good proof of the "inefficacy" of England's "prohibitory policy"; what "further measures" would Russell advise Her Majesty to adopt? The answer developed slowly over the next eleven months and proved to be thoroughly consistent with Russell's two early statements elicited by Confederate navy activity in Europe.

How had Bulloch sent the ship to Nassau? Who was to command her? Bulloch learned while in the Confederacy that a new communications system was established between various Southern ports and the West Indies. He knew also that CSN Lieutenant John N. Maffitt commanded the ship making the dispatch runs. Well acquainted with Maffitt, Bulloch considered him to be "a man of great natural resources, self-reliant and fearless of responsibility."[20] So he decided to send the *Florida* under the English merchant captain's command to Maffitt in Nassau. It was a risky undertaking. He could not notify Maffitt of the plan; would he be in Nassau? Would the temporary captain faithfully execute Bulloch's directives? Indeed, would a Confederate navy officer ever again set foot on the *Florida*'s decks?

To assure delivery of the ship to Maffitt and to protect his government's interests, Bulloch detailed John Low to sail with the ship ostensibly as a passenger.[21] Low's life and career cast much light on human relations involved in the Civil War. Family traditions, historians, popular novels, and movies long have taught us of the pathos of divided families.

There were many businesses whose personnel served overseas: Americans in Europe, and Europeans in America. This situation was especially prevalent in shipping and banking, which were closely related. Such Southern port cities as Charleston, Savannah, and New Orleans naturally attracted these interests. Many families living in those cities had relatives in Great Britain; indeed some of them, such as John Low, were themselves newly arrived from England. Moreover, many of them were involved in shipping as sea captains, harbor pilots, ships chandlers, or bankers; the interest that bound them together was in most cases the trade in cotton. Could not these human relations explain the warmth and cooperation some English afforded to the Confederates and especially to the Confederate naval efforts? And might not the same apply to the French in France and in New Orleans?

Born in Aberdeen and reared in Liverpool, John Low went to sea at the age of sixteen.[22] After a Far Eastern voyage, Low accompanied a well-to-do uncle, Andrew Low, who was a Liverpool-Savannah businessman, to Georgia.

In Savannah twenty-year-old John Low found the good life: a pleasant climate, a busy harbor, and a group of friends all like himself fresh from the British Isles. He formed a partnership with a newly arrived Scotsman, Robert Hardy, and their ship chandler business prospered. Andrew Low was in partnership with another Englishman, Charles Green. Their business, Andrew Low and Company, was a subsidiary of two Liverpool export-import houses and of a London insurance company. Soon young John, now prosperous and socially prominent, married Charles Green's sister, Eliza, who recently had arrived from England.

Thus, just three years before the firing upon Fort Sumter, John Low was settled in Savannah and related through business, family, or marriage to at least four other recent arrivals, all of whom had close relatives in England.[23]

James Bulloch had known the Low family in Savannah and England for about six years. He asked Secretary Mallory to appoint John Low to the rank of acting mate and to assign him to Europe. Bulloch put him to work supervising the loading of the *Fingal*. Low's competency during that trip convinced Bulloch in March 1862 to entrust the safety of the *Florida* to him. His successful delivery of the ship to Maffitt later led Semmes to request Low as a lieutenant on the *Alabama*. In June 1863 Semmes appointed Low commander of the C.S.S. *Tuscaloosa,* a cruiser born from the *Alabama*'s capture of a United States merchantman. After almost six months at sea Low was forced to give up his ship to British authorities in South Africa, and he returned to Liverpool to report to Bulloch. He later commanded the *Ajax,* but the war was almost over and John Low never reached the Confederate States. After the war he settled in the Liverpool area and enjoyed a successful career as a textile manufacturer and agent for ship petroleum and marine insurance companies.

Low was a good selection, then, for the *Florida* assignment and completed it just as Bulloch directed. Bulloch's happy facility of choosing the right man for the job materially reduced the inherent risks in delivering the ship without prior notice to Maffitt some three thousand miles distant.

Because he had not dared to arm the *Florida* within English territorial jurisdiction, Bulloch hit upon a technique that he would use later for other ships and that would cause the European diplomats many problems. He sent four seven-inch rifled guns and the necessary equipment in a British ship, the *Bahama,* to rendezvous with the *Florida*. Although this method of sending out an unarmed ship with her arms in another ship for rendezvous later brought successful United States charges of neutrality violations against the British government, at the time Bulloch honestly considered the action to be within the international laws of neutrality.[24] More immediately, the scheme worked and ships were in fact put to sea with arms and crews to engage the enemy.

Once clear of Nassau, the *Florida*'s career until her arrival at a French port in October 1863 is outside the scope of this study. It does serve to confirm Bulloch's judgment about Maffitt. The skipper of this first raider built in Europe managed to survive an outbreak of yellow fever among his crew, run the Federal blockade at Mobile, Alabama, outfit and rearm his vessel, and prey upon Northern shipping for ten months prior to returning to European waters.[25] Bulloch indeed had succeeded in Mallory's first assignment.

Confederate Naval Policy: Reflections

The memoirs, letters, and diaries of the effective navy officers in Europe reveal men not only of action but also of high intellect and moral integrity. Semmes's *Service Afloat* is filled with reflections on moral dilemmas about burning peaceful merchant ships, treatment of the common sailor, barroom brawls, and international law. Commander Matthew Fontaine Maury's diary and letters are not infrequently meditations on the moral issues of the war, of scientific developments, and of human tragedy. James Bulloch also often reflected on such issues. In the spring of 1862, just after he succeeded in getting the *Florida* out of England, he took time to evaluate the Confederate navy posture.

Were sea raiders such as the *Florida* really effective instruments of war? Was the ship construction program in Europe feasible financially? Would the European governments allow the ships armored with iron and constructed as fighting vessels, not merchantmen, to enter the service of the South? What alternatives were available to the Confederates? Some of these questions Bulloch answered by his actions and some by his pen.

Bulloch entertained no illusions about winning the war with sea raiders. In his instructions to Maffitt he wrote that, even if the two of them could coordinate the activities of the *Florida* and the *Alabama,* the most they could hope to accomplish would be "to illustrate the spirit and energy of our people" and to "repay upon the enemy some of the injuries his vastly superior forces alone had enabled him to inflict upon the states of the Confederacy." At about the same time, referring to the February Federal captures of Fort Donelson and of Nashville, Bulloch commented that although the news was saddening he thought the reverses would "do our people good . . . [because] they were too confident and too careless of the necessary precautions." He developed such firm reservations about the effectiveness of the sea raider activities and the efficaciousness of the ship construction program that he recommended the latter's abandonment. Meanwhile, he quietly went about his dual missions of contracting for ironclad ships and completing the *Alabama.*[26] His most immediate need was money.

Indeed, this last item was becoming a real problem to all Confederate agents in Europe and especially to the naval personnel whose most important purchases involved long-term, high-cost contracts. There was no central financial officer in Europe in 1862, and the government sent funds or cotton consignments to Fraser, Trenholm and Company as it could and designated these funds for specific agents in Europe.[27] This system was spasmodic and inefficient; it hardly provided the kind of funds needed to meet the long-range contracts involved in ship construction. Nevertheless, in the spring of 1862 Bulloch managed to put two wooden raiders to sea and to contract for two ironclad rams. Success rested upon his reputation for honesty and his own thorough preparation. The Lairds, for instance, so trusted Bulloch that they devoted man-hours and materials to the designs of the rams without any payment; this preparation in turn made it possible to begin construction on the rams when Bulloch was able to make just a small payment toward the total cost of the ships. By committing the available funds piecemeal, Bulloch could sustain several costly contracts at the same time with relatively little capital. He constantly owed vast amounts of money, much more than he ever had on hand; yet not only did he put ships to sea, purchase arms and munitions, and pay naval salaries, but when the war ended his books were balanced and he owed not a penny.

Disheartened by what he considered to be an unproductive policy, Bulloch nonetheless continued to execute his duties with candor and effectiveness. Despite his reservations about the use of sea raiders, he set about arranging for the launching of the *Alabama,* whose very success would substantitate his apprehensions.[28] What a consummate actor Bulloch must have been to play out the remaining years of the war in a role he saw as useless and for a cause he saw as hopeless!

The *Alabama:* Command Confusion

James Bulloch was inadvertently responsible for one of the chief problems concerning the *Alabama*—the question of a commander. Secretary Mallory, it will be recalled, on 20 January had ordered North to take the first ship completed (the *Florida*) and Bulloch to take the second one (the *Alabama*). But these orders did not reach North until Bulloch showed copies to him in London, and he did this only on 26 March, after he had sent the *Florida* to Nassau. This delay, misunderstanding, and bad timing contributed to North's anger and frustration and led to his outbursts about rank as well as ship commands. To North it seemed that Bulloch purposely had delayed conveying Mallory's changed orders until it was too late—until, that is, the *Florida* had sailed. To Bulloch, who assumed North had received the original orders and who marveled that North had refused the *Florida,* his colleague appeared to be a stubborn bungler. Immediately after Bulloch's return on 10 March, and as long as he remained in Liverpool, the two exchanged cordial letters; but after 26

March their relationship was strained over the questions of ship command, rank, and the type of ironclad ship most suitable to Confederate needs. As events turned out, neither officer received a ship.

Bulloch, however, assumed that he would command the *Alabama* and while he worked out the details of the ironclads with the Lairds he also supervised the completion of the cruiser. This task was complicated and delayed because the builders, insisting upon using the finest timber available, rejected "two or three" stern posts before they were satisfied. During this delay Bulloch busied himself purchasing gunpowder, revolvers, and rod lead and arranging to ship these goods on the steamship *Melita*. More pertinent to the *Alabama* story, when the *Melita* sailed on 12 April 1862 Semmes and his lieutenant, John M. Kell, sailed on her as passengers[29] and missed the *Alabama*'s launching by only one month. The confusion in command orders would cause Semmes to recross the Atlantic within four months and would cause Bulloch great personal disappointment.

Meanwhile Lieutenant North interpreted his loss of the *Florida* command as a signal to return to his original orders and he negotiated with James and George Thomson, shipbuilders on the Clyde River, Glasgow, for the construction of an ironclad warship. The size and deep draft of the Clyde River ship elicited Bulloch's opposition and he advised North to amend the contract. But Lieutenant North persisted, and on 21 May 1862 he signed with the Thomsons.[30] This action deepened the schism between the two officers.

The North-Thomson contract had an immediate impact on the question of the *Alabama* command. This problem is difficult to sort out even for the historian who has the documents before him; little wonder that in 1862 the men involved became confused and baffled, little wonder that they worked at cross purposes and came near to having no commander at all. Yet, from the records, the finger of culpability can point at no single individual. Slow and uncertain communications and Federal and British surveillance were the real culprits. The greater wonder is that Semmes ever managed to board the ship at all and that the *Alabama* ever became a Confederate weapon of war.

Working on the assumption that he would command the ship, Bulloch made detailed plans for its completion and sailing. He carefully selected the personnel needed to prepare for its launching, equipment, and trials. He hired two men who had been with him on the *Fingal* and had proven their abilities and loyalties: Coxswain George Freemantle, an Englishman, to supervise the deck preparations, and Engineer Angus McNair, a Scotsman, to oversee the installations of the engines. In addition, while in the Confederacy Bulloch had promised CSN Lieutenant John R. Hamilton sea duty and accordingly requested him as the

Alabama's first lieutenant. Hamilton arrived at the end of April and because he was not well known in Liverpool Bulloch placed him in charge of the on-site activities. These three men Bulloch trusted implicitly. His most difficult personnel decision was to appoint the right man to act as captain. In keeping with the fiction that the *Alabama* was a merchant ship being built for a nonbelligerent foreign interest, the captain would have to hold a British Board of Trade certificate and be capable of working with the builders in the final stages of preparing the ship for sea. He also would engage the crew and "transact all such business as by law and custom falls within the office of the commander of a vessel." Thus the captain would have to be English, would have to conduct daily business with the Lairds, and would have to follow Bulloch's instructions as delivered by Hamilton. Bulloch needed a man of discretion. Through a friend he contacted Captain Matthew J. Butcher of the Cunard line whom he had met several years earlier in Havana. After only a fifteen-minute conversation Bulloch knew he had found his man.[31]

Mindful that the *Florida* might have alerted the British to Confederate activity in Liverpool and aware that the *Alabama*'s structure was more clearly military, Bulloch and his assistants worked with discretion as they prepared the *Alabama* for launching. Bulloch avoided direct contact with the three British subjects; each had a specific area of responsibility and reported individually to Hamilton, who in turn informed Bulloch of the ship's progress.[32] As it turned out, this extra care was important to Bulloch because United States Consul Thomas H. Dudley was perfecting his surveillance techniques and the British government, after the *Trent* affair, and the escape of the *Florida*, was more conscious of its neutral obligations. Dudley hired private detectives to spy on the activities aboard the *Alabama*, he bribed employees of the Laird company, and he tried to bribe Bulloch's personnel. Bulloch knew the danger of detention or confiscation of the vessel, and he stayed within the British law as at that time interpreted and as counsel advised him. He even had inside information as to the state of negotiations between United States Minister Adams and the British Foreign Office, though this source has not yet been revealed. Bulloch later attributed his success in getting the *Alabama* to sea to the "fact that no mystery or disguise was attempted."[33] He and his men went about the job quietly and efficiently, within their understanding of the limits of the British neutrality law. Only at the last moment did he depart from his plans and, as he says, "with some precipitancy" put the ship to sea. He beat a detention order only by a matter of hours.

The delicacy and balance required to prepare the *Alabama* was precarious enough when Bulloch assumed he would be the captain; imagine his consternation when in mid-June he received directives indicating that someone else would command the ship. By that time the *Alabama* had been launched (15 May), her engines and equipment had been installed, and several trial runs had been made. Surveillance was strict, and Bulloch was anxious to take the vessel beyond British jurisdiction. He was within a week of sailing when two dispatches from Mallory arrived, which, he later wrote, "greatly disappointed my hopes and expectations in reference to getting afloat,"[34] and which seriously complicated his duties and endangered the ship. The old question of who would command the *Alabama* once again became critical.

In late April and early May Secretary Mallory wrote four dispatches addressed to North, Bulloch, and Semmes. He ordered Semmes, who was in Nassau on his way to Richmond, to take command of the *Alabama;* he informed North, who thought he had missed out on both cruisers, that $150,000 was sent to him to "fit out your vessel"; he informed Bulloch, who thought that within a week he would be commanding the *Alabama* on the high seas, that Semmes now had that assignment.[35] The letters, arriving in mid-June, filled the officers with bewilderment. Mallory had written the dispatches based on knowledge received in Richmond as of early May; he did not then know of Semmes's decision to leave the *Sumter* and return to the Confederacy, nor of Bulloch's disposition of the *Florida* and of the assignment of Maffitt as her captain (he learned this fact only on 28 May).[36] The recipients, on the other hand, did know of these arrangements by the time they received Mallory's orders. It is this knowledge sequence that accounts for the confusion among the officers and the near calamitous delay in getting the ship to sea.

In Nassau Semmes was delighted to receive the orders to return to England to assume command of the *Alabama*. While in London he had discussed the ship with Bulloch and already had concluded that she "will be a fine ship, quite equal to encounter any of the enemy's steam-sloops of the class of the [U.S.S.] *Iroquois*." He would, he wrote, "feel much more independent in her, upon the high seas," than he had in the little *Sumter*.[37] Unfortunately, he had to wait several weeks before he could book passage to Europe. Lieutenant Arthur Sinclair already had arranged passage to England by way of Halifax, and Semmes sent with him a letter to Bulloch informing him of his appointment to command the *Alabama* and urging him to get the ship out of British waters and to some rendezvous without waiting for his arrival. It undoubtedly was this letter, delivered by Sinclair to Bulloch about 8 July that finally settled the confusion concerning the command assignment and that both permitted and encouraged Bulloch to get the ship to sea.

Meanwhile in England, Bulloch and North, knowing nothing about Semmes except that he was in Nassau, were perplexed and uncertain. Bulloch, thinking that within a week he would be on the high seas as commander of his own ship, on 11 June received the Mallory letters dated 30 April and 3 May. In the first the secretary directed Bulloch to devote himself to the speedy construction of two ironclad rams and informed him that Captain Semmes was ordered to take the largest of the two cruisers, transferring his *Sumter* officers and crew to the new ship, and that Lieutenant North should take command of the other one. This meant that Mallory expected North to command the *Florida* and Semmes the *Alabama*. Bulloch's reaction was one of shock and dismay; he would have no ship and would be forced to remain ashore supervising the construction of the rams. Reading on he saw the short letter dated 3 May that appeared ambiguous in view of events already transpired; it informed Bulloch that Semmes should transfer his command to the second vessel "if he should be unable to refit and repair the *Sumter*." Bulloch knew that Semmes was already in Nassau and that North had missed his opportunity to sail on the *Florida*. The secretary's orders, then, could not be executed exactly. In these circumstances, what would be the best solution? Since the *Florida* was already away, should North be given the *Alabama*?

Bulloch's first thought was to retain command of the ship and turn over to North the supervision of all of the ironclads. He reasoned that this duty, after all, had been North's original assignment; furthermore, because the two disagreed on the class of ironclad ship most suitable to Confederate needs, and because North already had contracted for one in accordance with his own views, then he was the logical person to see it through.[38] But these thoughts occurred to Bulloch before he had heard from North.

On 11 June, the day he received the letters from Mallory, Bulloch wrote to North in London stating that the secretary had instructed him that Semmes was to take command of the second ship (the *Alabama*) and North the first ship (the *Florida,* already in Nassau), while Bulloch himself was to remain in England to build two ironclad ships. "You will perceive," he wrote to North, "that we should see each other as soon as possible." He set the meeting for Friday, 13 June, at noon in the office of Fraser, Trenholm and Company.[39]

Oddly, James North never responded to Bulloch's urgent request. Instead, three days later, on Saturday, 14 June, he informed Bulloch of his own letter from Mallory dated 2 May, the contents of which, as North reported them, tended to contradict Mallory's letters to Bulloch. The secretary referred to the $150,000 as funds to outfit the cruiser North was to command. Since the *Florida* already had sailed, North wrote, "I am ready to take command of the one you have in Liverpool or I am ready to continue the work on the armor-plated begun by myself near one month since." He would not go to Liverpool but would leave

London on Monday (16 June) to go to Glasgow, where he would await communication from Bulloch.[40]

This situation was just the beginning of the confusion that would follow. Bulloch noted the key phrase in Mallory's letter to North as quoted by North—" . . . you were to take command of the vessel built by Captain Bulloch"—and North's own statement that he was "now ready to take command of the one you have in Liverpool." There is no evidence that Bulloch ever saw the actual letter from Mallory to North. He rather hastily concluded that inasmuch as Semmes was nowhere about, North should command the *Alabama,* and he wrote to North in Glasgow to come at once to Liverpool "to discuss and arrange the manner of getting to sea." North himself concluded as of 18 June that he would soon have to leave the British Isles and indicated to the Glasgow builders that he would have to transfer the construction contract to another party.[41] Yet he lingered in Scotland for a full week before going to Liverpool. This delay possibly cost him the command of the *Alabama* because it allowed time for Semmes's letter to reach Bulloch.

North arrived in Liverpool on 26 June, but because of the estrangement between the two men he did not meet with Bulloch. Instead he wrote a letter. On the next day Bulloch replied also by letter: "A detailed statement of the condition of the ship and the plans heretofor devised for getting her out of English waters would be too lengthy for a letter of this character, but I hold myself ready to make verbal explanations upon all points upon which you may desire information, and I will yield you willing assistance in consummating the objects of your approaching cruise." He "formally and officially" transferred command of the ship to North and declared himself ready to assume responsibility for North's ironclad ship. Both men wrote to Secretary Mallory informing him of the exchange of duties.[42]

Had the two men been on good terms personally they quickly could have concluded arrangements for the ship's sailing. Indeed it was desirable for the *Alabama* to leave in June because, as Bulloch noted in his memoirs, the Federal minister was "pressing the Government to seize the vessel"; the delay was "very embarrassing" because the ship was "ready for sea, and had been delivered . . . by the builders."[43] Once again, as in the *Florida* case, North's procrastination and his resentment of Bulloch cost him command of a cruiser. A week and a half slipped by while, presumably, Bulloch briefed North on the ship and his arrangements to put her to sea. An officer more forceful and perceptive than North would have had the *Alabama* away before Semmes's letter reached Bulloch on 8 July.

That letter drastically changed the plans for both men. For the first time Bulloch realized that Secretary Mallory had made the command assignments before learning of the *Florida*'s sailing and that this accounted for his apparent contradictions. Bulloch now realized that North's assignment was voided by events while Semmes's assignment remained valid. He also must have chided himself for so precipitately transferring command of the *Alabama* to North, because he had acted simply on North's own interpretation of Mallory's letter. The situation required corrective action and Bulloch wasted no time in self-recrimination. He immediately wrote to North, still in Liverpool, revoking his transfer letter of 28 June[44] and thus resolved the question of who, as captain, would share the fame of the ship destined to become the South's most destructive cruiser.

James North, however, did not accept this decision without complaint. The Liverpool scenario of October 1861 was reenacted. On 9 July he wrote Bulloch a letter that unfortunately has not survived. On the tenth, the two passed in the street without a greeting. Later that day Bulloch wrote North a letter that reflects not only the content of North's complaints but also the tensions, frustration, and personal resentments the complicated question of the *Alabama*'s command had created.

He had not intended "to exercize any 'authority' " over North, Bulloch wrote; it was, in effect, a matter of receiving "later authentic and even official information" (Semmes's letter) that had prompted the revocation of North's command. Bulloch maintained that he was acting merely as a Navy Department agent, preparing a ship for whatever skipper the department designated; it seemed to him "useless and absurd" that a third officer "should for a few short days appear upon paper as her commander." If North could produce an order from the Navy Department appointing him commander of the ship "not rendered void by later instructions," Bulloch said he would immediately "with cheerfulness and without one pang of envy or jealousy" help him get the ship away. But, he continued, all his information indicated that "Commander Semmes is more fortunate than either of us." Bulloch's own frustration began to seep through his pen: "Heretofore I have had neither assistance nor advice, there seeming to be a strange feeling among the majority of naval officers who have been in England that my position in the service was incompatible with their own dignity and that I must therefore be regarded as one to be left alone."[45] This rare outburst of self-pity is unlike the cool and effective agent reflected in most of Bulloch's correspondence. The exhaustion of hard work, the uncertainty of the ship's command, the disappointment at losing that command, and the strain of working with the disaffected James North all had taken a toll on Bulloch.

However, the coolness quickly returned. He concluded the letter to North with these words: "but you and myself are of an age to be above the display of childish jealousies and offishness, and I propose that we continue to meet as our first acquaintance, and not to avoid each other's glance as was the case this morning." And indeed, Bulloch's correspondence until 1865 contains no disparaging remarks to or about James North. He put personal feelings aside and set about the delicate and intricate task of getting the *Alabama* to sea for Captain Semmes.

He described in detail the plan and its execution.[46] It was a variation of the *Florida* theme. He sent the *Alabama* to sea under Captain Butcher, rented and supplied another ship, the *Agrippina,* as her tender, and ordered the two to rendezvous at Praya Bay on the island of Terceira, one of the Azores. Bulloch had discovered this "inviting shelter" when he had put in there for water with the *Fingal* in 1861. Also as with the *Florida,* he sent John Low aboard the *Alabama* to act in behalf of the Navy Department. Bulloch himself remained in Liverpool awaiting Semmes's arrival.

There were several humorous incidents in getting the *Alabama* to sea. The Federal consul had kept her under close surveillance and United States Minister Adams had for months bombarded Foreign Minister Lord John Russell with demands to seize the ship. Bulloch knew from his inside source that, despite all of his own care, detention orders would be issued within a matter of days. He had to act swiftly and deftly. So he staged the ship's departure to appear as a gala trial run. He invited local dignitaries for a festive cruise down the Mersey River, then he returned with them to Liverpool on a drab tugboat, leaving the trim ship just off the coast of Wales at Moelfra Bay. The next day, 30 July 1862, when Bulloch arrived at the same tugboat to ship a crew of seamen for the *Alabama,* he was shocked to see as many women as men; they were the seamen's "ladies," who refused to allow their men to ship out until the articles of the cruise were duly signed and the first month's wage safely tucked into their own bodices. Bulloch protested, but he had to submit: steam downriver, women and all, to the Confederate ship, pay the women, and return them to Liverpool where they could work their charms on other seamen still ashore. But the women were not Bulloch's chief worry; just before leaving the dock, he received a message that the U.S.S. *Tuscarora* was looking for the *Alabama* and was working her way up the western English coast, ducking in and out of bays and hiding places. How long did he have before the Federal ship appeared in Moelfra Bay? As the seamen, baited by the women, dickered with Captain Butcher over wages, Bulloch's anxiety grew until finally the irony of the situation struck him as humorous. His tensions relieved, he ordered a meal and drink for all the seamen and the women. After a small feast, terms were quickly struck; the seamen signed on for a voyage as if to Havana, the first month's wages were given to the women, farewells were said, and at about midnight the tugboat left Moelfra Bay with its pulchritudinous cargo. Although a gale was blowing, Bulloch ordered Butcher to set sail and get up steam: he could chance the *Tuscarora* no longer. The course was set northward, away from the *Tuscarora*'s last reported position, and the *Alabama* made good time, reaching the coast of Northern Ireland by 8:00 A.M. on 31 July. Bulloch's caution and haste were justified because the *Tuscarora* looked into Moelfra Bay just twenty-four hours after his departure.

Bulloch stayed with the ship until it reached Giant's Causeway. There he hailed a fishing vessel, went ashore, and took a room in an inn. Although he had slept only a few hours in the last forty-eight, he could not help but brood about "the little ship buffeting her way around that rugged . . . coast" on her course to the Azores. The next day broke clear and, as Bulloch began his return trip to Liverpool, the sun's rays chased away his gloom. He was confident that the *Alabama*, now out of English waters, would reach its destination. In Liverpool, he learned "with satisfaction" that the *Agrippina* had cleared the channel and thus he knew that the two ships were "safely on their way to the rendezvous." He had done his job: the *Alabama* was at sea and soon would be armed and equipped to move against Federal shipping—and all because of the staged, festive, "trial run" and despite the women who so jealously had guarded the rights of the seamen.

In all this delicate maneuvering—moving two ships in full view of Northern and British officials, beating a detention order only by hours, escaping from a Union man-of-war by a day, handling his disputes with Commander North—Bulloch had made one serious slip. He had misjudged the character and loyalty of a Confederate navy officer. Bulloch had chosen Clarence R. Yonge as acting assistant paymaster on the *Alabama*. In his letter of instruction, given to Yonge as the *Alabama* sailed down the Mersey River, Bulloch assigned him two duties that specifically violated British neutrality law. He gave him a list of the *Agrippina*'s cargo, "every case and bale" and "the contents of each," and made him responsible for giving "efficient aid" in transferring the stores and munitions to the *Alabama*. He also instructed Yonge to attempt to recruit for the Confederate navy from among the warrant and petty officers who had signed aboard for a voyage to Havana. Yonge was to "talk to them of the Southern States, and how they were fighting against great odds for only what every Englishman enjoys—liberty!"[47]

Within a year Semmes was forced to dismiss Yonge from the service for drunkenness and failure to perform his duties. In disgrace and without funds, Yonge returned to England, where he sold his knowledge concerning the *Alabama* and Bulloch's instructions to Charles Francis Adams. He became a chief witness against the *Alexandra* and although his testimony was ineffective in that case it was later decisive in the ironclad rams case and was cited in 1872 by the United States before the Geneva Arbitration Commission. Yonge was one of the few serious errors Bulloch made, but it was a costly one. Nevertheless, in the summer of 1862 Bulloch succeeded not only in getting the *Alabama* to sea fully equipped and armed but also in getting the assigned captain aboard her.

While waiting for Semmes to arrive in England, Bulloch was not idle. He learned, somehow, that Semmes would come on the *Bahama*, the ship Bulloch sent out as the tender to the *Florida*. Already enjoying good relations with the owners, Bulloch chartered the ship as if for a return voyage to Nassau. His purpose, of course, was to use her to convey Semmes and his officers to the *Alabama*. He also arranged for "additional stores and two 32 pounder guns" and he picked up a "few good men" to ship as if to Nassau.[48] All of this was arranged and ready when Captain Semmes and Lieutenant Kell reached Liverpool on 8 August 1862.

For five days Bulloch and Semmes were busy preparing for the trip to the Azores. Bulloch supervised the loading of the *Bahama:* the additional crew, coal, and supplies. Then on 11 August, the night before the ship was to sail, as Captain Semmes was busy with his officer crew preparing to assume command of the *Alabama*, Bulloch sat down and wrote a long letter to Secretary Mallory.[49] All of the pent-up frustration and disappointment the past few months had created poured from his pen: the accusations and complaints of Commander North, the tensions involved in the delicacies of getting the *Alabama* to sea, and especially the letdown in seeing another receive her command. He referred to the jealousies that his appointment to the rank of commander created among certain navy officers, which he regretted; but, worse, he also learned from "private advices" that some officers considered him as "an interloper in the navy" and used their influence to prevent his "being employed in the active duties of the sea." While he never wanted to cause any friction in the service, still he "would rather be a private in one of the numerous regiments of my native State than to hold the highest commission in the Navy if I am never to exercize its legitimate functions." Referring to the two ironclad ships he was then building, Bulloch requested complete freedom in completing them and urged his "claim to command one of these ships in person." Thinking ahead to the next day when he would escort Semmes to the *Alabama,* a ship that he, Bulloch, had designed and nursed to life from the drawing board to the sea, he stated that he had no objection to the person who was to command the ship, that on the contrary he thought Semmes especially well suited and qualified for the job; he would follow Semmes's career aboard the *Alabama* "with unalloyed interest, and hear of his successes with pleasure, on private as well as public grounds." But what of himself, he wondered. Would he spend the rest of the war in England, building ships for others to fight, buying guns for others to shoot? That is what his critics were urging. The prospect seemed grim. "If I had no ambition beyond that of a private agent to do the work assigned him properly, I should be content to labor in a quiet sphere, but I aspire to purely professional distinction, and I feel that to toil here, as it were, in exile and then to turn over the result of my labors for the use of others is willingly to consign myself to oblivion." He appealed, again, for a fair chance to command a ship at sea. Having so strongly expressed this personal wish, having in effect lifted the weights bearing so heavily upon him, Bulloch turned to the duties that required him to do exactly what he did not want to do: turn over the fruits of his labors to another. Neither Semmes nor anyone else who wrote about the cruisers gave Bulloch the credit he was due; perhaps that is why he wrote his own memoirs, which are so detailed and so basically honest. In doing what he had to do, in the long run Commander Bulloch achieved not oblivion as he feared but the distinction in history of being the most effective overseas agent for a losing cause.

Captain Semmes meanwhile spent those August days gathering the officers from the *Sumter* who were still in England, making financial arrangements for the cruise with Fraser, Trenholm and Company, and consulting with Commander North.[50]

Semmes apparently had no difficulty in arranging funds for his cruise. Strangely, the records that are otherwise so profuse with Confederate money problems cast little light on the *Alabama*'s cruising funds, and Semmes himself is no help. Commander Bulloch provided $100,000 to Semmes through credit with Fraser, Trenholm and Company, but no records indicate whether Richmond or Prioleau advanced the money. Arthur Sinclair a lieutenant aboard the *Alabama,* mentioned in his book almost offhandedly that in ports Semmes always drew bills "on Liverpool" that amounted "generally to about ten thousand dollars at each coaling port." Semmes also, according to Sinclair, had a "considerable sum of gold" as a cruising fund but seldom had to use it.[51] At any rate, Semmes seems to have been careful in arranging for adequate funds. He remembered his financial embarrassment at Cadiz aboard the *Sumter;* none of the various accounts of the *Alabama*'s two-year cruise mentions the recurrence of such a situation. If Commanders North and Bulloch constantly felt a financial squeeze during 1862–64, Semmes never did so.

Semmes had an easy time also in gathering his officers. He had kept in close touch with those from the *Sumter* and managed to ship many of them aboard the *Alabama.* Of these, three had been with him since he left the *Sumter:* Lieutenant John M. Kell, the first officer; Marine Lieutenant

Becket K. Howell; and Surgeon Francis L. Galt. Three others had remained in Europe awaiting further orders and immediately responded to his summons: Richard F. Armstrong, for instance, had remained aboard the *Sumter* in Gibraltar until just prior to Semmes's return to Liverpool, and Semmes promoted him from midshipman to lieutenant and appointed him second officer of the *Alabama;* Lieutenant Joseph M. Wilson, third officer, had awaited Semmes's return in London, where he had reported to James Mason, as had Chief Engineer Miles J. Freeman. Two of these officers, Kell and Freeman, had worked with Semmes in New Orleans to convert the *Sumter* into a cruiser.[52]

Five of the lower ranking officers, referred to as steerage officers, and three warrant officers also had awaited in England for Semmes's orders. Two of the steerage officers—W. B. Smith, captain's clerk, and Matthew O'Brien, third assistant engineer—were later to serve aboard the *Shenandoah,* thus staying afloat longer than any other Confederate naval personnel assigned to Europe. Altogether, fourteen former *Sumter* officers followed Semmes to the *Alabama.* All had entered the service from Southern states. Only two lost their lives during the war: Assistant Engineer Simon W. Cummings of Louisiana accidentally shot himself during a hunting expedition in South Africa, and William Robinson, carpenter, of Louisiana drowned after the *Alabama* sank off Cherbourg on 19 June 1864.

Fourteen officers were not enough to man a ship as large as the *Alabama.* Commander Bulloch, however, during the months he had expected to command the ship, had begun to gather officers. Semmes inherited these and used those whom he needed. John Low became the *Alabama*'s fourth officer and an Englishman, Dr. David Herbert Llewellyn, became the acting assistant surgeon. Bulloch probably also personally recruited E. Maffitt Anderson, who had arrived in Liverpool the previous February. James Evans, a pilot in Charleston harbor, had sailed on the *Nashville,* remained in England, and, obviously in close touch with Bulloch during the intervening months, became Semmes's master's mate. Bulloch provided two other steerage officers and a warrant officer, all Englishmen.

Finally, the Navy Department ordered to the *Alabama* four other officers who by some lucky magic arrived in Nassau in time to join Captain Semmes. Lieutenant Arthur Sinclair, who carried dispatches from the Navy Department to Semmes in Nassau, and Midshipmen Irvine S. Bulloch, William H. Sinclair (Arthur's cousin), and E. Anderson Maffitt also joined Semmes in Nassau. They all sailed with Semmes aboard the *Bahama* from Nassau to Liverpool, then on to the Azores.

Apparently it was well understood that Semmes would use his *Sumter* crew as the nucleus for the *Alabama* crew. The officers represented the best families of American naval traditions. The Sinclairs were both grandsons of Commodore Arthur Sinclair, who became famous during the War of 1812, and their fathers were both United States Navy veterans and commanders in the Confederate navy. There are seven Sinclairs listed as officers in the Confederate navy.[53] Midshipman Maffitt was the son of the *Florida*'s skipper (John N. Maffitt), and Midshipman Anderson was the same skipper's nephew and Major Edward C. Anderson's son. Midshipman Bulloch was Commander Bulloch's half-brother and the uncle of Theodore Roosevelt, Jr. But perhaps the most illustrious Confederate family connection was Marine Lieutenant Howell's, for he was brother-in-law to President Jefferson Davis. Because he had no marine detachment on board, Howell drilled the seamen in small arms fire, and according to Lieutenant Sinclair he was Semmes's favorite throughout the two-year cruise. The only black sheep on the entire officer roster was the future traitor, Clarence R. Yonge. To preserve the purity of the *Alabama*'s roster of officers, of its members who wrote of the cruise—Semmes, Kell, Sinclair, and Low—only Sinclair even mentions Yonge's name. Thus purged, the galaxy of names leading the motley crew of English, Irish, and Scottish seamen did create a Confederate sea-weapon worthy of their family distinctions.

Bulloch's arrangement for the three ships to meet at Praya Bay was accomplished without a hitch. Captain Butcher already had begun the transfer of weapons and stores from the *Agrippina* by the time the *Bahama* arrived with the officers and additional crew and guns. By Friday, 22 August, the *Alabama* was fully prepared to sail as a Confederate man-of-war. After two days of coaling, on Sunday, 24 August 1862, she sailed out of the harbor, the Confederate flag was raised for the first time, and the crew was enlisted. Fully commissioned, the first completely European-built, -equipped, -armed, and -manned Confederate naval vessel sailed into the open seas.[54] To the cheers of the men about to return to shore, the trim ship now under full sail and with banners flying entered upon her unique and destructive career. The *Alabama*'s two-year raid upon United States commerce is a story already told many times, filled with adventure and glory, and it lies outside the scope of this study. Not until June 1864 when the *Alabama* returned to European waters does the ship reenter this story.

In his efforts to put both the *Florida* and *Alabama* to sea Commander Bulloch was careful in all his actions to avoid any violation of England's neutrality law insofar as he could discern its meaning and application. His purpose was self-serving: he wanted to assure the success of many similar operations in the future. To this end he sought and followed the advice of a British solicitor. Thus he armed ships only on the high seas outside English jurisdiction; he signed crewmen in England for legitimate cruises, then once in international waters offered them the opportunity to enlist aboard an avowedly Confederate warship. His chief problem was that the law had never been tested by the principles of intended use or ship structure; it merely prohibited a belligerent from outfitting, arming, and manning a ship of war on or from English territory. The solicitor's advice was good only if the British courts and government interpreted the law in the same narrow way he did. As a matter of fact, given the Northern victory in the war and the principle enunciated by Lord John Russell in both the *Nashville* and *Florida* cases, the Geneva Arbitration Commission in 1872 determined that such action as Bulloch had taken did not relieve the British government from its neutral duty of prohibiting one belligerent from making war on the other from British territory, and the commission awarded an indemnity of $15 million to the United States as compensation for losses inflicted by three European-originated Confederate cruisers. The United States claims were known as the "*Alabama* Claims," reflecting the extent of that ship's destructive two-year cruise.

The arbitration award was based on rules agreed to by the United States and Great Britain in the Treaty of Washington in 1871. These rules are listed in Article 6 under the heading: "A Neutral Government is bound—"; the treaty makes no reference to the neutral's domestic law. The first rule is: "First: to use due diligence to prevent the fitting-out, arming, or equipment, of any vessel which it has reasonable ground to believe is intended to cruise or to carry on war against a Power with which it is at peace; and also to use like diligence to prevent the departure from its jurisdiction of any vessel intended to cruise or carry on war as above, such vessel having been specially adapted, in whole or in part, within such jurisdiction, to warlike use." The final arbitral decision based in part on this rule lays down as a principle of international law this statement: "The obligation of a neutral state to prevent the violation of the neutrality of its soil is independent of all interior or local law."[55] It is the very principle that the *Nashville* and *Florida* correspondence had elicited from Lord John Russell.

Taken together, this rule and principle render void the Nassau decision on the *Florida*. The Foreign Enlistment Act could not be interpreted in a narrow manner if Great Britain were to meet its neutral obligations, which it was bound to do. The rule stressed two concepts: the intended use of the ship, that is *intent;* and the *structure* of the ship "in whole or in part." The rule also stipulated that it would be sufficient to detain a vessel on "reasonable ground to believe" the intent or structure was warlike. Why would the British government agree to such a broad interpretation of its neutrality law as a basis for the arbitration?

One authority maintains that Great Britain did so for diplomatic reasons and to establish its rules "as rules of International Law for the future."[56] Yet the essence of the new rules was recommended by parliamentary commissions in 1868 and 1869 and, spurred by the Franco-Prussian War, enacted into law in 1870.[57] The creation of the parliamentary commissions in turn had been spurred by Confederate naval activities as early as 1861 when Russell admitted that the Foreign Enlistment Act might need amending. Indeed the detention order for the *Alabama* was based on the law officers' 29 July 1862 opinion that the *Alabama* "is intended for warlike use against citizens of the United States" and "is constructed and adapted as a vessel of war."[58] The law officers therefore recommended that the ship should be detained so that this broader interpretation of the 1819 law could be tested in the courts. The detention order for the *Alabama* arrived one day too late, due to Bulloch's "precipitancy" in putting the ship to sea. But the government, having failed in the case of the *Alabama*, seized the opportunity in the case of the *Alexandra*. Changing naval technology, United States diplomatic pressure, and British common sense thus combined to formulate the 1871 rules as early as 1862. Bulloch, North, and Slidell had no knowledge of this British line of thought, but they experienced a stricter British neutrality from the moment the *Alabama* sailed from Moelfra Bay. It is remarkable that under such conditions they were able in the coming months to accomplish as much as they did.

CHAPTER 3

The Hope-filled Era:
First Ironclad Construction,
July-December 1862

The Confederate ironclad construction program in Europe originated in Secretary Mallory's orders to Lieutenant James North on 17 May 1861.[1] Its roots, however, go far back in history. As early as the third century B.C. the king of Syracuse sheathed his vessels with lead, probably to protect them from sea-worms and accumulated marine growths. The sixteenth-century French and Spanish used the same technique to protect their ships against enemy fire, and in 1592 a Korean "tortoise-ship" with an iron-plated turtle-back deck defended against a Japanese invasion.[2] The immediate roots of Mallory's orders, however, rose from the earlier nineteenth century.

There were "five great naval revolutions of the nineteenth century"[3] that culminated in the 1850s and 1860s. The application of the steam engine increasingly freed the ship from the vagaries of winds and currents on the high seas and gave it maneuverability and power within the confines of rivers and harbors. The screw propeller permitted the designers to place the engines below the waterline for the first time and reduced the dangers to which the paddle wheels had been exposed. Rifled artillery pieces increased the range and accuracy of naval ordnance. Although the average wooden ship-of-the-line with its strong wooden walls still could withstand the solid shot even from a rifled gun, the introduction of the shell exploding on contact destroyed the balance between offense and defense in sea warfare, and it doomed the wooden warship. The offensive destructive power of the exploding shell on a wooden ship created the need for a defensive response: the armored ship. These five interrelated developments—steam, screw propeller, rifled ordnance, explosive shells, and armor—were all products of the nineteenth-century industrial revolution that produced the necessary metallurgical technology. As techniques of production improved during the decades prior to the Civil War, the five developments coalesced and gave birth in the 1860s to the most advanced naval architecture then known to man. With the questions of intent and structure already raised by the *Florida* and the *Alabama* this new naval architecture made the British Foreign Enlistment Act of 1819 obsolete. It threatened British sea supremacy and created an intense naval race between France and Great Britain, recent allies in the Crimean War, and inspired naval strategists to flights of imagination that even this new technology could not realize.

The decade of the 1840s was one of extensive experimentation. Unarmored iron ships, using steam and the screw propeller as auxiliary to sail, were built. Te ts that pitted shot and shell against wood and iron were conducted in France and England. Throughout this period, conservative naval experts resisted the growing evidence that exploding shells were more deadly against wooden ships than against metal armored ones. There were problems of size, speed, maneuverability, and general seaworthiness of large ironclad ships. The revolutionary era that began to sweep across Europe in 1848, with all of its political and social implications, temporarily delayed the experiments and slowed the data-gathering process; indeed, at that time the British navy decided against further consideration of the armored fighting vessel.

War, however, soon stimulated further development in the use of armored naval vessels. During the Crimean War, Russian forts proved that accurate shell firing could neutralize even large wooden ships-of-the-line. French Emperor Napoleon III suggested that floating armored batteries would be more successful than his major war vessels in reducing the forts. French naval designers soon built self-propelled, shallow-draft ironclad batteries armed with shell-firing cannon. On 15 October 1855 three such vessels, towed by steam frigates to the scene of hostilities, made their way to their posts of combat under their own steam, withstood the Russian shot and shell, and reduced the fortress at Kinbun. The fighting value of the armored ship was proven once and for all.

Certain design problems remained; they were solved by the French naval architect Dupuy de Lôme, working closely under Emperor Napoleon III. In 1847 Dupuy de Lôme already had designed the *Napoleon* as the first major war vessel to utilize screw propeller and steam as the chief motive source, with sails as auxiliary only. In 1857, as Napoleon III's chief navy designer, he advocated a fleet of seagoing screw-propeller and steam-powered armored ships. He solved the design problems of weight distribution, balance, and speed. The result was the first seagoing, steam-powered, screw-propeller, armored fighting ship, the *Gloire*, launched on 24 November 1859. In August 1860 the emperor and empress crossed the Mediterranean to Algiers in it; it handled well in

moderate seas, attained a speed of over thirteen knots, and showed no
signs of stress. The emperor in 1855 already had ordered that all new
naval ships be of iron only, and by 1860 the French navy had in being or
under construction six seagoing and nine coast-defense ironclad ships;
only the great cost prevented the completion of a projected forty-one
additional vessels. This first "French ironclad fleet was far more homo-
geneous than the British fleet designed to cope with it." It was in fact a
revolution in naval construction and was "due to the will of Napoleon III
and to the genius of Dupuy de Lôme."[4] Secretary Mallory had indeed
selected the right country for Lieutenant North's activities.

The French "revolution in naval construction" seriously affected
diplomatic relations between France and England, the two leading naval
powers, which in turn affected the Confederate European ironclad
procurement program. Step by step as each technological advance
occurred in the nineteenth century, officials on both sides of the English
Channel acknowledged the military and diplomatic implications. With
the eighteenth-century wars and Napoleon's experiences fresh in their
memories, the French in the 1820s could not help but exult that their
new naval guns would "sweep away England's superiority." The French
adoption of steam power in the 1840s led Lord Palmerston to announce
that the channel was no longer a protective barrier but simply "a river
passable by a steam bridge."[5] Stilled by the 1848 revolutions and the later
Crimean War alliance, the British anxiety over French naval power was
rekindled by the successes of the *Gloire* and her sister ironclads. The
British government responded with a crash program to construct its own
ironclad fleet; the *Warrior,* the *Black Prince,* and eleven other seagoing
iron ships were the result. The feverish activity in shipyards on both
sides of the channel made it difficult for the Southerners to schedule
construction, and it drove up costs and extended building time. Without
adequate funds, with almost no ready cash, it is a wonder the Confederate agents were able to contract for any ironclad ships.

Simultaneously with the testing of shell against armor, the development of the screw propeller and steam power, and the construction of
the French ironclad fleet, two other significant naval architectural
changes occurred: the reintroduction of the ram and the invention of
the gun turret.

Ancients, using oarsmen for power, had utilized the ramming technique to damage enemy vessels. When sails supplanted oars as the main
motive power for warships, ramming became impossible. Navy officers
of various nations, however, saw early that steam power retrieved for the
helmsman control of ship movement from the fickleness of the winds. As
iron steamships were adopted for naval use, the ram almost automatically reappeared; hundreds of ram designs and scores of ramming tests
marked the 1840s and 1850s. Although the *Gloire* was not armed with a

ram, its sister ship the *Couronne* and the British *Warrior* were. The smaller French coastal defense ships and all subsequent ones also were similarly equipped.

The notion of naval weapons mounted on a revolving platform in order to allow a sweeping field of fire was also an ancient naval idea. The nineteenth-century contribution was to perfect this notion in relation to armor and to the newer and larger guns. The desirability of utilizing this arrangement on smaller ironclads designed for harbor and coastal defense raised the problem of weight distribution. Many designers in various countries vied to perfect the gun turret, but the most successful was Commander Cowper Phipps Coles of the British navy, whose design was successfully tested by 1861 to handle guns as large as hundred pounders. The revolving gun turret was applied more easily to the smaller vessel than to the larger seagoing one; however, by early 1862 plans for a mastless ironclad seagoing ship were approved in England prior to the Hampton Roads battle.

Certain difficulties with ironclad ships still existed when the Civil War began, difficulties of which Secretary Mallory was not fully aware. He ordered Lieutenant North to try to purchase the *Gloire,* which he thought could range along the American coast and utterly destroy the Union fleet. What Mallory did not realize is that, although the *Gloire* was indeed a seagoing vessel, her creator, Dupuy de Lôme, had stipulated that she was not designed to go everywhere on the seven seas and that, indeed, she was "not destined to act far from European waters." Even within the relative calm of the Mediterranean, "she rolled a good deal and shipped considerable water in bad weather."[6] Such limitations of the excellently designed *Gloire* forebode ill for the Confederate European ironclad construction program because the Southerners would have to steam even their smaller vessels across the Atlantic, which later proved to be a most dangerous task.

The South's decision to use the smaller ironclad vessels was not a unanimous one, as we shall see, but rather was the decision of Bulloch and Maury, the leading Confederate navy agents in Europe. That decision was reached just after the *Virginia-Monitor* battle in Hampton Roads in March 1862 and as a result of Bulloch's careful analysis of the South's naval needs. The Hampton Roads battle was the first between two ironclad war ships. It proved, first, the superiority of the ironclad over the wooden ship when the *Virginia* destroyed the *Cumberland* and the *Congress* with such ease, and second, the value of the turret gun mounting. The first was no surprise to any naval designer; the second spurred the development of the turret gun-mounting system.[7] Because this system was most practicable on a smaller, harbor-defense vessel, Commander Bulloch was forced to reevaluate the Confederate naval needs in accordance with the feasibility of procurement.

James D. Bulloch's statement is a thoughtful and penetrating evaluation of the Confederate naval needs. Its broad sweep includes the effect of cruiser activity, the European public and governmental reactions and policies, his own experience in Europe, the latest naval technological developments—all in relation to the most efficacious role the navy could play in establishing the independence of the Confederate States. In both depth and scope, this analysis of the Confederate navy's situation almost a year into the war and of its potential is more important even than Secretary Mallory's early statement of naval strategy. Bulloch stated his ideas in two letters to the Secretary of the Navy in March and April 1862.

Analyzing the early 1862 European reaction to the *Sumter*'s depredations against unarmed Northern shipping, Bulloch concluded that the anti-Southern feeling was in truth a threat to the South's naval program in Europe. "The feeling everywhere in Europe," he wrote, "is strongly against the simple destruction of private property at sea . . . and the cruise of the *Sumter,* although evincing great energy, skill, and tact on the part of Captain Semmes, has resulted in no profit; but on the contrary has tended to incite some feeling against us among the commercial classes in Europe."[8] He had put his finger on a sector of English opinion most likely to influence the British government. British insurers and commercial agents as early as the spring of 1862 registered their complaints to the government. They wanted better protection for their property. One way to provide that protection would be to prevent Confederate ships from "escaping" from British territory. In view of public opinion, Bulloch urged not only that the Confederacy's assault against Northern merchantmen should be discontinued but that its "naval resources should be concentrated on defense."

Such a major change in naval strategy required a change in naval procurement. Bulloch maintained that seagoing cruisers, wooden or ironclad, no longer were needed. The *Virginia-Monitor* battle furthermore had proven the value of turret-placed guns in recognition of which the British government had "changed the entire plan of iron shipbuilding for the British Navy." The British now were cutting down their large wooden ships and converting them into ironsides with turret-mounted guns.[9] Because the turrets required low decks for a proper field of shot to avoid excessive armor weight and to assure proper handling of the ship, such vessels could not be seagoing cruisers. They would, however, serve well as harbor and coastal defense ships.

Combining the factors of emerging government attitudes toward greater restriction of Confederate activity in Europe, the defensive naval needs of the South, and the new naval technology favoring the required small, shallow-draft armored ships, Bulloch asked the essential question: how can the South safely and quickly acquire such vessels? His answer was radical: abandon the ship construction program in Europe and combine the South's timber resources with Europe's metallurgical technology to produce the ironclad ships. It was an alternative that even the new technology had not yet produced and that nonetheless was possible only with the new technology: lay the wooden frames of ships in the Confederacy where materials were plentiful; send to Europe the scale drawings or working plans of the ships; and Bulloch, following the specific designs, could order the iron plates openly and freely because this violated neither British nor French neutrality restrictions. He would mark and ship the plates to the Confederacy and the armored and armed ships could be completed in record time—in time, Bulloch felt, to do some good. This novel suggestion, a kind of prefabrication of an ironclad fleet, was never acknowledged by Secretary Mallory.

What if it had been? Would it decisively have benefited the South? Certainly the Southern harbor defense forces would have been strengthened. Perhaps the blockade at certain ports could have been lifted and internal rivers better protected. Southern metal, which the Confederate navy eventually used to plate many ships, would have been available to the army for munition manufacture, and the matériel gap between the South and the North, which Bulloch already recognized as decisive, could have been narrowed. But in the long run it was the moral leadership of Lincoln, the military strategy of Grant and Sherman, and the manpower advantage of the North that prevailed. Even Bulloch's ingenious and innovative plan could not have saved the Confederacy. However, in the spring of 1862, before Antietam, Gettysburg, and Vicksburg, the plan had merit and would have produced more positive results than the continuation of a policy that was already bankrupt. On the spot, working with the British shipbuilders, careful of the British neutrality law, and without sufficient funds or capable personnel, Bulloch could see what Mallory in Richmond could not see. It would have been better to have tried the scheme than to have ignored it.

Secretary Mallory had little time for such untried schemes. At the beginning of the war he had expected an ironclad of the *Gloire* class to clear Federal blockading fleets from Southern waters and to range along the Northern coasts destroying ships and laying siege to cities. North's inability to procure such a ship and the Anglo-French naval race had led him in late 1861 to rescind North's orders and to try to build the ships in the Confederacy;[10] but the expectations created by the *Trent* affair induced him to reverse himself and in January 1862 he had "associated" Bulloch with North in the duty of initiating the ironclad construction program in England. By the spring of 1862 the Confederate war posture was deteriorating. General McClellan was at Fortress Monroe (2 April) with a Federal fleet controlling Hampton Roads, and Union forces moving by sea occupied New Orleans (1 May). Still the South had no ironclad ships; Mallory felt the need more than ever. Goaded into fervent action, he signed contracts with irresponsible civilians who promised to deliver completed ironclads to the navy, and he sent special agents to England to negotiate for the construction of such ships. In September, after the first European naval contracts for ironclads had been signed, he exhorted Bulloch to exert every effort to get the ships to sea in the shortest possible time. "Not a day, not an hour, must be lost in getting those ships over," he wrote. With "those ships" he envisioned a reversal of the war's trends: "If we can succeed in getting them to sea armed, manned, equipped, we would go to New Orleans at once and regain the Mississippi."[11]

Under such urgent orders Commander Bulloch had no choice. He had to abandon his own scheme, applying his coastal defense theories only to the ships he ordered, and cooperate with the other naval agents in getting ironclads to sea. It was under these conditions—the Anglo-French naval race, the changing technology, and the urgency expressed by Mallory—that the Confederate navy in Europe entered into the first ironclad contracts. Bulloch signed with the Laird shipyard in Birkenhead for two small rams, and North and Lieutenant George T. Sinclair, a special agent, each signed with George Thomson in Glasgow, Scotland, for a frigate-class armored cruiser.

The First Contract: North's Number 61

Ironically and yet appropriately enough, the first Confederate contract for an ironclad vessel was concluded by Commander James H. North.[12] As in his other dealings, this one also was a confused and confusing affair. The contract was hurriedly drawn, the funding was inexact and uncertain, the command responsibility fluctuated from North to Bulloch, and worst of all the ship's design did not satisfy the South's needs. North had bungled the job. But the fault lies not totally on his shoulders. James North was the victim of the command confusion surrounding the *Florida* and the *Alabama* and of conflicting orders from Mallory as well as his own indecision.

After the *Florida*'s departure from Liverpool, North at first was unsure of his mission. He had received his orders to go to sea too late and he had no new orders; what to do? In April he consulted Captain Semmes, then in London after having left the *Sumter*. After examining North's conflicting orders, Semmes advised him to "await for the arrival of those funds" for a reasonable period.[13] Thus reassured, North remained still without a command, without funds, without a contract; but he did have hope.

North began to translate the hope into action. During his sojourn in the British Isles and probably through the efforts of E. P. Stringer, North met George Thomson, a Glasgow shipbuilder whose yards were on the Clyde River.

In early April, North and Thomson first discussed the building of an "armor-clad steamship." Encouraged by Thomson's interest, North wrote to Mallory once again asking for the two million dollars promised almost a year earlier. This time he expected to receive the money at once because he "had partially arranged" a contract "and Mr. Stringer had arranged to get my letter forwarded." He asked Thomson "to go on and make a model, plans, and specifications of such vessel as we have had conversation about."[14] That Thomson did so attests to his confidence in Stringer as much as in North. There still remained the problem of cash in hand.

Imagine James North's joy when the next month, probably just prior to 20 May, Fraser, Trenholm and Company forwarded to him "thirty odd thousand pounds." Because there were no instructions concerning the money North quite naturally assumed the funds were sent for the armored ship. He signed the contract with Thomson on 21 May 1862 and made a first payment of eighteen thousand pounds.

Actually, on 17 March Mallory sent the money for use in fitting out the *Alabama,* to which command he was assigning North; but North never received Mallory's original letter of 17 March and learned of the purpose of the funds only in late June, long after he had spent them.[15] Thus North's contract initially was financed by money intended for the *Alabama;* North never did receive the two million dollars promised by Mallory. The origin of North's ship was illegitimate; it was born of the unhappy mating of hope and misunderstanding, midwifed by good intentions.

The circumstances of its birth and fate denied the ship any real name. It is referred to in the letters of the day as Number 61 or as the Clyde River ram; later historians bestowed on it the bastard name of the "Scottish Sea Monster."[16] At first Number 61 seemed to deserve a better fate. The contract agreement called for it to be completed by 1 June 1863 at a cost of 182,000 pounds with payment to be made in ten installments according to construction progress. Although smaller than the *Gloire,* it was of the frigate class and was more akin to the newer *Couronne.* It was an armored seagoing ram warship, designed to encounter the enemy's navy, not just to prey on merchant ships. It would be better armored and more heavily armed than any Union ship in its class. In fairness to James North, then, it must be reported that Number 61 came closer to fulfilling his original orders than any other ship available to the South; by entering into this contract he felt he finally had complied with Secretary Mallory's orders of 17 May 1861. All he had to do now was to await the completion of Number 61, see to her arming, and arrange for her funding. But in wartime men's plans seldom work smoothly; certainly Commander North's would not.

When Bulloch read the specifications of the "Scottish Sea Monster" he was astounded. According to his analysis of the South's changing needs and in view of his newly developed defensive philosophy, he considered a seagoing frigate of 3,200 tons (fully equipped, 4,747 tons), 270 feet in length, with a draft of 20 feet to be precisely the kind of ironclad the Confederacy did *not* need. He tried to persuade North not to sign the contract: "I cannot help thinking . . . that in the present aspect of affairs, as well as in view of the unsettled opinions on the subject of ironclad ships, that it would not be advisable to go into a heavy contract for a cruising ship of that material." Commander Bulloch also was astounded at the low cost of such a large ironclad. His own inquiries had convinced him that no seagoing ironclad, even somewhat smaller ones, could be had for less than 200,000 pounds. In light of North's total cost of only 182,000 pounds, Bulloch's suspicions were aroused and he advised North "to stipulate for a forfeiture for nonfulfillment of contract." In terms of the much smaller ships needed for coastal defense, Bulloch further advised North that a "ship of less size, cost, and draft could be built." But North was adamant, claiming his "orders specific and preemptory."[17] After all the months of frustrating inactivity Commander North would not be denied this opportunity, and he happily entered into the contract for the ill-fated Clyde River ram.

Commander Bulloch's criticisms of North's ship and of the contract have led to recent harsh evaluations of North's efforts. In respect to the ship's size and to the Confederacy's needs as of mid-1862, the evaluation is justified and is reinforced by the ship's ultimate performance at sea. And on the face of it the contract did contain "imprudent clauses" and through "expensive omissions" did fail to protect the South's interests. To this extent it is apparent that "North had little bargaining ability and remained uncomfortable and off-balance in the complicated business negotiations surrounding this deal."[18] Yet there were extenuating circumstances. The clauses in question proved to be less imprudent than they might have been and the omissions were less important and thus not as expensive as they might have been.

North's inexperience in negotiating a ship construction contract led him to ask Bulloch for copies of his contracts for the *Florida* and the *Alabama*. The request was made at the height of the estrangement between the two officers and Bulloch contented himself with the reply that specifications for "wooden ships would be no guide" in negotiating for an ironclad.[19] North then turned to the man who was his original contact with the builders, the elusive and mysterious E. P. Stringer.

Stringer was a representative of the highly respectable London banking firm of W. S. Lindsay and Company. This firm, according to James Mason, "acted entirely in the interest of the South." Indeed, William S. Lindsay, a member of Parliament and the largest shipowner in England, was a confidant of French Emperor Napoleon III. During the war years he conferred with the emperor four times on means of forcing a joint British and French recognition of the Confederate States.[20] Lindsay also had strong ties with the English cotton manufacturers and his pro-Southern inclinations, despite Mason's notion, seem to have been as much financial as ideological. Vaguely floating through the documents of the period was a name variously listed as Edgar P., E. P., or H. E. Stringer; Stringer was Lindsay's chief liaison with the Confederates. Not only did he introduce North to George Thomson, the builder, but he also witnessed the North-Thomson contract for Number 61. Although Lindsay's financial interests dictated the Lindsay-Stringer activities, they did serve the South; Stringer's self-interest was involved also because it was the custom to pay a handsome finder's fee for such contracts.[21] Mason's evaluation, perhaps, was not entirely naive. Could Commander North have found a better adviser?

He was not, himself, sure of the arrangement; indeed, North's ardor to do something for the South and his high hopes for Number 61 were constantly in conflict with his self-doubt. When he sent a copy of the contract to Secretary Mallory he revealed his anxiety: "As I am dealing with first-class builders, I had the contract drawn up more loosely than I otherwise should have done. But as I had not a cent of money when I first agreed with the constructor, I thought it best not to be too exacting." To cover his position he also sought James Mason's opinion. "All that I did, however, met with the approval of Mr. Mason," he wrote to Mallory, "and I hope that it will also meet with that of the department."[22] North's contract, then, was negotiated in the absence of Bulloch's advice and through the auspices of a self-interested employee of a member of Parliament who openly espoused the Southern cause, and it was approved by the highest-ranking Confederate government agent in England. Whatever imprudence it contained cannot be laid solely at North's feet.

Those "imprudent clauses" pertain primarily to the payments and construction schedules, which were interrelated. The contract was precise. The first payment of 18,000 pounds was made on the signing of the contract; a second one of 12,000 pounds would be due in one month, when the vessel's keel was laid; a third payment of 18,000 pounds would be due the third month after the contract date if the ship was in half-frame. Each payment then was tied to both a time and a building schedule. Should the building fall behind the time schedule, the payment too would be delayed. Such an arrangement was common in shipbuilding and held advantages for both parties. The buyer's heavy expenses were stretched out over the whole building time and the payment schedule served as an incentive for the builder to meet the construction schedule. On the other hand, the builder always had in hand the capital for each stage of construction. At first all went well. Commander North's 30,000 pounds was exactly enough to meet the first two payments, and the Scottish spring and summer good weather allowed Thomson to meet the construction schedule.

When North signed the contract he was confident that the 30,000 pounds was just the first of a series of installments of the 200,000 pounds he expected from Richmond. There was really no reason for him to think otherwise because the Navy Department's credit in England was "very sound" with "all liabilities" being paid "very promptly."[23] Thus James North had high hopes.

George Thomson, on the other hand, was not so optimistic. Because the payments depended upon an unrecognized government still fighting for its independence, Thomson had to protect himself against financial loss. The fifth clause of the contract provided Thomson's protection. It stipulated that should North fail to meet the third payment, Thomson would "be at liberty" to stop the work on the ship and at the end of an additional two months to cancel the contract.[24] If North were to make the payment on schedule, then Thomson's fears of dealing with the Confederacy would be allayed; he then could proceed with the contract in confidence.

The hedge was well taken but poorly placed. Thomson had omitted Bulloch from his calculations. Despite North's worries and despite Richmond's growing difficulties in transferring funds to England, Commander Bulloch with funds in hand made the third payment on schedule. Construction did not stop; the contract's integrity passed Thomson's test. The South's funding crisis occurred just after the third payment was made. By the end of September the Confederacy's domestic exchange was practically exhausted. The money shortage lasted throughout the autumn of 1862 and into the winter of 1863. It obviously affected the fourth payment to Thomson; not until 23 December did Bulloch pay the 22,000 pounds that were due at the end of October. In the meantime Thomson, committed to the contract by the third payment, continued work on the ship although he was slowed by bad weather.[25] If the contract contained an "imprudent clause" in the payment schedule it was the wiley Scotsman, not North, who suffered from it.

One of the "expensive omissions" in North's contract was his failure "to insist that the builders provide protection against the elements." He had not heeded Bulloch's admonition to stipulate for a "forfeiture of nonfulfillment of contract." Again at first glance this omission does appear to be costly because the adverse weather of the Scottish winter slowed construction; men could not work in the cold rains. Yet the facts of the construction of Number 61 indicate that this omission really did no harm. First, the payment schedule mitigated the omission; in order to receive payment Thomson had to complete a certain amount of work, regardless of weather conditions. In December North visited the shipyards and reported satisfaction with the progress because "as many men [are] being employed to work on her as is possible to work to any advantage in this season of the year."[26] How could North, behind in his fourth payment, criticize Thomson for being behind in the building schedule? Indeed, by late December the ship was only one month off the scheduled stage of completion. Even if he had had a forfeiture clause in the contract, North could not have enforced it.

Another omission refers to the ship's specifications, not to the contract itself. Because it was designed as both a sailing and a steam vessel, it should have had a device known as a "lifting screw" or, as North called it, "a propeller for tricing up." The purpose was to prevent propeller drag when the ship was under sail only. The device would increase the ship's sailing speed by several knots and thus reduce its sailing time and coal consumption. This latter was very important for Confederate ships, which were experiencing increasing difficulties in finding friendly neutral ports for coaling.[27] The arrangement had to be part of the original ship's design because it affected the construction of the stern. North was aware of all this but failed to stipulate it. On 15 August 1862, when Number 61's hull was almost half completed, Commander North suddenly noticed that the propeller was to be fixed in place. He immediately wrote to George Thomson: "In all our conversations I thought I had endeavored to convey the idea that the ship was to be fitted with a propeller for tricing up when not under steam or [when] under canvas alone." Because it was too late to make the change, North requested the installation of a clutch action that would allow the propeller to rotate freely when the ship was under sail alone. Yet much of the disadvantage of a fixed propeller remained. How had he permitted such an omission? As usual North shifted the blame: "The only way that I can account for not having seen it before was that the propeller was included in the machinery, and as I know very little about engines, etc., it entirely escaped my notice."[28] He had overlooked a vital factor of ship design and no explanation can relieve him of the responsibility for reducing the efficiency of a costly vessel.

During the last four months of 1862 North was filled with hope for his ship. He busied himself by inspecting guns to be placed on it and by requesting officer personnel for it. In September he urged Secretary Mallory "to send out suitable officers and enough of them so that I may do credit to them, myself, and country." In December he specified that Number 61 would require six lieutenants, one paymaster, one surgeon with one or two assistants, one master, one engineer with "about six assistants," a marine officer, and "some eight or ten midshipmen."[29]

If North had received the maximum number of officers requested, he would have had two more officers than Semmes had aboard the *Alabama*. While this seems to be an unusually large number of officers for a frigate, it pales beside the number of seamen North requested. To operate the ship properly he called for 500 men. Twenty-nine officers for 500 men is relatively few when compared to Semmes's twenty-seven officers for 150 seamen. The personnel requirement reflects that the Clyde River ram was too large and too expensive to serve the Confederacy's naval needs in 1862–63. North's ship was not the right sort.

In addition to the contractual and structural problems he faced, Commander North throughout the latter six months of 1862 was confronted with career problems that culminated in late December. These stemmed from the question of rank, responsibility for ironclad construction, and North's own dilatory approach to his duties. It all started with the cruiser command confusion and Bulloch's prior rank as commander. For a while North was busy and happy working with Number 61. But all the events still rankled; his pride in his career was hurt.

In late August, while Bulloch was on the *Bahama* seeing to the proper equipment and commissioning of the *Alabama,* North sent a cyphered message to Secretary Mallory: "You will please inform me as early as possible who is the senior or ranking officer out here. I understand in our army the regular officers take precedence and rank over the Provisional officer of the same grade. Is such to be the case in the Navy? As this is a matter of great importance, I beg that you will not fail to inform me in your next communication." He also complained two weeks later of having had no word from Mallory since 2 May and he again requested more money.[30] His messages to Mallory often were couched in accusative terms of complaint, as if the secretary were purposely evading him. It developed into almost a persecution complex. He had opened his 30 August message with these words: "I have written you so often upon the same subject that I hardly know if it will be worthwhile to intrude myself upon you again." That same feeling carried over to his ship. It had to be the best and it had to be ready when Bulloch's were completed. In early November, writing to George Thomson, he reported on the progress of the ironclads Bulloch was building and urged Thomson to "please not let him get ahead of us as I am so anxious that we should be ready at about the same time." A couple of weeks later he expressed fear that Bulloch was getting ahead of him with his ships.[31] That all of these matters in North's mind affected his career and his pride is revealed in his language when he requested the officers for his ship: "send out good officers . . . so that I may do credit to them, *myself*, and country." Commander North also suffered the misfortune of having many of his reports go astray.

All of these tendencies and symptoms along with North's long delay in arranging a contract finally led Secretary Mallory to write a series of letters that were critical and curt. It was just North's luck to receive on 22 December 1862 Mallory's letter of 26 October, which enclosed copies of letters of 17 March, 21 September, and 2 October. North had never received the originals and so the full impact of Mallory's opinion of him hit him at once. The hope Number 61 had given him was dashed into despair by the secretary's words. At one sitting Commander North had to read of reprimands, threatened recalls, and other rebuffs.

In the copy of the 17 March 1862 letter North learned that Secretary Mallory as early as July 1861 had ordered him to return to the Confederacy if he "could not buy or build ironclad vessels," and that on 27 September 1861 Mallory would have recalled him again had Bulloch not been absent from Europe. "Your remark in the brief note received last night," Mallory wrote, "upon the cruelty of keeping you abroad surprises me greatly." The letter of 21 September 1862 was milder in tone, except that from it North learned of the financial problems of the Confederacy. Also, Mallory concluded it with this curt reminder: "You have never acknowledged the receipt of your commission as a commander for the war."[32] So for the first time, on 22 December 1862, North learned that the secretary of the navy had twice wanted to recall him for failure to fulfill his original assignment; no action could so damage an officer's career as that one, no action could so damage an officer's pride and self-esteem as to learn much later that his superior had for months considered him to have failed in an assignment. But more hurt and pain greeted Commander North as he read the secretary's words under the date of 2 October 1862.

Quoting North's opening sentence of the 30 August dispatch, Mallory harshly reprimanded the commander: "Under any circumstances the appropriateness of this language by one whose duty it is to embrace every opportunity to keep his Government advised of his action is not

perceived . . . the dispatches received from you are few and not sufficiently in detail." If these words were cutting, the last three paragraphs
of the letter were devastating.

> You request to be informed "who is the ranking officer," you or
> Commander Bulloch, and you state that "it is a matter of great impor-
> tance." From your request I infer that you have received the commission
> of commander in the Navy, transmitted to you on the 5th of May last, and
> which your dispatches do not mention, and you are again requested to
> acknowledge receipt.
> The department does not regard the question of rank among its agents
> abroad charged with the specific duties of building and equipping vessels
> as a matter of great importance, and it does not suppose that any
> difference as to rank between you and Commander Bulloch is of any
> importance whatever in comparison with the public interests, or that it will
> be suffered in the slightest degree to interfere with them.
> In compliance with your request, however, you are informed that
> Commander Bulloch is senior in rank.[33]

Commander North, the traditions-following career officer, could have
received no greater rebuff than to learn once and for all that Bulloch,
until recently a civilian, now outranked him.

The letter of 26 October 1862, which had contained the copies of
these earlier ones, was almost as cruel, but on a slightly different order
of things. The secretary was concerned here with North's attitudes as
reflected in the dispatches already characterized as "few and not sufficiently in detail." Mallory opened the body of this letter with this
sentence: "I regret to perceive that your dispatches, though very brief,
seem to be conceived in spirit of complaint, which I deem uncalled for."
After citing his care in keeping North informed of his various assignments Mallory returned to the commander's uncommunicative nature.

> I regret that you have not furnished me with information in detail
> relative to your ship. From two interesting letters from Lieutenant Sinclair
> I have acquired some knowledge of her construction; but you will forward
> drawings and specifications and a copy of your contract by the first safe
> opportunity.
> I presume, of course, that you were not informed of the departure from
> England of Mr. Sanders, as he brought nothing from you.
> Ceaseless diligence, prudence, and ardor in all efforts for the construc-
> tion, equipment, manning and getting this ship to sea, without so violating
> British neutrality and foreign enlistment acts as to call for British interfer-
> ence, are demanded.
> Without the exercise of the utmost vigilance, caution, and zeal, and,
> possibly, with their exercise, serious embarassments may arise before these
> can be accomplished. I am unwilling therefore to retain in such a position

any officer one moment beyond his wishes, and if, from any cause, as the
tone of your letters lead me to apprehend, you prefer relief from this duty,
there are other fields of usefulness and honor to which the department will
promptly assign you.

You will number your letters in the future.[34]

Could even Commander North, as egocentric and unimaginative as he
was, not help but understand the secretary's meaning? Of course Mallory was implying that even a lieutenant was a more effective officer than
the commander; of course the secretary thought that North had known
of Sanders's departure and had failed out of indifference or procrastination to send letters; of course the secretary thought North lacked the
qualities to get his ship safely to sea without arousing British interference; of course the secretary was inviting North to request reassignment.

Commander North, as a proud navy officer, took the only course he
could. He replied as if he accepted Mallory's words at face value. In a
long and sometimes rambling letter he endeavored to answer point by
point.[35] His wording was at times contrite, but surprisingly he gave little
ground. By citing various dispatches he showed that the secretary had
known of the ship prior to Sinclair's letters; he explained how Mallory's
various orders concerning the commands of the two cruisers had been
contradictory; he explained how Sanders had changed his plans for
departure, making it impossible to get a letter to him. Interspersed
throughout were saving phrases, compliant in nature: "I regret very
much . . . to find how completely I have been misunderstood by you";
he seized on Mallory's use of "*seem* to be conceived in a spirit of
complaint," adding that Mallory was kind enough in using the term to
give North an "opportunity to clear away" what seemed to be the spirit
of complaint.

Mallory's attack forced North into some introspective objectivity: "I
am not a fluent writer; I write with difficulty, and do most earnestly beg
that you will not judge me by the length or frequency of my dispatches."
As to the brevity of his letters, he stated that "in such times as these I
thought it best if we could make ourselves understood, to be as laconic as
possible, but as it is your wish that I write more fully, I will endeavor to
do so in future." And he did so, beginning with this letter.

Despite the introspective nature of some phrases, Commander North
refused to budge on the question of rank. While agreeing that it should
never interfere with his work with Bulloch in "the public interest," North
added: "Still as a military man, I must feel that the question is in that
view one of importance, and I did hope that an ambition of thirty-odd
years might have been spared the shock of seeing the dearest hopes
crushed by finding myself made subordinate to one who was my junior

by many years, and who has not, by any act of professional distinction, won a place above his former superiors." In defiance of Mallory's comments, North was going to make that civilian understand the importance of rank to a military man; he would not give up. Perhaps North's sentence on Bulloch and rank reveals more of his character than all his letters together. Note the use of emotive words: ambition, shock, dearest hopes, crushed. Note, too, that Bulloch's achievements in procuring the two cruisers was not an "act of professional distinction." Commander North's own work in procuring a ship then logically would be outside the bounds of military professionalism. Perhaps that was why he looked forward to doing "credit . . . to myself" only after he had reached the high seas. Could he truly have been so blind to the exigencies of the war?

He would not give up his duty. He promised to exercise diligence, prudence, and ardor in seeing his ship to completion: "need I say to you that you greatly misapprehend the tone of my dispatches, if you can for one moment suppose, that I would desire to be relieved from duty, the consummation of which I can now for the first time see in the future." North, having written such a long letter, could not help but relapse into an old theme about which Mallory had warned him. In effect, North wrote, if Mallory had sent the two million dollars promised long ago in Montgomery when the two men first discussed this mission, then North could have accomplished as much as the others had. The accusative complaint, the excuses, were still there. Mallory must have sighed in hopeless resignation when he read Commander North's reply.

North himself, bravado aside, could not help but realize as 1862 drew to a close that his work in Europe had been unsatisfactory. The hope that he placed in the Clyde River ram was his last one; he would hold to it desperately. And yet 1862 had been a good year for the Confederate navy in Europe: two ships put to sea and goods and supplies sent to the soldiers on the battlefields. Commander North, however, had contributed nothing to those successes. Whether or not he would admit it, he had little prospect of contributing to it in the future. Bulloch and Mallory were right: the ship was too big for the job, and the man was too small.

Bulloch: The Laird Rams

Commander Bulloch's experiences with ironclad shipbuilding were no happier than were Commander North's. He suffered some of the same psychological problems that plagued his colleague. Disappointment at losing the command of the *Alabama* led him, as we have seen, to blame his isolation from his fellow officers in England on his appointment as a commander and further to express his suspicions that those officers were conspiring to prevent him from receiving a ship's command. He even offered to accept a reduced rank or to resign his commission altogether unless he was allowed to command a ship at sea.

In addition to these psychological problems, Bulloch daily faced real problems that might have overwhelmed a lesser man. Unlike North or Sinclair, Bulloch's experiences with two cruisers had made him aware of the British and United States efforts to prevent the "escape" of Confederate vessels from England. He took extra care therefore to cover his actions and he took extra precautions by seeking legal advice. The fear that he might do something to justify the detention of the ships was ever with him. Furthermore, as Mallory's most trusted agent in Europe, he faced from many different sources constant demands on his time and on his mental efforts. The special civilian and naval agents whom Mallory sent to Europe after the fall of New Orleans in his desperate efforts to procure ships and turn the tide of the war all depended upon Bulloch for advice on ship designs, living expenses, introductions to British arms manufacturers and shipbuilders, and especially for funds. Money, the getting of it and the accounting for it, was an incessant and time-consuming problem. It was at this time, after making North's fourth payment to Thomson, that Bulloch had only 4,000 pounds to meet all the Confederate navy expenses in Europe.[36] Such issues were a constant drain on his mental and physical energies.

Bulloch's own concern over the role the navy should play in the Confederate cause created inner conflicts. Despite his conviction that cruising against Northern shipping was counterproductive and that the South should limit its naval efforts to a coastal defensive policy, his professional training and ambition led him in May, while still expecting to command the *Alabama,* to admit: "Every aspiration in my heart is bound up in her, and I pray God to help me use her profitably in our country's cause."[37] And just as he devised his prefabrication scheme he learned of North's contract to build the large Number 61. The next month he himself contracted to build the Laird rams. Emotionally driven to fulfill the navy officer's professional desire to command a ship on the high seas, intellectually compelled toward a defensive posture using prefabricated ships completed in the Confederate States, ordered to oversee the construction of ironclad vessels in the British Isles, Commander Bulloch faced a vexatious dilemma. Secretary Mallory's order in July to turn over the *Alabama* to Captain Semmes partly solved the dilemma. Bulloch concluded "that at any rate" it was his "duty to carry out the orders of the Executive Government."[38] He then concentrated on the Laird ram contract.

Commander Bulloch's involvement in the Laird contract began in January as a mere collateral duty; by July it was his primary function. Originally charged with getting raiders to sea and expecting to command one of them Bulloch was still in Savannah on board the *Fingal* when he received the letter from Mallory that eventually changed his career. Having reversed himself during the *Trent* crisis, Mallory merely "associated" Bulloch with North in the reestablished ironclad ship construction program in Europe. He neither defined their relationship nor provided a timetable. When Bulloch returned to Liverpool his most urgent problems were the *Florida* and *Alabama*. Yet he dutifully studied the latest reports on ironclad ships and inquired about their cost and performance. His work with the Lairds on the *Alabama* naturally led him to consult them.

The Laird company was not only a natural choice but an exceptionally wise one for many reasons. Bulloch had established very good personal relations with John Laird, Jr., and with William Laird. He could speak freely with them, he trusted their technical knowledge, and they trusted him. There was another even more important reason. The William Laird and Sons Company under the direction of the elder William Laird had a long history of successful, innovative work. It built the first iron ship in 1829 and by 1842 had to its credit forty-four iron vessels built or under construction. It built iron war vessels for the East India Company and the Mexican and British governments. More to Bulloch's immediate interest, however, was the "iron-built ironclad" ordered by the British Admiralty on 30 August 1861.[39] This work in addition to the experience entitled the Lairds to receive the latest results of the tests that still were being conducted on armor plate resistance to shot and shell, the turret design, the latest guns and their efficiency against metal armor, and the latest structural designs of ironclad vessels. It was Bulloch's good fortune that he already had established a close personal relationship with owners of a company so experienced and so well informed.

The function and design of ironclad ships was still a matter of dispute even among the well-experienced and well-informed builders. Commander Bulloch's own ideas were based on what he now considered to be the most pressing Confederate naval needs: the protection of the ports and coasts. He therefore wanted small ships of shallow draft, well balanced to facilitate maneuverability in such waters. Yet he had another problem. These ships would have to cross the Atlantic Ocean, so they had to be large enough to be seaworthy. Working with the Lairds, Bulloch finally arrived at a satisfactory design. To have a ship "capable of acting efficiently either in the attack or defence of our coast," by a "close calculation of weights and form of model," they settled upon the following dimensions: "length, 230 feet; beam, extreme, 42 feet; draft, with crew and stores for three months, 15 feet; engines, 350-horse-power nominal; speed, 10 ½ knots; tonnage, 1,850." Thus did the future Laird rams reach the design stage.[40]

At this time, however, Bulloch had no order to begin construction and he still anticipated taking command of the *Alabama*. Yet his relations with the Lairds were so good and their trust in him so strong that on his request and without any payment they made plans and scale drawings of a ship to fit the agreed-to dimensions. On 10 June Bulloch received Mallory's letter of 30 April containing the order for two ironclads and announcing Semmes's assignment to the *Alabama*. Hiding his disappointment, not knowing the reasoning of the secretary, the commander immediately asked the Lairds "to make a tender for the contract." Because plans and drawings were completed, the builders easily could figure the costs. Within a few days the price was settled, verbal orders for the materials were made, and the contract was signed.[41] Thus so efficiently and quickly Bulloch fulfilled a collateral assignment that now became his primary duty.

Commander Bulloch, without naming the Lairds, informed Mallory that the builders had "shown great faith in the stability of the Confederate Government" and "great confidence" in him personally. Later he wrote that the contract arrangements were made "in the same way" as those for the *Alabama*. That is, Bulloch contracted as an individual for an unarmed ship to be delivered in Liverpool. It was, in his words, a "purely commercial transaction" and the Lairds never knew from Bulloch that he was acting for the Confederate government.[42] By contracting for two identical vessels, Bulloch received a total reduction in price of 2,500 pounds; the cost of each ship was set at 93,750 pounds, considerably below the 182,000 pounds of North's Number 61. The completion dates were set for March and May 1863. Furthermore, Bulloch reserved the right to make changes in the structure "as experience during the progress of the work may suggest." This stipulation was a concession to the ever-changing technology of ironclad ship architecture and allowed Bulloch to take advantage of any new developments that might emerge within the next several months.

Oddly, the physical feature of the ships by which they were to become famous in history, the rams, were but indirectly mentioned in Bulloch's long descriptive letter to Mallory: "The bowsprit will be fitted with a hinge so as to be turned inboard when the ship is to be used as a ram." No other reference appears in Bulloch's detailed account of the vessels. What were they like? Even now the ram measurements are unsure: they "protruded some six or seven feet beyond the prow" and when the ships were in motion their rams "remained three or four feet below the water line."[43] Bulloch referred to the ships in his correspondence of the day mostly as "my armored-clad ships," seldom as the rams. Yet history identifies them consistently as the "Laird rams." The ram was a feature of many ships already existing or under construction; to naval contemporaries it was not the ships' "most distinguished feature." To Bulloch and other naval experts the most impressive offensive features were the two gun turrets on each ship; turret-mounted guns had proven their worth in the *Virginia-Monitor* battle, and Bulloch's were the only Confederate ships being built in Europe with them. As construction progressed Bulloch spent more time studying the various turret arrangements then proposed than he did on any other aspect of the ships. Tests conducted by the British navy, designs sent by Mallory, consultations with the Lairds—all concerned the most effective turrets to be used on the ships according to size, ship gravity center, the field of fire, and accuracy in heavy waters. Finally Bulloch decided on the Coles turret design, generally accepted as the best of the day. Indeed, if Bulloch's interest and time spent are any gauge of the ships' "most distinguished feature," then they should be called not the Laird rams but the "Laird turret-ships." In fact, most naval contemporaries referred to them, as did Bulloch, simply as Bulloch's "armored-clad ships" or according to the Laird yard designation, Numbers 294 and 295. It was the laymen, the diplomats, and the journalists in 1863, when the ships' existence became common knowledge, who emphasized the ram feature and from whom history has taken its cue.

Compared to other ships afloat or under construction, Bulloch's were not particularly impressive. Each was fifty feet shorter than the French *Couronne* or North's Number 61, displaced 1,400 tons less, and had a draft of five feet less. All of these had armor plate and rams. But Numbers 294 and 295 were larger than the Union *Monitor:* forty-one feet longer, slightly wider amidship, about 550 tons more displacement, with a deeper draft of almost five feet. Neither the smallest nor the largest, Bulloch's ships were nonetheless unique in a most important facet because they were the only ships to contain all five of the nineteenth century's contributions to naval architecture plus the turret-mounting system for the rifled guns firing both shot and shell. Furthermore, and Bulloch and Mallory most appreciated this fact, they were designed specifically to serve the naval function at the moment most needed by the Confederacy. The monitors with their low freeboard could not fight in the open waters, and Number 61 as large as it was could not enter inland waters to encounter the monitors. Only Bulloch's armor-clad ships, necessarily capable of crossing the Atlantic, were designed to do both. Herein lay their potential threat to the United States.

The anticipation of putting such formidable ships into service led the secretary and his chief European agent into creative flights of fancy. They could visualize the tide of war turning. Secretary Mallory's imagination knew no bounds when he learned of the ships. They should, he wrote Bulloch, "go to New Orleans at once and regain the Mississippi . . . the river would be open to you and you would reap imperishable renown in restoring the Crescent City to our arms." At the same time, Bulloch hinted at other uses for the ironclads: "I think they will be as near in approach to cruising ships as can be devised, when the powers of offence and defence are considered in conjunction with their light draft of water." Before receiving Mallory's suggestions, Bulloch elaborated on the cruising qualities of the vessels, a characteristic almost ignored by history. "As their life must necessarily begin with a sea voyage of over 3000 miles, it was absolutely necessary to secure good seagoing qualities and fair speed, which I think I could not have done on less draft and dimensions."[44] Bulloch had created weapons of war that in the minds of his contemporaries could cross the ocean, maneuver the Mississippi River, and clear the Southern coast of Union blockaders; they contained all the latest technology—the turret-mounted shot and shell guns that all naval men feared and admired, the iron plate protection, the steam and screw propulsion, the auxiliary sail, the formidable ram. Numbers 294 and 295 were weapons of war that in 1863 would become, next to the *Alabama*, the greatest diplomatic problem of the war.

Their very design portended their seizure by Great Britain. Bulloch himself worried lest their obvious warlike qualities should attract the attention of the Federal spies and the British port officials. In the spring of 1862, while he and the Lairds were developing the ironclad design, he consulted a British solicitor to determine "whether armour-plating a ship could be considered 'equipment' within the meaning of the Foreign Enlistment Act." After studying the opinions on the *Alabama* the solicitor informed Bulloch that "the statute did not forbid the building of any description of ship, that the prohibitory clauses referred to the arming or furnishing a vessel with ammunition and ordnance stores for warlike purposes." Bulloch carefully arranged with the Lairds to have no magazines placed in the ship nor to provide any special places to store any shells or other ordnance. He also carefully maintained the pretense with the Lairds that the ships were not destined for a state then at war, that his order for them was in the nature of a purely commercial venture. Still he worried that their warlike features would attract the attention of the Northern spies and that the very structure of the ships would be sufficient cause for the British authorities to detain them. In early December, when the vessels were almost fully plated, Bulloch's apprehensions rose to the surface. "The two armor-clad turret-armed ships are progressing satisfactorily. I begin to fear that the Government will interfere with any attempt to get them out. The United States minister is pressing hard to induce the authorities to interfere. . . . However, I will go on as if still confident of success."[45] Commander Bulloch recognized that the new naval technology had made the Foreign Enlistment Act obsolete. No other Confederate navy agent realized this; indeed, even the British courts refused to admit it. Only Bulloch and the crown lawyers were perceptive enough to understand the full impact that nineteenth-century innovations necessarily would have on the existing domestic and international laws, especially after the questions of intent and structure had been raised by the *Florida* and *Alabama*. It took the British government many months to devise the methods to meet the new challenges. Bulloch, despite all his precautions, worried about losing the ships. At the end of 1862, however, good actor that he was, he carried on "as if still confident of success."

Not only did he speculate on how the ships would be used but he also suggested to Secretary Mallory who should command them. In early August, just after he had seen the *Alabama* safely away from the British Isles and just before he would turn her over to Semmes off the Madeira Islands and obviously still resentful at having lost her to Semmes, Bulloch wrote his report to Mallory: "Having already built two ships for the Navy, the second of which is as fine a vessel of her class as any service can show, and which I was to command myself, I am, as you have been informed, busily at work upon two armor-clad ships of entirely new design. . . . I earnestly beg leave to urge my claim to command one of these ships in person." A month later he returned to his desire to command one of them in a roundabout fashion: "As Captain Semmes will soon have a thoroughly organized crew, I respectfully suggest that one of these ships be put at his disposal. . . . I am sure that Captain Semmes would be pleased with such an arrangement, and I have written him that it was my intention to bring the matter to your consideration." Having so unselfishly raised the question of command, he noted: "I will not add anything on the subject of my being detailed to the command of one of these ships, but I beg to refer you to a previous letter in which I set forth my feelings and hopes. My ambition is to get afloat." In his response Mallory made no mention of Semmes. But he had to respond to Bulloch's own request and in doing so he was not unsympathetic. He understood Bulloch's personal and professional disappointment at losing the cruiser he had designed and nursed to life. "You were relieved of the *Alabama*," the secretary wrote, "only and exclusively because I did not feel that I could dispense with your services or supply your place in a position of far greater importance to the country than the command of a ship, and wherein you have rendered such good service."[46] Bulloch seems to have been mollified; after receiving this complimentary letter he never again requested the assignment. Mallory's truthful praise of work so well done was reward enough.

As 1862 drew to a close Bulloch was satisfied with the ships. Their progress was good; the Lairds even lighted the protective sheds with gas "so as to assure additional hours of work during the short, foggy days" of the winter season. Appeased on the matter of command and excited by the innovative features of the ships, he studied various turret designs, inspected the ships, planned their escape, and plotted their cruises against the Union blockading fleet. He did worry about the Northern agents' close watch over the ships. But while the ships remained unfinished and until the British government took some action, there was little he could do about it. The year ended with Commander Bulloch playing his role "as if still confident of success."

George T. Sinclair: The *Canton*

In August 1862 Lieutenant George T. Sinclair signed a contract with the James and George Thomson Shipbuilding Company for the construction of a cruiser named the *Canton*.[47] It was to be the last Confederate contract to build a major war vessel in the British Isles.

Strictly speaking the *Canton* was not to be an armored ironclad ship in the same sense as the Laird rams or North's Number 61. Yet it did incorporate some of the new technological features and Secretary Mallory expected it to operate in conjunction with the other three vessels. It was what Bulloch referred to as a "composite ship." Similar to the *Alabama* in design, it was a bark-rigged cruiser, 231 feet long, 33 feet wide, powered by both sail and steam. It differed from the *Alabama* in that it had an iron frame, partial iron plating, and telescopic masts as well as a lifting screw propeller. Its original purpose was to prey on Northern shipping. Despite the differences, Sinclair's ship construction coincided in time with that of Bulloch's and North's ships, was subject to many of the same problems, and ultimately shared the same fate. The *Canton* then must be considered along with the Birkenhead rams and with Number 61.

Canton's 1862 story is brief; its real importance to Confederate navy history during the last months of that year relates to the relationships among Sinclair, North, and Bulloch, and to Sinclair's unique financial arrangements.

George T. Sinclair, one of the seven Sinclairs who held commissions as officers in the Confederate navy, was a native of Norfolk, Virginia. He came from a family with a long navy tradition. Such families often intermarried or developed close family friendships that lasted over several generations. Such was the relationship between the Sinclairs and the Norths. On his return from his futile buying trip to the Northern states in March 1861, James H. North stayed at the Sinclair Norfolk home, where his children were visiting. He lingered longer than he had intended, enjoying their company and receiving the calls of many old friends.[48] When James North and George Sinclair separated in Norfolk, they had little notion that they would next meet in England some sixteen months later.

George T. Sinclair had been a lieutenant in the United States Navy and, like so many others, had followed his native state into the Confederacy in April 1861. His first assignment was at the Gosport Navy Yard, near his home. Later he was transferred to the Savannah station, where he first met James Bulloch, who was there on his *Fingal* trip. When the Union blockade prevented that ship's return to Europe, Sinclair became its commander and supervised its conversion into the ironclad *Atlanta*. What kind of officer was he? The documents of the day give little insight into his abilities. Like James North, his rise in the United States Navy had been unspectacular but regular. His subsequent career in the Confederate navy offers little information. He perhaps had more initiative than North and assumed personal responsibility more readily; but he was no James Bulloch or Matthew Maury. One comment offers a suggestion of the opinion at least one other Confederate officer held of Sinclair. Major Edward C. Anderson, who had returned to the Confederacy on the *Fingal* and expected to go back on her, criticized him for failing to get her through the blockading ships: "Sinclair had neither brains nor dash enough to get her safely clear of them," Anderson noted in his diary, "and yet I feel sure that either Bulloch or I could carry her out."[49] Anderson, himself a man of considerable energy and aggression, tended to be impatient with anyone who did not share those qualities, as evidenced by his comments concerning James North's visit aboard the *Camilla*. Yet he could be very positive toward those he considered intelligent and hard working, such as Major Huse and James Bulloch. His evaluation of Sinclair, then, cannot be taken at face value. Sinclair, unlike Bulloch and North, left too few letters for a penetrating analysis of his personality and abilities except to mention that his old navy ties tended to thrust him into association with the James Norths more than with the James Bullochs.

Secretary Mallory apparently entertained a high opinion of Sinclair because on 7 May 1862 he ordered the lieutenant from the *Atlanta* to duty in Europe with specific instructions to "construct or purchase a clipper propeller for cruising purposes" and to command her. Mallory directed Bulloch to render all aid necessary and to offer all financial assistance needed. Sinclair's European assignment fell within the designation of a "special service," that is, a navy officer whose duty was specific and whose authority derived directly from the Navy Department. Such an officer did not fit into the European activity pattern nor the command chain as did those who were assigned on a more permanent basis. Sinclair's assignment falls more in the category of Mallory's desperate response to Northern victories, such as the capture of New Orleans on 1 May 1862, than in the category of the secretary's strategic approach to Confederate naval needs. Indeed, at the time Mallory sent Sinclair to Europe he also was sending civilian special agents, referred to as "private contractors." They reflect one of the Confederate navy's chief weaknesses in Europe—a lack of clear-cut authority and organization. Perhaps Commander North had been right: the question of rank—that is, authority—was a most important matter to the navy in Europe.

Lieutenant Sinclair's status came close to being changed prior to his arrival in mid-July 1862. If communications between Richmond and Europe had been more sure, he would have replaced James North. On 12 July, before he learned of North's contract, and disgusted with North's complaints and inactivity, Mallory ordered North to "turn over to Lieutenant G. T. Sinclair the instructions you may have received, together with any public funds in your hands, and return to the Confederate States."[50] If Sinclair had replaced North, his status would have been more regular and he would have come under Bulloch's command. The drama of the subsequent Confederate navy history then would have had a different cast, but the plot probably would have been unchanged.

Sinclair's role as a special service officer placed him in the same category, in Bulloch's mind, as the Confederate civilian "private contractors."[51] Both types made demands on his time, funds, and energy, and as such they affected the Confederate navy story in Europe.

"Private contractors" were basically speculators who offered fanciful plans to the government and duped the officials into supporting them. Mallory's concern over the Union victories made him especially susceptible to such schemes. The pattern was this: a private contractor offered to procure a ship, deliver it to a navy representative on the high seas for a set price, and pocket the profit. But he needed official approval and financial support; Secretary Mallory provided the former and delegated the latter to Bulloch. But because there were never sufficient funds in Europe after late 1862, no such private contract ship was ever constructed in Europe. Private contractors' activities, however, often were reported in the London press and the contractors were described as Confederate agents. This publicity, Bulloch claimed, strengthened the United States's protests against Southern ship construction in Great Britain and influenced the stricter application of the British neutrality law. Obviously, he thought little of the idea of "private contractors" and urged Mallory to stop sending them to England.[52]

Naval officers on special assignments of course were not the same as the private contractors. Nevertheless they were an aberration in the pattern of the Confederate navy's European operations. As did their civilian counterparts, they made demands on Bulloch's energies and ever-dwindling funds; they attracted the attention of Federal consuls and British authorities; they thus disrupted regular naval activities. That undoubtedly is why Bulloch in his memoirs covers private contractors, Sinclair, and Matthew Fontaine Maury[53] in the same chapter. Sinclair arrived in England in the midst of the *Alabama* command confusion and at a time when Bulloch had little funds to finance the construction of another cruiser. If Bulloch shared Anderson's opinion of Sinclair, he probably was even less happy to have another officer to care for—North was proving to be quite a handful. Sinclair, nonetheless, managed to secure finances and contracted with North's builders for the *Canton*. Because the contract came only in October, the ship made little impact on events during the next two months. There are, however, significant and revealing subcurrents that Bulloch and other contemporaries completely ignored in their writings.

First there is the manner in which Sinclair managed to finance the construction of the *Canton*. Bulloch refused to aid Sinclair because of his own financial obligations on existing contracts. Neither the money nor credit existed. Yet during this time Sinclair found sufficient funds to pay cash for the *Canton*. How did he do it?

Sinclair managed the financing through a fortunate happenstance involving Commander North, private contractor George N. Sanders of Virginia, and the same E. P. Stringer who represented W. S. Lindsay and Company and was North's intermediary with Thomson. George Sanders, like Stringer, was a shadowy figure whose name weaves in and out of the documents. He proposed to the Confederate government a scheme to establish postal service between Europe and the South—something much to be desired. His idea was to combine state postal service with his own profit-making passenger and freight service by using "perfect self-protecting freight transport vessels" with six heavy guns. Such an armed ship also would act as a cruiser during its mail-freight runs, and Sanders would retain one-third value of all prizes taken. This combined postal-freight-naval vessel would be commanded by a government-appointed officer, presumably from the navy, and manned by Sanders's own employees.[54] Sanders somehow persuaded the Confederate government to give him a supply of cotton certificates to finance the purchase and outfitting of the necessary vessels. When Sanders arrived in England, he went directly to the Confederate State Department's agent, James Mason, to enlist his help in peddling the certificates.[55] It was at this time, around the beginning of September 1862, that events concerning Sinclair's finances chanced to coalesce.

As Sanders approached Mason, Stringer approached North with another suggestion for using cotton certificates to raise funds for the construction of Confederate ships. This suggestion could be the plan North later said he received from William S. Lindsay and Company. In September, receiving no encouragement from Mason, already busy with his Clyde River ram, and "having no authority to build more than one ship," North passed the Stringer plan to Sinclair, who turned to Mason for approval. Mason, suddenly faced with two different cotton certificate schemes, one from Richmond and one from London, chose the course of least responsibility. He delayed Sanders's proposal and approved Sinclair's because it involved less money, and he immediately wrote to Secretary of State Benjamin asking for instructions on certain conditions Sanders's would-be creditors demanded.[56]

Those instructions never arrived; Mason's actions condemned Sanders to history's oblivion. It was perhaps just as well because the mail-freight-cruiser scheme was too innovative to have been accepted. Not only did Mason and Bulloch not understand Sanders's idea, but recent historians have failed to explain it clearly.[57] He was and is treated as having connections only with the Confederate Navy Department, when in reality he was supported more by the State and Treasury departments. Sanders's importance to the navy is simply that Richmond's approval of his cotton certificates led Mason, who believed it was policy supported by the government, to approve the Stringer-Lindsay cotton certificate scheme for Sinclair.

Lindsay's reputation as a man of integrity, a member of Parliament, and a confidant of Emperor Napoleon III opened many doors to him. The plan was to produce ready cash through the simple expedient of getting the cotton manufacturers to advance money on the cotton certificates. This maneuver adroitly avoided the vagaries of the London stock market and more importantly maintained a curtain of secrecy about the whole thing. It worked well; without ever transferring money to Sinclair or to any Confederate official, the sale provided 62,000 pounds for the construction of a ship to be paid for and owned by a combine of seven British subjects. This combine contracted immediately with the Thomsons, already at work on North's ship, to build the *Canton*. Bulloch and Sinclair provided the ship's design and Sinclair became the responsible officer. No Confederate money was paid to the contractors.[58] Thus, because of North's nonchalant passing of Stringer to Sinclair, the Confederacy potentially gained a formidable warship without any immediate cost or obligation. The important thing for the Confederate navy was that Lieutenant Sinclair would supervise the construction of a paid-for ship that was intended to sail under his command against the enemy.

Yet Sinclair's success caused problems for the Confederate navy program in Europe. He was the only Confederate navy agent up to that time who had available cash equal to the total construction cost of his ship, and this disturbed and embarrassed Bulloch. One officer's payments in cash contrasted starkly with another's payments in arrears. Bulloch argued that this situation would make it difficult to place future orders on credit because "a creditor will not be satisfied to wait indefinitely for payment when he finds his debtor (the Navy Department) making purchases elsewhere for cash."[59] In effect Bulloch was chastising Secretary Mallory for sending individual agents whose successes would vary; he was reminding the secretary of the need for centralized authority and for consistent and coordinated efforts.

Nonetheless Sinclair's success in raising money through the cotton certificates had significant implications for Confederate naval operations in Europe. First, it confirmed that cotton could be converted into European currency by such a paper transaction. Already the government had determined to try this procedure, and several different forms of certificates and different methods of disposing of them had been suggested. For each of the various Confederate agents to compete with one another, obviously, was ridiculous. So the government appointed one agent, James Spence of Liverpool, to handle all of the certificates. This was not altogether successful, and eventually the now-famous Erlanger loan, which despite its limitations did make possible the bulk of the navy's construction in France, was tried.[60] Second, Sinclair's particular method of financing his ship led also to the ingenious contractural procedure that actually as well as legally bestowed ownership of the *Canton* upon seven British investors and relieved the Confederacy of all monetary responsibility. Furthermore, one of the owners was James Galbraith, North's lawyer and like Stringer a witness to the North-Thomson contract. Stringer, the fixer, did not have a share of ownership, but he must have profited from the deals. These close connections between North, Galbraith, Stringer, and Lindsay cannot be traced with precise accuracy, but they did make possible the construction of the *Canton*.

The fact that Sinclair had turned to North when he had discovered Bulloch could not furnish him with funds reflects the close relationship between the old friends. They lived in the same building at Bridge of Allan near Glasgow and their two ships. Together they inspected the two vessels under construction, attempted to place orders for cannon with the same manufacturer to save money, addressed one another in their correspondence as "Jim" and "Terry," and Terry constantly sent warm greetings to Jim's wife and daughter, Em and Annie. The personal clash between North and Bulloch implicitly included Sinclair. It was just after Sinclair's arrival in England that Bulloch spoke of the conspiracy among his fellow officers to prevent him from receiving a sea command. On one occasion Sinclair wrote to North: "Bulloch is here. I have seen much of him, and have a great deal to tell you when we meet."[61] These undercurrents of Sinclair's activities in the long run contributed to Bulloch's troubles and hampered Confederate navy activities in Europe in a way Secretary Mallory in Richmond never really understood.

As 1862 drew to a close the Confederate navy agents in Europe could view their year's efforts with a good deal of hope. The year had not gone badly for the South. At home the army had proved it could repel Northern challenges. The Peninsular battles had forced the Union army back to the coast, and the clear-cut victory at Second Manassas had led to Lee's abortive attempt to invade Maryland. Lee later balanced defeat at Antietam by staunch defense of Fredericksburg. Except in Tennessee and northern Mississippi, the South in the main still stood free from the Union army. Only from the sea had the South suffered losses. The Union fleet stood in Hampton Roads, and other Northern ships forcing Confederate defenses on the Mississippi River had taken New Orleans. Still the *Virginia*'s stand against the *Monitor* provided hope that the tide yet could be turned. In England the navy had sent supplies and munitions into the South and had constructed and put to sea two cruisers. The *Alabama* carried the Confederate flag against enemy shipping. Even more exciting, agents in England had contracted for three ironclad warships and one composite vessel, all of which were capable of carrying the war directly to the enemy's warships. Commanders Bulloch and North along with Lieutenant Sinclair seemed to sense the urgency of their missions. Hope and anxiety filled their chests.

The hope was mixed with a latent foreboding. The two commanders had suffered severe disappointments when Semmes sailed as captain of the *Alabama*. Their personalities clashed. Mutual suspicion arose between them. They had not cooperated as closely as they should have and this behavior had hurt their country in delays and costly contracts. As 1862 drew to a close their chief fear was that a lack of money would delay further the ship construction or perhaps even force them to forfeit the vessels. James D. Bulloch sensed an even greater threat to his work. During December he noted a growing number of United States Consul Dudley's agents in and around the Laird shipyard in Birkenhead. Despite his minute and legalistic precautions to hide the ultimate destination of Numbers 294 and 295, Bulloch's fears mounted at this indication of tightened British neutrality. The new year would bring those fears to culmination. Not only would Gettysburg and Vicksburg place a noose of defeat around the South, but the loss of the ironclads to British policy would spell the doom of Bulloch's efforts to build an ironclad fleet in Great Britain.

CHAPTER 4

British Neutrality Tightens: 1863-1864

The International Setting

The year 1863 was considered to be the turning point in the American Civil War.[1] It began well for the Confederacy. Lee defeated Hooker at Chancellorsville in early May and despite Stonewall Jackson's death still felt strong enough to challenge the North in its own territory. Crossing the Potomac on 15 June, Lee marched northward only to suffer defeat in the three-day Battle of Gettysburg on 1–3 July. Almost simultaneously in the west, Vicksburg fell on 4 July. The Southern high-water mark was reached. Even so, Lee's defensive genius repulsed General Meade at the Rapidan River in northern Virginia and the year ended in an apparent stand-off. The armies faced one another in almost the same positions as the previous May. The differences, however, were real. Manpower and matériel sacrificed in the Pennsylvania hills could not be replaced.

In Europe the Confederate navy also experienced setbacks just as irreversible. The armored ironclad shipbuilding program, once so promising, in early 1863 began to suffer construction delays, then investigations; diplomatic exchanges led to British detention and seizure of each ship. By year's end it became increasingly clear that the British government intended to deny the ships to the Confederates.

At the same time European international relations shifted from an uneasy tension into full-blown crises. British concern over French annexations of Savoy and Nice was intensified by the Polish Insurrection and by growing signs of Scandinavian nationalism clashing with the German confederation over the complicated question of rightful rule in the Schleswig-Holstein provinces. Furthermore, Napoleon III extended his unilateral intervention in Mexico. The American struggle, until 1863 the main disturbance on the international scene, was now but one of several problems. This change inevitably affected the Confederate navy agents in Europe.

The Polish Insurrection, lasting from February to November, contributed to further estrangement between France and England. Russian methods of suppression were harsh and French sympathies were almost united in favor of the Polish people. Foreign Minister Drouyn de Lhuys, encouraged by Lord John Russell, made three distinct efforts to arrange an international diplomatic intervention but each time the British cabinet forced Russell to back down. The Austrian government, willing to act only in conjunction with London and Paris, blamed the British cabinet's reluctance on fear of a war with the United States. For whatever reason, the diplomatic differences between London and Paris grew greater in the course of the year.[2]

French involvement in Mexico developed gradually during the first six months of 1863. The defeat before Puebla in May 1862 prompted Napoleon III to send reinforcements under General Forey during that summer. Forey's progress was slow. After a long siege he finally captured Puebla in May 1863, and his movements toward Mexico City were just as deliberate. Not until 10 June 1863 did he enter the Mexican capital; the emperor learned of the success at about the same time he learned of Gettysburg and Vicksburg.[3] The impact of the American struggle on his views was to affect Confederate ship use of French ports and the South's attempt to save the Laird rams through a French connection. But most importantly it diminished the ability and the will of France to exert influence on the British government's policies toward the Civil War and especially toward Confederate naval activity within the British Isles.

One other factor reached a turning point in 1863. In 1861 the surplus cotton in the British warehouses had frustrated Secretary Mallory's expectations of an early European intervention in the war. But by the autumn of 1862 the surplus cotton was exhausted. The worst period of unemployment in England and France were the winter months of 1862–63. Precisely during those months the South experienced its greatest success in raising money on cotton credit: Bulloch and Prioleau financed the Laird rams on cotton certificates; Matthew Fontaine Maury, as we shall see in Chapter 5, easily secured funds to purchase the *Georgia;* the Stringer-Lindsay-Sinclair deal made the *Canton* contract possible; and, most useful, the Erlanger loan was negotiated and floated. But by the end of 1863 new cotton sources—especially India, Egypt, and Brazil—had begun to take up the slack, unemployment was reduced, and production was increased.[4] Furthermore, President Lincoln's Emancipation Proclamation, effective on 1 January 1863, went far during the worst months of unemployment to allay the British workers' cry for intervention. Popular meetings, pamphlets, and political pressures publicized this humanitarian side of the American war. Public opinion, as Bulloch had noted, also was aroused over the *Alabama*'s sinking of merchant ships, and insurers complained to Palmerston's government. When cotton began to reach Europe from the new sources, pressure on British and French attitudes began to change. In both countries policy decisions led to ship detentions and seizures. By year's end Confederate naval agents in Europe realized that their dream to construct a navy in Europe was over; but they never gave up the effort.

The Confederate navy suffered its initial setback in Europe not as the result of any one event but from a coalescence of many things: fortune of battle in the Pennsylvania hills and along the Mississippi River; resistance of a far-off people in Poland to Russian rule; clash of Scandinavian and German nationalism over two obscure northwest German-Danish provinces; French involvement in Mexico; growth of cotton in remote lands; emancipation of slaves in America and changing public opinion in England; and, most of all, the construction of ships that directly challenged the Foreign Enlistment Act.

All those factors undoubtedly influenced the British decision that more immediately affected Bulloch, North, and Sinclair. It was a decision reached only after much trial and error, only after great legal and political introspection, and through extensive judicial action. The British government determined, despite the cotton shortage, before Gettysburg and Vicksburg, and perhaps because of the new naval technology and public pressures, to reinterpret its 1819 domestic law regulating the actions of the queen's subjects toward the belligerents of a war in which the government maintained a posture of neutrality.

The Legal Setting

Commander Bulloch claimed that among the various reasons the Confederates chose to operate in England was their expectation of "more liberty of action . . . and surer means of discovering what might be safely attempted," whereas in France "everything . . . would depend upon the secret purposes of the Chief of State."[5] In effect, he was saying that it was easier to work within the known law of a liberal society than to try to anticipate the whims of an absolute ruler. At first he was probably right; the *Florida* and the *Alabama* reflect that. But circumstances were soon to change.

During the Crimean conflict in the 1850s Great Britain had been "a liberal state at war."[6] Liberal principles, placing individual rights above the state, had limited the government's war-making powers. Only the forceful and sometimes arbitrary leadership of Lord Palmerston had seen England through then. Now, in the 1860s, England was a neutral liberal state enmeshed in the logistics of a distant civil war and tied to the outdated 1819 domestic law of neutrality. As the American Civil War continued and reports of the *Alabama*'s victims mounted, as the Federal espionage system became more efficient and diplomatic pressures more insistent, the deficiencies of the Foreign Enlistment Act became more apparent. The British government either had to change its domestic law or find some other way to meet its international obligations.

After the *Alabama*'s departure from Liverpool, United States Minister Adams vigorously protested the British failure to detain the ship. He submitted depositions of sailors who refused to sign with Semmes and returned with Bulloch to Liverpool; he even provided Russell with the opinion of a learned counsel that the Foreign Enlistment Act had been violated. Russell responded on 4 September 1862. He recounted his government's investigation of the ship and explained the law officers' recommendation to detain it on the basis of intended use and structure. He expressed regret that the ship escaped detention by surreptitious means. On 4 October he wrote Adams that as much as "Her Majesty's Government desire to prevent such occurences, they are unable to go beyond the law, municipal and international."[7] This promising exchange on legal aspects of ship construction was interrupted in the autumn of 1862 by a threat of international intervention in the Civil War.

In both London and Paris serious movements to mediate the war dominated the diplomatic scene throughout October and most of November 1862. The cotton shortage in Europe and Lee's victory at Chancellorsville combined to stimulate these projects. Led by Russell the British ministry in late September and early October began to consider informally the feasibility of mediating between the two belligerents. Lee's defeat at Antietam, however, convinced Lord Palmerston by 22 October that the time was not yet right for a direct act. But then Emperor Napoleon III, under internal pressures, on 31 October revived the intervention question when he invited Great Britain and Russia to join him in suggesting a six-month cessation of hostilities in America during which time the Southern ports would be open to commerce. This created a second crisis of decision within the British cabinet. After a two-day discussion the cabinet on 12 November rejected the French proposal.[8] With this threat of European intervention over and with Lee pushed back to a defensive posture in Virginia, Adams followed Seward's instructions to return to the question of the *Alabama*.

On 20 November 1862 Adams raised issues that forced a British reconsideration of the "efficacy of its prohibitory law" and led to an open parliamentary debate on the subject. As a result, the queen's law officers and foreign minister later departed from domestic law and followed policy in order to fulfill British neutral obligations under international law. The Adams-Russell exchanges in late 1862 and early 1863 coupled with the parliamentary debates were decisive in destroying the Confederate ship construction program in Great Britain.

Adams reopened the *Alabama* correspondence by referring to the widespread destruction of Northern commerce and public reaction to it. He raised the question of the United States's "right of reclamation . . . for the grievous damage done" and, after reviewing historical precedent, he informed Russell "of the direction which I have received from my Government to solicit redress for the national and private injuries already thus sustained, as well as a more effective prevention of any repetition of such lawless and injurious proceedings in Her Majesty's ports hereafter." The American minister thus raised two issues that would dominate British–United States diplomacy on Confederate navy activity in Europe throughout the next eleven years. Russell took almost a month to respond. On 19 December he rejected British responsibility for damages caused by British-built Confederate ships, but he acknowledged his government's obligation on the second point. He was very specific:

> As regards your demand for a more effective prevention for the future fitting out of such vessels in British Ports, I have the honor to inform you that Her Majesty's Government, after consultation with Law Officers of the Crown, are of opinion that certain amendments might be introduced into the Foreign Enlistment Act, which, if sanctioned by Parliament, would have effect of giving greater power to the Executive to prevent the construction in British Ports of ships destined for the use of belligerents.

He conditioned this as an offer for a similar change in United States law.[9] This necessitated a delay for Washington's response.

Throughout the first three months of 1863 diplomacy tended to concentrate on matters not directly related to the Confederate navy in England. Secretary of State Seward, for instance, interjected the possibility of creating Northern privateers to help enforce the blockade and Adams complained of Southern fund raising through the sale of cotton certificates.[10] Until mid-March Confederate shipbuilding was an undercurrent in diplomatic exchanges. Yet several references were made to that activity and the inefficacy of the Foreign Enlistment Act. In February Seward justified possible Northern use of privateers because "the law did not appear to enable the British Government to prevent" the construction and departure of Southern ships. And Russell in early March stated that "the building of ironclad steamers for either belligerent Government . . . is clearly prohibited by the Foreign Enlistment

Act."[11] Finally on 14 March Adams, referring specifically to Confederate ironclad construction, stated that thus far he had found the British government "without power to take the necessary steps"to prevent "this system of warfare notoriously established in some of the ports of the kingdom."[12] At the same time public opinion in England, even in Liverpool, voiced objection to Confederate ship construction in Great Britain.[13]

Russell since 1861 had acknowledged the obligation of a neutral to enforce its neutrality regardless of domestic law. He now began to bend under the weight of Adams's evidence and British opinion. On 21 March he voluntarily informed Adams that two ships for the Confederate navy were under construction in Scotland.[14] Five days later the two men held a long conversation that cleared the air on many points. It left Adams convinced that the British "Government is really better disposed to exertion, and feels itself better sustained for action by the popular sentiment than ever before." As if to confirm Adams's belief, a question was scheduled in Parliament for the evening of 27 March 1863 on "The United States—The Foreign Enlistment Act." In preparation for the debate Russell advised Palmerston that because "the fitting out and escape of the *Alabama* . . . was clearly an evasion of our law" the prime minister should declare the government's disapproval "of such attempts to elude our law."[15]

The question was put by W. E. Forster, a foremost "friend of the North." He spoke at length on the "dangers to our friendly relations with the United States" created by the Confederate navy's ship construction within Great Britain. Describing the *Alabama,* which "had a magazine, shot, and cannister racks on deck, and was pierced for guns, and was built and fitted up as a fighting ship in all respects," he raised the issues of ship structure and intended use. Forster concluded that all Adams had asked was that the British government "carry out the law, and if the law were not sufficiently powerful, they should come to the House and demand further powers." Solicitor General Sir Roundell Palmer gave the government's response. He was among the crown's legal officers who already had recommended the broader interpretation of the 1819 law specifically by adding considerations of ship structure and intended use. Now he found it awkward to defend the ministry. Only by limiting his argument to narrow legalistic grounds did he brave it out. Basically he maintained that the British government had adopted the Foreign Enlistment Act of its own volition to protect its neutrality. The United States, he said, had no right to complain if the English law were enforced in the usual way against English subjects, that is, "on evidence, and not on suspicion; on facts, and not on presumption, on satisfactory testimony, and not on the mere accusations of a foreign minister or his agents. The act must be not only interpreted but executed according to law." He explained how the law had been applied in the *Alabama* case but omitted any reference to the law officers' advice. If, as Forster had implied, "our law is defective," Palmer continued, "it is for this House to consider whether it ought to be amended." John Bright spoke next, as he said, on moral not legal grounds. He called upon Palmerston to utter "genial and friendly" words to "send a message to the United States that would allay much irritation." The specter of acting in face of American irritation was all Palmerston needed. Sensitive to British opinion against submitting to foreign pressure on internal affairs, he rose "to deplore" the positions taken by Forster and Bright, those "mouthpieces of the North." He closed with a statement that moved the issue from legal and moral grounds to purely political ones.

> I do hope and trust that the people and Government of the United States will believe that we are doing our best in every case to execute the law; but they must not imagine that any cry that may be raised will induce us to come down to this House with a proposal to alter the law. We have had—I have had—some experience of what any attempt of that sort may be expected to lead to; and I think that there are several gentlemen sitting on this bench who would not be disposed, if I were so inclined myself, to concur in such a proposition.[16]

Palmerston was referring to an 1859 experience when at French insistence he had requested a law to limit the freedom of radical political refugees in England. Accusing him of submitting to Napoleon III, the House of Commons had overturned his ministry. Now in 1863, with just as slim a majority, he could not truckle to United States pressure; he refused to request Parliament to amend the Foreign Enlistment Act.

And yet the 1819 law in some way must be changed in order, as Russell put it, to give "greater power to the Executive." Greater power to do what? Greater power to fulfill its obligation under international law as a neutral.[17] The customs and treasury officials' interpretation of the law allowed any ship to be built and go to sea so long as it was not actually armed. But the law officers cognizant of international obligations advised a broader view of the law. They maintained that the government must prevent the departure of a belligerent ship on any reasonable suspicion that it was intended for warlike use or that it was even partially fitted out for warlike activities. The differences between these two interpretations created a need for a clarifying change in the law. A parliamentary act would be the simplest method to accomplish the change; but on political grounds Palmerston denied this to the government. Some other method had to be found. What were the alternatives?

According to international law and practices the British government had to deny warlike ships to the Confederacy. Given depredations of the *Alabama* and the United States demand for compensation, combined with changing British opinion and the dangerous European diplomatic situation, it was apparent to Russell and the law officers in the spring of 1863 that the neutral obligation had to be met. One alternative would be to act on policy, that is, to find some extralegal way in each particular case to deny that particular ship to the South. Such a rule of policy would amount, in Bulloch's words, to adopting the "secret purposes of state." But England was a liberal society based on rule by law, a tradition the government could not easily abandon. The most feasible alternative then would be to test the 1819 act in courts of law in hope of grafting to it the principles of intent and structure. To do this a specific ship must be brought to trial. Only eight days after the parliamentary debate on the United States and the Foreign Enlistment Act, a Confederate-bound ship was seized and the court case was prepared. This action created in the spring of 1863 what has been called erroneously the "curious case" of the *Alexandra*.[18]

The *Alexandra* on Trial

Commander Bulloch, unaware of the Russell-Adams correspondence, anticipated the changing British attitude. As early as January 1863 he realized from the "conduct of the British Government that the Foreign Enlistment Act will be very strictly construed when applied to our acts."[19] He was right.

United States Consul Dudley had been gathering information on the *Alexandra* and two other ships for many months. Adams sent Dudley's reports to the Foreign Office on 30 March 1863. The British government almost immediately instigated its own investigation, for on 3 April Russell wrote two letters to Adams. In the first he stated that the reports on one of the ships (the *Phantom*) indicated that by its very structure it could not be intended for warlike use and therefore it did not come under the Foreign Enlistment Act. In the second letter he stated that the government would continue its investigation of the *Alexandra* to determine whether that ship might violate the act.[20] Russell already had made up his mind to detain the ship and in still another letter of the same day he informed Lord Palmerston: "The Attorney General has been consulted and concurs in the measure, as one of policy, though not of strict law." The intention was to "test the law."[21] The next day Russell received the law officers' recommendation that on the basis of intent and structure the ship should be detained and brought to trial.[22] On 5 April, just eight days after Palmerston's speech, Russell notified Adams of the seizure of the *Alexandra* and requested Dudley's cooperation with the British officials in Liverpool in collecting evidence against the ship. Adams received this news "with the most lively satisfaction."[23]

Adams's satisfaction indeed must have been lively. The British detention of the ship proved several things. First, the government was ready to act even without full proof of violation of domestic law.[24] Second, the detention reversed the impact of Palmerston's speech of 27 March. And perhaps most welcome to Adams, the British now sought the cooperation of the United States. Northern diplomacy was beginning to bear fruit.

On the other side, Russell's action confirmed Bulloch's worst fears. The *Alexandra* was ordered and paid for by Charles K. Prioleau, a British subject, to be presented as a gift to the Confederacy. A small ship, her only warlike quality was use of reinforced wood in her structure. Compared to the Laird rams or the ships under construction on the Clyde River, the little vessel seemed innocent enough. Should the South lose this case those other ships certainly would be condemned. Bulloch therefore secured the best legal counsel available. Sir Hugh Cairns, a member of Parliament and highly esteemed barrister, and George Mellish, recognized as one of Britain's best trial lawyers, together assumed the responsibility of protecting Confederate shipbuilding interests in Great Britain. Although the ship was seized on 5 April the trial did not begin for several weeks, on 22 June.

Meanwhile, British detectives and agents for the United States everywhere were watching the Southerners. Lieutenant John R. Hamilton, earlier squeezed out of a slot on the *Alabama* and now captain-designate of the *Alexandra,* was followed constantly and kept under surveillance even when in his own living quarters. Such vigilance prevented the Southerners from going about their usual business and aroused apprehensions among both the Confederates and their British naval contractors. The latter, fearful of costly delays, suits, and liabilities, suspended work already under way. During the early weeks between the *Alexandra*'s seizure and the beginning of her trial, Bulloch's pessimism grew: the English, he accused, were enforcing the law "in a manner most injurious and damaging to us"; and Commander North, alarmed by the work stoppage on his Clyde River ram, was sure that no ship built for the Confederate States "would be allowed to leave the country."[25] Frustrated, frightened, and helpless, they could only await the trial.

The period between the ship's seizure and trial was used by government lawyers to prepare the case. They were reluctant to bring their suit before a Liverpool jury because, as Lord John Russell said, that city was "a port specially addicted to Southern proclivities, foreign slave trade, and domestic bribery."[26] A change of venue to the Court of Exchequer in London avoided Liverpool prejudices and assured the government, should it lose, of only small damages.

The government's legal efforts failed. According to the strict view of domestic law, its case was weak and its preparation inadequate. Within four days the defense, especially Sir Hugh Cairns, had demolished the prosecution's position. Using the legalistic arguments by which Solicitor General Palmer had justified the government's policy in the *Alabama* parliamentary debate, Sir Hugh appealed to equal enforcement of the law, English pride in resisting United States pressures, and economic benefits derived from the lively shipbuilding industry. In summation he said to the jurors that they had it in their power "to show the American government . . . that upon one thing you are determined, and that is, to have our laws applied, not upon suspicion or presumption, but upon clear legal proof." Even the judge to whose court the British government especially had transferred the case emerged during the trial as an ally of the South. Sir Jonathan Frederick Pollock, following a strict interpretation of the law, charged the jury in part with these words: if "the object really was to build a ship in obedience to an order in compliance with a contract, leaving to those who bought it to make what use they thought fit of it, then it appears . . . that the foreign enlistment act has not been broken," thus rejecting the government's view that the structure of the ship was sufficient proof of its warlike intent and character.[27] Commander Bulloch could not have stated his case better. The British rule of law, especially in this industrial liberal state, would prevail: within half an hour the jury, on 26 June 1863, returned a verdict against the crown. The decision had far-reaching ramifications.

One effect, not immediately apparent but as certain as if the jury had reached the opposite decision, was the restriction of Confederate shipbuilding in Great Britain. When the principles of intent and ship structure were rejected by the court, the government changed its stand; it would treat the Southern activities not according to law, but according to policy. If the ship could not be sequestered legally, the government would detain it, seize it, investigate, and try to build a legal case against it. Should this become impossible within the meaning of the *Alexandra* decision, then the government would negotiate with the owners (as in the *Canton* case) or simply purchase the vessel (as in the Laird rams case) but in each case the government by policy would deny the vessel to the Confederates. Soon, in the eyes of Bulloch, North, and Mallory, the British cabinet would become as capricious as any absolute ruler. If circumventing the law was tricky business, Bulloch was to find that anticipating policy was impossible. Not only did this change eventually condemn the Laird rams, but from the time of the *Alexandra* decision the Confederates did not construct a single major vessel in the British Isles. In theory Sir Hugh had won the case for the South and had struck a blow for the liberal rule of law; but in fact he had forced Lord John Russell and Lord Palmerston henceforth to make decisions without consulting the queen's law officers. In its efforts to fulfill neutral obligations the British government after 1863 schemed to circumvent its own law.[28]

The solicitor in his failure to create a broader interpretation of the 1819 law in the *Alexandra* case also unwittingly contributed to an ultimate financial cost to the British government. One of his chief witnesses was that renegade from the Confederate navy, Clarence R. Yonge, "the infamous traitor" as Bulloch called him. Having been cashiered from the navy by Semmes, having married a rich widow, found his way back to England, and spent his fortune, Yonge in May 1863 sold his knowledge about Bulloch's and Prioleau's activities.[29] The solicitor general used his statement in the trial, but all that Yonge could testify to were the events surrounding the *Alabama*'s departure. He had no personal knowledge of the *Alexandra* and his testimony was useless. In 1872, however, when the United States presented its case in Geneva before the Tribunal of Arbitration, it included Yonge's *Alexandra* deposition. Yonge's words were cited in the final Geneva arbitration, "by whose judgment the British taxpayer was mulcted in damages to the substantial amount of 3,000,000 pounds sterling," as Bulloch later put it.[30] The *Alexandra* was far more costly to Great Britain than to Charles K. Prioleau.

Prioleau, despite the jury's decision, did not get the ship immediately. When the trial ended on 26 June 1863 the British government could not purchase the *Alexandra* without going to Parliament for the necessary funds.[31] The solicitor general resorted to appeals to sequester the vessel until April 1864. Even then Lieutenant Hamilton did not get the command, because, outfitted as a blockade-runner later in 1864, the ship was seized by British authorities in Nassau and was detained until the war's end. From beginning to end the ship did no one any good, and to many caused much harm and anguish.

Much of that anguish was felt by Confederates during the weeks between the seizure and the trial. Not only did work cease on the Southern ships under construction during these pretrial weeks, but hope died of successfully getting any vessel out of Great Britain. Considering the money already spent on them and the possibility that the United States somehow might gain possession of them, Confederate diplomatic agents met in Paris to determine what should be done. Typically, Bulloch assumed the initiative and, as we shall see later, went through the legal fiction of transferring title of the Laird rams to a French house; just as typically Commander North awaited instructions. When they came he was disheartened: the diplomatic agents advised him to sell the Clyde River ironclad to Russian agents who were then in England attempting to buy warships. About mid-June, just prior to the *Alexandra* trial, North did visit a Russian in London who, however, "did not catch at the bait as readily as . . . expected."[32] Indeed, the Russian rejected the ship without ever seeing it—this at a time his government was facing an international crisis over the Polish Insurrection. Commander North was not a forceful salesman.

In the short run his failure as a salesman appeared to be a blessing because the jury's *Alexandra* verdict at first instilled new hope among the Confederates. Only Commander Bulloch was not misled by the jury's decision; he still was convinced that even to launch Confederate-built ships "would result in their seizure and indefinite detention by the means of the interminable procedures of the court of exchequer." Both Slidell and Mason, however, agreed that there was now no need to sell North's ship. North boasted that "we might build any kind of ship, provided we do not arm her." In his new-found elation North wrote to his builder: "I see nothing to prevent us from going ahead. So pray put on additional steam so that I may be off doing something for myself and my country. Don't forget that my reputation as an officer is at stake."[33] While his loyalty to the Southern cause cannot be questioned, North's emphasis on his own reputation is just one more example of his value priorities. He was as wrong in his expectations for himself and his ironclad as he was in his evaluation of the *Alexandra* decision.

During the long months of legalistic maneuvering in the government's appeal of the *Alexandra* decision, Confederates in Europe (except Bulloch) shared North's excitement. They did not realize that the appeal itself represented a change in British tactics, that the cabinet would not accept merely the judicial approach to the very serious matter of meeting its neutral obligations. The government would enforce its policy by whatever means might come to hand: by court appeal, by cooperating with Dudley's spies, by harassing British subjects, by sending agents to foreign countries to investigate shady business deals or to take sworn affidavits from a head of state. The *Alexandra* trial already had delayed construction on the Laird rams and on the Thomson ships; the government had time to implement its policy. As 1863 faded into 1864 that policy would deny to the Confederates the ships on which so many hopes depended.

One Policy: Different Ships, Different Techniques

THE LAIRD RAMS

The first Confederate ships under construction to which the British government applied the rule of policy instead of law were Bulloch's. Number 294 was the first launched. Federal officials intensified their surveillance along the Mersey River and immediately lodged protests with the British. The very structure of the ships aroused fears that fed the Northern imaginations. Turret-mounted guns, the armor, and the rams all led to exaggerated speculation as to the damage the ship would inflict against the Union cause. The recent *Alexandra* decision enhanced these fears and drove Charles Francis Adams to make extreme charges and implied threats to Earl Russell, who answered in kind, and a veritable diplomatic war of words ensued. By early September the Laird rams became a cause célèbre.

James Bulloch even prior to the *Alexandra* decision understood the new British rule by policy. "I am convinced that the British ministry will do almost anything the United States Government asks," he wrote to Mallory, "and you are aware that an order in council will override the ordinary rules of law." Dudley's agents increased their activities in and around the Laird yards and, more importantly, English officials ordered frequent reports from the customs officials on all ships under construction in their districts. Fearful that the warlike features of his turret armorclads could not escape notice, Bulloch warned Mallory of impending dangers. All of the Confederate agents were "closely watched." He became convinced his rams would not be allowed to leave. "Wooden ships," he reported in the cryptic wording of cypher, "could evade the law, but object of armored ships too evident for disguise."[34] Still, he hoped; perhaps Numbers 294 and 295 could be completed and, unarmed, steam away from the Mersey River before the clumsy machinery of the British government could detain them.

This possibility raised another question concerning the ships. If they were completed on schedule and did manage to evade detention, who would command them? What enlisted personnel would man them? In September and November 1862 Bulloch had suggested to Mallory a rendezvous to meet officers and "leading men and noncommissioned officers who are natives of the South." The secretary's response reached Liverpool in early March 1863 and set off a chain of events that, independent of the ships, was to affect the lives of many Confederate navy officers, change the pattern of Confederate navy structure and command in Europe, and incidentally reveal potential additional obstacles to the fulfillment of the navy's European mission. The delays in communication that forced Mallory in Richmond to make decisions and take actions while ignorant of the changing situation in Europe place the sequence of events concerning the manning of the ships in an unrealistic, almost dreamlike setting. It is necessary then, in order to gain some perspective on Mallory's and Bulloch's problem, to leave Numbers 294 and 295 and to follow to completion this particular story. The two threads—the ironclad rams and the men to sail them—will become entwined once again later in the year.

Mallory rejected Bulloch's rendezvous scheme. Instead, influenced by a recently received report of a conversation John Slidell had with Emperor Napoleon III, he decided to send the officers directly "to

France incog., via England in the ordinary way." Bulloch should consult with Slidell to understand that Mallory had good reason to expect that in France the officers would find "no obstacle" in boarding the ships. He left undecided Bulloch's expressed need for native Southerners to fill the enlisted slots on the ships. Bulloch had no objections to Mallory's proposal because the "completion of the armored ships having been delayed, the change can be made." He urged the secretary to send the officers "as soon as possible."[35] Not until July, just as Number 294 was launched, did Bulloch again raise the question of the enlisted crew. He knew by then of Lee's victory at Chancellorsville and of his movement into Maryland and Pennsylvania, but he had not yet heard about Gettysburg and Vicksburg. Riding the crest of the Confederacy's high-water military tide, Bulloch was confident of successfully getting the armor-clad rams to sea. He worried only about the quality of their crews.

"I do not think reliable crews could be obtained from among the floating population of European ports," he wrote.[36] The adventure of cruising against commercial vessels and the possibility of sharing prize money had facilitated recruitment of such men for the *Florida* and the *Alabama*, "but the ironclads are too manifestly for other purposes" to attract such adventurers. Besides, the nature of the ships' riggings was such as to "require but few able seamen." The men needed to man the rams should be artillerists who were "willing to fight for the sake of their country alone." In a ship designed for naval combat, patriotic seamen were required; they obviously could not be found in the European ports. Where, then, and how could they be recruited?

Bulloch had a plan. By paying enough he could get sufficient man-power to take the ships to Wilmington, North Carolina, where they could sink or disperse the Federal blockading fleet. At that point, Mallory should have crews ready at Smithville or Fort Caswell, at the mouth of the Cape Fear River, who would be "actuated by the same spirit which has converted our farmers and backwoodsmen into the veterans who are now sweeping irresistibly through Maryland and Southern Pennsylvania." These dedicated men could in a few hours ready the vessel "to strike a decisive blow in any direction, north or south." Bulloch was "earnest and anxious on the subject of crews because the ships are too formidable and too valuable to be trusted in the hands of a mere set of adventurers."[37]

The commander's earnestness and anxiety were well placed. The problem of loyal, experienced seamen had plagued the South ever since Semmes sailed the *Sumter* from New Orleans. These men from the "floating population" of the world's seaports required constant and strict discipline, were prone to desert at any given moment at any given port; they hardly could be expected to live willingly within the rams' cramped and damp quarters or to expose themselves willingly to the dangers of combat. Only spirited Southerners could be counted on to render the kind of service the new ships required. The problem, to which Bulloch's optimistic view of Lee's Pennsylvania campaign blinded him, was to find even within the Confederacy such spirited artillerists with experience at sea. Could Mallory have found trained artillery soldiers willing or able to live aboard one of the small rams, to fire the guns from the turrets? Would such soldiers have been able to adapt their skills to the guns of a moving, bobbing ship? Would they have required less training, less discipline than the *Sumter* crew?

Bulloch was right in stipulating the quality of patriotism for the crew. But he was stipulating a commodity as scarce in the Confederacy as the natural resources, the shipyards, the skilled workers, and the astute management he had gone to England to purchase with the cotton produced by the slave labor of the plantations. The Confederacy was no more able to produce the required numbers of skilled personnel to operate the products of advanced technology than it was the personnel to produce those products. This lack of trained and patriotic seamen raises a strong doubt as to the efficacy of the service the rams or any other ship of advanced technology could have rendered to the South.

The South, however, did not lack trained naval officers to serve on the new-model ships. In August 1862, as we have seen, Bulloch had recommended that he and Semmes command the two vessels. When Mallory expressed his desire for Bulloch to remain in Europe as an agent to procure more ships, the commander acquiesced. But Number 294's approaching launching excited his seaman's ambitions once again; he could not help expressing his feelings, and they are not unlike those of Commander North: "I accept the sphere of duty you have thought proper to assign me . . . by thus doing I am giving up all my chances of acquiring professional distinction and advancement . . . I must henceforth be content with the self-assurance that I have only been an humble means to an end."[38] Still unsure who would command Number 294, the day after the launching, on 10 July 1863, he sent Lieutenant W. C. Whittle, Jr., to Richmond with detailed specifications of the ships. Secretary Mallory meanwhile had resolved the command question and when Whittle arrived was able immediately to issue the necessary orders.

The choice fell to Captain Samuel R. Barron, Sr. Barron came from a long naval tradition. His father, by the same name, had commanded the United States naval forces off Tripoli in 1804 and his Uncle James had the misfortune three years later to be in command of the U.S.S. *Chesapeake* when the British man-of-war *Leopard* bombarded her and impressed seamen from her. Samuel, following in his father's wake, entered the United States Navy as a boy and by 1861 held the rank of captain. On 11 June 1861 he received a commission in the Confederate States Navy at the same rank. This made him one of the three or four highest ranking officers in the service.

Barron's abilities are hard to evaluate. His letters, both official and private, are all proper and fitting. He seems always to have been in agreement with higher authorities and at the same time to have maintained a fraternal feeling toward other naval officers. His association with Secretary Mallory reached back to 1855. In that year, at then-Senator Mallory's insistence, a navy retirement board acted to weed out incompetent or unfit officers, and Barron served on the board to Mallory's complete satisfaction. In March 1861, just prior to the firing on Fort Sumter, he served at Mallory's request in Pensacola, Florida, to divert several United States naval vessels from taking possession of that military post. It is not surprising then to find Captain Samuel Barron assigned to the Richmond station in charge of detail and equipment. He did see combat in coastal defense activity early in the war and was captured in the fighting at Fort Hatteras on 29 August 1861. After parole he also served in the defenses of the Cumberland and Tennessee rivers in 1863.[39] Just two years after his capture, to the day, he received Mallory's orders to proceed to Europe.

The Barron family long had resided in Norfolk, Virginia, where so many navy families lived. Among their friends for at least two generations were the Whittles. Like Samuel, W. C. Whittle, Sr., was also a captain in both the old and the new navies. The two had sons, each named for his father, who were about the same age and who also transferred to the Confederate navy at about the same time as their fathers. Although the older Whittle never saw service abroad, the younger one did; both he and young Barron were in Europe and afloat during the war years. Indeed it was the younger Whittle who, serving as Bulloch's messenger, briefed Mallory on the armor-clad ships. When Captain Barron departed for Europe young Whittle accompanied him as his aide.

Mallory's orders to Barron were at once simple and broad. He was to proceed to England where Numbers 294 and 295 were expected to be ready in October. Commander Bulloch would deliver the ships to him at sea and Barron would take command and hoist his flag on either of the ships. He was admonished that in Europe he should "not interfere with the special duties to which Commander Bulloch has been assigned," but as the ranking navy officer he "should make such disposition of the officers abroad" as in his judgment would best serve the country. He also was ordered to inspect and report on North's and Sinclair's ships and later was ordered to assume command of the latter.[40] In effect, Barron was to command both Laird rams, the *Canton,* and possibly North's

Number 61. In truth, he would have a formidable ironclad fleet at sea and justify fully his designation as "Flag Officer Afloat" with the temporary rank of commodore.

The trip from Richmond to Liverpool was not without excitement. Barron and Whittle arrived in Wilmington, North Carolina, in the early morning of 1 September 1863 "after a tedious trip of a little more than 24 hours" from Richmond "over the rough railroad."[41] They ate at the City of Carolina Hotel "as miserable a breakfast as I ever saw in my life." Lieutenant Whittle found that the Navy Department had failed to secure a boat ticket for him and he had to pay in gold for passage aboard the government steamer *Cornelia*. The disgruntled lieutenant considered Wilmington to be "the meanest place I have been in the Confederacy." Wartime life in the South was getting unpleasant: unnecessarily long trips over rough rails, bad food, nervy ticket agents imposing bureaucratic regulations. Even the other passengers aboard the *Cornelia* came under Whittle's scrutiny: a "contemplatable [*sic*] red tape fellow of Jewish extraction," a professor of math from the University of Virginia, an artist sent to Europe "to cast the bronze statue of our noble 'Stonewall' Jackson," and, among others, a Swede suspected to be "in the Yankee service." No one was above suspicion. Finally, during the night of 5 September the *Cornelia* eased into the blockade area and within thirty minutes passed both the Union's inner and outer lines. The flag officer of the South's formidable ironclad fleet was en route to assume command.

Running at about ten miles an hour, the *Cornelia* made Saint George's, Bermuda, in four days. The travelers had to wait ten days before they could take passage on the British steamer *Florida*. The time passed quickly. They lunched and dined with Southerners living on the island: the Walkers, the Robinsons, and with Mrs. Taylor and Mrs. Harwood at their hotel in Hamilton. They shopped for relatives in Norfolk. They attended Church of England services. They studied the flora of the island. They commented upon the "idle, dissolute and profligate race" of recently (1834) emancipated blacks, who, according to Lieutenant Whittle, "are more respectful to Southerners than to any other white person and all are Simpathisers [*sic*] with the Confederate cause."[42] Finally, with the memory of the bad Wilmington food displaced by Bermuda's cuisine and with their closed minds strengthened by the sympathy of the Bermuda blacks, the officers began the last leg of their journey to Liverpool. It was to be arduous and long.

For three weeks and a day the *Florida* was buffeted by gales; it ran low on coal, the food was bad, tempers frayed. Commodore Barron, who had been seasick between Wilmington and Saint George's was ill most of the time. No one enjoyed the trip. On 12 October, Barron and Whittle went ashore at Beaumaris, where the people were "rough, healthy looking Welshmen." After a three-hour train ride, they arrived in Liverpool at 11:00 p.m. and took rooms in the Angel Hotel. They had been traveling for six weeks.[43]

Two days later, after conferring with Bulloch and learning of the British detention of the ironclads, Commodore Barron proceeded to Glasgow. On 15 October Barron and Whittle inspected the two ships, "just to see how work is carried on in this great country," as the naive lieutenant put it. He thought both were "fine vessels, perfect beauties." After conferring with Sinclair (North was out of town), they met the Blakely gun inventor and had tea with Mrs. North, who complained about the living conditions in Scotland. The next day they left for London and within a week were in Paris. Commodore Barron engaged a flat at 30 rue Drouot, where he would live for the remainder of the war. Given his proclivity for seasickness, perhaps he was just as well off.[44]

Barron's story overlapped that of the vessels he was supposed to command by several months. While he was journeying from Richmond, the status of the ships had undergone a drastic change. Number 294's launching on 9 July had touched off a diplomatic flurry of unusual intensity.[45] The awesome new features of the war vessel—the armor, turrets, and ram—aroused in the United States agents an acute fear of war between their country and England. Adams wrote Earl Russell that the construction of the ships, which incorporated "all the appliances of British skill to the arts of destruction," was the "gravest act of international hostility yet committed." Among other charges he aptly placed the blame where it belonged; the British reluctance to act, he told Russell, was not for lack of will but from "absence of power in . . . existing laws to reach a remedy." Russell's replies at first were reasonable appeals to the law, but Adams continued his blistering attack. Rumors spread among all parties, from the wharfs of Liverpool to the halls of Whitehall. During the first week of September 1863 the diplomatic crisis reached its climax. On 1 September Russell informed Adams that there was no legal evidence sufficient to seize the vessels; on the fifth, Adams wrote his famous "superfluous note": should the ships be allowed to depart, "It would be superfluous in me to point out to your Lordship that this means war." But before receiving this letter Lord John Russell had reached his decision, which was as much determined by the *Alexandra* case as by all the fiery letters from Adams. Russell ordered the ships stopped "as soon as there is reason to believe that they are about to put to sea, and to detain them until further notice." The next day he assumed personal responsibility for the detention, regardless of the consequences. He had, he informed Lord Palmerston, the solicitor general's approval "as one of policy, though not of strict law." The die was cast; Sir

Hugh Cairns' arguments and Judge Pollock's instructions in the *Alexandra* case effectively ended the South's naval construction program in Great Britain: no major Confederate-built vessel would ever again leave the British Isles. This was not to be a judicial test of the Foreign Enlistment Act; the rams would never reach the courts. Thus Earl Russell led the English government to a determination to fulfill its international obligations despite the domestic law.

This policy was backed by force, not legal warrants. The government notified the Lairds of the detention on the "9th or 19th of September" and effected the formal seizure on 9 October 1863. On 27 October detachments of marines were put aboard the two ships, "the workmen being sent on shore," and two British navy gunboats were stationed in the Mersey River to prevent the ironclads from moving.[46] By the time Barron was settled in his rue Drouot flat, the Laird rams were sequestered beyond his reach. Bulloch, however, still hoped he could evade the new policy by a clever ruse he had devised prior to the seizure. On this thin thread the Southerners placed their hopes for the rams.

Secretary Mallory had instructed Bulloch in March to consult in Paris with John Slidell on the best means to man and equip the ironclads from France. By the time Bulloch reached Paris he knew of the intense British investigation of the small wooden *Alexandra*. Worried already that the warlike character of his rams would be used by the port authorities to justify seizure, he now became convinced of that possibility. It was useless to talk of outfitting in France ships that probably would never leave England. He consulted with Slidell not on ways to outfit the rams but on ways to prevent British seizure of them. The shrewd diplomatic agent had a contact who just might help. He introduced Bulloch to a "distinguished naval architect of Bordeaux" with whom he had already discussed the possibility of building ships for the Confederacy. That gentleman, Lucien Arman, had good credentials. He was a member of the French legislative body and a confidant of the emperor. Anxious to please the Southerners, he introduced them to the partners of Bravay and Company of Paris. Bulloch, as it turned out, had his alternative ruse.

The *Alexandra* was seized by British officials on 5 April, just a few days later. All of the Confederates were frightened; only Bulloch had a way out. During the following weeks before the trial began, he negotiated a mutually satisfactory agreement with the Bravays. It was in every detail a meticulously legal arrangement. Bulloch cancelled his own contract with the Lairds, and Bravay and Company signed a new one with the builders. Bravay claimed to be acting as an agent for the ruler of Egypt, who would use the ships along the Nile River for internal security. It was a perfect dodge according to British law. Because the ships were no longer intended for a belligerent state, their warlike qualities now should be meaningless to the British government; the contract was transformed legally into "a purely commercial transaction."[47]

For Bulloch the months just prior to the rams' seizure in October 1863 and until their final disposition in May 1864 were times of hope and frustration. His hope lay in the Bravay ownership. When he sent Lieutenant Whittle to Mallory in July he referred to the "great probability that the two ironclads will ere long be released from the trammels of British interference." By August, however, the hope had changed to anxiety despite the Bravay contract because the British customs inspections had become intensified and actually interfered with the work progress on the ships. When the government took control of the vessels in October, Bulloch's worst fears were confirmed. His only hope lay in his French connection. To thwart the government he instructed the Lairds to announce the Bravay contract. He had wanted this done at the time the contract was made, but Mason and Slidell for reasons of their own had overruled him.[48] Bulloch felt that an earlier announcement of the Bravay ownership would have prevented the intense investigation and thus the seizure. And Bulloch was right if, as he expected, the British government were to act according to law. Even after the preliminary seizure Bulloch still did not realize that Palmerston's liberal government, in a liberal state, could act any other way. He attributed the seizure to Earl Russell's Northern partisanship. Bulloch should have known better. The act of purchase would be an obvious act of policy, not law. But Bulloch's whole mode of operation from the *Fingal* through Number 295 had been dependent on the law, and he could not now in October 1863 comprehend any other approach. If the English cabinet did not play by its own rules, then Bulloch found it impossible to play. "No amount of discretion or management on my part can effect the release of the ships," he admitted. He would have to turn to that power, earlier scorned, "where everything . . . would depend upon the secret purposes of the Chief of State." His only hope now lay in Emperor Napoleon III's willingness and determination to demand that the British government allow the ships "to leave Liverpool as the property of a French subject."[49]

This reliance on Napoleon III in late 1863 was poorly placed and ill-timed. It was poorly placed because, as Bulloch and all the other navy officers well knew, France and Britain were involved in a naval armaments race. It was one thing to construct vessels in France for Confederate use; Palmerston would have no objections. But he *had* objected as early as the late 1840s to the French "bridge of steam across the channel," and he still objected to the French iron fleet. To expect Palmerston's government to permit the sale of two ironclad, turret-gunned, steam-powered, screw-propellered, ram vessels to a subject of his archrival was expecting too much.[50] Palmerston and his officials suspected the Egyptian cover as much for the French as for the Confederates. Only if the pasha of Egypt would sign a sworn affidavit would they let the vessels fall into the hands of a Frenchman. Furthermore, the timing of the request, late 1863 and early 1864, was particularly unfortunate. The rancor over the Polish Insurrection diplomacy was fresh and the Danish question was rising to the surface. If Napoleon III's determination to maintain cordial relations had any substance, and it did, the most feasible area of diplomatic cooperation was precisely the American Civil War. Deeply involved in Mexico, the French government did not want to antagonize the United States. Thus, since September 1863 it had been investigating the Confederate shipbuilding at Bordeaux and Nantes and by January 1864 it detained those vessels. Also in January, John Slidell inquired as to the emperor's intention to intervene in the Laird rams case. "No less a personage than the Duke de Morny," the emperor's half-brother, informed the Southern commissioner that France could do nothing. Bulloch's expectations were "grievously disappointed."[51] At the same time, the English law officers were appealing the *Alexandra* case from the Court of Exchequer to the Exchequer Chamber and could yet go higher to the House of Lords itself. Convinced that the British government also in the case of the rams would "exhaust us by continual delays and appeals," Slidell, Mason, and Bulloch decided to sell the ships. In an act that, he wrote, "gave me greater pain and regret than I ever thought it possible to feel," Bulloch on 7 February 1864 instructed the Bravay company "to sell the rams in good faith and with as little delay as possible."[52]

Sell the rams in good faith to whom? Did the Egyptian ruler really want the ships after all? Were there Russian customers? Although Bulloch did not specify a particular buyer, the Bravays almost immediately contacted the British Admiralty and entered into negotiations for the sale of the rams.[53] Why did the French firm turn to London? Why not Cairo or Saint Petersburg? The 1863–64 winter months were a time of complicated and intertwining approaches to the rams problem. The Confederates were at once desperate to regain control of the ships and anxious to avoid losing their investment in them. The Northern diplomats maintained pressure on the British despite the October seizure. The English cabinet sought in two specific and different ways to effectively deny the ships to the South. The delays caused by slow communications created contradictions, which in turn led to false rumors and further anxieties. The different threads must be unraveled in order to clarify their impact upon the Confederate navy and to reveal the clarity and consistency of British policy.

British policy was clear: uphold the obligations of neutrality even if the 1819 Foreign Enlistment Act did not afford the means to do it. The intertwined threads of 1863–64 resulted from a search for the most

effective and least inconvenient means of enforcing the policy. The idea
of adopting the technique of purchasing the rams first surfaced in
September 1863. On 13 September Lord Palmerston suggested to
Admiralty officials that, because England had fewer ironclads than
France, the Royal Navy might buy the Laird rams, which could serve as
"peace keepers" in the channel. On 22 September, reacting to Adams's
bellicose letters, Palmerston suggested to Earl Russell that he should tell
Adams in civil terms "you be damned," because *"we are going to take the
Iron Clads away from the Confederates* and we might if we said nothing have
the appearance of humble submission to Yankee Bullying." Some weeks
later, after the seizure of the ships in October had forced the Confederates to reveal the Bravay contract, Captain Hoare, the Royal Navy
attaché to the British embassy in Paris, visited Bravay and "made a direct
offer to purchase them for the British Admiralty."⁵⁴ The policy established, one probe to find a technique was set in motion.

The seizure itself stimulated another probe in a different direction. If
the neutral obligation could be sustained through legal and judicial
means, the crown law officers were determined to do it and the foreign
office would not deter them. Almost as if conscience-stricken, the law
officers expressed the "opinion that the evidence does not justify the
interference of Government." But because the foreign office persisted,
the law officers began a search for substantive evidence that in the face
of the *Alexandra* decision would stand up in court. The obvious warlike
quality of the rams, as opposed to the little wooden *Alexandra,* should
help establish the principle of ship structure; but to prove intent they
had to show definitely that the vessels' destination was the Confederacy.
They already had good circumstantial evidence that Confederates originally ordered the ships and they suspected the transfer to Bravay to be
fictitious. To prove the latter point, and thus Confederate destination,
the British government instigated an intricate and prolonged effort in
Egypt to determine the validity of Bravay's claim to be acting as the
agent for that country's ruler. The story is almost a spy-thriller tale. The
reigning pasha refused to swear to any affidavit, and the Egyptian caper
reaped only legal whirlwinds. It was April 1864 before the tenacious law
officers admitted defeat.⁵⁵ The demand that the British government
placed on its diplomatic agents to procure legal proof of the ships' true
ownership is a tribute to English law and to the commitment to rule by
law. Such a tribute, however, does not change the fact that the government simultaneously was pursuing another technique to enforce its
policy.

That technique was revived in February 1864, not because of the
Egyptian investigations, which were still going on, but because of the
appeals procedures in the *Alexandra* case. Convinced of the futility of

fighting the rams case through court appeals and delay, Bulloch in that month ordered Bravay to sell the rams. Having been approached by Captain Hoare in October, the French agent contacted the British Admiralty in February 1864. The duke of Somerset, acting with Russell's approval, evaluated the rams and concluded that they were "not good for much" but had an "intrinsic worth" of about 200,000 pounds. When Bravay on 11 March asked 300,000 for them, negotiations slowed. Rumors were flying—there were, it was said, documents laid before the Confederate Congress that would prove the South's ownership; the foreign minister of Egypt was willing to stipulate against Bravay; some other French agent was involved—but all were false. Furthermore, Secretary Mallory, unaware of the recent developments in England, France, and Egypt, urged Commander Bulloch to retain possession of the ships at all costs.[56]

Southern hope died hard especially when laced with pain. Bulloch made one last desperate effort to verify the Egyptian sale. When it failed, he had no choice but to allow Bravay to sell the rams to the British. He made the offer on 4 May.[57]

Counsel representing the Lairds, the Bravays, and the British government negotiated a mutually acceptable price for the ships: 195,000 pounds for the vessels as they lay, plus 25,000 pounds for their completion. The deal was made. Confederate control over the rams was ended and Bulloch's despair was complete. "No one," he wrote Mallory, "could have had stronger inducements to get the rams to sea than I had." The service the rams would have rendered to the South would have redounded to his professional credit, he was sure, and he deplored the loss of that. His sense of his country's loss was mingled with "one of purely selfish disappointment."[58] Bulloch found little solace in the 180,000 pounds Bravay returned to him.

British policy had prevailed. Doubtless, the government would have preferred to condemn the ironclads in a law court, but even before the law officers admitted failure in their effort to build a solid legal case against the ships the foreign office did not hesitate to purchase them. Either technique would have fulfilled British policy, but purchase was more sure and no more inconvenient. That policy prevailed over law was made clear by the duke of Somerset. As first lord of the Admiralty, he was a member of Palmerston's cabinet along with Russell. In a letter to William Gladstone, another cabinet colleague, he reflected on the purchase of the rams:

The purchase of the ironclads in the Mersey was made at last unexpectedly, as I suppose that if they were to be purchased, we should have bought them, whereas the F.O. completed the purchase. I consider however that the price is fair and reasonable . . . we shall have the advantages

of an earlier trial of a smaller class of ironclad vessel: a matter of great
importance on grounds of economy as well as efficiency. In addition to
these reasons for the purchase, *there is the policy* of putting an end to the
complication of affairs which abroad was a source of difficulty, and at
home a matter of party attacks. . . . Thus the purchase was effected in a
manner somewhat unusual, as I did not know that the ironclads had been
bought. I consider however the result is the most satisfactory which under
the circumstances could have been attained.[59]

Lords Palmerston and John Russell had been the strongest advocates of
denying the ships to the Confederates. As foreign minister, Russell had
the duty of implementing the policy and his department (the "F.O.")
actually purchased the rams without even informing the Admiralty.
Furthermore, Somerset, a loyal member of the cabinet, changed his
opinion of the rams after the fact. They had not been "good for much"
upon earlier investigation, but now they provided the Royal Navy with
"advantages of an earlier trial of a smaller class of ironclad vessel."

The Southerners deplored their country's loss of the ships' service.
Just what did the Confederate States lose in the way of service? Just what
service had Bulloch expected from the two ships?

The most recent and best commentators have accepted without quali-
fication that the rams were expected to operate in the "rivers and
harbors of the South" or in the "coastal waters and rivers."[60] And this
seems to have been the assumption of the contemporaries, including
both Mallory and Adams. But the man who designed them and who had
spent years sailing the American coastal and inland waters had certain
specific reservations concerning the best service to expect from the rams.

Commander Bulloch hinted at these reservations as early as September 1862, but when Number 294 was launched he completely recast his
thinking about the ships' use and expressed a very different notion
about the function they could render.

The size and draft of Numbers 294 and 295 had been dictated by the
fact they had to cross 3,000 miles of ocean before reaching their battle
stations. They were smaller than North's Number 61 or the French
Couronne, but larger than the Union *Monitor*. Their cruising size made it
possible for them, Bulloch earlier had stated, to "sweep away the entire
blockading fleet of the enemy." But what of Secretary Mallory's suggestion that they should go to New Orleans and regain the Mississippi
River? On 9 July, before he had learned of the Confederate losses at
Gettysburg and Vicksburg, and in the exuberance of 294's launching,
Bulloch detailed his mature plans for the two ships.[61] Based upon his
"intimate knowledge . . . of the construction and capabilities of the
ironclads 294 and 295," Bulloch rejected any role for them on the
Mississippi River: "they are large ships, both in length and in breadth,

and in the rapid current and short turnings of the Mississippi, they would be at great disadvantage." What then? Would they enter the protected waters along the Atlantic coast to "sweep away the *entire blockading fleet of the enemy*"? Bulloch's answer is disappointing; it ignores his defensive theory so carefully enunciated in March 1862. The iron-clads would not enter those protected waters; they merely would "sweep the blockading fleet from the *sea-front* of every harbour from the capes of Virginia to the Sabine Pass, and cruising up and down the coast could prevent anything like a *permanent systematic* interruption of our foreign trade for the future." Although Bulloch's ships might clear the seafront of the enemy, how did he propose to deal with the Northern ironclads that were so "wonderfully serviceable in the shoal-water fighting of the Civil War"?[62] Bulloch had no illusion about the result of a "smooth water" engagement: the rams' "plates would have been loosened and the backing splintered." But "in open water, with room to maneuver, they would have had no difficulty in running down any *Monitor* [sic] then afloat." Did he expect to lure them out to the seafront? And if not, then what vessels would escort through the shoal waters those merchant ships bearing the South's "foreign trade"? Bulloch had no answers to these questions. The fact is, any ironclad built in Europe large enough to cross the Atlantic could *not* enter the shoal waters to encounter the smaller Union ironclads. Once Number 294 was launched, Bulloch realized he had perforce designed a vessel too large to do the job he originally had intended it to do. He was faced with a dilemma. The real defensive need of the Confederacy—ridding the inner waters of Northern warships—could not be met; what to do?

Bulloch's answer was immediate: transform his ironclad armored ships into offensive weapons; make them coastal cruisers that could take the war to the Northern cities. "Should Washington still be held by the enemy, our ironclads could ascend the Potomac . . . and could render Washington itself untenable." Portsmouth, New Hampshire, could be besieged and forced to pay $1,000,000 in gold as ransom; Philadelphia and Baltimore offered tempting images also. The cruising qualities by July 1863 had all but obliterated Bulloch's original defensive theories.

The rams' cruising qualities, necessitated by the ocean crossing, con-sisted of heavy rigging on tripod masts and a unique arrangement to increase the height of the freeboard. Hinged iron bulwarks amidships raised the distance between the waterline and the deck from six to eleven feet; when lowered they provided a field of fire for the turret guns. Furthermore, because turret guns would not be effective weapons while chasing a ship, the rams were constructed with emplacements fore and aft for future installation of proper chase guns. The features gave the Laird rams seagoing qualities possessed by none of the United States ironclads.[63] Bulloch intended that the rams should be used not just against wooden commercial ships but against the best and newest Union naval vessels. He also intended that the rams should operate not individually nor even as a pair but in conjunction with North's Number 61 and Sinclair's *Canton*. These in turn would be joined later by two smaller ironclads and four composite corvettes then under construction in France.[64] Bulloch planned to send a fleet of naval vessels to carry the war to the enemy.

But was Bulloch justified in his revised expectations? Given the rams' novel architectural features and lack of sea trials, was he being realistic? Only the ships' service in the British navy can afford even a hint of the answer.

At first glance the rams' record indicates that Commander Bulloch had overestimated their abilities. The seagoing quality was limited; the Admiralty found that one of them "rolled 18 to 20 degrees, often had her decks awash, and in heavy swells her hull was almost completely hidden from observers in other ships." One night the other one accidentally rammed a ship that "did not seem to know anything about it, just went on and took no notice" while the ram herself "had her forecastle ripped open" and could not steam ahead for danger of swamping.[65] Later, however, the British captain of Number 294 reported: "I found her at all times buoyant and seaworthy and should have no hesitation in taking her anywhere for passage; but as a cruising man-o'-war the discomfort from constantly wet decks would have materially interfered with her efficiency." The British experienced difficulty steering before the wind "owing to a flat floor and small rudder area." And under sail the three-bladed screw made the ships "erratic to the helm."[66] Used by the British navy for local defense duty, Number 294 was active for five years and then steamed to Bermuda, where she remained as a harbor ship for thirty years. Number 295 was active for over ten years and closed her service as a Hong Kong defense ship. The record, then, is not definitive. The ships had shortcomings that would have hindered their use as cruisers, yet they had better seagoing qualities than any Union ironclad.

Bulloch was probably more optimistic than realistic in his expectations for the ships. In the company of Number 61 and the *Canton* it is possible that they would have fulfilled some of his expectations. Indeed, it is probable that "they would have been exceedingly troublesome to the Federals."[67] But there is a vast difference between merely being "troublesome" and preventing "anything like a permanent and systematic interruption" of Southern trade. Was he then an inept designer? These ships incorporated the very latest technology, which was new and still changing. Under normal conditions the builders and owners would have subjected the ships to sea trials, adjustments, and further sea trials. But the South did not have the luxury of time required for such proper shipbuilding. The latest naval architectural technology in 1862 was not enough; trial and error soon produced better iron and armored ships than the Laird rams. But by then the South had lost the war. Given the Confederate needs and means, given the moment in the development of technical knowledge, Commander Bulloch had produced the best ships possible. No one knew their real capabilities and limitations, and as in all man's affairs it was ignorance that created the myth of the rams' awesomeness. The myth, in turn, lifted to their highest peaks the expectations of the Confederate officers in Europe; it created the most dangerous moment in British–United States relations since the *Trent* affair; it forced the English ministry to depart from its own liberal principles of government by law and to seize the ships according to policy, according to the secret purposes of state.

Lord John Russell and his cabinet colleagues had shown exceptional courage in detaining and purchasing the rams. Although they had gone beyond their own law, they had served their country's cause not only in this but in future wars. Henry Adams considered the diplomatic victory to be another Vicksburg; his father was deeply gratified. The Southerners, on the contrary, were not just disappointed but crushed. Mallory, Bulloch, and all the officers then in Europe felt that their war efforts had been unfairly frustrated and their country had suffered a severe, perhaps irreversible blow. There is an irony to all of this because when the Laird rams are studied in detail it is clear that acting alone they could not have punished the North; they merely would have been troublesome. In truth, they were of little more value than Commander North's much-maligned Number 61.

THE CLYDE RIVER SHIPS

Although Bulloch's rams received most attention and have attracted the bulk of historical notice, the British policy of neutrality was applied equally and simultaneously to Commander North's Number 61 and to Lieutenant Sinclair's *Canton,* both under construction in the Thomson Glasgow shipyards on the Clyde River. Differences in the original contracts, in Scottish law, and the ships' construction, however, led to different techniques of neutral enforcement.

Sinclair's unique method of financing his ship and his clever contract, which placed actual ownership in British hands, led to a negotiated compromise with the owners; North's Clyde River monster, so demonstratively unfit for the Royal Navy, induced government officials to allow its sale to Denmark. In both cases, however, the vessels were denied to the Confederates.

If the final settlements were different, the modes of procedure were strikingly similar to those used against the Laird rams. Federal officials and informants swarmed into Glasgow seeking information, British officials harassed British subjects, and the government threatened legal action and long court procedures. The *Alexandra* appeals were just as much a useful lever on the Clyde River as they were on the Mersey. On the same day it notified the Lairds of the rams' seizure (26 October 1863), the government notified the Thomsons of the *Canton*'s detention. Within a few weeks a British man-of-war steamed up the Clyde, and on 10 December the *Canton* officially was seized.[68]

Meanwhile, Commander North's optimism following the *Alexandra* decision in June 1863 gradually turned into despondency. The actions against the rams and the *Canton* finally convinced North that the British government intended to enforce its neutrality. By late November he recognized that "there is very little chance or hope of my getting out." Even his landlady had been summoned to testify before the sheriff's court. "Spies are dodging around from every direction; from one to two are generally on watch about this house." A British man-of-war, he informed James Mason, was keeping watch over the *Canton*. Despite such clear signs, North was uncertain as to his own proper course of action. "I should be much pleased," he solicited Mason, "to have your advice in this matter." On the same day he sought the orders of Commodore Barron in Paris: "I think I see quite enough in the trial of the *Alexandra* to convince me that I will never get my ship out." The dawn of truth was beginning to break. Finally, on Barron's and Mason's urging, North went to Paris to confer with them and Slidell. Four days after the seizure of Sinclair's *Canton*, on 14 December 1863, Commander North accepted the decision to sell his ship "without loss of time," and he obediently terminated his contract with Thomson on 21 December.[69] It undoubtedly was heartrending to admit defeat in a mission he had been pursuing, however desultorily, since May 1861.

Commander North had squandered twelve months in 1861–62 before he had found a builder for an ironclad ship in Europe; during that time and the months after May 1862, he had entered into a hasty contract with the builders, missed two opportunities to command a cruiser, contended with Secretary Mallory over rank, argued with Commander Bulloch, and still had no deck under his feet. With the decision to sell his still-incomplete "Scottish Sea Monster," he repeated the same pattern. He argued with Slidell concerning the broker fees for arranging the sale, and he allowed some five months to slip by before he received even a partial payment from the builder. In the long run he had to settle for far less money than he was due. Commander North's pattern of inefficiency, contentiousness, and failure remained the same whether he was attempting to procure or dispose of a Confederate navy vessel.

North's dispute with Slidell was not the officer's fault. In the December 1863 meeting the group had agreed that James Galbraith, long associated with North and the ship in Scotland, "should take charge of her and dispose of her to the best advantage." Galbraith, unable to journey to Paris, failed to confer on the project. Slidell took advantage of this and urged his son-in-law, Emile Erlanger, to act as broker; but neither North nor Commodore Barron understood that Erlanger should preempt or even join Galbraith in the business. Later in another meeting North informed Slidell of Galbraith's arrangements to sell the ship. To his "astonishment," North found Slidell "much annoyed" and "excited" because, Slidell said, "Mr. Erlanger and Mr. Galbraith were to attend to this business jointly and to divide the commissions."[70] The navy officer seems to have accepted Slidell's harshness docilely, realizing that it resulted not from his own mistake but from the diplomatic agent's greed. Nevertheless the pattern of personal conflict and animosity had been repeated.

Commander North's difficulties in disposing of Number 61 stemmed from Thomson's unexpected delays in completing the ship, and then international affairs intervened to further delay delivery. These delays increased the South's share of costs.[71]

Europe in that age of nationalism provided a ready market for machines of war. Just as James Galbraith began to seek a buyer for Number 61, the long-brewing dispute between German and Scandinavian national aims reached a diplomatic point of no return. Commissioned by the German confederation to prevent Denmark from annexing the duchies of Schleswig-Holstein, Prussia was looking for ironclad vessels to bolster its navy. Denmark had to do the same. Prussian naval agents contacted by Erlanger rejected the Clyde River ship, but Danish ones contacted by Galbraith accepted it; at the end of December 1863 the Danes agreed to pay Thomson 240,000 pounds for the vessel. War broke out before Thomson launched the ship on 24 February 1864; delivery therefore had to be delayed until peace was established on 31 October. By that time Thomson had added costs and commissions to the Confederacy's portion of the bill, Sherman was marching through Georgia, and Commander North had to accept less money than he had put into the ship. This final settlement was made sometime in December 1864, twelve months after the decision to sell the ship.[72]

These events were beyond Commander North's control. Commodore Barron was "distressed and annoyed" at Thomson's "outrageous" demands; he acknowledged that North had completed his mission "in as satisfactory a manner as seems possible under the circumstances." No one blamed North, but his reactions were predictable. He fumed at Earl Russell for being "bitterly opposed to us in everything," he hoped to receive command of one of the ships then abuilding in France, he complained that his "trust of honor" in Thomson was being violated, and he convinced himself that the builder "means to act improperly." He traveled from Glasgow to Paris and back again, always anxious over the sale of the ship and the money due him. He did manage to send cannon and blankets to the Confederacy, but he spent most of his time awaiting events, just as he had done in 1861–62. North's reaction was, in sum, a long, passive complaint. He received no ship to command; the war gradually wound down. On 2 January 1865, Commodore Barron authorized him to "return to the Confederacy by any route . . . deemed best." James D. North had arrived in Europe in May 1861, he remained there until January 1865, and the Confederacy was none the better for it. Yet he felt that his Scottish Sea Monster was a "noble ship" that "would have done us most valuable service."[73]

Suppose North had gotten Number 61 to sea; would she have rendered good service to the Confederacy? Several naval officers and naval architects examined the ship and expressed strong reservations about her effectiveness. Commodore Barron reported as early as November 1863 that the ship's size, deep draft, fuel needs, and manpower requirements led him "to doubt very much the expediency or propriety of ever owning her." The Prussian naval architect who inspected the Clyde River ram considered her to be "useless" and "a poor example of a covered corvette." James D. Bulloch's objections to the ship were well known even to James North. Still, North knew the ship better than anyone else and he was an experienced naval officer; in this light his opinion might easily balance that of the other three experts. The final judgment of the ram, then, must rest on her performance at sea. As the Danish naval vessel Danmark, North's ironclad made only one cruise, from June to October 1869, and her performance in bad weather (rolls of 45 degrees, sails blown away, coal consumed) led the Danes to decommission her immediately.[74] Had James North managed by some miracle to get her to sea, his luck and the ship's undesirable qualities probably would have brought disaster to the Southern cause and probably would have covered his name not with glory but with ignominy. It was his good luck and the South's good fortune, then, to have been caught in the squeeze of the British-tightened neutrality, to have understood, even belatedly, the true implications of the Alexandra decision and of the Laird rams' seizure, and to have sold the vessel to the Danes. In this way only the Danes were the losers.

Meanwhile George T. Sinclair ostensibly had given up his ship and retired to Paris to serve Commodore Barron. Before leaving, however, his very presence already had damaged North's position. The two men lived in the same house, which, as North put it, spies watched constantly.

If the Union and British officials suspected Sinclair and his ship as they did, the close association with North confirmed their suspicions of both men. Sinclair's transfer to Paris was effected too late to help either man or ship.

Having seized the *Canton* on 10 December 1863, the British officials began to make a case against her. Scottish law permitted the seizure prior to submitting evidence, so the matter was easier within the law than was that of the Laird rams. Investigation led the officials eventually to the intricacies of Sinclair's Sanders-Stringer-Lindsay financial arrangements and thus to the question of true ownership. Once they accepted the fact that British subjects were the actual owners, the law officers realized they had no case in court. They had to adopt a different technique to enforce British neutrality. They threatened the owners with court action, then they negotiated an out-of-court settlement with them. The owners could retain possession of the vessel on three conditions: that they alter the ship to assure its peaceful use; that they give bond for its proper employment; and that they change its registry so as to preclude transfer of ownership.[75] The *Canton*, then, passed forever from Confederate control. British neutrality again was upheld.

The ship does enjoy a unique place among all of those the Confederates contracted to be built in the British Isles: it did not cost the South one penny. The contract, more carefully drawn then either North's or Bulloch's, provided that the actual owners pay for the construction. It was for this reason, perhaps, the easiest ship for the British government to deny to the South because legal pressure to negotiate a settlement could more effectively be applied against British subjects than against the Confederate navy. But the Confederate navy agents in Europe refused to recognize this and schemed to get the ship to sea under Sinclair's command.

The Confederate hope sprang from Sinclair's unique contractual arrangements with the British subjects. Commodore Barron, convinced that the ship would be safe if only Sinclair's connection to it could be concealed, twice suggested that the lieutenant absent himself with all of his papers from Glasgow.[76] After the government's compromise arrangement in March 1864, Commander Bulloch tried his hand. Bulloch's plan was to feign acceptance of the *Canton*'s fate and then secretly arrange with the owners for delivery of the ship outside British waters. First he had to get Sinclair out of the way because that officer was always too excitable to carry out such a secretive deal; so Barron ordered Sinclair to Paris in June 1864. Then in August Bulloch discovered that he would have to act through Sinclair's friend Galbraith before he could approach the owners. So he had to take Sinclair into his confidence. The plan then, according to Bulloch, had two problems. First, would the

owners be willing to part with their four-pence-per-pound cotton certificates? Second, would the irrepressible Sinclair be able to play the cloak
and dagger role? The second question was answered first; as soon as
Bulloch confided in Sinclair, "he at once began to detail the matter of
engaging engineers, carpenters, etc." You must, Bulloch implored Barron, "get him away from this neighborhood, at least while negotiations
are going on; if matters begin to look favorable, he will not be able to
contain himself."[77] But matters did not begin to look favorable; the
owners undoubtedly felt their investment to be safer with their compromise with the government than with any shady dealings with the Confederates. At least Bulloch's plan is not mentioned again; still, it had
been a good rehearsal for the C.S.S. *Stonewall* episode later in the year.

Secretary Mallory insisted that Barron should not give up on the
Canton. The commodore was willing to humor the secretary "since we
have nothing to lose by her; no money has been paid out." He had no
illusion, however; "We certainly can never get her out during the
continuance of hostilities." Then, anticipating his government's action a
few months later, he added that because the *Canton* was a "fine vessel
and in the event of an armistice she could be got out in a week," he
would keep Lieutenant Sinclair in Europe ready for such an eventual-
ity.[78] Hope died hard in the Southern hearts, but it did die. Two months
later, even before the Hampton Roads Conference, the Confederate
navy officers in Europe were seeking ways to go home, and within
another month, they were ordered home. The *Canton* still sat on the
Clyde River, still owned by the British combine of seven investors in the
now worthless cotton certificates. For the Southerners, the "fine vessel"
provided a sad end to a story that had such exciting beginnings; for the
British, she was a floating monument to their flexible policy of denying
warships to the Confederacy.

British neutrality during 1863–64 was effective. The "fleet" that
Commodore Barron was to have commanded had been destroyed
without firing a shot.

Why had British neutrality begun to tighten as early as March 1863?
In that month, just after Lee had beaten Burnside from the heights of
Fredericksburg, long before Gettysburg and Vicksburg; in that month,
before the Polish Insurrection had reached a contentious point between
Paris and London, before the Schleswig-Holstein question attracted the
attention of the European great powers; in that month Lord John
Russell instituted the investigation of a small, wooden ship ostensibly
intended for use by the Confederacy. With this investigation of the
Alexandra British neutrality began to tighten not because of the ironclad
rams at Birkenhead, not because of distant and future battles, nor even
because of delicate European problems; why then?

British neutrality tightened because Lord John Russell recognized that the British Foreign Enlistment Act of 1819 was insufficient to enable the government to meet its neutral obligations. He and the law officers were anxious to test the 1819 act in the *Alexandra* trial; when Judge Pollock and Sir Hugh Cairns refuted them, they appealed. During the appeal process, customs officials and special detectives probed to find evidence that would stand up in court in other and similar cases. Commander Bulloch was right when he wrote in January 1863: "Lord Russell says in effect that the *Alabama* evaded the law, and rather intimates that it shall not be done again."[79] And it never was done again.

Earl Russell faced difficulties, however, in preventing any other *Alabama*s. He believed in the rule of law as much as anyone, so he turned almost automatically to the law officers. When they failed him with the *Alexandra*, he took full responsibility for detaining the rams. He still expected to prevail legally, but he already had adopted a policy of assuring that Great Britain's neutral obligations would be fulfilled. Others gradually came to his side. Lord Palmerston, ever ready to use unorthodox methods to achieve his purposes, first suggested extralegal means of fulfilling the neutral obligations: buy the rams.[80] It was after the adoption of Russell's policy that Commander North felt it necessary to sell his Clyde River ironclad and that Lieutenant Sinclair lost control of the *Canton*. His policy also led to changes in the 1819 law designed to meet the needs of a modern world, that England insisted in writing the strengthened neutrality into international law in the Treaty of Washington and then accepting that as the basis for the Geneva arbitration. But Lord John Russell had recognized the principle as early as November 1861.

There was, of course, self-interest in observing the principle that a sovereign state has an obligation toward other states to enforce its declared neutrality. Great Britain was the greatest sea power in the world; in any future war in which Britain might be a belligerent, it would want to prevent an enemy from being armed in neutral lands. Lord Palmerston, taxed with the problems of the Danish War, understood this; so did Disraeli and Gladstone, later, when the new law was passed and incorporated into the Treaty of Washington. But it was a good law because it would protect weaker neutrals from bullying belligerents. And Commander Bulloch, Captain Semmes, and Secretary Mallory— the Confederate navy in Europe—largely had been responsible for forcing the issue. Had their ships not been constructed in the Birkenhead yards and if at least one of them had sailed the seas, the modernization of neutral obligations might have come too late to match the growing technology of war. Great Britain's indemnity of $15,000,000 to the United States was in the long run a small amount to pay.

Throughout the year 1863 and afterward, Commander Bulloch failed to understand Russell's position. He constantly and consistently accused him of being pro-Northern, favorable to the Federals, a partisan of the United States. It wasn't true, for it was Russell who pushed hard in the autumn of 1862 for some sort of cabinet debate on intervention in the Civil War. Bulloch's attitude created its own pain and blinded him to the reality of his position. He always thought that if he stayed within the 1819 law, by whatever ruse, then his work would be unassailable. He did not count on the liberal state's becoming arbitrary. When it did, he took his business to France, where he thought he could assay the whims of an arbitrary ruler; he was to be as frustrated there as ever he was in Liverpool.

After the seizure of the *Alexandra* in March 1863, only one other cruiser reached the seas for the Confederacy in that year. It was a small, comparatively ineffective ship known as the C.S.S. *Georgia*. Her story coming in the midst of Bulloch's gigantic struggles would seem anticlimactic if it were not part of another larger story—that of CSN Commander Matthew Fontaine Maury, scientist of the seas.

CHAPTER 5

Matthew Fontaine Maury in England

The most interesting of the "special service" naval officers is Commander Matthew Fontaine Maury. That interest is increased precisely because historians writing on Confederate naval activity in England consistently have overlooked Maury's full mission in Europe and even have failed to appreciate fully his success in acquiring vessels for the navy.[1] His contemporaries in Europe—Bulloch, Semmes, Sinclair, Anderson—barely mention him. Yet he was the only Confederate official other than Bulloch to get a naval cruiser to sea, and he did this under the eyes of Federal spies and British officials at a time when Bulloch had given up hope. It is hard to account for these oversights of Maury's extensive activities except to acknowledge that the *Official Records of the Union and Confederate Navies in the War of the Rebellion* contains little information on him. It published only fourteen of his letters covering the period from January 1862 to April 1865. Among the literally thousands of other letters in the *Official Records*, Maury is mentioned only thirty-four times.[2] Little wonder the naval historians have slighted him.

Save for only James D. Bulloch, Maury's experience, knowledge, and reputation made him the best prepared of all Confederate agents in Europe. He was born in Virginia (14 January 1806) and raised in Tennessee until the age of nineteen, when he entered the navy as a midshipman.[3] His naval career was marked by high controversy and great achievement. He was aboard the first United States naval vessel to circumnavigate the globe; he was an activist in a personnel reform movement; he suffered a crippling accident that left him marked for life and relegated him to shore duty. This duty led to an assignment first as superintendent of the navy's Depot of Charts and Instruments (July 1842) and later (October 1844) as the first superintendent of the new

Naval Observatory. In this dual capacity Lieutenant Maury with a salary of $1,500 a year and no formal higher education began a scientific career that would lead to world renown among marine scientists and meteorologists and honors from half a dozen foreign governments including England, France, Belgium, and Russia. His was a reputation in Europe that would survive the stigma of Southern service during the Civil War, exemplified by perhaps his most cherished award—an honorary doctorate from Cambridge University in 1868. Yet throughout his career in the United States Navy he was opposed step by step by those scientists who considered him to be unfit because of his lack of higher education.

Lieutenant Maury never backed off from this criticism. He was caustic and sharp in his responses. Thus by 1861 he had made many enemies in Washington, some of whom would serve in high places in Richmond: Jefferson Davis, Judah P. Benjamin, and Stephen R. Mallory.[4] Three naval officers who served on a so-called plucking board in 1855 and who voted to place Maury on the retirement list at half pay later turned up as his Confederate navy colleagues in Europe: Samuel Barron, Richard L. Page, and William L. Maury, a distant cousin.

Maury's scientific career began that day in 1842 when he became head of the Depot of Charts and Instruments. The facility previously was just a depository of sea charts, with which little if anything had been done. His experience sailing around the world and on the seas in general had aroused his curiosity about currents and winds. He now had at hand years of records from which could be extracted much information, and he set to work. He began at once to publish articles and eventually a *Guide to Navigation* based on those charts. He devised blank forms that the navy required all captains to complete, and thus he established a source of continuing information about currents, wind direction and velocity, storms, air and water temperatures and pressures. His publications attracted the attention of mariners all over the world but especially of the seagoing nations of Europe. He pushed for scientific cooperation between nations and finally in 1853 succeeded in bringing about the first International Maritime Meteorological Conference, known as the Brussels Conference. High-ranking navy and government engineers gathered from all the maritime powers—Belgium, Denmark, France, Great Britain, the Netherlands, Norway, Portugal, Russia, and Sweden—to hear Lieutenant Maury of the United States deliver the opening address.[5] They must have been impressed because they adopted for all their countries the recording forms devised by Maury, and mankind's knowledge of the sea-lanes began to grow ever faster and vaster. Sailing and steaming time was reduced; lives were saved. So great was the respect for Maury at Brussels that some of the delegates became his friends for life, and one of these would later cooperate with Maury in getting a Confederate cruiser to sea. The ensuing years brought acclaim from abroad and jealousy and reduction of pay at home.

Not satisfied to write only for seamen, Maury also wrote for the general public. His *Physical Geography of the Sea* and school texts on geography, couched in laymen's terms, were exciting reading and made him the first widely known marine biologist. He always realized the danger of errors, yet his domestic enemies seized on these, ignoring his contributions, to condemn him.

Maury's work consisted in part in discovering the North Atlantic shelf and in determining that the ocean floor was without currents or tidal effects. This led to the 1858–60 attempts by Cyrus Field to lay the first Atlantic cable. Had Field followed Maury's specifications as to the weight of the cable, success would have come sooner than it did in 1866. This earlier intercontinental communication undoubtedly would have affected the European response to the American Civil War and well might have affected its outcome.

By 1861, then, Matthew Fontaine Maury had served mankind by making the sea-lanes known, saving both time and lives. He had come close to making the world smaller through quicker communication. He had established a European-wide reputation and had won many friends among European naval officers and scientists. He, of all the Confederate agents in Europe, had credentials that opened doors and created opportunities. He became the only naval officer besides Bulloch to put a naval vessel to sea that successfully harassed Union shipping.

Maury had additional advantages by the accident of birth and marriage. A close family man, he could count relatives in the Confederacy, the United States, Great Britain, and France. Unlike Bulloch he did not have to hide his presence in Europe; unlike Commander North he did not have to let opportunities slip by for want of money or of initiative; unlike even the Southern political agents he did not have to use back stairs to confer with the European governmental or military officials. Maury's presence in England and France served the Confederate cause best when he maintained a high profile, and in this respect he was unique. Perhaps this uniqueness explains why the other naval agents practically ignored him; it most certainly explains in part the ambiguity of his assignment to Europe and of his "special mission" there.

That assignment sprang from Maury's early service to the Confederacy. The morning after learning of Virginia's secession from the Union, Maury turned over command of the Naval Observatory to a subordinate, relinquished his sword as an officer of the United States Navy, and wrote his resignation to President Lincoln. The decision had not been an easy one. He would be leaving his scientific work, the source of his achievements and fame. As he left the observatory on that Saturday afternoon, 20 April 1861, he fully realized that the life and career he had struggled to create was now at an end; he would never be able to turn back to it. Within twenty-four hours he met with Virginia Governor John Letcher and accepted appointment to the governor's advisory council.

This position thrust Maury to the highest level of the frenzied activities to mobilize the state for war. For the next six weeks he excitedly participated in a myriad of the council's activities: recommended military appointments to the governor including that of Robert E. Lee as "Commander of the Military and Naval Forces of Virginia"; surveyed the pitifully inadequate supply of munitions and armaments available to the state; evaluated the United States naval capabilities; assigned Virginia naval personnel to command the defense batteries along the state's coastal waters; and personally established a laboratory for experiments to perfect underwater mines, called torpedoes, to protect the state's waterways from Federal naval incursions. Although some of these activities were disheartening and frustrating—the scarcity of munitions and the lack of simple materials to make the torpedoes—others were rewarding and heady. Maury sat with the governor as Robert E. Lee was sworn in as commander of Virginia's military forces; he was in daily contact with the state's highest officials; he was consulted constantly on the most urgent matters. But such stimulating activities soon came to an abrupt end.

When on 23 May 1861 the voters ratified Virginia's Act of Secession, the Confederate government began its relocation from the provisional capital of Montgomery, Alabama, to Richmond. By 2 June Maury's old enemies—Davis, Benjamin, and Mallory—were ensconced in Richmond. Although he was appointed a commander in the Confederate States Navy on 11 June, Maury sensed that his role in the war effort would change: "I begin to feel very useless," he wrote to a relative. "Davis, it appears to me, is grasping after patronage. Don't think he likes Lee. Lee told me yesterday he did not know where he was—nor do I."[6] On 19 June the governor's advisory council held its last meeting. Maury had no assignment, no mission. From the center of decision-making power, he moved to the periphery of activity. For the next fourteen months Commander Maury would work in almost obscure isolation trying to perfect the electric torpedo and to construct a fleet of small wooden gunboats designed to protect the Virginia waters by harassing enemy vessels through use of hit and run tactics.

As usual Maury did not accept his new role passively. He wrote stinging articles published in the *Richmond Enquirer* suggesting ways to improve the Confederate navy and proposing peace overtures to Washington following the South's victory at First Manassas (21 July 1861); he contested with a former subordinate in the Naval Observatory, John M. Brooke, over the validity of the small wooden fleet;[7] he argued with Secretary Mallory over the efficacy of the electric torpedo. Although he received an authorization of $50,000 for its development, he had a long wait before the Confederate Congress actually appropriated the money. None of this endeared him to his superiors.

Indeed, Secretary Mallory in September removed Maury from the torpedo work and ordered him to a routine assignment in Cuba. But the scientist–navy officer still had political support, and the secretary, rescinding the order, had to put up with Maury for another year.

Those months, too, were filled with controversy. Maury's small wooden fleet was under construction and he had developed a theme to justify it: "big guns, little ships." Meanwhile, John M. Brooke and Secretary Mallory were directing the conversion of the former *Merrimack* into the ironclad *Virginia*; they were convinced that Maury's small "mosquito" boats would prove ineffective against Northern naval vessels. Their slogan, had they adopted one, would have been "iron ships and direct combat." Maury once again was on a collision course with the secretary of the navy. On 9 March 1862 the *Virginia* and the U.S.S. *Monitor* cast their shadows onto the future of naval warfare as they met in that momentous first battle of ironclads. Maury's fate was sealed. George T. Sinclair, later to be in Europe with Maury, wrote: "As to the wooden gunboats we are building, they are not worth a cent." Brooke immediately submitted plans to Mallory for iron-plated gunboats and received the approval within a fortnight.[8] Without torpedoes, without support for his "big guns, little ships," Maury's value to the Confederacy in Richmond came to an end.

As if to underscore the irony of his situation at home, Commander Maury in the late summer of 1861 received a letter from the Archduke Constantine, Grand Admiral of Russia. In part, he read, "your name is well known in Russia . . . and . . . we have been taught to honor in your person disinterested and eminent services to science and to mankind." The archduke invited Maury "to take up your residence in this country, where you may in peace continue your favorite and useful occupations." What a contrast to the lack of appreciation at home. The offer was tempting: Mrs. Maury urged her husband to accept. Yet, "though Mallory is trifling with me," Maury turned down the Russian offer in order to find some way of "rendering the [Confederate] state good service."[9] The archduke's offer was not the only one Maury would receive from foreign dignitaries before the American Civil War ended; it reflects the worldwide implications of the struggle. It perhaps also, by indicating the high esteem Maury commanded abroad, contributed to Mallory's decision to send him on a special mission to Europe.

Another factor, perhaps as decisive, developed in the late summer of 1862. The Confederate Congress established by joint resolution a select committee to "investigate the administration of the Navy Department under its present head."[10] No one within the navy had been more outspokenly critical of Mallory's leadership than had Maury; it was good strategy to ship him out of reach of the select committee. Within twenty-four hours after the joint resolution, Maury received orders to proceed to Charleston, South Carolina, and thence to Europe on secret service. Although he considered this to be a "banishment" by President Davis and Secretary Mallory, Maury accepted the assignment. After settling some family matters and after a long delay caused by the Federal blockading fleet, Matthew Fontaine Maury and his thirteen-year-old son Matthew on 9 October 1862 sailed on the *Herald* for Bermuda. Still another new career was about to begin.

Had the assignment resulted from Mallory's spite and fear? Could the secretary have used Maury to any better advantage? There was nothing more Maury could have done within the Confederacy; other men could develop his torpedoes, given the limited laboratory and production equipment available; other men could skipper a ship, if one were available. But did other men have Maury's international reputation? Could they as well introduce new finance methods in England, procure needed scientific equipment for the torpedoes, meet government officials in London and Paris on equal terms, write effective propaganda to the *Times* of London, procure ships to cruise against Northern shipping? If Mallory's fear of Maury's possible testimony before the select committee had prompted Maury's European assignment, then it had sparked a mighty deed for the Confederacy. Save only for James D. Bulloch, Maury would become the South's most effective naval agent abroad.

It took Maury almost three months from the date of his orders (24 August) to make the trip to Liverpool, where he arrived on 23 November 1862. As he settled his family affairs in Fredericksburg, Virginia, General Lee won the Second Manassas battle and followed it by crossing the Potomac River into Maryland. But by the time Maury left Charleston, Lee had been turned back at Antietam on 17 September and had recrossed the river with his tattered army. Bulloch's *Florida* long since had sailed from England and was undergoing repairs and receiving her armament in Mobile harbor; the *Alabama* too had sailed from the Mersey River, but Maury hardly could know of her whereabouts on that moonless night when he left Charleston. Perhaps he received word of her commissioning off Terceira Island (24 August) while he waited in Bermuda two weeks for the British mail steamer *Delta*. Certainly, as he contemplated the South's chances in the war, like James Bulloch, he must have concluded that they were slight. Maury well knew his country's desperate need for arms and munitions, for scientific equipment, for supplies of all sorts, and for ships. Despondent, nonetheless he determined while abroad to do all he could to remedy the situation.

Maury's reception in Bermuda undoubtedly lifted some of his despondency. He was received by the governor of the island, called upon by the commandant of Fort Saint George, and honored at a dinner aboard H.M.S. *Immortality*. But the British officials always made it clear that they were recognizing the "scientist of the sea," not the Confederate navy commander. This recognition was a foretaste of his receptions in Europe.

Secretary Mallory's exact orders are nowhere to be found in the published or unpublished documents. He did inform Commander Bulloch in a general letter: "Commander Maury goes to England on special service, and you will please advance to him his current expenses and pay."[11] This statement is the only historical record of any official nature concerning the origins of Maury's European assignment. James D. Bulloch in his memoirs did speculate: "The Confederate Government very probably had a political purpose in sending Commander Maury to Europe." He added that the "duty chiefly assigned" to Maury was scientific in nature: "to investigate the subject of submarine defences." To this end, Bulloch stated, Maury "gave much time to researches into electricity, the manufacture and use of gun-cotton, torpedoes, magnetic exploders, and insulated wire." And finally, according to Bulloch, Maury "had also general authority to buy and dispatch a vessel to cruise against the commerce of the United States."[12] Bulloch's comments appear to be based not on documents but on memory of what Maury actually did while in Europe.

Bulloch's memory was good. Maury more than any other Confederate naval officer identified himself with public causes, both propagandistic and political in nature; he did conduct scientific research and send to Richmond specimens, especially for electrical torpedoes; and he did procure two ships for the purpose of cruising against Northern commerce. He did more, however. He introduced an efficient and quick way to finance ship purchases; he consulted with and advised the Confederate diplomatic commissioners; he analyzed European political attitudes toward the American strife. He also suffered anxieties created by the war: the death of a son and the capture of a son-in-law and the worry, the constant worry over his wife's and daughter's welfare. His one consolation was young Matthew, Jr., whom he called Brave and whose youth and love sustained the commander. His two and a half years in Europe were busy, at once frustrating, rewarding, and personally tragic.

Seven weeks after he had sailed from Charleston, Matthew Fontaine Maury arrived in Liverpool. It was a city even more crowded, a harbor even more busy than the one Bulloch had encountered some eighteen months earlier. To the thirteen-year-old Brave, the wagons and carts, the ships and steam engines, and the street hawkers' cries must have been exciting; the city was both larger and louder than the Washington he knew so well. But his father allowed him no time for wonderment; holding the boy's hand, Commander Maury limped on his game leg directly from the ship and through the crowds to the offices of Fraser, Trenholm and Company. There, Maury and Bulloch met for the first time on 23 November 1862.

Bulloch received Secretary Mallory's letter of 20 September from Maury's hand[13] and learned of his obligation to pay Maury's expenses and salary. Perhaps it was at this meeting that Maury outlined the purposes of his special mission. Later Bulloch was to write of Maury's prewar scientific work with great respect and high praise; nowhere in his memoirs does he specifically criticize Maury. This attitude, so different from his comments on Stringer, Sanders, and Sinclair, reflects Bulloch's understanding of Maury's political and scientific duties—his nonnaval activities. Except for a very brief outline of one of Maury's ships, Bulloch had little else to write about the scientist–naval agent. Still he must have provided Maury with salary and travel expenses, for although often low on personal funds Maury managed to live well enough to ship clothing to his family in Virginia and to send Brave to a private school in England.

Indeed the Maurys' life-pattern in England developed quickly. After a few days in Liverpool, they moved to London, to Sackville Street, where Commander Maury engaged inexpensive third-floor rooms. Almost immediately he was besieged with visitors: lords and admirals, scientists and naval officers from the Brussels Conference days. Most significant for his work was the visit of Captain Marin H. Jansen of the Royal Navy of the Netherlands. The two had met in 1853 in Brussels and had maintained a correspondence ever since. Their letters and their mutual relations reflect a genuine affection, and Jansen was among the first to climb the stairs to Maury's rooms on Sackville Street.

In England on official Dutch naval business, Jansen nonetheless found time to entertain Brave by showing him around Victorian London, then the largest city in the Western world with almost four million inhabitants. If Liverpool had excited the young boy, London must have overwhelmed him. It stretched from Greenwich in the east, along both sides of the Thames to Kensington in the west, and beyond to Hammer-smith. It was the financial center of British commerce and "no light from whatever source came unfiltered or unenriched by steam, mist, haze, smoke or fog." Recalling the relative pastoral setting of his homes in Washington and Fredericksburg, a sensitive youth such as Brave must have noticed the abject poverty and magnificent wealth existing side by side. Certainly his father would have felt in such a city a loneliness among the millions of nameless people and would have agreed with Henry James's observation that London "was as indifferent as nature herself to the single life." This "dreadful, delightful city" would be their home for most of the next two years.[14]

While Brave was sight-seeing, Commander Maury set about his business. He arrived in Europe during the diplomatic flurry over possible European intervention in American affairs. The English refusal of the French mediation proposal had just been made public. As he talked with Mason, Rear Admiral Robert Fitzroy, Lord Wrattesley, Sir Henry Holland, and an unnamed member of Parliament,[15] he tried to gauge the depth of interventionism in England.

Confederate diplomatic agent to London James Mason undoubtedly repeated the impressions he already had written to Secretary of State Benjamin in Richmond. By 11 December 1862, when Maury was conducting his interviews, Mason felt that despite the British rejection of the French suggestion, "events are maturing which must lead to some change in the attitude of England." He argued that the economic privations could not be met through private contributions and that in February when the government would have to seek treasury appropriations from Parliament, "a potent argument will be drawn thence, in support of the relief that would be extended, by the termination, in some ways, of the American war."[16]

When Maury probed his British friends, however, he found little to support Mason's optimism: "the sympathy here is mostly confined to the upper classes and . . . this sympathy is in the main more apparent than real. It is not that the sympathisers love us or our cause more, but they hate us less than they hate the Yankees, and as for the cause, they like ours less than they do the Yankee cause with its abolition and the like. We are gaining ground here, it is true, but before we can expect any aid or comfort we must show our ability to get along without it—then it will be offered right and left."[17] Maury understood better than James Mason did that the British government, aristocratic though it was, still depended on the British people. Over 1.5 million people, he wrote, had emigrated to the United States since 1850, and the government "can't go against them." Speculators "are in favor of the war and against peace" precisely because of the textile situation. At the wartime price of cotton in England, the 400,000 bales then in the realm, he maintained, were worth $100 million, but "would fall to $15 or $20 million if peace were established." Even the upper-class Southern sympathizers "generally are what we should call abolitionists." The South had few friends in the British Isles because "many of our friends here have mistaken British admiration of Southern 'pluck' and newspaper spite at Yankee insolence as Southern sympathy. No such thing. There is no love for the South here. In its American policy the British Government fairly represents the people." In this light, Maury concluded, because the government does represent the people, "there is no hope for recognition here, therefore *I* say withdraw *Mason*."[18]

Within a matter of a few weeks, after talking with his British friends and evaluating conditions in England, Maury had come to a more realistic assessment of the situation than either Mason or John Slidell in France.[19]

Maury's perceptive evaluation of the diplomatic picture convinced him that the South had to prove that it could "get along without" Great Britain's "comfort and aid." His instructions, partly political, enabled him to contribute to this effort, and he set about the job he had to do. His reputation as a scientist and his public meetings with British naval officials lent an authority to his words that no other Confederate agent, naval or diplomatic, enjoyed. His pen perhaps could persuade public opinion. As he had done in Washington and in Richmond, he chose to write to the newspapers. On 22 December 1862 he sent a letter that appeared in the *Times* of London.

The letter was designed to revive and encourage the issue of intervention in the American war, to show the relative strength of the South as opposed to the North, and to refute stories of Southern hardships caused by scarcity of food and clothing. Referring to Secretary of State Seward's recent argument that foreign intervention in the war would only "afford an additional motive for America to sustain her resolution to remain united," and to President Lincoln's oft-spoken determination to reunite the country, Maury asked: "Then, why dread intervention? If such are to be its effects it should be courted by Mr. Lincoln, one would suppose." Maury also claimed that Lincoln's recent offer of gradual emancipation of the slaves with compensation to the owners "is certainly a bid for the South to come back, and it looks very much like a practical admission on his part that the cause of subjugation and reunion is becoming desperate."[20] In essence, Maury was saying to the *Times*-reading English public: do not let Yankee bluster deter your government from recognizing the Confederacy; the bluster flows from desperation.

Furthermore, Maury wrote, the rumor that Southern merchants were "making overtures for a return to political union with the Yankees" was "only a Yankee trick" to delay an intervention. It was a false rumor, he said, because the Southern war effort, "consecrated by the best blood in the land," was based on "our self-reliance, the faith we have in our cause and leaders." The Federal constitution, Maury claimed, had been overthrown and the Northern government was "but a mob, with Lincoln at the head of it." Rather than the South's seeking a return to union with the North, it would prefer to "be received again as British plantations."

Citing customs receipts in Charleston, Maury endeavored to prove that the South lacked no clothing and he stated simply: "There is not lack of food among us." His final sentence summarized the impact of the letter: "Events now transpiring in America show that we are quite as able to keep the field as is the enemy, and far more united."

This one letter was but a small contribution to the overall Confederate propaganda operation in England, but it is unique as the only self-identified effort by a Confederate naval officer to influence the English public. It served to establish Maury's high public profile and in so doing distinguishes him from all other naval agents in Europe. Only Captain Semmes, just after his dramatic battle with the U.S.S. *Kearsarge*, was to challenge Maury in this, and Semmes never acted to procure ships and munitions for the South. Despite his conviction that there is "no love lost for the South here," Maury purposely had sought publicity; was it a preconceived scheme to cover his ship procurements?

Slightly over a month after he had written to the *Times*, Maury received his first specific orders to procure a ship. In early February 1863 Secretary Mallory instructed him to seek out a ship suitable for cruising against Northern commerce.[21] Commander Bulloch recited the facts of this first vessel obtained by Maury.[22] She was a new iron steamship with a screw propeller. He purchased her in Dumbarton, on the Clyde River in Scotland. As the *Japan* she sailed on 1 April 1863, an ordinary ship of commerce, cleared and approved by the British customs authorities. She met a tender, the *Alar*, off the coast of Brest, France, transferred armaments and stores, and was duly commissioned the C.S.S. *Georgia*. Between May and the end of October 1863, she cruised the South Atlantic and "captured and destroyed six or seven American vessels." But the *Georgia*'s inadequate sail power necessitated frequent coaling stops, and her skipper returned to Europe. On 28 October 1863 the *Georgia* put into Cherbourg, France; she never again cruised against Northern commerce, and her existence and her disposal caused Bulloch many anxious moments during the next year.

Bulloch's bare account of the ship hardly does justice to Maury's role. At a time (early spring 1863) when Bulloch was desperate for funds, how did Maury purchase the ship outright? At a time when British officials were investigating the *Alexandra* and were preparing the legal documents to seize her (5 April 1863), how did Maury manage to obtain British customs' approval and clearance for the ship? At time of intense

Union consulate vigilance, how did Maury avoid detection? Indeed, how did he manage in less than two months to locate and to put to sea a vessel suitable for cruising against enemy shipping? It is this kind of omission in both the official records and in Bulloch's memoirs that is puzzling and that has led scholars to ignore or to deprecate Maury's role in Confederate naval affairs in Europe.[23]

Commander Maury was well prepared to execute Mallory's instructions to procure a vessel to cruise against Northern shipping. Even before he received the secretary's orders Maury had instigated a search for a proper ship. Just as he was preparing to thrust himself onto the British public by writing to the *Times*, on 20 December 1862 he wrote Marin Jansen, his friend in the Royal Netherlands Navy:

> Let me be frank and friendly and to the point, with the condition if you don't like this proposition, that you will commit this to the flames and to oblivion.
>
> You are visiting for your own information the building yards. . . . Will you not visit all of them? And in your mind note every vessel that they have in progress—from the frames to completion—Her size and draft and fitness for armaments. She should be not over 15 ft. draft—good under canvass, fast under steam—with the ability to keep the sea for a year—using steam only when necessary for the chase.
>
> Also note any gunboats or ironclads that you may come across. In short make a note of all that comes under your observation upon a subject which you know is a hobby with me.
>
> As soon as you find one which you think would interest me particularly and fulfill certain conditions, please drop me a line.[24]

Captain Jansen served his American friend loyally. By early 1863 Maury knew of several potentially suitable ships under construction in the yards of England and Scotland. All he needed were the secretary's orders and the necessary funds, which Lieutenant William Lewis Maury delivered in early February 1863. Matthew Fontaine Maury was ready to act quickly.

Maury's own words retain over the span of time the excitement and urgency he felt as he read the secretary's letter: "Lewis Maury brought me $1,500,000 cotton certificates. He arrived about 1st February. This was the first . . . pounds I could lay hands on since leaving Richmond. These certificates to be valid require the signature of Mr. Mason." But Mason, concerned over the effect the cotton warrants would have on the $15,000,000–Erlanger loan that John Slidell was then negotiating in France, refused to sign them. Impatient with such a view, Maury pressed upon Mason the need for quick action, and "after awhile he [Mason] agreed to sign them on condition I would not put them on the market for 60 days. . . . So I took them and raised money on them for 60 days by depositing them in a bank for 60 days as collateral and in six weeks had a fine cruiser out to sea under Lewis Maury."[25] It was as simple as that; without reference to Bulloch or any other Confederate navy officer, Maury had reached into his own resources and accomplished the task.

But even Maury does not tell his full story. He was careful, given his own high public profile and the British and Union vigilance over Confederate activities, not to handle the money matters personally nor to risk being involved in the ship purchase. Instead, he turned to yet another cousin, Thomas Bold of Liverpool. Bold, already involved in supplying Confederate armament needs, was employed by Fraser, Trenholm and Company and was a member of Jones and Company, a Liverpool shipstore supplier and ship chandler. Through his own companies Bold arranged Maury's loan with the London House of J. H. Schroder and Company.[26] With the Confederate origin of the money thus concealed, Bold purchased the still uncompleted vessel ostensibly for use as a merchantman.

Although he had purchased the ship, Commander Maury did not go near Scotland, much less Dumbarton, during the finishing and equipping of the vessel. Instead, he sent cousin William Lewis, captain-designate of the ship, to a small village near the shipbuilder. Lieutenant Maury, incognito, posed as a man on a quiet holiday who received an occasional visitor. He never left the village. Unlike Commander North, he never visited the ship or communicated directly with the builders. Instead—and here Commander Maury's prewar career again paid off— Captain Jansen tended to the details of completing the ship for a cruise. Not one Confederate went near the ship or the shipyard. Jansen later admitted that he had played "a dangerous part" in the *Georgia* case.[27] Dangerous though his part may have been, it was effective. By early March Jansen informed Maury that the ship would be ready to sail "any day after the 18th." The commander was thrilled: "A thousand thanks my good friend for going ahead with such vision. I am charmed with the prospects of your being ready so early. I shall give the passengers notice."[28]

The "passengers" were the Confederate officers Maury contacted discreetly and individually so that none knew of each other's orders. Where did he find them? He had no time to request them from Richmond and there was not yet in Europe a pool of officers awaiting assignment. He was, in this instance, lucky. Commander Bulloch and Lieutenant John R. Hamilton quietly had gathered the officer complement for the *Alexandra*. Maury simply exercised his prerogative based both on his own rank and the military principle of immediate need, and he assumed command of Hamilton's officers. Later, referring to the British government's seizure of the *Alexandra*, Maury wrote: "They have seized Hamilton's vessel. They can do nothing with her at present. But if they let her go, he can do nothing with her for want of officers. I had to take those that had been sent to him, and sent them out with Lewis Maury."[29]

Of the nine officers Commander Maury procured to serve under Lewis Maury, two (Lieutenants Robert T. Chapman and William E. Evans) had been in Europe since arriving there on board the C.S.S. *Sumter;* from all indications the other seven had been sent at Bulloch's request.[30] Even with these nine Southerners to assign to the *Georgia,* Commander Maury was perturbed that Secretary Mallory had not sent "plenty of officers" to Europe because "Lewis Maury has, counting commissioned and warrant officers, more Englishmen than Americans."[31] He thus had to sign on approximately eleven Englishmen of various commissioned and warrant ranks. The enlisted sailors, according to custom, were picked up by the vessel when she left Scotland as the commercial ship *Japan.*

To convert the peaceful *Japan* into the Confederate warship *Georgia,* Maury took a leaf from Bulloch's book of operations. He bought arms, munitions, and supplies in London and engaged the *Alar* to convey them and the men to a rendezvous with the *Japan.* Some ten days prior to the *Japan*'s sailing, William Lewis left Scotland and joined Matthew Fontaine in London, where the two made the final arrangements. They planned well.

The *Alar* was a small vessel regularly engaged in trade between New Haven, England, and the Channel Islands. On Saturday, 4 April, about twenty men arrived at New Haven, heavily laden with baggage and supplies; while they boarded the vessel, "a man, rather lame, superintended them."[32] This is the only indication that Matthew Fontaine Maury involved himself personally with either ship or with a group of the officers and men. Apparently his love of the sea got the better of his caution; after that Saturday he could have been identified with the Confederate cruiser, but in neither case submitted to the Geneva Arbitration Tribunal did the United States or Great Britain connect the "rather lame" superintendent to the marine scientist. As he intended, his public profile in London placed him above suspicion. In none of the official documents concerning the ship is his name even mentioned.

It would have worked even better had all the men who shipped on the *Japan* stayed on the *Georgia.* But about ten refused to sail under the Confederate colors and returned to Liverpool to demand their pay from Jones and Company. This led, eventually, to the prosecution of two of Bold's partners—a Mr. Jones and a Mr. Highatt—for having violated England's neutrality law by engaging men to serve on a Confederate vessel. Each was fined fifty pounds.[33] Still, Thomas Bold was not prosecuted, and his relationship to Matthew Fontaine Maury was never revealed. The hundred-pound sacrifice of Jones and Highatt was a sound investment.

After some difficulty and almost five nights of work off the coast of Brest, France, the *Georgia* was commissioned by William Lewis Maury and sailed into the South Atlantic. Within six months she would destroy Northern shipping valued at $406,000. Commander Maury's unusual financial arrangements and his shrewd use of cousins and a Dutch friend served the Confederate cause well. Even if the *Georgia* was not as spectacular a cruiser as the *Alabama,* even if she could not keep to sail well, she played a role in the war during the months prior to the battles of Gettysburg and Vicksburg. She was the last cruiser whose depredations could have contributed to a Southern victory. And Maury had accomplished the launching of the *Georgia* within two months under the watchful eyes of the Federal consuls and the British officials so cleverly that despite the sailors' depositions, the Geneva tribunal in 1872 found that the government of Great Britain had not failed in its neutral obligations in the *Georgia* case and so rejected the United States claim for compensation for damages inflicted during her cruise.[34]

Maury's second ship presents a story with a different flavor—a taste of failure, not success. The ship was originally the British dispatch vessel H.M.S. *Victor.* Maury renamed her the C.S.S. *Rappahannock,* after the river in his beloved northern Virginia. As a Confederate cruiser she managed to stay at sea only about forty-eight hours; she put into Calais, France, for repairs and was detained dockside for the duration of the war. The unsavory side of the *Rappahannock* was seasoned more by her French experience than her English one; yet, history has attributed her failure to Maury. Contemporary documents and accounts are scarce and vague at best, which has resulted in a confusing and sometimes contradictory historical literature on the ship.[35]

The big facts are clear enough. Maury, using an English front, purchased the ship while she was undergoing repairs. In November 1863, while workmen were on the ship, he sent her to sea from the royal dockyard at Sheerness near London; in the English Channel Southern officers boarded and commissioned her as a Confederate naval vessel and then immediately sailed into Calais. Claiming right of haven from distress, her captain asked for repair facilities at the French imperial dockyard. At that point Maury assigned control of the vessel to Commodore Barron. It was after this time that the *Rappahannock* became a burden to the Confederates; that story is related later, for Maury had nothing to do with it.

These facts, clear as they are, reflect little of the manner in which the Confederate navy operated in Europe; they leave all important questions unanswered. How did Maury pay for the vessel?[36] How, at a time of acute Federal and British watch over Confederate activities, did Maury manage to buy the ship from the Royal Navy and get her to sea? What were the Confederate expectations at Calais? The answers to these questions cast Matthew Fontaine Maury in a positive and imaginative role especially in the exploitation of his British connections.

First, Maury in acquiring the *Victor* was following orders directly from Secretary Mallory. Upon his return to London after seeing the *Georgia* off, he received further orders from Mallory to procure more "anti-mercantile cruisers."[37] The moment was not propitious for the work. Maury himself could not scout about for such a ship, so he ordered Lieutenant W. F. Carter "to visit the shipyards on the Thames, examine the vessels there for sale, and report such as may be suitable for our purposes."[38] It was Carter who first suggested that the *Victor* met Maury's requirements. The ship had been retired from British service because she was "defective and wornout beyond economic repair." In 1862 an agent acting for the Chinese government had refused to buy her because "she was rotten." Maury, well known as he was, never visited the ship. He did send others to inspect the *Victor* and at least one reported favorably: "This is a fine ship and we will do well to get her."[39] Even if he had seen the ship personally he probably would have approved her because the South was finding it ever more difficult to build or buy vessels in Great Britain. Indeed, at that moment the *Alexandra* was being held while Her Majesty's solicitors prepared to appeal the case. Under the circumstances even a ship needing repairs was better than none.

Finding a ship was the easy part of carrying out Mallory's orders. Finding funds and arranging the purchase in such a way as to hide the Confederate navy's role were the hard parts. Although the Erlanger loan had by July 1863 produced large funds there is no indication that Maury received any of that money from Commander Bulloch or from any other Confederate agent.[40] Maury went once again to his British cousin, Thomas Bold. The two devised a scheme that resulted in the successful purchase of the *Victor* by the Confederate navy directly from the British navy. Even Bulloch never attempted such a provocatively daring act.

Bold arranged for a British firm, Gordon Coleman and Company, to bid on the ship. The Admiralty accepted Coleman's offer of 9,375 pounds as equal to the value of the ship with fixtures. The needed repairs according to custom were performed at Sheerness; Royal Navy equipment and manpower were even used for some of the more difficult tasks. The repair work continued from late July until early October 1863.[41]

Meanwhile events in America prompted the British authorities to tighten even more securely their guard over Confederate activities.

News of the Northern victories at Vicksburg and Gettysburg had reached London. The Erlanger bonds had begun their plunge on the London stock exchange. Lord Palmerston and Earl Russell, more sensitive to United States Minister Adams's protests, detained Bulloch's Laird rams in early September.

Even in the midst of such unfavorable conditions, Maury quietly gave 100 cotton certificates to Thomas Bold, who in turn somehow converted them into English currency used by Gordon Coleman to pay for the *Victor*. A partial payment on 6 October and a final payment on 24 November completed the transaction.[42] Maury and his cotton certificates were in no way connected to the vessel. Yet the Federal consul in London, Freeman H. Morse, and the British Admiralty itself, ever alert, began to question whether the ship might be destined for Confederate use; nonetheless a British customs official inspection on 23 November gave the ship clearance. Maury, apprehensive, ordered the ship to sea the next day. So sudden was her departure that some twenty British workmen remained aboard. Somehow—the existing documents are not clear—Maury had arranged for CSN Lieutenant William P. A. Campbell to board the ship, and in mid-channel he commissioned her a Confederate man-of-war. Faulty boilers and other problems forced Campbell to put into Calais on 27 November.[43] Commander Maury was "taken aback by a telegram from Campbell saying the ship was in Calais unseaworthy." He sent Lieutenant Carter "with orders for C. to go ashore and wait orders and then to see what could be done with ship." Maury then turned the vessel over to Commodore Barron, who expected within a few weeks to put the *Rappahannock* to sea fully armed, equipped, and manned.[44] Commander Maury's responsibility for the ship was ended as he noted in his diary: "I have had nothing to do about the ship since she went to Calais."[45]

Under the most adverse circumstances Commander Maury had done his job. Without benefit of Erlanger money, during the time of heightened British and Northern vigilance, he actually purchased a ship directly from the British navy and sent it to a port whence other Confederate officials fully expected to place it into operation. The fact that the *Rappahannock* never went to sea, never fired a round against the North, and eventually became an embarrassment to Bulloch and was considered even by the Federal officials to be "a miserable affair at best"[46] was no fault of Matthew Fontaine Maury.

There was a flurry of diplomatic exchange between Charles Francis Adams and Lord John Russell once the identity of the *Rappahannock* was discovered. One British naval officer was reprimanded for using a Sheerness dockyard crane to place a new mast on the ship, and one worker was dismissed.[47] But no Confederate naval officer ever was involved in any of this; Maury again covered his tracks successfully and was free in the later months of 1863 to pursue his scientific interests.

In truth it may have been Maury's scientific activities that helped conceal his involvement in the *Victor-Rappahannock* affair. The simultaneous timing even raises the question as to Maury's principal duty in Europe: was it to purchase ships under cover of science or was it to gather scientific data and equipment under cover of purchasing ships? Surviving documents do not afford a definitive answer. At any rate, in August 1863 while the *Victor* was undergoing repairs, Maury began laboratory experiments on torpedoes.[48] Drawing upon his prewar friends in the world of science, Maury himself analyzed a magnetic exploder and a phosphide fuse, both of which had been developed by Europeans. He sent his results to Richmond, hoping that the necessary materials to duplicate the devices could be procured.

By mid-1864 Maury had sent valuable new information on improvements in the use of undersea torpedoes and even new and highly effective electric exploders. His own previous experiments on the James River prior to his departure for Europe, his knowledge of the latest developments in Europe, and his scientist friends all enabled him to continue these experiments and procurements. He cooperated with British military officials who, grateful for his help, gave him information on guncotton, which he advised the Confederate Navy Department to use for mines floating near the surface of the water. In August and October 1864 he shipped "a great deal" of torpedo supplies and equipment to Richmond and he urged General Lee to use torpedoes on land as well as underwater.

These 1864 experiments proved to be very valuable to the Confederacy. Secretary of the Navy Mallory wrote in June 1864 that the torpedoes used as directed by Maury had prevented the Union fleet from "sweeping up the James River to Richmond."[49] Maury also played a role in the defense of Wilmington, North Carolina. That city, the last port on the Atlantic open to Southern shipping, lay up the Cape Fear River, whose estuary was guarded by Forts Fisher and Caswell. In January 1865 six thousand Union troops, after concentrated shelling by the largest fleet ever assembled in America, stormed and captured the two forts. They found Fort Fisher protected by land mines, unexploded because the shelling had cut the wires accidentally, and by underwater mines with wires strung to Fort Caswell. Upriver the marines found wires that led them to "the most advanced electrical torpedo system the war produced." The land end "was of English manufacture" and had been "devised by Matthew F. Maury in England." The detonator consisted of three magnetos set off by a crank that fired as many as twenty-five circuits so rapidly that the effect was as one explosion.[50] Three thousand miles of water did not prevent Maury from contributing essentially to the defense of two of the most important cities in the Confederacy during the last year of the war.

While his scientific efforts helped prolong the war, Maury simultaneously acted politically to end it without reunification. He worked with William S. Lindsay, who had helped finance the *Georgia* purchase, and with the "Society for Promoting the Cessation of Hostilities in America." On the face of it, 1864 was an unlikely time for England to take such action. Grant was already pressing toward Richmond, and Sherman was about to begin his move against Atlanta. But in mid-1864 European affairs and Palmerston's slim majority in the House of Commons coalesced to create an atmosphere of hope. The Danish War and the Anglo-French maladroit handling of the London Conference (summer 1864) appeared to endanger Lord Palmerston's slight majority. A vote of censure was threatened, and Palmerston sought as much support as he could muster. Lindsay, a member of Parliament who also had a heavy investment in Southern cotton certificates, organized pressure groups designed to influence the House of Commons toward intervention in the American war. As parliamentary maneuvering developed in the house, Lindsay chose to use the "Society for Promoting the Cessation of Hostilities in America" as a lever.[51]

Maury reentered the public arena in January 1864. In response to a false document pretending to be a report by Secretary Mallory on the Confederate navy and circulated in the English press, Maury wrote once again of "Yankee tricks." The letter along with the false report was published in the *London Standard* in early February. Maury denounced the so-called report: "It is a take-in, it bears internal evidence of a hoax, and I know of many of its statements to be false." In justifying his action to Mallory, the commander perhaps unconsciously revealed much of his feelings of isolation from naval affairs: "I know little or nothing of the transactions of the department at home and almost as little of items abroad."[52] Still he acted when no other Confederate navy official would do so.

This same letter probably played a role in Maury's association with the "Society for Promoting the Cessation of Hostilities in America." Maury had a good friend in the society—the Reverend Francis W. Tremlett, who was its honorary secretary. At any rate, after Lindsay laid the political foundations, at the height of Palmerston's parliamentary crisis, Maury joined with the Reverend Mr. Tremlett and other members of the society to call on Lord Palmerston. Their purpose was to submit signed petitions to prove the existence of a strong British public desire for peace in America. The audience, originally scheduled for 9 June, was postponed by the politically wise Palmerston; the censure motion failed by only eighteen votes on 8 July, and on 15 July the prime minister received Maury and the others. The effective moment had passed; Palmerston no longer needed the votes of the pro-Southern members of the House of Commons. Still, the society made one last effort, aimed directly to the House of Commons through an appeal drafted by Confederate Navy Commander Maury.[53] Like the others, it failed; Lindsay and the Confederates had been outmaneuvered by Lord Palmerston. Futility aside, Maury was the only Confederate navy officer to have an interview with the British prime minister.

Throughout all these activities, Maury continued his scientific work. Indeed, at the very end, on 2 May 1865, having learned already of the fall of Richmond and of Lee's surrender at Appomattox, Maury sailed for Texas with torpedo equipment worth some $40,000.[54] He hoped, somehow, to keep Galveston harbor open and the Confederate cause alive. It was too late. By the time he reached Havana Johnston had surrendered and Davis had been captured. Maury's service to the Confederacy had ended.

That service rendered in Europe has received little historical notice. He succeeded in Commander Bulloch's own special area by putting the *Georgia* to sea, and he did more. Propagandist for the Confederate cause, and friend of scientists, statesmen, and military figures, he shared his work with the British government, and from England he contributed to the defenses of Wilmington and Richmond. No other Confederate navy agent had done as much, yet his European role in the South's conduct of the war has been misunderstood and unappreciated.

CHAPTER 6

Confederate Naval Operations in France

In April 1863 James D. Bulloch traveled from Liverpool to Paris and there signed a contract with Lucien Arman of Bordeaux for the construction of four ships. Events leading to this transfer of the Confederate naval construction program to the Continent were many and varied. Initiative for the change came from both sides of the Atlantic Ocean.

In Great Britain the Confederate naval program seemed to be going well. Commander North's Number 61 and Lieutenant Sinclair's *Canton* were under construction on the Clyde River in Scotland and Commander Bulloch's two ironclads were well under way in the Laird yards on the Mersey River. Still, Bulloch feared that his ships might be delayed or even seized by the British government because of their obvious warlike characteristics. As early as January, anticipating such problems, he determined that "if we get money and I contract for other ships I should go to French builders." Two weeks later he had concluded that "the British Government will prevent iron ships leaving because their object is too evident for disguise."[1] Iron ships designed to lift the Federal blockade of Southern ports, as we have seen, were Bulloch's top procurement priority. Even before the British government confirmed his worst fears by seizing the *Alexandra* (5 April 1863), Bulloch made his move.

Bulloch's action was suggested by the Confederate diplomatic commissioner to France, John Slidell. The previous October, during an interview on purely diplomatic matters, Emperor Napoleon III suddenly asked why the Confederacy did not build a navy in Europe sufficient to lift the blockade at several Southern ports. Slidell explained the construction under way in England and stated that the South would institute a similar program in France if the emperor could assure that his police would not interfere. "Why do you not build them as for the Italian

Government?" Napoleon III responded. "I do not think it will be difficult, but I will consult the minister of marine about it." Slidell passed this on to Benjamin in Richmond and to Bulloch in England. The latter's work in Liverpool and lack of funds prevented him from taking action at the time.[2]

Bulloch's confidence in the safety of construction in France was premature. Slidell checked with Napoleon III's personal secretary only to learn that the emperor had backed off from his October suggestion. Obviously the minister of marine saw more difficulty in the Confederates' building "as for the Italian Government" than the ruler had anticipated. Slidell was perplexed and despondent. But at just that moment the Bordeaux shipbuilder Lucien Arman approached him with assurances that he could build ships so long as they were represented as destined for some other service. The implication was clear: if Confederate ownership were discovered, then the French government would act according to its interests and to the law, both domestic and international. Slidell was not satisfied. He consulted Napoleon III's ministers of state, marine, and foreign affairs; only from the first two did he receive encouragement. Still, Arman was known to be a consultant to the emperor, and he remained confident that he could build, arm, and equip the vessels. Slidell cautiously advised Bulloch that he should investigate Arman's proposition. When the Erlanger loan seemed assured in mid-March, Arman sent his business agent Henri Arnous de Rivière to Liverpool with definite proposals and an invitation for Bulloch to visit the Bordeaux yards.

Responding to Arman's initiative and with Slidell's tentative approval, Bulloch went to Bordeaux. He spent several days there inspecting the shipyards and discussing ship designs with the French builder. The two came to an "arrangement" concerning the construction of four ships. Carefully, Bulloch questioned Arman on French neutrality laws and received assurances that Minister of State Eugene Rouher understood the situation. So long as the ships were proposed for service on the China seas, where piracy was rampant, they could be armed and could sail under the French flag. Because these assurances coincided with those Slidell had received, Bulloch felt safe in making the arrangement. This arrangement of mid-March was a preliminary contract; Slidell insisted on further proof of the French government's good intention before assenting to a formal commitment. Meanwhile, Arman showed his own good intentions by preparing for construction immediately. When the financial arrangements were settled on 15 April 1863, the contract was signed and construction begun. By June, "good progress had been made."[3]

Why had the French officials gone out of their way to assure such safe violation of the French domestic laws? To Bulloch and Slidell it must have seemed a particularly happy situation in face of the British seizure of the *Alexandra* and the activities of the Federal spies in Liverpool and Glasgow. They had not accepted the assurances lightly, however; they knew the emperor himself had made the first suggestion; they had the word of the minister of state, a veritable prime minister to the emperor, and still they waited to approve the contract until Arman received permission from Minister of Marine Prosper Chasseloup-Laubat to arm the ships. That permission, granted on 6 June 1863, convinced Slidell and he gave his full sanction of the 15 April contract.[4]

There seemed to be obvious reasons for the French actions. The emperor had hinted, not too subtly, at a primary reason when he spoke in October of opening several Southern ports: the French lack of cotton. The interdependency of the industrial world finally had begun to affect the French economy: cotton imports were down, unemployment was up. Approximately 223,336 persons, for whose relief the French spent over twelve million francs in a seven-month period, were out of work. Exports were down and the port cities Bordeaux and Nantes, normally active in shipping to America, were stilled.[5] In a country where everything would "depend on the secret purposes of the Chief of the State," as Bulloch put it, certainly the economic crisis was enough to justify ministerial actions. But there were further reasons.

Napoleon III's deepening involvement in Mexico led the Southerners to believe that when successful he would prefer his Central American dependency to be surrounded by "weak states," as Maury put it,[6] rather than by a victorious United States. The construction of Confederate ships in France logically might be tied to a forthcoming recognition of the Confederacy.

Indeed, in the month of June this was a headline topic for the newspapers in Paris, London, and New York. When Southern sympathizer John A. Roebuck quoted Napoleon III in the House of Commons as merely awaiting a British initiative to extend full diplomatic relations to the Confederate government, Southern hopes and Northern fears both rose. Secretary of State William H. Seward reacted by instructing his minister in Paris, William L. Dayton, to suspend his functions.[7] Had Slidell and Bulloch known of this, Slidell's later actions in regard to ship construction in France might have been more aggressive. The episode ended, however, without lasting benefit to the South.

Even the French posture in Europe gave the Confederates hope. The Polish Insurrection with its resultant diplomacy threatened to destroy the close Franco-British cooperation in American affairs—an event for which Slidell much hoped. Well into the autumn of 1863 this problem persisted; but once again it ended without lasting benefit to the South.

John Slidell and James Bulloch did not have to read the diplomatic correspondence during the first half of 1863 to know that conditions in

Paris were favorable to the South. They could add the factors—unemployment, the Roebuck affair, the Mexican situation, the Polish Insurrection—and logically conclude that Napoleon III, with or without Great Britain, would favor two republics in North America. They could hope and even scheme for official recognition and ultimate intervention in the Civil War. King Cotton had not yet been dethroned.

Still another reason existed for French actions. President Lincoln had his own troubles. General Lee's victory at Chancellorsville in April and his preparation throughout May and June to invade Pennsylvania were well known within the French government. The November 1862 elections in various Northern states had revealed strong peace feelings, especially among the Democrats of the West; United States Congressman Clement L. Vallandigham and the Copperhead peace movement were visual and vocal well into the summer of 1863; antidraft riots in June merely dramatized the North's internal troubles. In Europe Napoleon III was closely informed on all of this, and the Confederates tried their best to make propaganda capital out of it. The American minister in Paris reflected the Union despondency: "Our delays, disasters, and constant changes have been such as to make our best friends abroad almost despair of our final success." It was in this diplomatic atmosphere that Napoleon III, just a few days after suggesting to Slidell that the Confederates build ships in France, proposed that the maritime powers of Russia, Great Britain, and France jointly advocate a six-month armistice in America, and, in January 1863, unilaterally offered French good offices for North-South peace negotiations.[8]

Slidell and Bulloch in Europe, Mallory and Benjamin in Richmond knew of these proposals by early spring. Their optimism rose to such heights that Mallory reverted to his 1861 scheme of buying French navy ships, and Bulloch rejected the notion not because it was impracticable but because those ships would not be useful in the South's rivers and harbors.[9] Slidell, apparently with Bulloch's concurrence, jeopardized a navy contract in an effort to force the emperor's hand in the diplomatic question of recognizing the South. Bulloch had never allowed this conflict of activities in England; only unbounded confidence and optimism led him to do so in France.

The First Construction Contract

France did not possess the significant number of large shipyards that existed in England. But Napoleon III's crash program to build an all-ironclad fleet had stimulated the industry since about 1850. Government yards and private yards, equally, had received contracts and had gained much experience in the new naval technology. One such private yard was Lucien Arman's in Bordeaux. Although Arman had gone bankrupt in 1848, the government's needs during the Crimean and Italian wars had revived him. He did not have the long experience of the Lairds in iron ship construction, but even prior to the Crimean War he had established a sound reputation for building mixed or composite ships. During that war the Department of Marine had selected his works to build the emperor's floating iron batteries, and in 1859–60 he contracted for four others designed for French coastal defense. At the same time he was busy constructing three iron ships for Russia.

Bulloch, remembering his own plan for a Confederate prefabricated ironclad navy, probably was most impressed by Arman's contribution to a naval sectional construction of four wooden ships for lake use during the Italian War. The sections were shipped in pieces to Garda and there assembled into ships. The scheme worked well, each piece fitting the others as it should.[10] Such precise, innovative work could not help but appeal to James Bulloch.

Bulloch inspected Arman's workshops carefully in mid-March and also took measure of the man himself. He liked the short, rotund Frenchman almost immediately and found him to be "shrewd and exacting" and "an artist in his profession." Furthermore, he was "liberal and obliging in the execution of his work" so that Bulloch was able, as the ships progressed, "to modify the internal arrangements, if desirable, to suit any improvements that may be suggested while the ships are under construction." Bulloch compared Arman favorably with Laird, especially because his "desire to give satisfaction in the character of his work is greater than the inclination to screw an extra profit out of it."[11]

In addition to these professional qualities, Arman possessed certain political advantages. He was a member of the French legislative body, first elected when only government-approved candidates could serve. An obvious beneficiary of the emperor's naval construction program, Arman supported Napoleon III uncritically in other programs. He enjoyed a confidential relationship with the emperor that inspired Confederate confidence in all he said. Of all the private shipbuilders in France, Lucien Arman seemed to Bulloch and Slidell to be the best qualified to execute in their behalf the secret purposes of the chief of state.

Ten days after the British had seized the *Alexandra*, Bulloch formalized the "arrangements" of mid-March. On 15 April 1863 he signed a contract with Arman for the construction of four ships to cruise against Northern commerce. Because the plans had been settled earlier, construction on the ships began immediately. No copy of this contract exists; the only description of the ships is a general one in Bulloch's memoirs. They were of composite construction—that is, iron frames with wooden hulls and some armor amidships. Bulloch calls them "clipper corvettes of about 1500 tons and 400 horsepower." They were to be armed with "twelve or fourteen 6-inch rifled guns." No length or breadth is available. Slidell referred to them as "steamers of the *Alabama* class on a larger scale." Arman consigned the ships to "Messrs. A. Eymand and Delphin Henry, shippers at Bordeaux" as agents for a foreign shipper. The vessels were, according to this blind, destined for use in the "Chinese and Pacific seas, between China, Japan, and San Francisco."[12]

The arrangement seemed complete and foolproof. They were, according to contract, purely merchant vessels ordered through a Bordeaux agency by a foreign shipper for use abroad. Normally, these ships unarmed would have required no permit to construct or to deliver. Why, then, did Bulloch and Arman stipulate arming them? Why did they not plan from the beginning to arm them from, say, England at some rendezvous, as Bulloch had done with the *Alabama*? Arman appears to have been assured that commercial ships operating in the pirate-infested Chinese waters could be armed without arousing suspicion. Bulloch mentions only a point of convenience: the rifled guns were to be the " 'canon rayé de trente' of the French Navy, that gun being adopted because of the facility of having the batteries constructed in France from the official patterns."[13] It was a blatant violation of French neutrality, a most unlikely Bulloch mistake, and it could have been born only from extreme overconfidence in Arman's assurances of ministerial and imperial connivance. It was an act of hubris that would cost Bulloch dearly.

Why had Bulloch contracted for cruisers? Had he foregone his own preference for small iron ships that could enter Southern harbors and raise the Yankee blockade? Not really. The cruisers seemed a safer beginning in France. They were the kind of vessel for which both Slidell and Arman had received French official promises. They also could serve as a beginning point; once committed to allowing cruisers for the Confederate navy, the French would find it easier to allow the smaller warships. Indeed, Bulloch began to make plans for such ships almost immediately. Besides, as he says, he was obeying his instructions, which "were to keep as many cruisers at sea as possible."[14]

The Southerners insisted on the necessity of speedy construction and stipulated delivery within ten months from the dated contract. This time element forced an additional complication that in the long run was to be just as fatal to the Confederate cause as was the hubris of arming the vessels. Arman's yards were busy, so to assure delivery on schedule he arranged for the construction of two of the vessels in Nantes. In that city "an eminent ironfounder and engineer," who was also a member of the legislative body, undertook the production of two of the ships simultaneously with Arman's efforts. He was J. Voruz, to whose "business capacity, commercial and personal integrity, and kindly social qualities" Bulloch was happy to testify. Voruz himself was not a shipbuilder. He farmed out the actual construction of the hulls to the yards of Jollet et Babin and of Dubigeon, both of Nantes. Thus if the purchasing blind of Eymand and Henry is included, five different French companies were involved in the corvette building and all corresponded on every aspect of the project: procurement of materials, delivery date, armaments procurement, and financing.[15] The opportunities for a security leak, then, were legion. It fell to Voruz's unfortunate lot, despite his kindly qualities, to suffer the indignity of having an employee expose to United States Minister Dayton the whole scheme. A more simple production procedure well might have assured delivery of the corvettes to the South. Bulloch, however, seems never to have worried about this aspect of the project; his more immediate concern had been its financing.

Financing had been a cause of the delay from mid-March to mid-April. Although Arman began construction on 15 April, he did not settle this question until 10 June, four days after Slidell's final approval of the contract. Arman had rejected unsecured installment payments from the Erlanger loan proceeds. Voruz and Arman played the major roles in solving the problem. They went directly to Emile Erlanger and made a mutually satisfactory arrangement. As Erlanger wrote to Arman: "I engage to guarantee the first two payments for the ships which you are constructing for the Confederates for a commission of five per cent." This "security" was simply a promise by Erlanger to make the payments to Arman in case Bulloch's funds, already in Erlanger's hands from the bond sales, should fail. It was, in other words, merely a 5 percent windfall to Erlanger in addition to the fees he already had charged the Confederacy for handling the loan. The first payment was 720,000 francs, so a valid assumption is that Erlanger would receive 36,000 francs for guaranteeing a transaction already assured. And who paid this money? Bulloch was not fooled. "I am quite sure," he reported to Mallory, "that some how or other the commission has been included in the estimate of prices, so that after all we will pay it. . . . In fine, we are in the condition of all purchasers on credit—we must pay the creditor for the risk he runs in trusting us."[16] Despite his self-proclaimed love for the South and his upcoming marriage to Slidell's daughter, Erlanger did not hesitate to exploit the South's needs.

Arming the corvettes presented two problems. The first, getting official permission, was easy. On 1 June 1863, as required by French law, Arman identified the four ships under construction and requested authorization to arm them with "from twelve to fourteen thirty pounders" each. Such heavy arms required some justification and Arman, as we have seen, emphasized the China Sea service for which he purported the ships to be built and, additionally, the ultimate sale of the ships to the governments of China and Japan. Arman also indicated in his request that the cannon would be made "under the care of M. Voruz" of Nantes. On the surface, this request appeared routine: a French business was building merchant ships for use in dangerous waters and planned to arm them for self-defense against piracy and with the expectation that the new owners eventually would sell them to governments with which France was at peace and who themselves were not at war. Minister of Marine Chasseloup-Laubat, even had he not been privy to the Arman-Bulloch scheme, would have granted the builder's request, and he did so just five days after receiving the request.[17] The official records in the Marine Department, at least, contained no reference to the Confederate States; Bulloch's camouflage of his violation of neutrality laws seemed to be as foolproof in France as his work on the *Alabama* had been in England—except now he considered the government to be his partner, not his opponent.

In England, as we have seen, custom allowed the payment of finders' fees for contracts. The money, however, came out of the seller's profit and was not passed on to the buyer. A different and much more costly custom prevailed in France. Such go-betweens were called agents and they acted strictly on percentage fees that were calculated into the total cost of the product. In the case of the corvettes, Bulloch had to swallow hard to accept the 5 percent fee Erlanger charged for guaranteeing the installment payments. Bulloch, though, does not mention that Erlanger received also a 3.8 percent fee on the cost of all machinery. Nor does he mention fees paid to Henri Arnous de Rivière, who acted as agent for Arman and Voruz at a cost to Bulloch of at least 3 percent. Nor does Bulloch mention the 10 percent fee paid to the Blakely Company of England for Voruz's right to manufacture the cannon in Nantes. In the Blakely case, for instance, Bulloch paid 7,000 francs per gun; 700 francs went to Blakely immediately with the difference between the cost of production and the remaining 6,300 francs being divided equally between Voruz and Arnous de Rivière.[18]

There was an additional cost of the fee system that Bulloch never acknowledged in his correspondence or in his memoirs. The papers purloined from Voruz's files and that on the face proved that the ships were constructed for the Confederate navy contained letters that discussed the fees the Southerners owed to the various agents. In the long run, then, it was the French agents' fee system that defeated Bulloch's efforts in France—a most costly system.

The decision to arm the corvettes and the agents' fee system ultimately forced France to sequester all the ships built to the credit of the Confederacy. But in 1863 before Gettysburg and Vicksburg, while the cotton shortage still hurt France, the Confederates did not know this. They expanded their program in France by contracting for ironclad rams designed to engage the enemy navy, carry the war into the rivers and harbors of America, and to lay siege to Northern cities.

The Ironclad Contracts

Commander James D. Bulloch considered the Confederacy's greatest naval need to be small ironclad ships that could raise the enemy's blockade of the Southern ports. When he first inspected Arman's shipyards in Bordeaux in March he had initiated the stream of events that culminated in a contract on 16 July 1863 for the construction of two ironclad rams. He carefully inspected the two "armor-cased batteries" then under construction for the French navy and discussed with Arman the details of ironclad ships suitable for "service on the Southern coast." Arman at that time even made drawings of such ships. But just as the need for money delayed the beginning of the corvettes, so it also postponed a contract for the ironclads. Bulloch, furthermore, did not have orders from Mallory to enter into the ironclad construction program. Only near the end of June did Bulloch learn from Mallory that the Confederate Congress on 1 May had appropriated two million pounds for the "construction of ironclads in Southern Europe." The act was "induced by the belief that we can have such vessels constructed and equipped in France and delivered to us on the high seas or elsewhere."[19] Still, it was one thing for Congress in Richmond to appropriate the money and quite another for Bulloch in Europe to have the money to spend. Eventually Bulloch had to use funds from the Erlanger loan to pay for the ships.

Although Commander Bulloch was unable to begin an ironclad construction program in France during the spring of 1863, another Confederate officer, Commander Matthew Fontaine Maury, did initiate such an effort. Maury, as we have seen by his work in England, always enjoyed a special relationship with the Confederate Navy Department and he was not subject to Bulloch's control as were the other officers. In procuring the *Georgia*, Maury made his own financial arrangements and preempted the officer personnel from those originally assigned to the *Alexandra*. Furthermore, he carefully used his cousin, Thomas Bold, and his Dutch navy friend, Marin H. Jansen, to carry out the whole scheme. Even before the *Georgia* was commissioned and safely at sea and without any specific authorization, Maury's thoughts turned to ironclad construction in France. He had, as it turned out, merely anticipated Secretary Mallory by a matter of three days. Maury's efforts, although futile, reveal a facet of Confederate diplomacy unknown to Paris, London, and

Washington and even to history, which nonetheless was brilliant in concept and for a brief period gave hope for a decisive Confederate diplomatic victory.

Maury's operation in France followed a strikingly familiar pattern. He used relatives and friends to make the initial and possibly dangerous contacts and maintained a high public profile to cover his own activity. Only in the area of finance did he depart from his English pattern of operations. In this detail, the Confederate commissioners intervened and came near pulling off what would have been the war's diplomatic coup.

Maury and Jansen obviously discussed the notion of building an ironclad in Europe. Just after the *Georgia* was commissioned Maury made his first move toward the French project. On 21 April 1863 he wrote Jansen that he expected funds to arrive soon and he was ready now to "go to France and contract for a cupola ram which I have asked to have command of." He requested Jansen to investigate the situation in France to determine if certain conditions could be met: the ship must have "ability to cross the Atlantic—high spread—I do not care for more than one turret—greatest draft not over 15 ft.—if with twin screws the requisite speed can be got out of her, say 15 or 16 knots." He wanted a ship "that will push into the wooden ships and ricketty monitors of the Yankees. . . . They want to be stronger than those you saw in Lairds' yard." So, he asked Jansen, "put on your thinking cap and go to work with your plans."[20] Maury, it seems, was dissatisfied with Bulloch's Laird rams; he wanted a stronger ship capable of ramming the monitor-class ironclads of the United States and he wanted to command the ship himself.

Eight days later he wrote more specifically to Captain Jansen:

> I am now in hopes of going ahead with that shot-proof and ram-proof in France. I wish to have the benefit of your professional knowledge and skill in helping me to plan and assisting me to carry out. I wish you to superintend the work during its progress to see that it is properly and faithfully carried out.
>
> And for your services I offer you $250 a month from the receipt of this to the completion of the vessel.[21]

Before Jansen responded, Maury received Mallory's instructions "to build in France." His own inclinations thus confirmed, he and Jansen steamed full speed with the French project.

Jansen accepted Maury's offer, even taking an official leave of absence from the Royal Netherlands Navy. By 4 May he informed Maury that the French builders were ready to provide five or six ironclad rams for six million dollars. This news from France set Maury in motion in England. He asked Thomas Bold to get from Laird a model of the twin-screw ship, and from Commander Bulloch he sought a set of drawings of Bulloch's variations on Coles's turret. He also wrote to Commander North requesting a copy of his contract with the builders of Number 61.[22] This French ironclad would be Maury's building endeavor and he consulted all appropriate authorities to assure a successful project. He intended to command the ship and he wanted it to be as near perfect as possible.

Matters moved swiftly in France. Jansen went to Bordeaux on 18 May, prepared to negotiate for several ironclads, but on 21 May Maury drew in the reins. Lee's victory at Chancellorsville earlier in the month had sparked newspaper reports of an armistice, and after a conference with General McRae, the newly appointed Confederate comptroller of the Erlanger and other funds, Maury telegraphed Jansen "to commit himself to nothing."[23] A hiatus set in; for a week no agreements, no progress occurred.

Finally Commander Maury decided to take a personal role in the negotiations. He went to Paris. On 4 June he met Lucien Arman and the two men struck a bargain. Arman promised to build a double stern-post ironclad—"two screws—1280 tons displacement—220 H.P.—eight guns—for 60,000 pounds." The ship would be delivered at sea in seven months. More importantly, General McRae promised Maury the money out of the Erlanger proceeds.[24] Jansen had laid the groundwork, McRae had promised the money, and now Maury and Arman had agreed in principle on the kind of ship and the financial terms. All seemed set for Maury to return to England, leaving Jansen to work out the details of construction—weight of iron, size of guns, internal fixtures and furnishings—and to superintend the quality of workmanship. And so it would have been if Maury had been in sole control of the money. But the Erlanger loan was a Confederate government project; John Slidell had urged its signing on purely political grounds. Maury and McRae had to submit the spending of the 60,000 pounds to the political commissioners for their approval.

On 5 June 1863, then, the two military officers presented the case for building an ironclad ship in the Bordeaux yards of Arman. Three commissioners heard the arguments. As they did, they considered many facets of the Confederacy's posture in the world. They certainly understood naval needs, but one ship more or less—even such a formidable one as Maury described—was just one of their considerations. They looked at the total international picture and their decision changed the nature of Maury's activities. It raised them from a purely military level to the heights of statesmanship.

The commissioners were John Slidell, James Mason, and L. Q. C. Lamar, who was then in Paris on his way to Russia. John Slidell, the strongest personality of the three, was of all the Confederate diplomatic commissioners in Europe the only one to have gained access to a head of state. He had discussed naval policy with Emperor Napoleon III the previous October and he had talked with three ministers about it in January and February. He was on most friendly terms with the emperor's close friend and oft-times official, Count Persigny. Undoubtedly, Slidell led the review of the situation. The discussion must have ranged over France's ever-deepening involvement in Mexico and of the Polish Insurrection; combined with the cotton shortage–induced unemployment in France, these factors indicated that the time was ripe for Napoleon III to act in American affairs. Furthermore, Mason was well aware of the Lindsay-Roebuck plan to force Palmerston's government to take a stand on extending recognition to Richmond, and Slidell was in correspondence with Roebuck on the subject. Realistically, however, Slidell knew the Polish and Mexican problems tended to distract the French from American affairs and he had little confidence in the Roebuck overture. He saw the South's best chance through separating France's American policy from England's.[25] Given Lee's posture following Chancellorsville, one more Confederate victory might serve as Sarotoga had in 1777 to bring France into the war. What could the Confederates in Europe do to apply pressure on the French ruler?

The Confederate navy's operations in France suddenly seemed to provide an answer. The corvettes, already well under way with Napoleon's tacit approval, were the bait. Now Arman was willing to undertake construction of an obvious warship, one impossible to disguise. Could the commissioners chance such a large sum of money without certain assurance that they could get the ship? Of course not; the thing to do was to get the assurance from the emperor himself. So they approved Maury's request for the 60,000 pounds provided the emperor would give his personal permission *"that the vessel is to be built for us openly."*[26]

Now, suppose the emperor gave such permission. If done at the time Roebuck in the House of Commons introduced a motion that Great Britain should extend full diplomatic recognition to President Jefferson Davis and his government in Richmond—what would be the effect on President Abraham Lincoln, Secretary of State William H. Seward, and members of the United States Congress, who just months earlier had passed resolutions against the French in Mexico? These Union officials, concerned over Vallandigham and the Copperhead movement and the need to draft young men into an army that seemed unable to defeat the South, would have no choice but to react quickly and decisively. At the least the United States would have to break diplomatic relations with France; at the most it would have to declare war on France. Either way John Slidell would have fulfilled his mission to Paris. In all probability, even the shrewd Lord Palmerston would follow France into either recognition or war. Commander Maury's ironclad was now an instrument of international politics at the highest level; it was pregnant with potential.

All that remained was for John Slidell to ask the emperor about constructing the ironclad in Arman's Bordeaux yards. He arranged a meeting for 18 June 1863.

In the meantime Maury and Arman continued their work. On 12 June Arman submitted a "final plan of a gun battery drawn according to the design that Captain Jansen explained to me." This battery necessitated a redistribution of weight throughout the ship, which in turn raised the displacement from 1,280 tons to 1,358 tons, yet increased the draft by only seven centimeters. It would increase the cost to approximately 87,500 pounds and extend the time of construction to eight months. Despite this progress Maury was pessimistic. He wrote that the "conditions attached to this loan will prevent me from doing anything."[27] More than just a naval officer anxious to get a command at sea, Maury was also a scientist with a worldwide horizon and an unusually fine insight into political matters. He knew that France could not hazard a war with the United States and he saw the commissioners' efforts to guarantee the 60,000 pounds as misguided prudence. It is most likely that he was not privy to Slidell's involved diplomacy. In a sense, Maury was playing the high-stake game hand by hand, while Slidell was placing all bets on the one hand he now held.

The drama played out on 18 June. Slidell was cordially received by Napoleon III in the Tuileries Palace at ten o'clock that morning. The emperor stated that he "was more convinced than ever of the propriety of the general recognition by European powers of the Confederate States," but that he faced certain difficulties. The conversation then ranged over the whole diplomatic scale: French-English relations, the Polish and Mexican situations, and then Slidell's own proposal that France should act to recognize the South in conjunction with certain continental powers and independently of England. When the emperor did not rise to that bait, Slidell read extracts of a letter from Roebuck and the emperor did agree to receive the two English pro-South members of the House of Commons. Then, and only then, did Slidell raise the matter of Confederate shipbuilding in France.

> I expressed my thanks to him for his sanction of the contract made for the building of four ships of war at Bordeaux and Nantes. I then informed him that we were prepared to build several ironclad ships in France, and that I required *only his verbal assurance that they should be allowed to proceed to sea under the Confederate flag* to enter into contracts for that purpose.

Slidell had begun the play by showing a hand of strength—the bait of the corvettes; then he had revealed his highest cards—open construction of ironclad Confederate warships. His inner tension must have been great as the emperor, with eyelids heavy and half-closed, contemplated Slidell's move. Finally, with the reserve strength always held by a chief of state, Napoleon III remarked: "You may build the ships, but it is necessary that their destination be concealed."[28] Slidell had lost. Never again would he be so close to victory; never again would he hold such a strong hand. The diplomatic game was played out that June morning in the Tuileries. The Confederacy would have to fight on alone.

Slidell's losing ploy also cost Commander Maury a powerful ship. He knew this. On 22 June he noted in his diary, in the informal, broken syntax of a broken hope: "Saw Slidell about the Emperor and the ironclads—Emperor would give no more assurances than he had already given—This would not satisfy condition placed on loan—No money for me." He accepted French Admiral Charbonnes's invitation to visit Cherbourg, and then he returned to London. The next month he made one last effort. He must have been desperate, for he sought a copy of Commander North's contract to raise "funds by cotton certificates" because he had a proposal "for a tremendous ironclad armored ram." But nothing came of this and Maury henceforth limited his not inconsiderable activities to the British Isles. Later, in November, he apologized to Jansen for using him in the abortive French affair, but the cordial Dutchman denied that he ever was in danger and continued to help his friend.[29]

The Confederate navy was not through in France even though Maury's ironclad was sacrificed by Slidell to higher political ends. Commander Bulloch, in Maury's wake, undertook an uncomplicated military arrangement with Arman.

When at the end of June Bulloch received Secretary Mallory's instructions to build ironclads in France, he was prepared to act immediately. He continued his contacts with Arman and Voruz through his agent, Captain Eugene L. Tessier, a Frenchman who also held British master's papers. By mid-July, despite the arrival of the news of Southern defeats at Gettysburg and Vicksburg, Bulloch went to France to settle the details and sign the contract. On 14 July 1863 Bulloch, Erlanger, and Arnous de Rivière left Paris for Bordeaux. Two days later Bulloch contracted with Arman for two ironclads to cost about a hundred thousand pounds each.[30] The ships included several features that suited them better than the Laird rams for harbor and river actions. They were shorter by fifty-nine feet, ten feet narrower, more heavily armored, and drew eight inches less water. More exciting were the twin sternposts and twin screws that Maury had wanted; this meant that by operating the screws in opposite directions simultaneously the ship would be able to turn within its own length, a property much to be desired in river and small harbor action. Each ship would be armed with two six-inch guns in an aft turret and two seventy-pounder Armstrong guns in a forward turret. These larger guns had a fixed lateral position in line with the keel and were aimed by operation of the double screws, thus, according to Bulloch, assuring that the ship always presented to the enemy the smallest possible target. The ships were designed to withstand the 3,000-mile ocean voyage necessary to reach their fighting grounds. Bulloch fully expected these rams, unlike the Laird ones, to enter the Southern rivers and harbors and to lift the blockades and even recover New Orleans. Indeed, the two rams and four corvettes constituted a fleet under construction in France more formidable even than the one more nearly completed in the British Isles. For a few months in the summer of 1863, after the *Alexandra* decision, the Confederate navy in Europe had four ironclad rams, North's larger ironclad, and five composite cruisers all under construction. Such a fleet, had it ever reached American waters, certainly would have affected the course of the war.

Bulloch was able to finance his ironclads where Maury could not because the commissioners were willing to advance installment payments from the Erlanger loan against the appropriated two million pounds reported by Mallory. It was, in effect, a loan from one Confederate fund to another. Even so, Bulloch had to agree to Erlanger's securing the installment payments as had been arranged for the corvettes and to accept the additional 5 percent as part of the vessels' cost.[31] The commissioners approved this higher cost not only because they antici- pated reimbursement from congressional appropriations, but also be- cause they had no diplomatic use for Bulloch's ships. When the news of Gettysburg and Vicksburg arrived in Europe, the time for such ploys was ended; Bulloch's ships, then, did not become a pawn in Slidell's schemes as had Maury's.

Summer and autumn months in France provided good construction weather. As the iron and wooden hulls took shape, ships' names were given to them. Recalling Arman's justification for arming the corvettes, they were appropriately called the *Yeddo* and the *Osacca* at Bordeaux and the *San Francisco* and the *Shanghai* at Nantes. When Arman applied to the marine ministry for permission to arm the ironclads, he represented the gunboats as being built for the viceroy of Egypt. They received the equally appropriate names of *Cheops* and *Sphinx*. By November the corvettes were nearly enough completed for delivery on schedule and the ironclads were "quite three-fifths finished," as Bulloch put it. The commander reported despondently, however, because "by that date affairs began to change in their aspect."[32] Indeed, September and

October 1863 were fatally decisive months for the Confederate naval construction program in Europe.

Changing Fortunes:
The C.S.S. *Florida* in Brest

In Great Britain, as we have seen, government action against Confederate naval activity began in April 1863, at the pinnacle of Southern military success, with the seizure of the *Alexandra*. Policy replaced legal action during the summer, and in September and October the Laird rams, despite Bulloch's Bravay scheme, were detained and seized. By the end of December both North's and Sinclair's ships were sequestered. The actions resulted from government policy even at the cost of circumventing British law. At almost the same time, the French government took similar procedures against Confederate naval activities in France. Southern fortunes were changing.

The French approach was as much a matter of policy as was the English, except the government under the direction of Foreign Minister Drouyn de Lhuys was able either to act under existing law or to change the law decisively in order to fulfill its neutral obligations. Despite the "secret purposes" of Napoleon III, Paris in the long run was a more successful neutral than London. The United States never brought postwar charges against France as it did against Great Britain in the Geneva arbitration.

Even so, France was more affected than England by the fortunes of the battlefields. Lee's defeat at Gettysburg and the division of the Confederacy by the fall of Vicksburg, combined with the French capture of Mexico City and European diplomatic developments, led Paris to reevaluate its relations with Washington. The probability of a Northern victory posed a definite threat to the French position in Mexico. It was necessary, then, to follow an honest neutrality in the American war and thus avoid agitating Washington. Neutrality, true neutrality, became a matter of French self-interest. The man who first understood this was Drouyn de Lhuys, but he had to struggle against the whims of his ruler before he won. In the long run, United States Secretary of State Seward, unable to intervene in Mexico anyway, accepted Drouyn de Lhuys's policy and Washington and Paris followed mutual postures of neutrality to the end of the war. The only diplomatic weapon at Drouyn de Lhuys's disposal was the Confederate navy and its activities in France.[33]

Until 1863 the Confederate navy, despite Mallory's early expectations, had not operated in France. James North's pitiful efforts in 1861 had gone unnoticed; no Confederate ship had touched at a French port.

Then the center of operations shifted across the channel: Bulloch's construction projects and Erlanger's financial projects were just the beginning. In August 1863 the C.S.S. *Florida* put into Brest for repairs; the *Georgia* arrived in Cherbourg in late October; and on 27 November the *Rappahannock* sought refuge in Calais. Suddenly, the French ports began to serve as Confederate naval repair and reprovisioning centers. Specific questions of belligerent rights and of neutral obligations were raised for the first time between Paris and Washington. And that was not all. On 23 October Flag Officer Samuel Barron settled in at 30 rue Drouot in Paris. At the moment France was attempting to establish a government in Mexico, and, when Drouyn de Lhuys was most preoccupied with Mexican affairs, the Confederates made Paris the European headquarters of their navy, the shipyards of Bordeaux and Nantes the production center of a formidable fleet to cruise against Union merchantmen and to carry the war against Federal warships, and the harbors of Brest, Cherbourg, and Calais their sustaining ports of call. Furthermore, they were using the Paris stock market to sustain the Erlanger loan, their most ambitious European fund-raising scheme. Could Drouyn de Lhuys long permit this in the face of Washington's objections?

Confederate leaders remained tenaciously blinded to the awkward position in which their activities placed their host. Slidell continued to hope that the Mexican venture would force Napoleon III to recognize the South and even the usually astute Matthew Fontaine Maury supported him. Writing to his friend Admiral Charbonnes, Maury expressed this attitude in sweeping terms. The letter is worth a close examination in that it reflects the scope of Confederate hopes. Maury recounted Lincoln's troubles in raising troops in face of the strong peace movement in the North. "Southern skies, my friend are very bright," he wrote. "What does that wise man and sagacious ruler, your Emperor, think?" Then Maury proceeded to outline a broad policy for that "sagacious ruler": "As long as France is identified with Mexico, it will be her desire to see Mexico surrounded by weak nations. This is already the case on the South, and will be the case on the North when California deems the time to have come for her to withdraw from the Lincoln government, and to set up for herself." The people there, he said, "are already nearly equally divided" and "it is well understood that the Pacific States intend to withdraw from political association with those of the Atlantic." The people in the West, he went on, want their coasts surveyed and protected by a navy, an army to protect them from the Indians, a railway from the Mississippi River to the Pacific Coast. They are watching their "chance for a slice off Mexico," which only good government in Mexico could prevent. The Lincoln administration, unable to fulfill the Californians' expectations, agitated them "to go in for a war with France, to March down into Mexico to help themselves." The emperor, Maury assumed, had already made up his mind.

> And if the Yankees choose to make war upon him because he may recognize the South, he will be prepared. If he will show himself ready they will be quiet, and let both him and Mexico alone.
> The Yankees have not a single ironclad that can double Cape Horn. A couple of yours sent to the Pacific would give you command of the whole coast. Their presence in San Francisco would arouse the state, and with a little persuasion, she with Oregon and Washington might be induced to withdraw from the Lincoln government and set up for themselves and as allies of yours.
> In this view the polygamous kingdom of Brigham Young assumes importance. He you know is in Eutaw, a central region midway between the Mississippi River and the Pacific Ocean. He can prevent the passage of an army from the Atlantic States across the country into California, and the ironclads can do the rest. There is room for diplomacy among the Latter Day Saints.
> Thus you see, my friend, there is a magnificant vista from that French point of view. . . . What France lacks is more fields of industry and enterprise for her young men: where are such fields? Never since the world began were such fields as are now before you ever presented to the imagination of rulers. There they are, you see them stretching along, and lining this vista.[34]

What a sweeping view of affairs on two continents: from Paris to Central America, up through Mexico to the Northwest, across the continent and through the Latter Day Saints to Washington! To what end? To encourage Napoleon III to recognize the Confederate States and to consider the value of war against the United States. Maury's confidence that his letter would influence French policy was not misplaced. Admiral Charbonnes did show the analysis to the emperor. Later, Maury noted on the same page in his diary, as if there were a cause-and-effect relationship, that three French ships had been sent to blockade Mexico's west coast as far as Acapulco.

The proposed naval policy for France, designed to detach California from the United States, was no idle suggestion on the part of the internationally recognized scientist of the seas. In the same month Maury wrote to Archduke Maximilian, an old correspondent who had just been called to the imperial throne of Mexico, offering his services as commander of an ironclad fleet. Such a fleet, he maintained, could serve to detach California from the Union. As a start, he urged Maximilian to purchase James North's Number 61 because the Confederacy could not have it.[35] Among the Confederate navy officers in Europe, Maury was unique in expressing such a comprehensive understanding of the international implications of the Civil War. He had no way of knowing yet that Napoleon III's designs on Mexico would fail, nor even that France's Mexican policy was already forcing Paris to adopt an honest neutrality toward the North and the South. He did have the vision, and the vision fed his hope.

Other officers maintained the hope and based it not on grand designs but on daily activity. The captains in Brest, Cherbourg, and Calais were busy with coaling, repairs, and personnel problems; Bulloch was busy in England buying supplies and, for the first time, acquiring ships to serve as Confederate government–owned blockade-runners; Barron was busy in Paris handling personnel and rendering aid to the ships in port. Unknowingly, these activities provided Drouyn de Lhuys with the opportunity to change French policy from one favorable to the South to one of strict neutrality.

It all began on 23 August 1863 when John N. Maffitt sailed the C.S.S. *Florida* into the harbor at Brest.[36] His cruise had been successful. The *Florida* had taken fifty-five victims since leaving Mobile, but the seven months at sea also had taken a toll on the ship and on the skipper.

Maffitt long had known that the engine and hull needed repair and that his own health was poor. After coaling in Bermuda on 26 July, he headed across the ocean to seek repair facilities. On 18 August he landed an officer in Ireland with a message for John Slidell in Paris forewarning him of the necessity of requesting docking privileges at Brest. The *Florida*, according to England's neutrality rules, could not enter another British port for two months after 26 July, and Maffitt considered the French government's repair facilities at Brest to be the next best equipped to do the work needed. He had no knowledge of Bulloch's construction program in France or of the supposedly favorable diplomatic atmosphere there. It was an innocent coincidence that he sought French aid on the eve of critical diplomatic decisions in Paris.

En route to Brest, Maffitt captured and burned the *Anglo-Saxon* in the English Channel. His ship appeared off Brest, as it were, silhouetted against the flames of his latest victim. The *Florida* was a large three-masted steamer, armed and flying the battle flag of the Confederate States. Excitement rippled through the port populace as they recognized the raider; anxiety spread to the port authorities as they realized the implications of this belligerent's presence. Maffitt respectfully requested of the station commander "the courtesy of the French Government in my present emergency." Vice Admiral Count de Gueyton was in a quandary. The *Florida* was testing, for the first time, the French neutral reaction to a belligerent's use of harbor facilities; he had no precedent, no specific regulations on which to act. Let the vessel sit, he decided, and seek instructions from the minister of marine. How should I receive this formidable vessel, as a pirate or as a regular warship? Chasseloup-Laubat was just as uncertain. He knew that neutral practices entitled the ship to certain privileges, but the only facilities in Brest were French government ones; what was the policy in this case? He equivocated: accept the ship as you would one of any country, he wired back, but make no commitments; all will depend on the foreign minister. Maffitt, unknowingly, created the diplomatic problem that eventually would lead to a statement of strict French rules regulating belligerents' use of ports and would complicate Bulloch's construction program. Meanwhile, he awaited Count de Gueyton's response.

Foreign Minister Drouyn de Lhuys took four days to render his decision. He received the unsolicited advice of William L. Dayton and of George Eustis, acting in Slidell's absence, and eventually decided in favor of the *Florida:* the ship was not a pirate, was not a privateer, and therefore was entitled to full use of the port facilities subject only to the general rules of the declaration of neutrality. She could receive the repairs and fuel necessary to make her seaworthy; she could not in any way enhance her manpower, her armor, or her armaments.[37] This decision opened French ports to all Confederate navy vessels and allowed them the same treatment as the ships of any nation with which France was at peace, including access to all port facilities and government shipyards, subject only to the general neutrality regulations. It was a right the Confederates would use extensively throughout the ensuing year.

The repair problems were greater than Maffitt anticipated. On 3 September he notified Bulloch in Liverpool of his mechanical needs; the next day Bulloch left for Brest with "competent representatives of the builders of the ship and the engine."[38] These experts supervised the repair work. As they worked they discovered additional defects. Not only did the boilers need cleaning and repairing, but a new blower had to be installed; the screw shaft was out of line and had to be straightened; the copper hull sheathing not only had to be repaired but in spots replaced. Permission had to be sought for each repair project and for each new piece of equipment. This took time because the prefect had to consult the minister of marine on each request. Maffitt originally had estimated that the repairs would require just eighteen days, but the ship remained in the dock for almost two months and in the harbor for two more. Finally, in early January 1864, she seemed to be complete. The trial run, however, only served to reveal additional defects in the engine. Not until 9 February 1864 did the *Florida* steam out of Brest after a stay of six months. Such an extensive delay exposed the *Florida* to several dangers: Federal surveillance, especially by a United States warship;

changing fortunes of wartime diplomacy; and problems of personnel.

Maffitt fully expected the personnel problems and was himself a part of them. During the seven-month cruise the enlistments of seventy-five crewmen had lapsed. They demanded their discharges. Maffitt had no choice but to comply, leaving the ship with only twenty-seven crewmen. This put the ship in great jeopardy. French rules forbade a belligerent's recruitment in France; without sufficient manpower, the *Florida* might have to remain in Brest for the remainder of the war. On the other hand, maritime practices permitted restoration of all defects that were an "act of God" and were necessary to make a ship seaworthy, and sufficient crew to operate the vessel safely was necessary for the ship to be seaworthy. Acting under this custom, Maffitt notified Vice Admiral Count de Gueyton that he was "compelled to discharge" the seventy-five men.[39] Having, he hoped, laid the foundation for recruiting seventy-five men, Maffitt then requested his own reassignment.

To whom should Maffitt address his request? He had just learned of his promotion the previous May to the rank of commander and there was no one in Europe of higher rank. Matthew Fontaine Maury, who had learned of the *Florida*'s expected arrival in Brest and had gone to France to see her, was the senior officer by date of rank. So Maffitt sent his request, along with a surgeon's certificate of ill health, to Maury. "Grieved to learn" that Maffitt's health had "given away under the severe trial it has undergone in the *Florida*," Maury relieved Maffitt of his command on 11 September 1863. His replacement, a newcomer to Europe, was Commander Joseph N. Barney. Barney's fate was no better; ill health forced his replacement on 5 January 1864 by Lieutenant C. Manigault Morris. Maffitt managed to leave Europe by mid-December 1863 and return to the Confederacy; he was on active duty in Nassau near the end of the war. Barney's luck remained bad; he did not recover his good health until December 1864 and then continued in Europe "awaiting assignment" and running errands for Commodore Barron. Morris, on the other hand, experienced some glory on the *Florida* prior to her capture in Brazil.[40]

Barney's health very likely was adversely affected by the stress of responsibility aboard the *Florida*. Frustrating repair delays caused by French bureaucracy and worry of having only a twenty-seven-man crew were magnified by the U.S.S. *Kearsarge*'s arrival in Brest on 18 September 1863. Even should the repairs be completed, what could he do with such a small crew? Fortunately the repairs dragged on and gave Barney and his successor Morris time to recruit replacements for the seventy-five discharged seamen. In early October the French Council of Ministers decided that because the discharge had been involuntary it should, as Maffitt had hoped, come under the "act of God" custom. The men could be replaced so long as they were not French and so long as the total number of men did not exceed the number aboard the *Florida* as of her arrival in Brest.[41] The *Florida*'s captain wanted English-speaking men and to get these he had to go to Great Britain. There, Bulloch contracted with agents to engage sailors in "small groups wherever they could be found." The men were sent to Calais, where the *Rappahannock* was by then docked, then by train to Brest. This activity aroused the suspicions of Federal officials, ever on the alert, who tried to prevent the "unusual but systematic movement of nautical-looking men." United States Minister Dayton protested this recruitment and John Slidell had to smooth over the surreptitious arrangements with Chasseloup-Laubat. Even so, when Morris finally steamed from Brest his crew was twenty to thirty men short and he was unable to man one of his guns.[42]

Guns and munitions presented another problem to Barney. The gun carriages were "so defective that they would not stand half an hours fighting." Port authorities denied improvements to this obvious fighting quality of the ship and Bulloch secretly ordered new ones made in Nantes. On 9 February 1864, as he left Brest, Morris after some difficulty met a boat from Nantes and took "all on board that was expected." This transfer included the new gun carriages, fuses, "and other contraband of war," according to Bulloch. Somehow he considered that this manufacture of armaments and their delivery within French waters did not in any way violate French neutrality.[43] But it is obvious that the *Florida* with all her problems had stretched the French rules and laws, and it is just as obvious that Confederate navy officers were almost arrogant in the excessive demands they made on their host.

The second major problem caused by the *Florida*'s long stay in Brest—surveillance by United States warships—began early and persisted until war's end. The *Florida* attracted the only major Northern vessel in European waters at that time. The indefinite French rules concerning belligerents' use of ports allowed frequent confrontations between the enemy vessels, and these confrontations escalated as additional Confederate ships sought refuge in French ports and as the Bordeaux and Nantes ships neared completion. Two important events resulted, one of which affected international law, and the other the course of naval warfare during the Civil War. France was forced to articulate in detail the rules of belligerents' port use. This articulation was so similar to the British statement that it became common usage during all subsequent wars. The scene of the naval war between the American belligerents, insofar as major vessel confrontations is concerned, was literally transferred to the European waters. Europe, used first as a Confederate naval procurement source, became by the winter of 1863–64 the sole locale of major naval combat. From the autumn of 1863 until the spring of 1865 major war vessels of both belligerents plied the seas from the Madeira Islands, around Portugal and Spain, and on into the Bay of Biscayne and the English Channel. These maritime hostilities in European waters climaxed dramatically in June 1864 with the decisive and classic *Kearsarge-Alabama* battle and continued with the United States vessels *Niagara, Sacramento,* and *Iroquois* keeping watch over the Bordeaux ironclads and in 1864 eventually confronting the only ironclad that fell into Confederate hands, the C.S.S. *Stonewall.* But it all began that September day when the *Kearsarge* dropped anchor not far from the docked *Florida.*

The *Kearsarge,* classified as a "screw-sloop" and about the same size as the *Florida* at 1,031 tons, carried seven guns. Her captain was a tough and shrewd patriot, Commander John A. Winslow, who fully exploited the vague French rules in his quest for Confederate vessels. He did not hesitate to enter French waters off the harbors of Brest, Cherbourg, and Calais or to dart across to an English leeward cove during high seas. He often went into Brest and anchored near the *Florida.* His men, on shore leave, brawled with the Southern ship's crewmen; he sought and got information from a Union sympathizer who also sold supplies to the *Florida.* His most flagrant abuse of French hospitality was necessitated by the arrival of two additional Confederate ships: the *Georgia* at Cherbourg on 28 October and the *Rappahannock* at Calais on 27 November. He then had three enemy ships to watch. He was handicapped by the rough waters in the channel and by the overly zealous Union informants who maintained a steady barrage of rumors that first one of the Southern ships and then another was ready for sea. Such news forced the *Kearsarge* in and out of various ports as Winslow tried, alone, to patrol all three harbor approaches. At one point in late January exaggerated reports of the Southern ships' powers and plans culminated in a false rumor that the *Florida,* the *Georgia,* and the *Rappahannock* were all three ready to converge on Winslow to destroy the *Kearsarge.* So persistent was this rumor that Winslow received warnings from Union officials in Paris, London, and Liverpool. No wonder he remained on the move, seeking accurate information where he could. He based his cruise in Brest, entering that harbor four times during November and December and remaining in port each time from three to fourteen days. Such frequent use of a port was prohibited by the British rules; such frequent use of a French port soon exasperated the French officials.

On one occasion Vice Admiral Count de Gueyton had to assign a French war vessel to stand between the *Kearsarge* and the *Florida;* this situation, he wrote to Chasseloup-Laubat, was "intolerable." The minister of marine concurred and immediately consulted Foreign Minister Drouyn de Lhuys. The two agreed that more specific rules governing belligerents' port use were necessary. Chasseloup-Laubat urged the adoption of the British rules including the provision that a ship could visit a port only every two months, but the foreign minister demurred. He preferred to prohibit a belligerent ship from using "a French port as the center of its cruise," whether for one or twenty visits a month. The new regulations were drawn up by the marine department and with Drouyn de Lhuys's approval were promulgated on 2 February 1864. The preamble stated that the two belligerents were making "the neighboring waters of the neutral states of Europe the scene of the maritime hostilities" and listed, then, specific regulations to control their movements in French waters.[44] Winslow considered the rules "nearly similar" to the British ones, and, as far as the record shows, he never again entered a French port except to land the wounded from the *Alabama*. The new restrictions were to apply also to Confederate vessels. Brest officials forced Morris to steam from the port within twenty-four hours after his repairs were finally completed, and Cherbourg officials applied the same rule to the *Georgia* once she was restored to a seaworthy condition. The warm hospitalities to the South had changed into a cool neutrality.

The French government's willingness to allow Confederate construction in Bordeaux and Nantes, the *Florida*'s long stay in Brest, and Commander Winslow's zealous efforts to capture the Confederate vessels all had contributed to the new French rules. Designed to control the naval activities of both belligerents, they did in fact force an even greater naval activity in French waters. Ironically, Winslow allowed the *Florida* to escape while he was chasing the *Georgia* on a false rumor.

Changing Fortunes: The Voruz Papers and a Lost Fleet

Commodore Samuel Barron arrived in Paris in October 1863 just after the British government had taken the Laird rams into custody. Affairs in France, however, still looked good. Four corvettes and two ironclads were under construction, the *Florida* was undergoing repairs at a government dockyard in Brest, and Barron had a sufficient number of officers to man the ships. Five days after his arrival, the *Georgia* put into Cherbourg and a month later the *Rappahannock* went into Calais. In all, counting the vessels under construction and those in ports, Barron had nine major warships under his command. No other Confederate navy officer could boast such a fleet; Barron's title of flag officer was no idle one. His immediate task was to get the ships to sea and in action against the enemy. As yet he had no indication of the navy's changing fortunes in France and he was optimistic. The corvette construction was on schedule and the ironclad ahead of schedule. So long as the French government maintained its present policy, he would be able in due time to lead a formidable fleet against the enemy's merchant ships, its blockading fleet, and perhaps even against the Northern coastal cities. The prospects, as Maury had put it, were never brighter.

Unknown to Barron a chain of events had started that would frustrate his bright expectations. On 9 September 1863 a Voruz office employee, acting from conviction and honest concern that his government had been duped, presented United States Minister Dayton with documental proof that the corvettes were being built for the Confederate navy. The papers consisted of various financial agreements between Erlanger, Arman, Arnous de Rivière, and Voruz; they referred to Bulloch by name; they detailed the armaments agreement between Voruz and Blakely. Later the employee submitted a copy of the Bulloch-Arman ironclad contract. There could be no doubt that the six ships were, indeed, destined for action against the United States. On 22 September Dayton presented copies of these papers to Drouyn de Lhuys, and three days later the foreign minister initiated an investigation through the Marine Department. Because the ships were still far from completion, the French investigation was not hurried. However, on 22 October 1863, the Marine Department withdrew permission to arm the corvettes and in December ordered Arman to seek other buyers for the ships. In February 1864 the department detained the ironclads and in early May detained the corvettes because by their very construction they were "veritable ships of war."[45] This decision on the corvettes provided the legal basis for the emperor's personal order to the builders to sell all of the ships to neutral governments. Arman, by two different contracts, sold the two Bordeaux-built corvettes and the ironclad *Cheops* to Prussia on 25 May 1864; he already had contracted to sell the *Sphinx* to Denmark on 31 March. However, because Prussia and Denmark were then at war, delivery was delayed for many months.[46]

During the months between November 1863, when the Southerners first learned of the Voruz Papers, and June 1864 the Confederate navy officers retained hope of getting the corvettes unarmed to sea, but they decided to sell the ironclads as early as February 1864 because Slidell admitted he had no imperial promise concerning them. During all of those months until the actual delivery of the ships the Northern officials remained skeptical: Dayton sustained diplomatic protests, reacting to every rumor; the U.S.S. *Kearsarge* and after June 1864 the *Niagara, Sacramento,* and *Iroquois* remained in European waters keeping watch over the Bordeaux-built ships until the war's end. All of this Union activity adversely affected Confederate control of both the C.S.S. *Georgia* and *Rappahannock* and caused the complete frustration of Barron's hopes.

Motivation for French action, like the British, was a matter of policy. Unlike the British, the French made straightforward changes in their rules and laws. They issued more rigid rules on belligerent use of ports, as we have seen; they determined the ironclads by their obvious warlike designs to be contraband; and they detained the corvettes through a new interpretation that a ship's structure, regardless of arms, indicated intent for war use—a rule required by the new naval architecture and yet rejected in the British courts. Like the British, the chief force behind the policy was the foreign minister. Drouyn de Lhuys, who considered the Mexican policy to be an overextension of French strength, felt he had to protect that weakness from the power of the United States, and the best way to do so would be to apply a strict neutrality in the matter of the Confederate ships in France. At a cabinet council meeting on 26 January 1864, presided over by Empress Eugénie in the emperor's absence, Drouyn de Lhuys prevailed. His policy was approved, and he gained full control over the ships, including the Bordeaux-Nantes ships abuilding and those in the French ports. Still, he had to overcome Napoleon III's personal policy toward the vessels. The fact that as of mid-February the Southern leaders decided to sell the ironclads but to retain the corvettes indicates that they still trusted in the emperor, that Drouyn de Lhuys had not yet converted him to the policy of strict neutrality. Slidell felt the emperor's initiative and implicit promises to be stronger than Drouyn de Lhuys; the latter felt the emperor's interest in Mexico to be stronger yet. Repeatedly in his informal correspondence with Chasseloup-Laubat, Drouyn de Lhuys related the Confederate ships to Mexico and to Washington. For instance, in February 1864, as Maximilian was preparing to go to Mexico, Drouyn de Lhuys urged the sale of the ships to neutral governments and admonished his cabinet colleague "to avoid all acts which would in the eyes of the United States constitute serious and founded complaints" because such might "adversely affect the enterprise which we pursue in Mexico." Eventually Drouyn de Lhuys convinced the emperor of the United States's threat to Mexico, and it was the fear for this pet project that led Napoleon III in May 1864 to order Arman to sell the ships at once.[47] Policy—French national policy as formulated by Foreign Minister Edouard Drouyn de Lhuys—now had become the "secret purposes of the Chief of State."

The Voruz Papers, the Mexican situation, the battlefields in Virginia, and the persistence of Drouyn de Lhuys over a period of eight months coalesced to defeat the Confederate navy program in Europe.

As early as February 1864, when the Southern leadership decided to sell the rams, however, differences arose between the political and the military leaders. Slidell insisted that the rams be sold and the corvettes retained; Barron and Bulloch argued that such an arrangement would defeat the whole purpose of the contracts. They saw the ships together forming a compact fleet, each type depending on the other. The rams were the offensive heart of the fleet; without them the corvettes would be just cruisers, destined to sail in the *Alabama*'s wake. Southern ports would remain blocked; Northern coasts would remain unthreatened. If the rams were to be given up, then so should the corvettes. Slidell, nonetheless, prevailed.[48] On the face of it, the affair was settled, but Bulloch had no intention of submitting so easily.

He and Arman arrived at a secret agreement. Bulloch would allow two of the corvettes and one ram to be sold to other governments; Arman would intrigue to deliver the other ram and corvettes to Bulloch. Neither, in February, expected difficulty concerning the corvettes: they were, after all, only unarmed merchant vessels. In order "that the builders might be able to make the transaction satisfactory to the authorities," Bulloch on 8 February 1864 gave Arman orders to sell the two ironclads. He even detailed the financial arrangements that should be followed. Throughout March, April, and into May this understanding prevailed; Bulloch was willing to take half a loaf because the three ships—one ram and two corvettes—would afford an offensive weapon whereas the four corvettes simply would enlarge a tactic that Bulloch long since had condemned. The only difficulty was that construction slowed and all the ships fell far behind schedule. Bulloch suspected government interference, and he probably was right.[49] During these months Bulloch did not inform any of his colleagues about his designs on one of the rams; along with Slidell he continued to act as if his only expectation was to get the corvettes as unarmed merchantmen to sea where he would arm and man them.

In early May Bulloch went to Paris for two meetings with Arman. He took George Eustis, Slidell's secretary, to the first one and Captain Eugene Tessier, his own French agent, to the second. In the first meeting Arman explained his scheme to assure delivery of one ram to Bulloch. He would, he said, sell the ship bona fide to Sweden. After the French government investigated and found the sale to be true, he would sail the vessel under a French crew and captain to Gottenburg. Thus assured, the French and United States officials, he maintained, would not be suspicious of the second ram: Arman's people then could deliver it to any point Bulloch might designate. Arman was fulfilling their secret agreement. They devoted the second meeting to a discussion of such details as the "best mode of shipping the guns, the engagement of reliable captains, and the possibility of getting seamen from the ports of Brittany." Bulloch insisted on the importance of timing and demanded assurance that the French government would, indeed, "permit the vessels to leave Bordeaux." Arman expressed "no doubt of the corvettes being allowed to sail unarmed" but would see the emperor within a fortnight to bring the matter to a close. Bulloch considered affairs to be in good state. He returned to Liverpool confident that the Confederate navy soon would have afloat if not a formidable fleet at least a semiformidable fleet.

The meetings in Paris undoubtedly revealed his now longstanding plot with Arman. Eustis certainly would tell Slidell who in turn would tell Barron. Arman's confidence spread to at least the top echelon of Confederate personnel in Europe. What none knew at the time was the changed status of the corvettes: no longer classified as unarmed merchant ships, they had become "veritable ships of war." Still if the emperor wanted the South to have the ships, he could approve their sailings. Arman, confident of success, saw Napoleon III in late May 1864, at the very time Maximilian was arriving in Mexico, Grant was pressing Lee in the Battle of the Wilderness and around Spottsylvania Court House, and Sherman was beginning his move from Chattanooga toward Atlanta. The moment was not auspicious for the French emperor to grant favors to the South, and he did not. When Arman made his request, the emperor "rated him severely, threatened imprisonment, ordered him to sell the ships at once, bona fide, and said if this were not done he would have them seized."[50] Arman, astounded, signed the contracts with Prussia on 25 May for the sale of one ironclad and two corvettes.

Captain Tessier hurried to Liverpool with the bad news. Bulloch was flabbergasted. He wrote to Barron that "our hopes of getting ships from France are nil."[51] From all evidence Bulloch gave up all hope of getting an ironclad or any corvettes. The *Stonewall* story is an entirely separate episode.

Later, analyzing the reasons for the French change of policy, James Bulloch touched upon all the main reasons but two. He recreated the relatively favorable Confederate military posture during the winter and spring of 1862–63, the fears of the Northern cities, especially Boston and New York, of Southern naval action, and recalled that Napoleon III's "invitation to build ships in France was given during the period of successful resistance at the South, and of apparent doubt and trepidation at the North." It was withdrawn, he wrote, when the fortunes of war shifted, that is, after Gettysburg and Vicksburg.

> It suited the Imperial policy, and appeared to be consistent with the designs upon Mexico, to extend a clandestine support to the South when the Confederate armies were still strong and exultant. It was neither prudent nor wise to maintain a doubtful or hesitating attitude towards the winning side when it became apparent that the prospect had changed, and

that neither Emperor Maximilian nor Mr. President Davis could probably maintain his position.[52]

Bulloch thus correctly concluded that French national policy changed between October 1862 and October 1863, and he explained that change by relating the French position in Mexico to the Confederate military fortunes in Mississippi and Pennsylvania. Indeed, if Lee had defeated Meade, then swung eastward to threaten Philadelphia and Baltimore, Drouyn de Lhuys probably would have reacted differently to the Voruz Papers in October 1863. Based solely on events in America and without a thorough understanding of the French evaluation of the Mexican situation, Bulloch's case rests on "iffy" history.

A wider perspective and a closer examination of the timing of events, however, affords a clearer assessment of the changing French national policy and at the same time avoids dependence on "iffy" history. The wider perspective includes Confederate errors in France and changing French domestic and diplomatic needs; the timing of events relates to the French evaluation of the Mexican situation in relation to Confederate ship construction.

The Confederates' confidence, almost amounting to arrogance, spawned their mistakes. Throughout the summer of 1863, while the ships abuilding in Nantes and Bordeaux were taking shape, Bulloch and Tessier openly visited the shipyards. Northern informants were active. Inevitably rumors spread of the ships being built for the Confederacy. John Bigelow at first had dismissed them as coming from "wholly irresponsible sources, usually needy Confederate refugees." But other nations took them more seriously. Prior to the Voruz Papers' revelations, Captain Hoare, the British naval attaché in Paris, decided to investigate the rumors. He visited Arman in early September at the Bordeaux yards "to see the vessels building for the CSA." The French builder proudly showed him the corvettes, which he said were designed for the China Sea service; he showed him through the partially completed ironclad rams and told him "with a smile that they are for the Pasha of Egypt." Captain Hoare read the smile correctly and concluded that the rams were "formidable ships ordered by Captain Bulloch of the Confederate Navy." Thus, even before Drouyn de Lhuys knew positively of the ships, the British government had this report. Later in the fall, Lord Cowley, the British ambassador in Paris, frequently prodded Drouyn de Lhuys concerning French policy toward this belligerent activity.[53] Such widespread knowledge of the construction program could not but cause embarrassment to Napoleon III and even resentment among his ministers. It undoubtedly affected France's leverage in European affairs and especially in dealing with Great Britain on American affairs, yet Bulloch does not mention it. The overuse of French ports since October 1863, as we have seen, so angered the French ministers that they tightened their rules to the South's detriment. Slidell, too, contributed to ministerial vexations by his direct access to the emperor; that was one reason Drouyn de Lhuys seized the moment of the emperor's absence to force his own policy on the ships through the cabinet council. Bulloch fails in his evaluation to consider all these Confederate errors, which in effect were unrelated to either Mexico or the battlefields.

France's domestic needs and her diplomatic posture in Europe both changed between October 1862 and October 1863. When the emperor extended an invitation to Slidell to build ships in France, the cotton shortage and unemployment were at their height; when Drouyn de Lhuys first learned of the Voruz Papers, the cotton supply had improved and unemployment had dropped. The domestic crisis was passed. Just so, the diplomatic picture changed. Prior to Vicksburg and Gettysburg, the Lindsay-Roebuck affair revealed a basic difference between British and French attitudes toward the Civil War. During the summer and fall of 1863, diplomacy surrounding the Polish Insurrection left France almost isolated in Europe and injured Drouyn de Lhuys's personal prestige among the Continent's diplomats. It convinced him that France needed all its power concentrated in Europe, that it had no business diluting that power in overseas adventures.

When Drouyn de Lhuys saw the Voruz Papers he alone among all the French officials understood their implications for Napoleon III's venture in Mexico. He alone saw the need to avoid agitating the United States by blatant violation of neutral obligations, regardless of the battlefields in America. And he alone forced the issue through the cabinet council and then convinced the emperor *prior* to Maximilian's arrival in Mexico, long before the fates of the Mexican emperor and the Confederate president could be equated.

Domestic and diplomatic needs, then, forced a change in French policy independently of the American battlefields; but when the two—French needs and Confederate defeats—are combined, all "ifs" are removed. Bulloch was right; the South's chances by June 1864 of getting ships from France were nil. The South's fortunes had changed as certainly in France as they had in England, yet Bulloch, Barron, and Maury with some surprising successes continued their desperate efforts.

CHAPTER 7

Last Desperate Hopes

Naval activities during the last twelve months of the Civil War were truly European in scope—they involved Great Britain, France, Denmark, Spain, and Portugal. In April 1864 Bulloch and Barron still held to a fading hope of getting some of the French-built ships to sea and of placing the *Rappahannock* in service as a cruiser. By the end of the summer, however, all such hope was dead and, worse, the *Alabama* lay in ten fathoms of water off the French coast. The Confederates' last desperate hopes were revived in the fall when Bulloch almost by accident sent the *Shenandoah* to prey upon Yankee whalers and, at the last minute, acquired one of the Bordeaux rams. Until the very end Barron remained busy with personnel assignments and Bulloch furiously bought and shipped blockade-runners.

During these same months when so many Confederate ships were in European waters, the United States responded. The U.S.S. *Kearsarge* remained on station, even after the C.S.S. *Florida*'s escape, in order to watch over the *Georgia*, the *Rappahannock*, and the Arman ships. The *Kearsarge* was ready when the C.S.S. *Alabama* appeared in French waters in June, and one of the two most famous naval battles of the war ensued. Afterwards, when the *Kearsarge* returned to the United States to lick her battle wounds, three other Northern ships, the *Niagara*, the *Sacramento*, and the *Iroquois*, replaced her and remained in European waters until the war's end.

In all, during that last year, some eleven oceangoing belligerent naval vessels were active in European waters and one major battle occurred there. The single most famous Confederate naval cruiser, the *Alabama*, lies not under American waters but under European waters. If the armies of Sherman and Grant during the same months gradually closed their pincer movements against the heart of the Southland, and defeated it, the South was fighting, and even winning some, with its navy in Europe.

The officer most responsible for the only Confederate offensive naval action during the last months of the war was Commander James D. Bulloch. He seemed to be everywhere at once, performing simultaneously a multitude of functions. Based in Liverpool, he traveled to Calais and Paris, bought ships in England and Scotland, paid the salaries of other navy personnel in Europe, assigned officers to two major vessels, arranged secret codes for safe communications and rendezvous for supply ships, sent mechanics to supervise repairs, and bought supplies of all sorts for the Confederacy to ship by whatever means he could find. The activities, the travel, and the decision making began in the last months to take their toll; he became impatient with those who failed, criticized fellow officers who could not keep his secrets, and became obsessed with the details of financial bookkeeping.

Throughout the last twelve months Bulloch alone of all the Confederate leaders in Europe maintained a positive attitude circumscribed only by his grasp of reality. He reestablished his 1861–62 role as the dominant naval personality and he reproduced some successes of the earlier period. But first he had to suffer the agonies of prospects vanished and of ships lost.

Three Ships Lost

The first half of the war's final year was a period of loss and near defeat for the Confederate navy in Europe. Its hopes for amassing a formidable fleet in Europe that could make a decisive thrust against the enemy were dissolved. Not only did the navy fail to acquire those vessels abuilding in Great Britain and France, but it lost three additional ships long in its possession: the *Georgia*, the *Rappahannock*, and the *Alabama*. Their story reflects less the failures of men and ships and more the impossibility of succeeding within the strictures of a strong nation's neutrality; it is a story basically of French domestic law applied with a gentle but deadly hand.

The C.S.S. *Georgia* was the first of the three to arrive in France, but her destiny soon came to be intertwined with that of the *Rappahannock*. Both vessels reached ports prior to the French determination to apply a strict neutrality and at first affairs seemed to move favorably for the Southerners.

Lieutenant William L. Maury sought and received permission at Cherbourg to effect repairs sufficient to make the *Georgia* seaworthy.

Maury was at first most interested in reporting her shortcomings as a cruiser. Her sails, he maintained, were insufficient to supply the speed needed in a chase or in rough weather, which led to an excessive consumption of coal. She could not stay at sea for long periods of time. To the higher officers, the *Rappahannock* seemed better suited for this service and, because they needed money and were experiencing difficulty in buying cannon for her, they hit upon the idea of transferring the armaments from the *Georgia* to the *Rappahannock* and then selling the *Georgia*. It seemed simple enough. Once the two ships were repaired, they could rendezvous at sea and easily and lawfully make the exchange.[1]

The *Rappahannock* had entered Calais in late November 1863. She was a handsome ship, three-masted with two smoke stacks; she looked the part of a cruiser. But she was not yet ready for sea and no one knew the extent of her needs. She had, it will be recalled, been purchased by Commander Matthew Fontaine Maury from the British navy and had left England hurriedly. When she arrived off Calais she had only thirty-five men aboard and fifteen of these were carpenters, employees of the British navy who had been caught in the swift move. The captain had joined her in the channel, but other officers Maury had assigned to her were unable to board her until she was in Calais—a violation of French neutrality law. Lieutenant William P. A. Campbell asked for repair facilities to make the ship seaworthy, a request automatically granted to any belligerent on the assumption that the damage was an act of God, that it had resulted from sea duty. It did not take the Union consuls long to report that the *Rappahannock* had left Sheerness, England, in the same condition she had entered Calais, and that officers and crewmen were added in the port. United States Minister to France William L. Dayton made his first protests to Drouyn de Lhuys in December, and he maintained the diplomatic pressure with every rumor, every report relayed to him.[2] The *Rappahannock* began her career as a cripple and she soon implicated the *Georgia* in her troubles.

Commodore Barron planned the exercise to transfer the *Georgia*'s guns to the *Rappahannock*. His first idea was to send the *Florida* along with the other two. They were to rendezvous off the northwest coast of Africa. He instructed Lieutenant Campbell, after he got the guns aboard, to cruise for whalers in the Western Islands, then to intercept ships on their homeward passage from the East Indies and California; in April he should "make a dash at the enemy's commerce on the New England coast." The *Florida* and the *Georgia* were ready at the same time and according to the new French rules they had to leave within twenty-four hours; they sailed from their French ports on 9 and 16 February 1864, respectively.[3] But the *Rappahannock* was unable to join her sister

ships. Coordinating the activities of three ships in different ports involved many people, and inevitably rumors spread. Dayton heard that
the *Rappahannock,* after being repaired in the French port, planned to
sail soon to meet a tender from England and take on her arms: he knew
nothing about the *Georgia.* On 2 February 1864 he threatened Drouyn
de Lhuys with United States claims against France for all losses caused by
the *Rappahannock.* Drouyn de Lhuys, already convinced that the ship
had not entered port out of distress and irritated with the ship for
remaining so long at Calais, at first ordered her out of the harbor within
twenty-four hours; but after talking with Dayton on the next day, 5
February, he instructed the port officials to permit the *Rappahannock* to
leave only upon the orders of the marine minister. The detention order
arrived on 15 February, the day before the *Georgia* had to sail from
Cherbourg. The first rendezvous effort was frustrated.[4]

When the *Georgia* steamed out of Cherbourg, she did so under a new
commander. W. L. Maury, as had happened with Maffitt earlier, had
requested and received release from the ship due to ill health. Lieutenant William E. Evans, who had sailed with Semmes on the *Sumter* and
who had served as first officer on the *Georgia,* replaced him on 19
January 1864.[5] Evans, young but seasoned, apparently had orders to
return to France as soon as practical; he made a meaningless five-week
voyage off North Africa before reappearing at Bordeaux on 25 March.
Evans's job must have been frustrating to him. Every naval officer
yearned to command a ship, but when Evans got his chance it was as a
caretaker of a vessel soon to be removed from service. Yet he performed
capably.

The *Rappahannock* meanwhile underwent a major change. Lieutenant
Commanding Campbell had had difficulty acquiring experienced engineers, and he proved to be somewhat a perfectionist. The personnel
problem led him to recommend on 29 February 1864 that at least
one-third of the crew should be natives of the Confederacy, a condition
Semmes had found impossible to meet even in New Orleans. Furthermore, Campbell was unable to fill the complement of engineers because
three deserted; at the time he was ordered out of Calais in early
February he had neither enough men nor enough coal aboard to
comply. Thus during the five days he was permitted to leave, he was
unable to do so. Slidell severely reprimanded him for this and Secretary
Mallory later suggested his replacement. Apparently Barron was also
unhappy, for on 18 March he gave Campbell permission to return to the
Confederacy and on 21 March Lieutenant Charles M. Fauntleroy relieved him of command.[6]

Perhaps Campbell's greatest error had been a failure to convey to
Barron the true condition of the ship. If so, Fauntleroy wasted little time
in doing so. He had arrived in Calais only on 20 March to assume

command by the twenty-first. On that day and the next he wrote reports on the ship's "present situation." Combined, these are the best evaluations of the situation in Calais and of the ship's potential as a cruiser.[7] Matthew Fontaine Maury, it will be recalled, had never seen the ship when he purchased it and he had been appalled that it was not in top condition when it first arrived at Calais. Barron should have been appalled when he read Fauntleroy's reports.

The new commander found the crew completely inadequate. He had but twelve deck hands; there were more officers—"too many idlers"— aboard than crewmen; one, "Sinlcair's acting boatswain," was "partially deranged" and would have to leave. The *Rappahannock*'s situation in the harbor was difficult if not impossible. She was in the inner basin and the open gates and changing tides left her "high and dry almost" for twelve of twenty-four hours. Furthermore, such grounding placed strains on the ship that, as Campbell already had reported, required frequent caulking. Fauntleroy further was worried that the grounding had "hogged" the ship—that is, had caused the keel to bend like the back of a hog. There was, Fauntleroy reported, "a large chain cable quite recently drawn across the gateway" that he suspected "was put there with views sinister to this vessel." The arrangement of the ship's interior left little storage space. The engines took up a large area, leaving only small quarters for the crew. The largest area was the magazine and shell room and when filled with munitions left storage space for only about a four-week supply of food. While the engines were in good shape, the coal storage area was sufficient for only "four days' coal for full steaming." Additionally, he wrote, "her sailing capacity must be small, as her masts are very low and no great spread to her sails." Fauntleroy explained the trouble with the coals, something Campbell should have done: the coal could not be placed on board during any one high tide; it would take longer and the additional weight would create additional strains to the ship during the low tide groundings. Had Campbell been equally articulate and thorough, he might not have lost his command. At any rate he did not have to pass his remaining war service on a ship tied to dock in a basin where she alternately grounded and floated according to the tides, as Fauntleroy did. Although the records do not inform us of Campbell's subsequent career, he probably contributed more to the Confederate war effort than did Fauntleroy.

Lieutenant Fauntleroy's reports have a far graver significance than applies to Lieutenant Campbell. One sentence should have alerted Commodore Barron: "I am satisfied that if a board of officers were ordered now to report or had looked into the vessel earlier she would never have been on our hands today." When Barron assumed responsibility for the ship, why did he not appoint a board of officers to appraise her? He would have saved himself—as well as Bulloch, Mallory, and

Slidell—much worry and time. Even Drouyn de Lhuys would have been happier. The report described a ship fit no better than the *Georgia* for cruising service: they had the *Georgia,* ready-armed and free to go to sea. Why sell her and keep the *Rappahannock*? Did Barron not read Fauntleroy's report; or if he did, did he simply not heed it?

Despite these reports Barron insisted on arming the *Rappahannock* from the *Georgia.* Evans returned to Bordeaux from the futile North African cruise on 25 March and at the commodore's suggestion met with Fauntleroy in Calais during the first week of April. Although they could not plan a rendezvous because of the *Rappahannock*'s detention, they discussed whether the *Georgia*'s arms would be sufficient for the larger ship. Fauntleroy implied some criticism on this topic: "From Lieutenant Commanding Evans I learn for the *first time* the character of the *Georgia*'s battery." Only one gun, he reported, could be used on his ship; the others were useless because of their carriages or their size. "It is," he wrote to the commodore, "for you to decide whether such a battery is in any way suitable for the *Rappahannock.* She cannot keep the sea for lack of fuel and provisions, and she will be unable to fight for lack of an armament." What clearer warning did Barron need? In all the plans for the two vessels, he had not before considered whether the armament would serve the purpose. It is almost as if Barron was so intent on getting another ship to sea that he failed to evaluate it properly. The young lieutenants were better informed and more realistic than the experienced commodore. Fauntleroy sent warning after warning to Paris. He especially stressed the insufficiency of the *Rappahannock,* should she ever be released from Calais, to face or flee the U.S.S. *Kearsarge,* which kept watch in the channel.[8]

In Paris, however, Fauntleroy's letters went unheeded. Barron and Slidell concentrated on getting the ship released. Throughout February and March they gathered affidavits to prove her distress upon entering Calais, and on 14 March 1864 Slidell submitted to Drouyn de Lhuys a direct request to know why the *Rappahannock* was still detained. In desperation, he and Barron tried to force the foreign minister's answer by ordering the ship's commander to strike his colors and leave the ship to the disposition of the authorities at Calais.[9] Slidell took one step further and appealed directly to Napoleon III.

By appealing to the emperor Slidell forced the foreign minister into an apparent compromise. The whole question of the *Rappahannock* would be turned over to a "Comité Consultatif du Contentieux," which served the French foreign ministry in the same capacity that the queen's law officers served the English foreign minister. Meanwhile, Commander Bulloch warned Barron that "such precipitant action as abandoning the ship might cause all of our other undertakings in that country to fail," and he suggested the alternative of simply selling the

Rappahannock. The French government, he felt, "would be well satisfied to end the matter in this way." This time Slidell and Barron compromised: through Bulloch they ordered Fauntleroy not to abandon the ship. This order, in turn, much agitated Fauntleroy, who protested that it "will appear in the future history of the ship that I alone am responsible for the course pursued—whereas it has been contrary to my own judgment from beginning to end."[10] The Confederate tempers were beginning to flare.

Running throughout the voluminous correspondence of this episode is an underlying current of weak leadership. Barron in Paris was intent upon getting the ship to sea regardless of her condition or her qualities; Bulloch thought the wisest policy in respect to the overall naval interests was to be rid of the ship; Fauntleroy, concerned with preparing an inadequate vessel for an operation he knew would fail, was caught in the middle. Slidell, in Paris with Barron, was obsessed with his clever diplomatic schemes, playing the emperor against the foreign minister. Drouyn de Lhuys, fending off the emperor's personal orders and needing time because of a delicate problem he was negotiating with United States Secretary of State Seward, instructed the advisory committee to delay its decision. With such crosscurrents and frictions, no real Confederate success possibly could have emerged. The Southerners were their own worst enemies. Days, even weeks passed, and the inadequate gunless ship sat in Calais.

The longer the *Rappahannock* sat, the more problems she accumulated. If Drouyn de Lhuys delayed a decision by referring the matter to a committee, minor events in the Calais basin almost as if by design aided and abetted him. The small basin was crowded with boats, and Fauntleroy had to move his large ship "backward and forward daily on some pretext or another"; he did not have room enough to turn his ship around and so from "the constant exposure of one side only to the sun" he had to "recaulk her entire starboard side." Because of "negligence" the basin gates were left open and the *Rappahannock* was grounded, and Fauntleroy had to off-load fifty-two tons of coal from her deck. As late as 25 May Fauntleroy reported that even if the committee released the ship he would "require some little time to make the necessary preparations" to sail. The crowded conditions on 27 April had caused a minor collision with a small French merchant ship, the *Nil,* which led to a minor court action, which Southern pride escalated into a major diplomatic affair,[11] which later actually contributed to the *Rappahannock*'s detention.

All of these incidents finally led Commodore Barron to cancel his plan to transfer the *Georgia*'s inadequate battery to Fauntleroy's ship. The second rendezvous was frustrated. Fauntleroy, who had opposed the plan all along and who also worried about the *Kearsarge* lurking in the channel, was "truly happy" because, he wrote, he was "convinced that we have avoided a most disastrous conclusion—jeopardizing both the safety of this vessel and the *Georgia* as well."[12]

The decision also affected the *Georgia*. Her sale could now be effected immediately. There had been much question as to where the sale should take place. Bulloch at first worried that the authorities would confiscate the ship should she appear in a British port, but in mid-April he decided the *Georgia* might as well be sold in Liverpool as any place else. It became Lieutenant Evans's job to elude the *Kearsarge* and take the vessel safely to port. Evans had indicated that he expected to leave on Sunday or Monday, 1 or 2 May. Bulloch, always busy, wanted him to arrive by Sunday. Because it was a two-day voyage and because he actually arrived in Liverpool on Monday, Evans must have heeded Bulloch's request and sailed sooner than planned. He was successful in avoiding the *Kearsarge* partly because of his earlier departure from Bordeaux and partly because the *Kearsarge* was watching the *Rappahannock* off Calais. At any rate, without interference from the authorities, Bulloch sold the ship on 1 June 1864; the *Georgia* fetched 15,000 pounds and was converted into an English merchantman. Evans's short career as captain of a warship was over; he, at least, had played his role well. He ordered the *Georgia*'s officers, except for the paymaster, to report to Barron in Paris, and her crew, who "almost without exception volunteered" to join another Confederate vessel, to Calais to report aboard the *Rappahannock*. The ship herself had one more note to add to her history; stigmatized by her Confederate navy career and despite her new civilian status, she was captured in mid-August and sent to the United States as a prize.[13] She was the first ship lost.

At a time when the Confederate navy had only two ships on the high seas—the *Alabama* and the *Florida*—was this loss necessary? The *Georgia* was not as good a raider as the two then on duty, but she had proven that she could destroy Northern merchant ships. She did have to make frequent coaling stops and neutrals were ever more reluctant to allow this. Furthermore, Union warships were becoming more active and the *Georgia* was no match for them. Yet her loss was intimately tied to Barron's efforts to put another vessel to sea—the *Rappahannock*—with the same cruising defects. Had he been successful in transferring the battery, he would have traded one for the other without gain. Such a useless expenditure of time and money and effort seems almost unexplainable. Why had he done it? Perhaps, simply, he unconsciously reacted to frustrations caused by the French government's denial of the Bordeaux and Nantes ships. If so, in the long run he lost even more. And the *Georgia*'s loss was just the beginning.

The C.S.S. *Alabama* was the second ship lost. The U.S.S. *Kearsarge,* stationed in the English Channel to watch over the *Rappahannock* and the

Bordeaux-Nantes vessels, sank her on 19 June 1864 off Cherbourg, France. The story has been told often—by participants, eyewitnesses, naval officers, and scholars.[14] The surface facts are clear enough. Captain Semmes put into Cherbourg on 11 June 1864 seeking needed repairs and rest. Three days later the *Kearsarge* appeared and Semmes challenged her to fight as soon as he took on coal. Word of the impending battle quickly spread; people came even from Paris to witness the struggle. On Sunday, 19 June, the *Alabama* steamed out of the harbor while crowds on the quays watched and cheered. About seven miles into the channel the two ships met and engaged in a sixty-five-minute running circular battle, each keeping the starboard broadsides in action against the other. By noon the *Alabama* was foundering, and she sank, stern first, at 12:24 P.M. On these facts all accounts agree. Yet questions remain.

Why did Semmes fight? Why did the *Alabama* lose? What happened to the men involved in the battle? What was the significance of the battle? These questions elicit no objective answers. All of the principal accounts are colored by allegiances, points of view, and mental conditions.

Why did Semmes fight? Arthur Sinclair, with thirty years of perspective, said that his captain had chosen the best possible time for the battle. If he had stayed for repairs, four or five United States vessels rather than just one would have been waiting outside Cherbourg for the *Alabama;* if he had a chance at all, Sinclair maintains, it was in June 1864. Bulloch mentions only that Semmes had to choose between a fight or completing his repairs and then slipping out on a dark night. George T. Sinclair, having arrived in Cherbourg after Winslow and the *Kearsarge* had accepted the challenge, never thought to ask Semmes *why;* he contented himself by offering advice on *how* to fight. Semmes, according to his written accounts, never faced the questions of whether or why he should fight; he saw the enemy and, simply, sent the message: "If you can wait until I receive some coal aboard I will come out and give you battle."[15] His reaction involved no serious deliberation, no careful weighing of the relative strengths of the two ships. It did, however, flow from a certain psychological posture, a certain unconscious mental preparedness.

Counting the *Sumter* and *Alabama* cruises, Semmes had been at sea almost constantly for three years. Inevitably a special relationship developed between him and his ship. In the weeks prior to and just after the battle he referred to the *Alabama* as a living thing with which he enjoyed an intimacy one finds only in a home:

> No one who is not a seaman can realize the blow that falls upon the heart
> of a commander, upon the sinking of his ship. *It is not merely the loss of a*
> *battle*—it is the overwhelming of his household, as it were, in a great

catastrophe. The *Alabama* had not only been my battlefield, but my home, in which I had lived two long years, and in which I had experienced many vicissitudes of pain and pleasure, sickness and health.[16]

Earlier, just before he turned the *Alabama*'s bow toward France, he gave chase throughout the night to a Northern merchant ship. The moon was bright, the breeze gentle, the sea smooth. "The Yankee worked like a good fellow to get away, piling clouds of canvas upon his ship . . . , but it was no use," Semmes wrote. "When the day dawned we were within a couple of miles of him. It was the old spectacle of the panting, breathless fawn, and the inexorable stag-hound." A week later the usual rough weather of an equator crossing reminded him of having passed the spot two years earlier; in one thought, falling into the use of the third person almost as if he were detached, viewing the scene from afar, he reflected upon his ship and himself:

> The poor old *Alabama* was not now what she had been then. She was like the wearied foxhound, limping back after a long chase, footsore and longing for quiet and repose. Her commander like herself was well-nigh worn down. Vigils by night and by day, the storm and the drenching rain, the frequent and the rapid change of climate, now freezing, now melting or broiling, and the constant excitment of the chase and the capture, had laid, in the three years of war he had been afloat, a load of a dozen years on his shoulders. The shadows of a sorrowful future, too, began to rest on his spirit.

From his last victim Semmes had acquired recent New York newspapers, and he read of the continuing Northern victories. "Might it not be," he asked himself, "that, after all our trials and sacrifices, the cause for which we were struggling would be lost? . . . The thought was hard to bear." From the review of the situation, "I was very apprehensive that the cruises of the *Alabama* were drawing to a close."

His work and that of his home, of his living companion, *were drawing to a close.* Before he ever entered Cherbourg, he realized the end was at hand. When the *Kearsarge* appeared, could he have allowed the *Alabama* to be bottled up in Cherbourg, as the *Rappahannock* was in Calais? Could he permit his gallant stag-hound, tail between her legs, in the face of the enemy to cringe behind the neutrality of France? What an inglorious end to a glorious cruise already "drawing to a close."

During the battle an unexploded shell lodged in the *Kearsarge*'s sternpost: "It was the only trophy they ever got of the *Alabama*! We fought her until she could no longer swim, and then we gave her to the waves." As she settled stern-first and the waters engulfed the taffrails, Semmes and John M. Kell, his well-tried executive officer, prepared themselves to abandon ship. They stripped their heavy coats and boots, and then in a last gesture of defiance against the accursed Yankee flag, Semmes hurled his sword, symbol of command, into the depths of the ocean; the two jumped and, side by side still, swam away to avoid the vortex of the waters:

> We then turned to get a last look of her and to see her go down. Just before she disappeared, her main topmast, which had been wounded, went by the board; and, like a living thing in agony, she threw up her bow high out of the water, and then descended rapidly, stern foremost, to her last resting-place. A noble Roman once stabbed his daughter, rather than she should be polluted by the foul embrace of a tyrant. It was with a similar feeling that Kell and I saw the *Alabama* go down. We buried her as we had christened her, and she was safe from the polluting touch of the hated Yankee!

That is why Semmes threw his sword into the water; the fox-hound had found her repose; the cruise was over.

Why did Semmes fight? Like Martin Luther, he "could do no other-wise."

Having decided to fight, why did Semmes lose? The two ships were about equal in speed and size. The answer is not simple. The accounts vary. Winslow in his matter-of-fact, descriptive report to the United States Navy Department does not bother with reasons, although he inadvertently affords one insight: "The fire of the *Alabama*, although it is stated that she discharged 370 or more shell and shot, was not of serious damage to the *Kearsarge*. Some thirteen or fourteen of these had taken effect in or about the hull and sixteen or seventeen about the masts or rigging." Only about 8.5 percent, at most, of the *Alabama*'s shots even touched the *Kearsarge*. Still, this might have been enough if the powder had been fresh and if upon contact the shells had exploded. Semmes himself claimed: "I should have beaten him in the first thirty minutes of the engagement, but for the defect of my ammunition, which had been two years on board, and become much deteriorated by cruising in a variety of climates." He was referring in particular to the unexploded shell that struck and lodged in the sternpost of the *Kearsarge*. "On so slight an incident—the defect of a percussion cap—did the battle hinge."[17] He says nothing of his gunners' marksmanship except that he had directed his men to fire low, depending on ricochet to injure the hull. Yet, of those shot that did strike the enemy ship, more hit the rigging than the hull; his men were firing high, not low. Commander Bulloch later picked up these two points and analyzed them as reasons for the loss. The men of the *Alabama*, he wrote, had not been trained at judging distance and had not practiced "firing at a visible target and noting the effect." Bulloch stated simply: "The result of the action was

determined by the superior accuracy of the firing from the *Kearsarge*."
What then of the unexploded shell? Bulloch admitted that "if it had not
failed to explode, the stern of the *Kearsarge* would have been shat-
tered . . . and she would have foundered instead of the *Alabama*." The
powder, then, was deteriorated; but Bulloch did not stop here, as
Semmes did. He asked the further question: why was the powder
allowed to deteriorate? Was it inevitable? Was it simply due to the
two-year cruise in varying climates? Bulloch had a stake in this; he had,
after all, designed the ship and arranged for its provisioning. He had
known it would be long at sea, moving from climate to climate. The
magazine, he said, was placed two and a half feet below the waterline
and protected by the iron freshwater tanks. Bulloch learned from the
engineer, after the battle, that it often had been "the habit to condense in
excess of the quantity which the cooling-tank held" and that pure steam
filled the iron tanks. "I think this practice contributed largely to the
deterioration of the powder," he concluded.[18] And so it was not just in
the nature of things, nor in the condition of the powder Bulloch had
purchased, nor in the storage arrangement he had designed; it was,
rather, in the engineer's "practice to condense" in excess of the cooling
tank capacity. That is why the shell failed to explode. There is in this
detailed analysis by Bulloch some self-service.

Captain Semmes in his official report written in Southampton two
days after the battle noted that much of his shot failed to penetrate the
Kearsarge amidships because Winslow had ironcoated her there by
hanging anchor chains from rail to water and covering the chains with
planks. This armor, as he called the vertical chains, gradually became
more important as a cause for his defeat. On 1 July 1864 he equated it
with his powder, and four years later in his memoirs he accused Captain
Winslow of ungentlemanly deceit and referred to the chains as "concealed armor." Because of the armor, Semmes wrote, "my shot and
shell . . . fell harmlessly into the sea."[19] The implication is clear: in a fair
fight between two wooden vessels, Semmes, regardless of his powder's
condition, would have defeated Winslow. Bulloch on the other hand
considered Winslow to have been "quite right" in increasing the defensive power of his ship. Semmes's comments permit the obvious inference
that he did not know about the armor and Bulloch makes no reference
to any Confederate having knowledge of it prior to the battle. Yet
Lieutenant Arthur Sinclair, who was there, states very clearly that the
French port admiral had informed "Semmes, a day or so before the
fight . . . of the chain-armor arranged on the ship, and strongly advised
Semmes not to engage her." He also states that Semmes's purpose in
alternating solid shot and shell was for "the former to pierce, if possible,
the cable chain-armor." Semmes officially reported: "Perceiving that our

shell, though apparently exploded against the enemy's sides, were doing but little damage, I returned to solid shot firing, and from this time onward alternated with shot and shell."[20] Who was right? Did Semmes know about the chain armor before or during the battle? If so, his later statements reflect an uncharacteristically acetous attitude toward his defeat. Sinclair's memory served him poorly in other details. Perhaps Bulloch, despite his self-serving analysis, was right: Semmes lost the fight because of his gunners' poor marksmanship using poor powder.

The *Kearsarge* suffered only three men wounded during the fight, one of whom died later.[21] The *Alabama* had forty-seven casualties, of whom twenty-six either were killed in the fighting or drowned after it. Among those who drowned was David H. Llewellyn, acting assistant surgeon, who had served with Bulloch prior to joining the *Alabama*. David Henry White, ship's boy, and Andrew Shilland, a fireman, also drowned. White and Shilland served the *Alabama* and Semmes well; they fought the Yankee *Kearsarge* with courage; both were listed, simply, as "colored slaves." It is ironic that two slaves fighting for the South against the North should have died in European waters less than ten months before their freedom would have been assured. Of the twenty-six dead, nine were killed aboard ship during the fighting. Of the wounded, nine were treated in the marine hospital in Cherbourg. George T. Sinclair stayed in Cherbourg to visit and see to the wounded; a Confederate navy surgeon was sent to tend them; Sinclair had to arrange for the burial of the dead whose bodies were recovered. Naval tradition for a moment conquered the war's passions: Sinclair visited the *Kearsarge* wounded and *Kearsarge* officers visited the *Alabama* wounded in the hospital.[22] The unwounded were scattered from Cherbourg to Southampton. *Kearsarge* boats and a French pilot boat took sixty-one men to the *Kearsarge;* they became prisoners of war, but Winslow, due to crowded conditions, battle damage, and lack of other transportation, paroled all but four officers. Six others, including Lieutenant R. F. Armstrong, were plucked from the water by another French pilot boat, which took them directly to Cherbourg, thus they were not prisoners of war. The others, including Captain Semmes and Lieutenant Kell, were saved by the boats from a British yacht, the *Deerhound,* and were taken to Southampton, England.[23]

These men—the dead, the wounded, the saved—were, in Semmes's words, "my" officers and crew who "formed a great military family, every face of which was familiar to me." During the two-year cruise Semmes had taken special care for the health of the crew, seeing to their food and even to frequent changes of clothing; he was especially proud that he had not "lost a single man by disease." Like a father, Semmes always applied discipline tempered with mercy, and like a father he loved his crew. The men reciprocated. Their affectionate nickname for the captain was "Old Beeswax." On the morning of the battle Semmes, exchanging pleasantries with Arthur Sinclair, asked how the lieutenant thought the battle would go. "I cannot answer the question, sir," Sinclair responded, "but I can assure you the crew will do their full duty, and follow you to the death." Supremely confident, Semmes replied as a matter of fact: "Yes, that is true." And so it was. "When I looked upon my gory deck," he wrote, "toward the close of the action, and saw so many manly forms stretched upon it, with the glazed eye of death, or agonizing with terrible wounds, I felt as a father feels who has lost his children—his children who have followed him to the uttermost ends of the earth, in sunshine and storm, and been always true to him."[24] It was not easy for Old Beeswax. He did what he could for his men. They were paid off in full, and so were the survivors of the dead when they could be located. The men, even White and Shilland, had followed him around the world; they had fought the battle, and some had died. He did not want to blame their poor marksmanship for the loss of his "fox-hound." Perhaps that is one reason he blamed the poor powder and Winslow's chain armor.

Semmes himself had entered the battle in ill health. Indeed, as Maffitt and W. L. Maury before him, he had requested of Barron to be relieved from command of the *Alabama*. The commodore already had selected Thomas J. Page to succeed Semmes.[25] But the battle intervened. Semmes was wounded in the right hand during the fighting, a fact he never mentioned in his memoirs. It was slight, he must have judged, compared to the terrible wounds of his men. The Confederate Congress promoted him to the rank of admiral and various British societies bestowed honors on him before he returned to the Confederacy.

The significance of the *Kearsarge-Alabama* struggle lies less in the battle itself than it does in the location of the battle. The course of the war was affected not one whit by the battle. Had Semmes won, he would have had to face the U.S.S. *Niagara,* which was then en route to Europe and more powerful still than the *Kearsarge.*[26] Semmes had been right; the *Alabama*'s cruise was over regardless of the battle's result and Grant and Sherman would have defeated Lee and Johnston even had the *Kearsarge* lost. But the battle was the only one fought on the high seas between two major warships. The very location of the battle reflects the international implications of the American Civil War because it dramatized the work of the Confederate navy in Europe. Designed by Commander Bulloch, built in Liverpool by the Laird shipyard, the *Alabama* for two years wreaked destruction upon Northern shipping. Needing rest and repair, she returned to France, where Bulloch and Barron had transferred their chief activities. Were she to lie under any waters except those of Europe, between the shores of England and France, it would be a historical injustice to the work of Bulloch, Barron, M. F. Maury, and, yes, even James H. North.

The war ended that nineteenth day of June in 1864 for the C.S.S. *Alabama* when like a living thing she threw her bow high and slipped beneath the waters, but for her progenitor the agony of war continued. Bulloch, with Barron, first had to try to get the *Rappahannock* to sea and then to make a last supreme effort in Europe to sustain the falling Confederacy.

The *Rappahannock* had not sat quietly in Calais during the excitement of the classic battle off Cherbourg. Her commander, claiming the national character of his ship, had rejected the port authority's finding in the *Nil* dispute and had refused to pay a fine of 200 francs. A plan developed to rendezvous with a tender sent by Bulloch, but Fauntleroy was skeptical, after 19 June, because the *Kearsarge* was still in the channel and the U.S.S. *Niagara* and *Sacramento* had joined her.[27]

The first big break came on 7 July when Slidell learned unofficially that Napoleon III, acting on the advisory committee's long-delayed report, had given the order to release the *Rappahannock*. This news caused some jubilation among the Confederates in Paris. Barron instructed Fauntleroy to complete his rendezvous plans with Bulloch because the *Rappahannock* was needed to take the place of the *Alabama*. This startled and even frightened the lieutenant. It was, he said, most difficult to communicate with Bulloch and, because all depended on his departure from Calais, he reminded the commodore that three Federal ships blocked him and with only two hours of darkness a night he did not see how he could elude them. "So far from this ship supplying the place of the *Alabama*, I very much apprehend that her only use is more likely to result in augmenting our naval disasters." He then reminded his superior that he had maintained all along that the *Rappahannock* was "worthless." Still Barron persisted. He instructed Fauntleroy to settle the *Nil* affair at any cost to national pride and be ready to leave on a moment's notice. The fine had increased daily and on 19 July Fauntleroy paid 730 francs under protest and effectively closed the case.[28] All seemed ready to make an attempt, which in Fauntleroy's mind would be suicidal, to leave Calais.

Then, on 28 July 1864, Slidell learned that Drouyn de Lhuys had convinced the cabinet council that the emperor's order to release the vessel was valid only on the condition that the number of men aboard ship were the same as were aboard when she had entered Calais. The French officials had proof that this number, at most, was thirty-five.[29] The emperor could offer no further help. Lieutenant Fauntleroy would have to operate the ship with only thirty-five men, or not at all. Fauntleroy, maintaining the "absolute impossibility of navigating the ship," refused "to take her out at all." Barron agreed and instructed him to discharge all but a few of the crew and to "lay up the ship until we can determine upon what course we shall pursue in regard to her." Fauntleroy, as if relieved and happy, proceeded "without any delay" to comply.[30] There was to be no new course pursued for the *Rappahannock*. She remained dockside in Calais, rising and falling with tides, rotting, until the end of the war. And Fauntleroy remained with her. It was an inglorious career for both the *Rappahannock* and Lieutenant Fauntleroy; it was a fate Captain Semmes had averted, for both himself and the *Alabama*, by doing battle. The *Rappahannock* was the third ship lost.

By the beginning of August 1864, just over a year after Bulloch had signed the corvette contracts and halfway through the last year of the war, the Confederate navy's grandiose plans in France collapsed. It had failed to get the six new ships out of Bordeaux and Nantes, and it had lost the *Georgia*, the *Alabama*, and now the *Rappahannock*. The whole scheme to build an offensive fleet in France and to carry the war to the enemy was symbolized by the *Rappahannock* rotting in Calais. The collapse dated back to the Voruz Papers, to Drouyn de Lhuys's determination to institute and pursue a policy of honest neutrality. It reflects the impotency of the Confederate navy to operate successfully in a strong country determined to maintain its neutrality. French neutrality, as the British, had denied the South the means of making naval war against the North. Chasseloup-Laubat referred to the *Rappahannock* as "an altogether unfortunate affair" and William L. Dayton called it "a miserable affair at best."[31] Indeed, as of August 1864 the Confederate navy in Europe was both unfortunate and miserable.

With Sherman in Atlanta (22 July) and Grant massing his forces on the south bank of the James River, disappointed and discouraged as the Confederate navy officers in Europe were, it would have been easy for them to give up. Yet Bulloch with much success during the last months of the war provided the South with ships, even then, to carry the battle to the enemy. Just as in the first months of the war he had dominated naval activities in Europe, so at the last he was the moving spirit. He aroused the navy in Europe from its unfortunate and miserable doldrums.

Bulloch and the Blockade-Runners

Blockade-running was of twofold value to the Confederacy: it brought goods and war materials into the South and it took cotton to Europe. Both became ever more essential as the Federal blockade became increasingly effective and as the Confederate dependence on foreign arms grew. The activity was carried on primarily by private individuals, both Southern and foreign. As the danger of capture and the Confederate need both increased, the opportunity for large profits also increased. One or two successful trips through the blockade would not only pay for a ship but would also provide large profits. So, with this attraction, and despite the dangers, the activity continued until the last port of entry fell to Union forces. The activity began early; in 1861 alone some 1,200 vessels carrying supplies for the Confederacy entered or left the harbor of Liverpool.[32] This contraband trade grew rapidly. In some instances individual Southern states chartered boats, but in most cases free-lance fortune hunters took the risks along with the earnings.

While there were many Rhett Butlers in the Confederacy, Great Britain had its own real versions of the dashing fictional Georgian, varying from individuals to shipbuilders to corporate investors. In one group of 105 blockade-runners identified as of British origin, only 28 were owned by the Confederate States. Among other owners were W. S. Lindsay, McConnell and Laird, Hayle and Bristol Company, Clyde Shipping Company, and London Street Navigation Company. William C. Miller and Sons Company, shipbuilders, built and owned 3 blockade-runners; Thomson, Commander North's builder, built 18 ships that became blockade-runners, but he did not retain ownership of any; Jones and Quiggin built 19 of which 6 were for Confederate States ownership. Laird shipyards built 5 and Thomson 4 that came into Confederate ownership. Many of these ships would make one or two successful runs, then convert to legitimate use. It is impossible, then, to say how many vessels operated at a given time as blockade-runners. One source estimates that a total of 111 ships of British origin, with over 60,000 gross tonnage and valued at 1.7 million pounds, were, at one time or another, put into the blockade-running business.[33]

The ingoing cargo consisted of some munitions and some luxury items; the outgoing cargo was almost always cotton, which sold at an inflated price in Europe. With such large profits at both ends of the voyage, one successful trip could bring a return on an investment of some 700 percent. No wonder the British investors jumped at the opportunity; they had found a substitute for the forbidden slave trade.

As the Union blockade became more effective, oceangoing vessels found it more and more hazardous to run into Southern ports. Smaller boats of lighter draft and swifter movement were needed to pass through the blockading fleet. Therefore a new pattern of shipping developed by late 1862. The Confederate government sent agents to Bermuda, Nassau, and Havana; larger vessels transhipped their cargoes at these island points onto the smaller ones. These agents who originally were to supervise only the movement of government goods came in time to handle all the goods consigned to the Confederacy.[34]

Until 1864 the Confederate navy in Europe was involved only incidentally in blockade-running. Commander Bulloch early had seen the need

for government-owned blockade-runners. He demonstrated the feasibility of this with the *Fingal* in 1861 and the *Coquette* in early 1863–64.[35]
Bulloch returned to the theme on 18 February 1864 in his report on the
sale of the Bordeaux rams. Those ships, designed to raise the blockade
and harass Northern coastal shipping, were lost; how to fill the void? "If
the Navy Department would take the blockade-running business into its
own hands," he wrote, it could soon have a fleet of shallow-draft screw
and paddle steamers with strong decks. Under civilian registry, they
could trade without interruption and one or two trips would more than
pay their costs. Then, when several happened to be in a harbor at one
time, "a few hours would suffice to mount a heavy gun on each, and at
early dawn a successful raid might be made upon the unsuspecting
blockaders." Furthermore, at irregular intervals one or two could be
supplied with coal for a cruise against Northern shipping off Hatteras or
in the Mexican gulf, especially against troop transports. The ships, he
maintained, could serve alternately as blockade-runners and as warships.[36] In this way at least part of the purpose of the ironclads would be
fulfilled. It was an audacious plan and lacked only two ingredients:
proof that ships of such size could, indeed, run the blockade, and
government support.

New Confederate laws (6 February 1864) regulating imports and
exports convinced Mallory of the need for government-owned vessels
specially designed for blockade-running. The Confederate navy in Europe, then, effectively was put into the business of procuring blockade-
runners and Bulloch was able to put his plan into effect.[37]

The 6 February laws prohibited the export of cotton except under
presidential permit, forbade the import of luxury items, and stipulated
that at least half of all incoming cargoes must be government orders.
This legislation placed all blockade-runners under government control.
The various departmental agents in Europe—representing the Treasury, War, and Navy departments—then merged their resources and
established a systematic arrangement. General McRae, the fiscal agent of
the Treasury Department, would arrange the financing, Bulloch would
select the type and structure of ship, and the navy would be responsible
for operations. This arrangement, during the last year of the war, gave
new life to Bulloch at a time when he had lost hope of getting a fighting
vessel to sea.[38]

While McRae made the financial arrangements and Bulloch sought
the ships, many months passed. During that time at least two ships of
British origin reached Wilmington, North Carolina, and were used both
as blockade-runners and as cruisers.[39] The records do not reflect
whether Bulloch was responsible for these ships, but their histories
prove the validity of the commander's proposal.

In early June General McRae notified Bulloch that he could proceed to purchase ships under their new arrangement. Bulloch already had surveyed the building yards and acted quickly; by 6 June he had let several contracts and was working on others. In mid-September he reported a total of "fourteen fine steamers either already completed or in course of construction for the Government."[40] Two, he indicated, already had sailed and he expected two others to leave in October, one in November, four in December, three in January 1865, and two in April. The first four were bought while under construction and too far advanced to effect any changes. Yet, they were excellent for blockade-running: steam side paddle wheels, capable of carrying 800 bales of cotton with a draft of less than seven and a half feet. All four—the *Owl,* the *Bat,* the *Stag,* and the *Deer*—saw service before the end of the war. The other ten ships were built specially for coastal service. Two of them were steel paddle-steamers with a capacity of 1,500 bales of cotton with about a nine-foot draft. Two others were smaller, with about a 350-bale capacity and a five-foot draft, designed to work the gulf shoal areas. The remaining four were of similar structure with varying capacities between the two extremes.

The ships so far acquired under the new arrangements were general blockade-runners. Bulloch was not satisfied; he still wanted ships capable of opening some of the Southern ports to commercial trade and capable, as well, of making effective attacks upon the Northern seacoast. His opportunity came in early October when Mallory directed him to use the McRae financial arrangement to build "four steamers especially for the Navy Department." Since Bulloch long had wanted this project, he already had consulted with builders as to design and structure. By late October he reported their details. All four were designed as tow boats "to deceive the Federal spies" but could be converted quickly and easily into gunboats. Two were small—only 170 feet long with a draft of less than 8 feet—and intended for harbor warfare. Fast at twelve knots, they could sneak out to the blockading fleet off the Cape Fear River and with their specially designed guns encounter the wooden ships and even, perhaps, the monitor-class ironclads. One of these, the *Ajax* under Lieutenant John Low's command, got as far as Bermuda by the war's end. The other two were larger (Bulloch does not give the details) and would have been sent "against one or more of the sea-ports along the Northern coast, that of Portsmouth, New Hampshire, especially." But only the *Ajax* was completed prior to Appomattox. None affected the war.

This account of Commander Bulloch's involvement in the business of blockade-runners is significant because it reveals that despite British neutrality the Confederates could finance and deliver warships right to the very end of the war. If in 1863 the South had had a dozen or so *Ajax*-type ships in Charleston and Wilmington, even in Hampton Roads, they could have affected the course of the war. Needed war materials could have been imported on a large scale, paid for by cotton exported on a large scale. Confederate government policy, however, until pressured by military events, prohibited the government regulations needed to supervise and protect the European lifeline. Not until the summer of 1864, as Sherman approached Atlanta and Grant crossed the James River, did a plan of ship construction become effective in England. Only then did the Southern leaders in Richmond realize that British investors were willing to take the risk for a quick return on their capital. Ships financed by English pounds could pay for themselves by a couple of successful trips into Southern ports; then, under Confederate ownership, they could be converted into harbor gunboats or even cruisers with the power to attack the Northern coast.

This scheme was a true navy activity, and James D. Bulloch was its architect. Despoiled of the ironclads in Liverpool and Bordeaux, he potentially had created another naval fleet with the capability of carrying the war to the enemy. Bulloch long had questioned the military value of cruisers on the high seas. Ever since the *Sumter*'s victims had cast their shadows on England he had opposed it. His suggestion for a prefabricated fleet of harbor defense vessels was in vain. Persistent, loyal, he carried out the department's orders; ironically, only at the end did the department come around to his views. It was too late, then, to do the South any good. As Lee grudgingly and brilliantly gave way before Grant's hammer blows, and as Sherman marched irresistibly to the sea then through the Carolinas, closing ports as he went, the Confederate navy officers in Europe continued to plan and work toward taking the offensive against the enemy.

The Last Confederate Offensive

John Slidell, back in July, had asked Drouyn de Lhuys if the *Rappahannock* would be released if Grant failed to take Richmond. He was basing his last hopes on military defensive success. Bulloch would have none of that; to the very end he based his hopes on offensive action and amazingly he succeeded in putting two offensive vessels to sea: the C.S.S. *Shenandoah*, a cruiser, and the C.S.S. *Stonewall*, an ironclad ram.

The story of the *Shenandoah*, as that of many other Confederate ships, has been told often, but never completely. The ship has been eulogized as a gallant rebel, her commander as an excellent navigator, loyal, proud, honorable; Bulloch's cleverness in getting her to sea and the futility of her career have been properly and well noted.[41] But nowhere have all of these factors been studied within the concepts of Confederate naval theory and needs.

James Bulloch's reservations about the value of cruisers were revised not only by the loss of the *Alabama* and the *Rappahannock*. True, only the *Florida* still preyed on Northern shipping and she needed help. But in his memoirs Bulloch introduced his role in acquiring the *Shenandoah* with a ten-page apology. He referred to the change in British opinion concerning the destruction of ships and property, the historic practice of such destruction by the United States in previous wars, and even its use by other countries. But he failed to mention perhaps his principal motivation: his conviction of the impossibility of getting warships to sea from European countries, a conviction he consistently stated in his correspondence of the day.[42] This rationalization, however, never changed his notion of the real Confederate need to carry the naval war to the Southern ports and against the enemy's warships, otherwise he would not have run the risks of obtaining the *Stonewall*. Still, he nowhere mentions the sole reason for putting ships to sea specifically during the autumn of 1864: the desperate military situation at home. Southerners in Europe after the fall of Atlanta spoke more and more of an armistice, less and less of a victory. Ships acting against the enemy—any kind of ship: blockade-runner, cruiser, ironclad warship—were the last desperate hope of avoiding total defeat. It was this strategic value of any possible kind of offensive military action that changed Bulloch's opinion on the use of cruisers.

Secretary Mallory did instruct Bulloch urgently to replace the lost *Alabama,* but it was unnecessary. The Southern leaders in Europe already had moved in that direction, even considering for awhile the *Rappahannock* in that role. Bulloch in England kept his agents busy scouring the shipyards and the docksides for likely ships. It was a new endeavor for the commander. He had *built* major ships before and had gotten them to sea; but only Matthew F. Maury had *bought* major vessels and had gotten one of them to sea. Now, because building was out of the question, in the *Shenandoah* case Bulloch followed what was for him a new methodology; it might be called a composite one because it combined some of his own *Alabama* techniques with some of Maury's *Georgia* techniques. The new method turned out to be quite effective: safe, smooth, and quick. Furthermore, Bulloch for once had sufficient money; refunds from the sale of the Laird rams, the Arman ships, and North's Number 61 enabled him to take immediate advantage of such an opportunity. From the records it appears that not more than four weeks lapsed between Bulloch's first knowledge of the *Shenandoah* (then the *Sea King*) and her safe departure from England.[43] There was, it must be said, a good deal of luck and what Bulloch called "interesting coincidence" in the undertaking.

In the summer of 1863 Bulloch and Lieutenant Robert R. Carter had seen a new composite ship, the *Sea King,* at dock on the Clyde River. Both realized she would make an excellent cruiser, but she was then about to embark on her maiden voyage and was not for sale. During the ensuing year, Carter returned to Richmond and after news of the *Alabama* loss discussed with Mallory the beautiful ship he had seen and suggested that such a ship could wreak havoc among the New England whaling fleet that worked in the North Pacific. At about the same time, Bulloch had enlisted Charles K. Prioleau's father-in-law, Richard Wright, as an agent to find a ship suitable to replace the *Alabama.* Sometime shortly after 1 September 1864 Wright reported that the *Sea King* was in Glasgow, just unloaded and available. Realizing his good luck, Bulloch telegraphed Wright to buy the ship in his own name. This done, the *Sea King,* now commanded by Captain Corbett, a British master and Bulloch's old friend, sailed to London and took on a cargo of coal. Simultaneously, Bulloch set in motion the details of procuring a tender, gathering an officer staff, and coordinating the movements of armaments, provisions, men, and ships. He was in his element. All worked to perfection and properly deceived the Northern spies.[44] The ships sailed on schedule, the *Sea King* slipping past two Federal warships at the mouth of the Thames River. They met as prearranged at Bulloch's favorite spot off the Madeira Islands, transferred title and command of the ship, transloaded the arms, and on 19 October 1864 the C.S.S. *Shenandoah* was born, full grown, like Venus, on the waters.

Like Venus, she was a beauty: graceful lines, sleek, and fast. A full-rigged three-master, she had been logged at thirteen and a half knots. With a lifting screw and full sails, she could stay long at sea without refueling. Having all the proper features the *Georgia* and the *Rappahannock* had lacked, she was almost perfect for service as a cruiser. She was, her commander reported, of "good sea quality" in rough weather, strong, fast, spacious, and well ventilated. He did note two "objectionable points": the boilers were eighteen inches above the water-line and the cylinders were five feet above it.[45] Still, W. L. Maury or Charles M. Fauntleroy would have been more than happy with her.

Given Sherman's and Grant's positions, given the enforcement of French and British neutrality, and given the *Kearsarge* victory, had the British and Federal officers fallen into complacency? Or had Bulloch, with ready cash, simply outmaneuvered them? There were similarities to the *Georgia* acquisition: like Maury, Bulloch did not go near the ship—indeed, no Confederate official did; Wright served Bulloch as Jansen had served Maury. Bulloch, Like Maury, made his own financial arrangement. All of these factors enabled Bulloch, like Maury, to complete the transaction in a matter of weeks, outstripping the slow process of Federal fact-finding and of British bureaucratic action. Even so, the Northerners had become suspicious, and only the quick sailings of both the *Sea King* and the tender made possible the *Shenandoah*'s birth.

One other factor contributed to Bulloch's success. The officers sent over for duty on the Laird and Arman ships were mostly still in Europe and readily available. Bulloch first requested Lieutenant William H. Murdaugh as the commander of the ship, but he was on special ordnance service, so instead Commodore Barron assigned Lieutenant James I. Waddell.[46] Waddell was a good choice. He had no qualms about destroying unarmed merchant ships. Indeed, he maintained that it was proper naval warfare to destroy the enemy's power "and burn, sink and destroy his vessels." There was, he thought, too great a risk in "getting to sea vessels of war" that could not "justify spending millions in that folly." He needed no apology, no rationalization to burn and sink defenseless merchant or whaling craft that flew the enemy flag. In taking over his first command, provided with orders by Bulloch and Barron, Waddell's only concern was getting sufficient crew to operate the ship. He had little worry about the *Shenandoah*'s teakwood siding or the unsafe locations of her boilers and engines, because unlike Semmes he intended "to not engage the enemy on the ocean."[47] He claimed several victims in the Atlantic and recruited needed crewmen from them. Then, sailing around Africa, he went to Australia, where he recruited additional seamen, and New Zealand, finding few enemy flags; he arrived at his assigned hunting grounds, the North Pacific, only in April 1865, where on the tenth he sank his first New England whaler. It was one day after Appomattox. Waddell's next conquest came on 27 May, seventeen days after Jefferson Davis's capture. Only in June did he learn of the war's end, and then he spiked his guns and made for Liverpool, where he arrived on 5 November. He destroyed or bonded Northern shipping worth $1,172,223, of which only $294,436 occurred prior to Davis's capture.[48] And still in his memoirs he expressed no regrets.

Given these rather tragic statistics, was the *Shenandoah* worth it all? Certainly her career did not delay the Confederacy's demise: it was, rather, a "sad futility" that contained "many of the leitmotifs of the larger, more sombre theme of the Confederacy's defeat."[49] Yet the *Shenandoah* demonstrated one incontestable fact: from the beginning even to the very end, and afterward, the Confederate navy in Europe and operating from Europe was able to mount and maintain offensive warfare against the commerce of the United States. Beginning with the *Sumter,* and from the *Alabama*'s first victim in 1862, there was a raider on the high seas. When the *Florida* left Brest, the *Alabama* shortly entered

Cherbourg; the *Shenandoah* was commissioned just twelve days prior to the *Florida*'s capture in Brazil. Bulloch was responsible for each of these ships. No other branch of the Confederate military was as successful. Taking full advantage of the international aspects of the conflict and despite sincere French and British neutrality, Bulloch rejected defeatism and continued to carry the war to the enemy. The *Shenandoah* was not his last effort.

The cruisers fought on the high seas, far from the scenes of battle in the South. Ever since 1862 Bulloch had advocated that naval activities at home against the enemy were more pressing than this kind of warfare. He thought, in the spring of 1863, that he finally had provided for a fleet that could raise the blockade at several ports and even take the war inland, especially into the Mississippi River and the coastal shoal waters. The two Laird rams, the two Arman rams, along with the Arman corvettes and the North and Sinclair Clyde River ships, certainly had that potential. Even after the British government had detained and then sequestered the ships in that country, even after the French government had forced the sale of the six ships abuilding, Bulloch still expected to regain one of the rams and one of the corvettes for use in Southern waters. Only in August of 1864 did he give up this plan. Arman had sold all of his ships, and Bulloch was left with the blockade-runners and the *Shenandoah*. A second opportunity, however, developed as the Danish War drew to a conclusion in the fall of 1864.

Arman had sold his vessels to two belligerents—Prussia and Denmark—thus he could not make delivery during the war. The two rams, as of October, were still in Bordeaux, the *Cheops* destined for Prussia and the *Sphinx* for Denmark. So far as the French, Prussian, and Danish governments were concerned, the sales were bona fide and final. Yet Arman, in October, sent his agent, Henri Arnous de Rivière, to offer the *Sphinx* to Bulloch. Time had run out on Denmark, which with the war drawing to an end had no more use for the ironclad; Bulloch knew that time also was running out on the Confederacy. He wanted the ship, but he distrusted Arnous de Rivière; besides, the ship was still in Bordeaux and he saw no way of getting her out. He refused the offer.[50] Circumstances changed within a month, however. Arman sent the ship to Copenhagen, where Danish officials were inspecting her with an eye, obviously, to canceling the order.[51] Arman saw an opportunity to please the Danish government by letting it off the hook, to please his Confederate friends by selling his ship to them, and to please himself as a businessman by saving his investment and turning a tidy profit. He sent Arnous de Rivière to Bulloch once again.

This time Bulloch listened more carefully, even though he still did not trust this suave Frenchman. He wanted the ship because his country needed it and because it was the kind of ship designed to operate in American rivers and harbors. Besides, now there were real possibilities of success because the vessel was no longer under French control. She sat in Copenhagen under the charge of Rudolph Puggard, a banker, while the government deliberated. There could be no question of violating French neutrality now. With his usual care and caution, Bulloch in early December 1864 set in motion the series of events that on the eve of defeat culminated in the addition of a formidable ironclad ship to the Confederate navy. The series of events was planned in a marvelously intricate manner, at the cost of large amounts of money, at the risk of many young men's lives. Why did he do it? Did he really expect one ship to turn the tide of war?

Bulloch was no fool. He knew the ship well because he had specified its qualities to the builder and he had seen the designs as they developed. Even after the Danish purchase, his trusted friend Captain Eugene Tessier had visited Bordeaux to observe the changes instituted by the Danish navy. Now, in December 1864, Tessier went to Copenhagen to examine the ship again and reported that "the *Sphinx* did then show no signs of weakness."[52] Good—the ship was strong and should be able to function as designed.

Bulloch then requested a conference in Paris. John Slidell, James Mason, Commodore Barron, and even Major Huse, Bulloch's army counterpart, discussed the various facets of "the proposed enterprise" with Bulloch. Conditions within the Confederacy were serious. Not only were the armies gradually being squeezed between Grant's and Sherman's forces, but the ports were falling one by one. Only Wilmington remained open, and they knew the North was planning a joint land-sea attack against Fort Fisher at the mouth of the Cape Fear River. Any possible aid from Europe should be rendered. Reports of the ship's power had been exaggerated, Bulloch knew, and disseminated among Union officials. If the ship could suddenly appear among the gathering Union fleet off Cape Fear, its effect would be greater than the ship itself. Furthermore, the psychological impact could encourage the South and strike fear throughout the North. Should the ship survive, it could take the offensive against Federal naval forces at other Southern ports, and, meanwhile, two other ships Bulloch had under construction in England for blockade-running could strike "a severe blow" at "New Bedford, Salem, Portland, and other New England towns" by use of "incendiary shells and Hall's rockets." Such an offensive action might—just might—induce Washington to accept an armistice for negotiating a peace; it was better than total defeat.[53]

Bulloch's views were accepted by his colleagues. On 16 December 1864 he signed with Arnous de Rivière a detailed agreement for the transfer of the *Sphinx* to the Confederate navy. Arnous de Rivière undertook to procure a Danish cancellation of the contract, which was easy, and to deliver the ship to any spot designated by Bulloch. His fee was large: 375,000 francs for himself and 80,000 for Puggard. Arnous de Rivière also promised to enroll an engineer and firemen at Copenhagen who would transfer along with the ship to Confederate service. On the same day Bulloch notified Arman of the arrangement. He released the builder from obligation to refund to the Confederate navy the value of the ship and promised to pay to Arman the costs incurred in delivering it to Copenhagen.[54] Bulloch now had control of the ironclad; all that remained was to assign officers and crew, to arrange for a tender to convey provisions and crew, and to coordinate the ship's movements.

The personnel operation was the easiest. Paroled officers and crewmen from the *Florida* had reached Europe and were temporarily housed on the *Rappahannock* at Calais. Commodore Barron took care of the paperwork in assigning the men to Bulloch. Three other officers played key roles. Lieutenant Samuel Barron, Jr., son of the commodore, served Bulloch as an aide during the planning stages; he then stayed aboard the *Stonewall* as a watch officer. To command the ship, Barron and Bulloch selected Captain Thomas J. Page, who had gone to Europe to command one of the Laird rams and later was designated by Barron to relieve Semmes on the *Alabama*. Page had played no role in naval activities since his arrival in Europe. He was by nature a taciturn, close-mouthed person whom Bulloch considered ideal for secret service. Bulloch briefed him in London, then sent him to Copenhagen to learn the ship and supervise local expenditures. One other quick consultation with Bulloch in London readied Page to sail the ship to the rendezvous and there assume command. Lieutenant Robert R. Carter, who had worked with Bulloch in the *Shenandoah* affair and whom Bulloch held in high esteem, became a key figure in the transfer of the *Stonewall*. Bulloch sent Carter to Niewe Diep, the Netherlands, to arrange for coaling the ship en route to the rendezvous at Quiberon Bay and to look after what Bulloch called "other matters in connection with her." Carter did his job well there and he later joined the ship as the first lieutenant, or executive officer. Bulloch seemed to have more confidence in Carter's judgment and opinions than in those of Page.[55]

Commander Bulloch was fortunate in his arrangement for a tender. His funds were low so he could not buy one, as he had done recently for the *Shenandoah;* besides, he really did not have the time to search for an appropriate ship. He had to take a civilian, W. G. Crenshaw of Richmond, into his confidence. Crenshaw was in England at the time to organize for the Confederate government a business company to run supplies through the blockade. Having included British businessmen in the company in order to gain funding, Crenshaw had to be very circumspect in any military activity that would violate British neutrality. Nonetheless, he agreed to place at Bulloch's disposal the *City of Richmond,* which was scheduled for immediate departure with a cargo of railway iron. The tight schedule of this ship, obligated as it was to private investors, forced Bulloch to act within an even tighter schedule than he had wanted.[56] Still there were unexpected advantages: the ship cost nothing and CSN Lieutenant Hunter Davidson was in charge of her for this particular voyage. He entered into Bulloch's plans with full enthusiasm.

With these arrangements made, Bulloch, by way of coded telegrams, coordinated the movements of the two ships. The *Stonewall* left Copenhagen on 7 January 1865; Bulloch awaited further word from her before sending off the *City of Richmond.* Only at this point did uncertainties enter into the execution of Bulloch's carefully laid plans. The *Stonewall* ran into heavy seas and snowstorms; she had to seek cover in Elsinore, Denmark. Under command of a Danish captain whose duty was to return the ship to Bordeaux in good condition, she lay in Elsinore, like Prince Hamlet, in a dark and brooding mood. The mood engulfed Bulloch. How long would be the delay? Can the *City of Richmond* wait? He made elaborate contingent plans with Davidson that involved alternative meeting places: Terceira and Bermuda. How the *Stonewall* would reach those places without officers and crew he could not yet even contemplate. He had other worries. His plans, so carefully and secretly laid, somehow had become "very generally talked about in Paris." Two officers from the *Rappahannock* had met him in a Paris railway station at 2:00 A.M. and boisterously asked about the ironclad. Lieutenant Arthur Sinclair had been guilty of loose talk. "The result of all this has been to bring the USS *Niagara* to Dover and spies have been sent from here to Calais to tamper with the men on board the *Rappahannock.*" Bulloch's plan was endangered, his temper was short: those responsible for such thoughtlessness "should forthwith be sent out of Europe." But the commander's anxieties proved to be unnecessary. The *Stonewall* and the *City of Richmond* finally did meet and despite bad weather made the transfers of command, men, ammunition, and provisions. They deposited the Danish crew and Arnous de Rivière and sailed from the French coast together on 28 January 1865.[57] Although some seventeen days behind schedule, Bulloch finally had his offensive ironclad ram at sea. His plans had worked! The dark mood lifted.

Confederate morale in Europe soared. Commodore Barron seemed justified in the elaborate instructions he had given to Captain Page: the *Stonewall* first should lift the blockade at Wilmington, sink a few of the California steamers coming up the coast, make "a dash at the New

England ports and commerce"; then, he suggested, "a few days cruising on the banks may inflict severe injury to the fisheries of the United States." What great expectations! Barron seemed to share the Northerners' exaggerated view of the little ship's power. Bulloch was more realistic. The delays already experienced foreshadowed even greater difficulties in crossing the ocean; he methodically went about the business of issuing instructions for the ship's refueling en route. Still, he had hopes that the *Stonewall* could arrive in time to make one telling blow. He recommended that this attack be not at Wilmington but at Port Royal, South Carolina, the last reported base of Sherman's operations.[58]

Then the euphoric bubble burst. Extremely rough weather in the Bay of Biscayne struck the two ships. The *Stonewall,* designed for river use, did not rise to the waves; rather she plowed through them, often submerged from bow to stern. Water rushed into the lower decks; a leak about the rudder casing occurred, allowing water into the bilge. The men and even the officers were alarmed. How could they ever fight with such an uncontrollable ship? Captain Page had no choice but to put into port. On 2 February he reached Coruña, on the northeastern corner of Spain. In five days at sea, he had not yet cleared European waters.

His junior officers drew up a complaint addressed to Commodore Barron. They claimed that the ship could carry coal for only four or five days of steaming and that even in mild weather water swamped the deck, making use of the guns impracticable except in smooth waters; even if she reached American shores the ship "would not be in condition to accomplish anything nearly adequate to the slight chances of success attending the efforts of making the passage." They demanded an inquiry before proceeding. Page blamed "everyone connected with her outfit and delivery" and claimed that they all were "guilty of neglect, deception, and cheating." He requested a meeting in Paris with Barron and Bulloch.[59]

Bulloch's reaction was almost immediate. He sent an engineer from England, he arranged for Tessier to go to Ferrol, and he advised Barron to reject the junior officers' petition. He also rather severely criticized Page for wanting to leave his ship in time of trouble. Barron, almost passive during this emergency, assented to the conference, and in March Page, Barron, Bulloch, and the two Confederate commissioners discussed the ship and her mission. Despite Page's misgivings—he seemed to agree more with the junior officers than with his superiors—they determined that the ship should cross the ocean and that Page, once in Nassau or Bermuda, should take whatever action he could against the enemy. Barron gently reprimanded the junior officers, and Page returned to Ferrol.[60]

Meanwhile, Bulloch's measures had been effective. On his return to Ferrol Page found the repairs completed; he also found the large U.S.S.

Niagara and the smaller U.S.S. *Sacramento* awaiting him. Bravely, Page
and his men made ready to do battle. Another major naval conflict in
European waters appeared to be imminent. Twice Page attempted to
leave port, but rough water turned him back. Finally, on 24 March 1865,
the weather cleared and the seas calmed. The ironclad slid easily
through the smooth sea, her men uneasily prepared for combat with the
two enemy warships. But Captain Thomas Craven of the *Niagara* believed all he had heard about the *Stonewall's* invincibility and refused to
accept Page's challenge. From 10:30 A.M. until 8:30 P.M. the *Stonewall*,
flying the Confederate flag, stood in full view of the *Niagara*. Page could
not believe that the two United States "heavily armed men-of-war" were
afraid of the *Stonewall*. Having lightened his ship to a fighting trim, Page
had little coal; so, shrugging his shoulders at Craven, he steamed to
Lisbon to refuel. The *Stonewall* left European waters on 28 March
1865.[61] The rest of her story is even sadder. Arriving at Nassau after
Appomattox and Davis's capture, she put into Havana. Page, completely
out of funds, turned his ship over to the Spanish authorities for just
enough money to pay off his crew, $16,000. The great hope, the
desperate effort made by Bulloch, Page, Carter, and the crew, was over.

It was over, but certain questions remained. Bulloch asked and answered two of the most important ones. Could any small ironclad ram,
designed for river and harbor action, ever have reached the Confederate waters from Europe? Certainly the *Stonewall's* damage from the
rough seas in the Danish waters and in the Bay of Biscayne deserve
explanation. Bulloch maintained that the original contract called for
delivery of the Arman ironclads in June precisely in order to enjoy the
smoother summer seas; he never expected to have to subject the small
craft to the winter blows. Even so he recognized the dangers of sailing
three thousand miles across the open ocean; this concern had been one
reason for much earlier suggesting the prefabricated iron fleet. The
Arman rams were constructed as well as the newest naval technology
would allow. Certain Danish changes from the original design had
weakened the ship. She still could have fought well in the smooth harbor
and river waters for which she was built. She probably survived the
rough winter gales better than Bulloch expected; his exasperation was
caused not by the ship, but by Arnous de Rivière and by Page's caution.
Bulloch must be exonerated from the charges of having produced an
inadequate ship.[62] The problem of getting a small, inland-water ship
across the ocean was one inherent in the Confederate dependence upon
Europe. The second question is subject to a hypothetical answer only:
could the *Stonewall* have imposed damage on the Northern blockading
fleet? Certainly under the most favorable conditions she could not have
fulfilled Commodore Barron's instructions. She could never have
cruised the fishing banks; without a coal tender she could never have

made a "dash against New England ports." Captain Page while in Ferrol had worried about such orders and rightly so. But, if the *Stonewall* had arrived in time to make repairs in a neutral port, if she could have had a tender, then she could most certainly have scattered the wooden block-aders; she probably could have fought the monitor-class United States ironclads. Two *Stonewalls* with escorting corvettes in the summer of 1864 could have caused much havoc among the blockaders and even on the Mississippi River. Bulloch's fleet approach was a sound one. In the long run, however, the monitors by sheer numbers could have defeated the two river rams. United States Acting Rear Admiral S. W. Godon saw the *Stonewall* in Havana and was impressed but still believed the U.S.S. *Monadnock* "would be more than her equal."[63] The question, as Bulloch well knew, reduces to a matter of industrial capacity. In the production of ironclads the North, as with all other war materials, had the upper hand.

One aspect of the *Stonewall*'s acquisition remains a mystery because Bulloch in all of his writings makes no mention of it. He carefully had selected the rendezvous for the *City of Richmond* and the *Stonewall*. It was, strangely, within French territorial waters, at Quiberon Bay just off Belle Isle. It was a remote spot, but news reached Paris through United States vice consuls and French marine ministry officials. This news sparked United States protests and even led to indirect French protests at Madrid, causing delay in Ferrol.[64] Although the *Stonewall* did manage to get to American waters, this delay was costly. Bulloch earlier had expressed fear of the *Niagara*'s presence at Dover. Why, then, did he select Quiberon Bay for the rendezvous? Perhaps, if he could, he would say it was on the route to Bordeaux and would arouse little suspicion among the Danish crew; but certainly Danish suspicions amounted to little. Perhaps he would say it was easy to get coal from Nantes; but coal could be obtained from almost any continental point. Certainly this was a costly mistake that Bulloch never recognized. He should have.

Both the *Shenandoah* and the *Stonewall,* as it turned out, were exercises in futility. But who could have known this when the decisions were made? Given his mission, could Bulloch have refused to make the efforts? The fact is, when Lee and Johnston and Davis surrendered, Bulloch was still fighting. There can be no denying that the last desperate hopes of the South sailed in Bulloch's two ships. The Confederate navy in Europe was the only military arm of the country capable of mounting offensive efforts against the enemy in March and April 1865, futile as they were.

There is nothing gallant about destroying private property on the high seas, especially after a war is over; there is nothing gallant about sending young men into hopeless battle. There is something admirable, however, in a man who never gives up and who despite all obstacles is able to take the battle bravely to the enemy. That is what James D. Bulloch did with the *Shenandoah* and the *Stonewall*.

CHAPTER 8

Evaluations

The Confederate navy in Europe was born in Montgomery, Alabama, from the coupling of the inferior Southern industrial potential and the fertile mind of Stephen R. Mallory. It grew eventually to encompass hundreds of officers and men, build ships that would cruise the world's oceans and others that would thrust innovative naval architecture ever forward, spend millions of dollars and destroy property worth millions more, and transfer the scene of major naval warfare to European waters. Naval officers, most separated from their families, suffered personal tragedies; their activities, impinging upon maritime practices and diplomacy, effected changes in domestic and international laws stemming from the highest British and French governmental decisions. The Confederate navy in Europe had a meaning beyond its own existence.

Although the navy started small in Europe with one officer and one civilian agent, by 1863 it had increased to several hundred people, including dependents and crewmen. There was tragedy in the lives of these people. They lost loved ones on the American battlefields, their homes were destroyed, and ultimately they lost the war. At the same time there was some levity in their lives and even some romances. Their story is the human meaning of the Confederate navy in Europe.

There were, first of all, Southern families who for whatever reason were unable to go to the Confederacy and stayed in Europe throughout the war. James T. Soutter of Virginia, for instance, had been a banker in New York when the war commenced and was obliged to leave the United States with his wife and daughter Sallie. They settled in Rome and made occasional visits to Paris. There was James M. Buchanan of Maryland, a former United States minister to Denmark, who settled in Paris.[1] With the families of various Confederate agents—Slidell, Mason,

Eustis—plus those of European relatives, sympathizers, and collabora-
tors—Prioleau, Green, Low, Bold, Spence, Lindsay, Roebuck, Tremlett,
Fontaine, Erlanger, and Maury—they constituted a large Southern
colony in Europe. Add to this group the wives and daughters of some of
the officers, such as North, Bulloch, and Page, and the colony grows.
London and Paris were the centers of happy gatherings. For instance,
one November day in 1863, young Lieutenant William C. Whittle, Jr.,
lost his heart to Miss Louisa Spence, who radiated the "gentleness of a
dove and the beauty of an angel."[2] Later, Lieutenant Charles M. Fauntleroy, who had elected to stay on the *Rappahannock* in Calais, found
warm compensation for such military boredom. In December 1864, as
Bulloch was assembling the *Stonewall* crew from his ship, Fauntleroy
spent a month in Rome wooing and winning Miss Sallie Soutter. Even
Commodore Barron, a widower and father of a *Stonewall* officer, met
and became engaged to a Mrs. Parker. Otherwise unidentified, Mrs.
Parker was warmly accepted by Mrs. Page and Mrs. North.[3] The correspondence is rife with references to dinner parties, outings, and sight-
seeing trips. Captain Semmes, for instance, after losing the *Alabama* and
before returning to Richmond, traveled with the Reverend Mr. Tremlett
and three Tremlett women on the Rhine River to Switzerland, where he
rested. M. F. Maury was a frequent guest at an English country estate;
young Brave Maury had school holidays in Paris, London, and Scotland.
Life was not all bad for the Confederate navy officers and friends.

As the end approached, however, new hardships arose. Secretary
Mallory began ordering his officers home and travel was difficult and
even dangerous. Barron and Mrs. Parker, the Sinclairs, uncle and
nephew, and most of the young officers all left for the Confederacy
during the last weeks. M. F. Maury elected to go to Mexico, where he
undertook to establish a colony of Southern plantation owners for his
old friend, Emperor Maximilian; fortunately, he left that country before
Maximilian's fall. Still fearing to return to the re-United States, Maury
went to England, where he received an honorary degree from Cambridge University. Finally, he did return and became a professor at
Virginia Military Institute, where he remained until his death. James H.
North seems to have been reluctant to leave Europe; he was still in
England as late as 2 April 1865. Of all the Confederate navy officers in
Europe, only two—Bulloch and Low—appear to have opted for postwar
careers in England. Both settled in Liverpool, active in maritime affairs
but never again going to sea. Two of the younger officers who were at
sea when the war ended chose not to go home immediately. Lieutenant
Barron, paid off at Havana from the *Stonewall*, went to Argentina, and
Lieutenant Whittle joined him there after the *Shenandoah* cruise. Years

later they returned to Norfolk, Virginia, where they settled.

In most cases the Confederate navy officers were able, despite deep scars, to put their lives back together. It is perhaps more than could have been expected during those dark and uncertain weeks of April and May 1865.

All these officers had gone to Europe with great expectations. They were going to buy or build ships with which they would fight the Yankees. Without exception, each of the major figures expected to command a ship at sea. Perhaps the most disappointed one was Bulloch; until the last minute, as it were, he was the designated captain of the *Alabama* and he had good reason to expect assignment to one of the Laird ironclads. Barron, of course, was supposed to command the fleet, hence his title of flag officer. North and George T. Sinclair came close to having their own ships but lost them to the British government. Not one major officer who went to Europe expecting to acquire and command a ship did so: Maffitt boarded the *Florida* in Bermuda; Semmes returned from Bermuda to accept the *Alabama* from Bulloch; W. L. Maury received the *Georgia* from his cousin. Waddell, sent to Europe to serve on an ironclad, was second choice for the *Shenandoah,* and Page finally commanded an Arman, not a Laird, ironclad. Bulloch, North, M. F. Maury, and Barron all suffered disappointments in their career aims.

Beyond these personal aspirations, however, lay the chief accomplishments of the leading figures. Commodore Barron served a positive function as the ranking officer in Europe: for the first time no one could quibble, as North had done in 1862, as to who should order whom. Still, Barron was no giant force in Confederate naval achievements. For a while in 1863–64, he played a leader's role, threatening even to eclipse Bulloch; but he became ever less assertive, never initiating policy and seldom affecting it. His handling of the *Rappahannock-Georgia* activities was especially inept; the younger officers, Evans and Fauntleroy, had a much stronger grasp of reality than the commodore. Barron, as it turns out, was more a passive symbol of authority than he was an active agent of it. Just as much would have been achieved in Europe if Barron had never gone there. It was Mrs. Parker, not the navy, who benefited from his tour of duty.

Commander James H. North was Mallory's most inept officer in Europe. He had arrived early in the war with perhaps the most important assignment of all: to buy or acquire an ironclad and to command it against the Federal blockaders. It is true that Mallory was unable to send him the promised two million dollars; it is true that Mallory's orders were based on a naive understanding of France's position. But North's dilatory approach to his assignment—sight-seeing in London and yacht racing among the Channel Islands—indicates that even with money, even with French cooperation, he never would have sustained the effort needed to acquire, arm, equip, and man an ironclad and then to sail her across the ocean and carry the battle to the enemy. Such finesse, such imagination, such persistence were just not part of his character. He amply illustrated this in the turmoil of the *Florida* and *Alabama* command issues. Even when he signed the contract for Number 61, unlike George T. Sinclair or M. F. Maury, he was completely dependent upon Mallory and Bulloch for funds. James H. North, as he complained, procrastinated, quibbled over rank and precedence, did more harm than good. Tradition-bound as he was, North could have commanded ships on the inland waters of the Confederacy more effectively than he served the navy in Europe.

The two most effective officers in Europe were James D. Bulloch and Matthew Fontaine Maury. Bulloch has dominated the pages of this study. Imaginative, innovative, knowledgeable, tireless, he served the navy as finance officer, supply officer, personnel officer, legal adviser, even at times adviser to diplomats. He put to sea four major vessels and more blockade-runners than the records tell us. Moreover, he studied, mastered, and applied the latest developments in the rapidly changing naval technology: naval architecture, naval armor, naval ordnance. And above all, he was a naval strategist. His theories on blockade-running, coastal offensive warfare, and fleet activities all were accepted by Mallory and the Richmond government, but too late to affect the outcome of the war. If his mission in Europe failed, it was not a personal failure. Yet Bulloch was not without fault. He tended to trust the law too much and did not fully understand the relationship between national interest and policy. He was himself an achiever and thus let short temper and impatience at times rule him. Withal, he was the one to whom the other officers turned; he was the one who made the final decisions. Never was his influence in Confederate naval affairs greater than during the last six months of the war, when Mallory looked to him for everything—personnel, ships, ordnance, clothing, shoes, blockade-runners—and that was when, against all odds and completely on his own initiative, he acquired two major warships and continued to plan offensive military actions.

Matthew Fontaine Maury's role as part of the Confederate navy in Europe has been practically ignored heretofore in historical literature. He, like Bulloch, did many things and he did them well. He was a publicist, a scientist, an unofficial diplomat, a naval architectural specialist, an imaginative fund raiser. At a time when Bulloch thought it impossible to get ships out of Great Britain, Maury got two out. He even purchased one of them directly from the British navy. He used friends such as Marin H. Jansen and relatives such as Thomas Bold as means to his ends. Perhaps his chief contribution to the Confederate war effort were the torpedoes or underwater mines that served so well, according to Mallory's testimony, in defending Richmond and keeping open the water approaches to Wilmington.

Raphael Semmes during his three trips to Europe played only a minor role, yet he was and is the most famous of all Confederate navy officers. He was a fighter, using ships supplied by someone else. His decision sparked the war's only great naval battle fought in the open seas, and it was fought in European waters. His fame best illustrates why each of the other officers wanted his own ship to command.

These three, Bulloch, Maury, and Semmes, came closest to fulfilling Mallory's original naval strategy: to drive the Union's commercial fleet from the seas and to lift the Union blockade. Semmes and the *Alabama* almost accomplished the first. Bulloch conceived of the means of accomplishing the second: offensive military action through fleet movement. For a short few weeks in the spring of 1863, he expected to put four ironclads and six composite escorts to sea. Such a fleet acting under a unified command would have been able, even if only temporarily, to lift the blockade at one or more Southern ports. Maury, thinking in broad terms, tied this activity to the world powers. Anchoring his concepts to French needs in Mexico, he could foresee the fragmentation of North America into western, eastern, and southern parts, each in counterpoise to the others and all supported by a strong Latin empire in Mexico. If these geopolitical notions in the fall of 1863 were hypothesized on unobtainable conditions, they were no more beyond fulfillment than Mallory's naval strategy had been in 1861.

In fact, as many excellent studies have shown,[4] the Confederate expectations from Europe in the form of favorable treatment or intervention in the war against the United States were misplaced from the beginning. It is the duty of heads of governments to conduct a foreign policy always in the interest of their own country, and Lord Palmerston and Earl Russell in London and Napoleon III and Drouyn de Lhuys in Paris reacted just that way to the American Civil War. In each case the needs of the countries dictated a policy designed to avoid war with the United States, but this policy was neither always easy nor apparent. The Confederate leaders by withholding cotton expected to change the British and French self-interest and to enlist their aid in lifting the blockade at least, or in joining them in the war against the North at most. But they had miscalculated. King Cotton diplomacy failed because the Southampton and Liverpool warehouses were filled with surplus imports from the previous two years. Self-interest, however, is a fragile thing; it depends on events and on changing circumstances. While the United States held the two Southern diplomats who had been taken on the high seas from the *Trent*, a British ship, certain English leaders saw it as in the self-interest of Great Britain to declare war on the United States, and they took steps to strengthen Canada militarily. This activity was perhaps the closest England ever came to intervening in the Civil War. By the fall of 1862 the cotton shortage had begun to pinch both the British and the French economies, and this situation led to diplomatic proposals to intervene in the American war. In London Lord John Russell asked the cabinet to consider such a step, and in Paris Napoleon III actually proposed a three-power overture for an armistice. But both moments passed without action. Lee's defeat at Antietam convinced Lord Palmerston that the issue in America was still too fluid, and French domestic relief measures reduced unemployment. Still, the self-interests of France and England varied from time to time, and John Slidell in particular seized the spring of 1863 to try to force the emperor's hand. He failed because he had misjudged the statesmanship of Drouyn de Lhuys and the power of the French cabinet over Napoleon III. These ministers, persuaded by Drouyn de Lhuys, were more concerned over the implications of the emperor's Mexican adventure than the flow of battles in Maryland and Virginia. And so it went, from circumstance to circumstance, from event to event. Both European governments followed policies of peace toward the United States, tempered with expediency. Drouyn de Lhuys was perfectly candid about this approach. When Dayton, during the Roebuck affair in the summer of 1863, asked him to explain the emperor's policy toward the United States, the foreign minister calmly replied: "He has none; he awaits events."[5]

Policies based on expediency are flexible. To maintain peace with the United States did not imply hostility toward the Confederate States; it implied neutrality. There can be no doubt that the battles of Antietam, Gettysburg, and Vicksburg were events that affected the expedient policies of London and Paris. The South still lives on the "ifs" of these campaigns. It is the consensus of those excellent studies mentioned earlier that the South is right and that if Lee had won at Antietam Russell's proposal might have prevailed in London, and that if Lee had prevailed at Gettysburg the Roebuck motion and Napoleon III might have persuaded Palmerston that the moment was then right to intervene in the American Civil War.[6] That consensus seems to be the decision of the historians.

What, then, of the Confederate navy in Europe so far from those battlefields? Did it play no role in determining the fate of the Confederate States of America? Were the activities of Bulloch and Maury and Semmes as futile as the cruise of the *Shenandoah*? Only if the historians' decision is true. What in an undecided war is the best expediency for a neutral? It is strict, honest, real neutrality. Did Paris and London adopt such enforcement of their neutral declarations in response only to the

American battlefields or in response also to Confederate naval activities in Europe?

Both countries acted on the same principle of international law: "The obligation of a neutral state to prevent the violation of the neutrality of its soil is independent of all interior or local law."[7] This principle was recognized as binding by Lord John Russell in the C.S.S. *Nashville* case as early as 1861 and reiterated in the C.S.S. *Florida* case in March 1862, long before Antietam. In its first test, the 1819 law proved insufficient to deal with the *Florida* and the *Alabama;* much less, then, could it handle Bulloch's ships, which were built according to the latest naval technology. The queen's law officers, agreeing with Russell, wanted to graft onto the 1819 Foreign Enlistment Act by court decision the additional prohibitions of intent and structure. These prohibitions would update the law and enable the government to prohibit delivery to either belligerent any ship that by its very structure was intended to be used as a warship. The desire to modernize the 1819 law through judicial action prompted the *Alexandra* case. When that ploy failed, Russell for purposes of state initiated the extralegal methods of buying the ship, threatening to seize the ship, or negotiating with the owners. In these ways the Laird rams, North's Number 61, and Sinclair's *Canton* all were denied to the South. The fact that these denials occurred after the key battles is coincidental; the policy of enforcing neutrality was articulated even before Antietam and acted upon before Gettysburg. In France the policy of strict neutrality developed later but also as a reaction to Confederate navy activity.

Confederate construction at Bordeaux and Nantes had begun only in the late spring of 1863. The first Confederate use of a French port was in August. Until September when the Voruz Papers exposed the extent of Confederate activities, there was no real need for French action. The French government was not hampered by an outdated law; instead the responsible ministers had to deal with an adventurer as their emperor. Drouyn de Lhuys, always opposed to Napoleon III's personal diplomacy, developed the French strict neutrality piecemeal. In December 1863 he ordered the Arman ironclad ships sold to nonbelligerent governments; in January 1864 he issued the stricter rules and regulations concerning belligerent use of French ports as centers of their cruises; in April 1864 he ordered the sale of the corvettes precisely because their structure manifested their intended use as warships. When the emperor showed signs of favoring the South in July 1864, more than a year after Gettysburg, Drouyn de Lhuys then used the Mexican situation to support his own position, and he applied this technique to prevent the *Rappahannock* from sailing.

He had done the same thing Lord John Russell had done: he had denied the ships to the Confederates. In both cases the denials were less an end than a means—a means of enforcing the neutrality of their soil. In Great Britain that policy was consistent; only the technique changed from event to event, from ship to ship. In France the policy was consistent with the foreign minister; it varied in application from event to event because of the emperor. The differences between substance and form created resentment and even fear in both belligerent camps. Any consistency in Russell's actions in the *Alexandra* court case and in his extralegal detention of the Laird rams was not readily evident to Charles Francis Adams or to James D. Bulloch. Adams resented Russell's apparent indifference to the rams and wrote his famous "superfluous" note; Bulloch resented Russell's extralegal approach to the rams and feared the implications for the other ships. The *Rappahannock* affair in France caused the same reactions. In that case Drouyn de Lhuys had to circumvent the emperor's desire to release the ship; thus he resorted to delay and technicalities. John Slidell took this tactic as weakness on Drouyn de Lhuys's part and as a show of ill will to the Confederacy; William L. Dayton saw it as indecision. Neither belligerent could discern a consistent policy in either country's approach to the ships. It was, then, the application of policy that agitated the Americans; this agitation carried over into the postwar era and created what has been called a "more frankly . . . power relationship" between the United States and Great Britain.[8] A true neutrality at best will elicit resentment from a government involved in the life and death struggles of a war; when it is applied with different techniques and with variations from event to event, it inevitably will create lasting resentments. Still, England and France did maintain a consistent neutrality toward the belligerents, and this policy was occasioned more by the Confederate navy in Europe than by the battlefields in America.

Conceivably, had Lee won at Antietam, the British would have demanded some change in the blockade system; but would this action have led to recognition of the Confederacy or to military intervention? If not after Antietam, then what of Gettysburg and Vicksburg? In Palmerston's view there always could be a next battle that might further clarify the issue. Only the last battle would have made it perfectly clear and then neutrality problems no longer would exist. The same logic can apply to France and to Gettysburg. If the Anglo-French inclination toward neutrality predated any of the so-called decisive battles, would one victory here or there have been significant enough for those governments to abandon their neutral postures?

It indeed was the activity of Bulloch and Maury and Semmes that occasioned the British and French action. This fact was something that Bulloch never comprehended. He argued in his memoirs[9] that the Geneva arbitration was wrong; that Great Britain had been more neutral than France because the *Florida* and the *Alabama* had been got to sea within British law and that Napoleon III had invited ship construction in France and had gone back on his word. Bulloch was right except that the government, following Drouyn de Lhuys's lead, had changed French local law as soon as events raised issues and, by using the Mexican problem, had prevailed on the emperor to enforce neutrality. In England Russell knew that the law was too weak and resorted to various techniques to enforce British neutrality. This overall approach becomes clear when the naval and governmental activities are viewed in their entirety, that is, from the C.S.S. *Nashville* case to the Geneva arbitration decision.

Russell's view of the 1819 Foreign Enlistment Act's inadequacy elicited by the *Nashville* in 1861 and the *Florida* in early 1862 was accepted by later English governments. In 1870 Parliament enacted a new law incorporating the principle that a neutral government is bound to protect its neutrality regardless of local law, and the government in 1871 accepted this principle as a basis to arbitrate the United States's claims against Great Britain arising out of Confederate navy activity during the Civil War. The Geneva Arbitration Tribunal awarded a "sum of 15,500,000 dollars in gold as the indemnity to be paid by Great Britain to the United States" in the cases of the *Florida, Alabama,* and *Shenandoah* precisely because "the Government of Her Britannic Majesty cannot justify itself for a failure in due diligence on a plea of the insufficiency of the legal means of action which it possessed." In the *Shenandoah* case the tribunal found that the British failure occurred only when additional crewmen were allowed to ship aboard the vessel at Melbourne, Australia, not when the ship left the British Isles. Furthermore, no award was allowed for damages claimed as a result of the *Georgia* cruise.[10] By the tribunal's decision, then, Russell and the law officers despite the inadequacies of the 1819 Foreign Enlistment Act had from the moment of the "curious case" of the *Alexandra* successfully enforced the British obligations of neutrality in the Home Islands. Their techniques of trial, seizure, threats, or negotiations were effective; no further violations of international law occurred after the *Alabama*'s departure.

Britain and France for reasons of self-interest articulated and enforced their neutrality precisely because of Confederate navy activity in Europe. In spite of themselves Bulloch and Semmes, Barron and Maury forced two great maritime powers to write new laws that entered the corpus of international jurisprudence. And they did not even realize it.

Suppose it had been otherwise. Suppose the two governments had not so articulated and imposed their neutrality. Could the Confederate navy in Europe then have put together a fleet that would have changed the war's outcome? There were too many negative forces aside from the French and British actions for the war to have been won from Europe.

Not the least of these was the Confederate government itself. Mallory had to fight for every dollar he got, and as Commander North reiterated over and over money was needed to coax cooperation out of the shipbuilders. Furthermore, until late in the war failure to establish a clear command structure in Europe stimulated the explosive personalities among the navy officers there and led to duplication of effort and financial waste. Even when they did succeed in getting the kind of ship most critically needed in the South—the shallow-draft, small ironclad for river and harbor use—they faced the problem of steaming across 3,000 miles of open ocean and arriving at the battle site in fighting trim. This problem, as the *Stonewall* demonstrated, was never solved. But the ultimate determining factor was the industrial supremacy of the United States backed and inspired by the moral leadership of President Lincoln and, after 1 January 1863, by the moral impact of emancipation. That combination could have produced enough *Monitor*s to overwhelm a dozen *Stonewall*s.

The futility of the *Shenandoah* as she sailed the 17,000 miles from the American northwestern waters, south around Cape Horn, then northward toward Liverpool, her skipper too fearful to hail any vessel she met, was symbolic of the Confederate navy in Europe. Yet that navy, those men, did suffer in a cause they freely had chosen to support. They did produce the *Alabama,* and Raphael Semmes remains an intriguing, romantic figure. They did produce fighting ships according to the latest technology, containing at once all the advantages and disadvantages of innovation; if only they could have built the *Stonewall* in Mobile or Charleston or Wilmington! But no, the small shallow-draft ironclads were beaten by the waters before they could ever meet the enemy. This futility itself is instructive. It teaches, down through the years, that if a people need a navy, whether in the birth pangs of their independence or in its sustenance, they must possess their own resources to build, equip, arm and man those ships. They must not depend on other powers for them.

During those last weeks in March and April 1865, Bulloch still was busy preparing a naval offensive strike against the North, Semmes still was fighting against the North in Virginia, and Maury was en route to Texas with equipment for torpedoes to keep open one last Southern port. Each in his own way continued the war he had chosen to fight. Bulloch and Semmes and Maury—yes, and North and Barron—already had made their imprints on history. They are interesting fellows, and good to have known.

ℕotes

Preface

1. Volume 2 of Series II contains the correspondence between Secretary of the Navy Stephen R. Mallory and his various agents in Europe; volume 3 of Series II contains the Confederate State Department diplomatic correspondence; volumes 1–3 of Series I contain ships' logs and correspondence pertaining to ship cruises. Full bibliographical data for this, other published works, and archives mentioned in this Preface can be found in the Bibliography.

Introduction

1. United States, Department of the Navy, *Official Records of the Union and Confederate Navies in the War of the Rebellion,* 30 vols. and index (Washington, 1894–1927), series II, 2:151, Mallory to Davis, first annual report, 27 February 1862. Hereafter cited as *ORN* with Roman numeral to indicate the series, followed by Arabic numerals to indicate the volume and then the page, thus: *ORN,* II, 2:151.

2. Mallory to North, 17 May 1861, ibid., p. 70.

3. These figures are derived from an analysis of the records in United States, Department of the Navy, Office of Naval Records and Library, *Register of Officers of the Confederate States Navy: 1861–1865* (Washington, 1931). Hereafter cited as *Register of Officers.*

4. For the Erlanger loan, see Judith Fenner Gentry, "A Confederate Success in Europe: The Erlanger Loan," *Journal of Southern History* 36, no. 2 (May 1970): 158–88. Gentry presents a good discussion of the literature and draws new conclusions concerning the loan's yield to the Confederacy. For the impact of the loan on overseas purchases, see Samuel Bernard Thompson, *Confederate Purchasing Operations Abroad* (Chapel Hill, 1935), pp. 54–55 ff., and Richard Cecil Todd, *Confederate Finance* (Athens, Georgia, 1954), pp. 182–86. For the loan and

purchases specifically in Great Britain, see Richard I. Lester, *Confederate Finance and Purchasing in Great Britain* (Charlottesville, 1975), chap. 2.

5. For the various phases of the Confederate financial European operations, see Todd, *Finance*, chap. 6, especially pp. 175–76; Thompson, *Purchasing Operations*, chaps. 1, 3, and 4; Lester, *Finance and Purchasing*, chap. 1. For the Fraser, Trenholm and Company, see Todd, *Finance*, pp. 178–79 ff., and Thompson, *Purchasing Operations*, p. 9.

6. Bulloch to North, 28 December 1862, *ORN*, II, 2:323.

7. Thompson, *Purchasing Operations*, p. 7.

8. Mallory to North, 17 May 1861, *ORN*, II, 2:70.

9. See Frank L. Owsley, *King Cotton Diplomacy* (2nd ed., Chicago, 1959), for the evolution and early application of the King Cotton theory. For the cotton industry in England and France, see Arthur L. Dunham, *The Anglo-French Treaty of Commerce of 1860 and the Progress of the Industrial Revolution in France* (Ann Arbor, 1930); Claude Fohlen, *L'industrie textile au temps du Second Empire* (Paris, 1956); William O. Henderson, *The Lancashire Cotton Famine 1860–1865* (Manchester, 1934).

10. For the early consultation, see Russell to Cowley, 6 May 1861, Great Britain, Public Record Office, London, Foreign Office Series (hereafter cited as PRO, FO), 27/1375/553, and Cowley to Russell 7 May 1861, ibid., 27/1390/677; Thouvenel to Count de Flahaut, 11 May 1861, Archives du Ministère des Affaires Etrangères, Paris (hereafter cited as AMAE), Fonds Divers, Guerre des Etats-Unis, carton 1861. The Davis proclamation is in *ORN*, II, 3:96–97; the Lincoln one is in James D. Richardson, ed., *A Compilation of Messages and Papers of the Presidents, 1789–1897* (New York, 1896–99), 7:3215. For the British proclamation of neutrality, see Ephraim Douglas Adams, *Great Britain and the American Civil War* (2 vols., New York, 1925), 1:94–95; for the French one, see Archives de la Marine, Paris (hereafter cited as AM), BB⁴/1345/I.

11. This discussion of international and domestic law is based on several letters exchanged between Russell and Adams and on parliamentary debates in 1863, both of which are cited in later chapters, and on the Geneva tribunal decision located in Great Britain, House of Commons, *Parliamentary Papers,* Irish University Press Area Studies Series (hereafter cited as IUP Area Studies), *The United States of America*, 58:13–18. The principle that a neutral government is obligated to protect its neutrality despite the inefficacy of its domestic law was long-standing. For the historical development of the principle, see Philip C. Jessup and Francis Deák, *Neutrality: Its History, Economics and Law* (4 vols., New York, 1935), vol. 1, chap. 8, pp. 249–50 ff. Case histories of the principle's development are in Publications of the Navy Records Society, vol. 49, *Documents Relating to Law and Custom of the Sea,* ed. Reginald G. Marsden (2 vols., London, 1915), vol. 1, especially pp. xxiv and 353–54 ff. Legal commentary on the principle prior to the Civil War can be found in Robert Phillimore, *Commentaries upon International Law* (3rd ed., Philadelphia, 1854), 1:79, 92. The only secondary discussion of the principle as it applied to the Civil War is Charles Francis Adams, Jr., "The Treaty of Washington," *Lee at Appomattox and Other Papers* (Cambridge, Mass., 1902), pp. 31–198. Lacking many pertinent documents, C. F. Adams, Jr., did not consistently apply the principle to British actions, but he did

prove that it was an issue during the war. This perceptive article is curiously overlooked by the historians mentioned above in the Preface and below in notes to Chapters 2 and 4. That the principle continued to be a live issue during the negotiation and ratification of the 1871 Treaty of Washington, which established the rules for the Geneva arbitration, is clearly illustrated in the parliamentary debates of 1870–71, especially the comments of Earl Russell (Great Britain, *Hansard Parliamentary Debates*, 3rd series, 206:1823–24 ff.) and Sir Roundell Palmer (ibid., 203:1378). For a complete account of the various issues in the negotiations and ratification of the Treaty of Washington, see Goldwin Smith, *The Treaty of Washington 1871* (Ithaca, N.Y., 1941), and Adrian Cook, *The Alabama Claims. American Politics and Anglo-American Relations, 1865–1872* (Ithaca, 1975).

12. These introductory comments are general knowledge. Allan Nevins, *The War for the Union* (New York, 1960), vol. 2, chap. 10, despite some errors is the best short account; he is especially good on Palmerston, Russell, and public opinion. See also E. D. Adams, *Britain and the Civil War*, and Owsley, *Cotton Diplomacy*. The more recent biographies of Palmerston are Jasper Ridley, *Lord Palmerston* (London, 1970), and Donald Southgate, *"The Most English Minister . . ." The Policies and Politics of Palmerston* (New York, 1966); for Russell, see Spencer Walpole, *Life of Lord John Russell* (2 vols., New York, 1889); A. Wyatt Tilby, *Lord John Russell: A Study in Civil and Religious Liberty* (New York, 1931); John M. Prest, *Lord John Russell* (London, 1972). See also Norman B. Ferris, *Desperate Diplomacy: William H. Seward's Foreign Policy, 1861* (Knoxville, 1976) and *The Trent Affair: A Diplomatic Crisis* (Knoxville, 1977).

13. For these introductory remarks on France, see Lynn M. Case, *French Opinion on War and Peace During the Second Empire* (Philadelphia, 1954); Lynn M. Case and Warren F. Spencer, *The United States and France: Civil War Diplomacy* (Philadelphia, 1970); Henry Blumenthal, *France and the United States: Their Diplomatic Relations, 1789–1914* (New York, 1970), bk. 1, chap. 5; Lynn M. Case, ed., *French Opinion on the United States and Mexico, 1861–1867. Reports of the procureurs généraux* (New York, 1936); Lynn M. Case, *Edouard Thouvenel et la Diplomatie du Second Empire* (Paris, 1976); Daniel B. Carroll, *Henri Mercier and the American Civil War* (Princeton, 1971); Warren R. West, *Contemporary French Opinion on the American Civil War* (Baltimore, 1924); Nancy Nichols Barker, "France, Austria and the Mexican Venture," *French Historical Studies* 3 (1963): 224–45; Alfred Jackson Hanna and Kathryn Abbey Hanna, *Napoleon III and Mexico* (Chapel Hill, 1971).

14. See Kenneth Bourne, *Britain and the Balance of Power in North America 1815–1908* (Berkeley and Los Angeles, 1967), chaps. 7 and 8, and Stuart L. Bernath, *Squall Across the Atlantic* (Berkeley and Los Angeles, 1970).

15. Palmerston to Russell, 30 December 1860 and 18 October 1861, Great Britain, Public Record Office, Russell Papers (hereafter cited as PRO, Russell Papers), 30/22/21 and 30/22/14.

16. See for instance James D. Bulloch, *The Secret Service of the Confederate States in Europe or How the Confederate Cruisers Were Equipped* (2 vols., Liverpool, 1883; reprint, New York and London, 1959), 2:48–51.

17. For Adams and Dudley in England, see Frank J. Merli, *Great Britain and the Confederate Navy 1861–1865* (Bloomington, 1970), especially his bibliographical essay on Adams. For Dayton and Bigelow in France, see Case and Spencer, *Civil War Diplomacy.*

18. For the first three commissioners see Owsley, *Cotton Diplomacy,* pp. 52–53 ff.; for a bibliographical treatment of Slidell and Mason, see Merli, *Britain and the Confederate Navy,* p. 276. My characterizations of Slidell and Mason are derived largely from their correspondence and will emerge in the following chapters.

Chapter 1
Confederate Naval Activity in Europe:
The First Phase, 1861

1. This biographical section is based on the introduction (pp. x–xi) by Philip Van Doren Stern to Bulloch, *Secret Service,* which in effect is Bulloch's memoir.

2. For the quotes see ibid., 1:31–32,33.

3. Ibid., p. 41. Bulloch does not mention his wife, yet she was with him in Liverpool.

4. Eric Midwinter, *Victorian Social Reform* (New York and London, 1968), p. 5.

5. Bulloch, *Secret Service,* 1:52–53 ff.

6. Ibid., pp. 57, 58–63. For the *Florida* and *Alabama* origins, see Bulloch to Mallory, 13 August 1861, *ORN,* II, 2:83–87. The *Florida* originally was called the *Oreto* and the *Alabama* frequently was referred to as Number 290; the ships will be referred to here by their final historical names only.

7. Bulloch to Mallory, 13 August 1861, *ORN,* II, 2:85.

8. Mallory to North, 17 May 1861, ibid., pp. 70–72.

9. James H. North Diary, University of North Carolina Library, Southern History Collection #862, Chapel Hill, enclosed passport for James H. North. Hereafter cited as North Diary followed by entry dates. The author is grateful to J. North Fletcher, Warrenton, Virginia, for permission to quote from the North Diary.

10. Ibid., 22 March and 4 April 1861.

11. Ibid., 13, 21, and 25 May 1861; telegram is enclosed in diary.

12. Edward C. Anderson, *Confederate Foreign Agent: The European Diary of Major Edward C. Anderson,* ed. with prologue and epilogue by W. Stanley Hoole (University, Ala., 1976), p. 2. Hereafter cited as Anderson Diary followed by entry dates.

13. Paragraph based on North Diary, last entry (undated) and various entries during June and July 1861.

14. Ibid., 25 and 26 July 1861.

15. North to Mallory, *ORN,* II, 2:87. Editor's date of 16 August 1861 is inaccurate because on that date North was at sea aboard the *Camilla* en route to France.

16. Anderson Diary, 2 August 1861.

17. North Diary, 8 and 6 August 1861.

18. Ibid., 7 and 16 August 1861.

19. North's Paris activities are covered in ibid., entries from 17 August through 15 November 1861.

20. Ibid., 25 September 1861, and North to Mallory, telegram, [n.d.] September 1861, *ORN*, II, 2:88.

21. North Diary, 5 October 1861.

22. Mallory to North, 27 September 1861, *ORN*, II, 2:95–96.

23. Anderson Diary, 2 and 11 September 1861.

24. North Diary, 8 and 9 October 1861; and North to Bulloch, 9 October 1861, *ORN*, II, 2:97–98.

25. Bulloch to North, 9 October 1861, *ORN*, II, 2:98–99.

26. North Diary, 8 and 10 October 1861; Anderson Diary, 10 October 1861, for "utterly demoralized."

27. Bulloch to Mallory, Richmond, 19 November 1861, *ORN*, II, 2:105.

28. See Bulloch, *Secret Service*, 1:132–41, for an account of Bulloch's activities within the Confederacy.

29. Mallory to North, 20 November 1861, *ORN*, II, 2:106.

30. The most complete account of the *Trent* affair is Ferris, *Trent Affair*. See Merli, *Britain and the Confederate Navy*, pp. 74–85, for a scholarly account and especially pp. 85–86 for the effect upon the Confederate navy in England. See also Case and Spencer, *Civil War Diplomacy*, pp. 191–94. For the British military decisions, see Ferris, *Trent Affair*, chap. 6, "England Mobilizes for War," especially pp. 65–66, and Bourne, *Britain and the Balance of Power*, pp. 251–87 for British military plans and concerns for Canada during the Civil War, and pp. 218–47 for British military and naval planning specifically in response to the *Trent* crisis. For reactions in Canada see Brian Jenkins, *Britain and the War for the Union* (2 vols., Montreal and London, 1974; Montreal, 1980), 1:199–203.

31. Mallory to Bulloch, 13 January 1862, *ORN*, II, 2:130.

32. Pegram to North, 20 November 1861, ibid., p. 112.

33. North to Mallory, 16 March 1862, ibid., p. 167.

34. Semmes to North, 26 February 1862, ibid., pp. 148–49. The Hotze quote is in E. D. Adams, *Britain and the Civil War*, 1:243.

35. This impression was derived from all of the above works cited on the *Trent* affair, especially Ferris, *Trent Affair*, p. 194. For the *Trent* affair's favorable impact on British officials, see Ferris's excellent evaluation (pp. 193–98); this case stimulated the British government's closer surveillance over Confederate naval activities in the British Isles.

36. Bulloch, *Secret Service*, 1:144–51.

37. This account of the *Nashville* is based on a long letter written 2 March 1862 by the *Nashville*'s third officer, CSN Lieutenant William C. Whittle, Jr., to his father in Beaufort, N.C.; the letter is in the William Conway Whittle Papers, University of Virginia Library, Manuscripts Department, No. 3973, MSS ViU 661233 (hereafter cited as William Conway Whittle Papers). The letter recounts the *Nashville*'s voyage across the Atlantic, her stay in Southampton, and her return to the Confederacy. Whittle's account is more detailed than Lieutenant Pegram's official reports, which are in *ORN*, I, 1:745–52.

38. David Paul Crook, *The North, the South, and the Powers 1861–1865* (New York, London, Sydney, and Toronto, 1974), p. 118, suggests the decoy mission. See also W. C. Whittle, Jr., to W. C. Whittle, Sr., 2 March 1862, William Conway Whittle Papers; Caleb Huse, *Supplies for the Confederate Army, How They Were Obtained in Europe and How Paid For. Personal Reminiscences and Unpublished History* (Boston, 1904), pp. 32–33; Ferris, *Trent Affair*, p. 213, n. 3.

39. G. G. Gardner to H. Waddington, Customs House, 6 December 1861, copy enclosed in Adams to Seward, 11 December 1861, no. 11, National Archives, Washington, Foreign Office Division, State Department Correspondence, Despatches from U.S. Ministers to Great Britain (hereafter cited as SDC Despatches Gr. Br.), vol. 78; and C. J. E. Patey, Southampton, to Secretary of the Admiralty, 23 December 1861, copy enclosed in Adams to Seward, 2 January 1862, no. 97, ibid.

40. Ferris, *Trent Affair*, pp. 37–41; Wilbur Devereux Jones, *The Confederate Rams at Birkenhead: A Chapter in Anglo-American Relations* (Tuscaloosa, 1961), pp. 27–28. Both books are based on extensive archival documentation but neither mentions Russell's statement on international law or that this was the first test of the Foreign Enlistment Act. Many of the documents used by Ferris and Jones are also in the State Department Correspondence as enclosures in Adams's dispatches to Seward. Other recent scholars have overlooked the *Nashville* episode. Neither Merli (*Britain and the Confederate Navy*) nor Lester (*Finance and Purchasing*) mentions the ship or the diplomatic exchanges it stimulated; Crook (*Powers*, p. 118) simply states the results of the exchanges as if they already were well-established and well-applied practices toward Confederate warships and he makes no references to the diplomacy involved. Jenkins (*Britain and the War*, vol. 1) does not mention the diplomatic exchanges prompted by the *Nashville*. See above, Introduction, n. 11.

41. Crook (*Powers*, p. 118) suggests this possibility. Adams did note that other issues such as the *Nashville* should be put aside in view of the *Trent* issues (Ferris, *Trent Affair*, p. 49 and n. 33).

42. Russell to Adams, 28 November 1861, copy enclosed in Adams to Seward, 29 November 1861, no. 79, SDC Despatches Gr. Br., vol. 78. This letter is reproduced in its entirety in Charles C. Beaman, Jr., *The National and Private "Alabama Claims" and Their "Final and Amicable Settlement"* (Washington, 1871), p. 203, but Beaman makes no specific references to the quoted sentence. Ferris (*Trent Affair*, pp. 37–41), whose emphasis is not on maritime activities and on whose work this paragraph largely is based, makes no reference to Russell's 28 November letter, nor does Jones (*Confederate Rams*, pp. 27–28) in his otherwise excellent discussion of the issues raised by the *Nashville*. The importance of this statement will be developed below in the sections on the *Florida* and in Chapter 2.

43. Adams to Seward, 2 January 1862, no. 97, SDC Despatches Gr. Br., vol. 78.

44. This account is based on W. C. Whittle, Jr., to his father, 2 March 1862, William Conway Whittle Papers. This account is more detailed than Pegram's official report, especially on crew activities.

45. Adams to Seward, 17 January 1862, no. 103, SDC Despatches Gr. Br., vol. 78, which enclosed a copy of Russell to Adams, 10 January 1862.

46. The material on Semmes and the cruise of the *Sumter* is based on Charles Grayson Summersell, *The Cruise of the C.S.S. Sumter* (Tuscaloosa, 1965), because it incorporates all the material from the previously published works on Semmes, and on Admiral Raphael Semmes, *Memoirs of Service Afloat During the War Between the States* (Baltimore, 1869), because it reflects Semmes's immediate wartime thoughts and contains many valuable documents. The memoirs of Semmes's first lieutenant are unfortunately very uninformative (John McIntosh Kell, *Recollections of a Naval Life Including the Cruises of the Confederate States Steamers "Sumter" and "Alabama"* [Washington, 1900]). See also *ORN*, I, 1:613–744, for the cruise of the *Sumter*.

47. Bulloch to Mallory, 11 April 1862, *ORN*, II, 2:183–84.

48. Ibid., pp. 284–97; *ORN*, I, 1:652–59.

49. Semmes, *Memoirs*, p. 304.

50. Summersell, *Cruise of the Sumter*, p. 154. If a U.S. merchant ship carried bona fide neutral goods, the Confederate cruiser captain could not destroy the ship or the goods. He then "bonded" the ship, which meant his government, when it was capable of doing so, would later claim the ship (but not the goods) as a prize in maritime court.

51. Semmes, *Memoirs*, chaps. 24–26.

52. Ibid., pp. 334–35.

53. Ibid., p. 347.

54. Summersell, *Cruise of the Sumter*, pp. 168–71, details the tragedy of Andrews and Hester; he uses the *ORN* plus United States State Department and British Foreign Office documents.

55. Summersell, *Cruise of the Sumter*, pp. 171–76.

56. Semmes, *Memoirs*, pp. 347–48 ff.

Chapter 2
The First Cruisers: January–July 1862

1. Various letters from North during January–March 1862, *ORN*, II, 2:125–47.

2. Bulloch to Mallory, Charleston, 22 January 1862, ibid., pp. 134–35.

3. North to Mallory, 29 March 1862, ibid., pp. 176–77.

4. Mallory to North, 5 May 1862, ibid., p. 191. There is no way of knowing when North received this letter because he did not acknowledge the promotion until late in 1862.

5. Bulloch's instructions of 10 October 1861, quoted in Fraser, Trenholm and Company to North, 5 February 1862, *ORN*, II, 2:142–43.

6. Mallory to North, 20 November 1861, *ORN*, II, 2:106, and Mallory to Bulloch, 30 November 1861, ibid., p. 113.

7. Bulloch to Mallory, Savannah, 13 January 1862, ibid., p. 130.

8. Prioleau to North, 9 January 1862, ibid., pp. 125–26; North to Mallory, 27 January 1862, ibid., p. 138; Semmes to North, telegram, 2 February 1862, ibid., p. 140.

9. Two letters, Prioleau to North, 3 and 5 February 1862, ibid., pp. 141–42.

10. Prioleau's two letters, ibid., and North to Mason, 6 February 1862, ibid., p. 144.

11. Based on two letters, Prioleau to North, 2 and 20 February 1862, and North to Mallory, 8 February 1862, ibid., pp. 145–47.

12. Merli, *Britain and the Confederate Navy*, pp. 67–68. Merli's research is thorough and fully establishes the fact of Dudley's activity; that material is all that is necessary to this story of the Confederate navy.

13. Huse to North, telegram, 22 February 1862, and North to Mallory, 22 February 1862, *ORN*, II, 2:147; North to W. T. Mann, 28 February 1862, Mann to North, 1 March 1862, and North to Mallory, 16 March 1862, ibid., pp. 160–61, 166–67.

14. Bulloch, *Secret Service*, 1:150–51.

15. This assignment was contained in a dispatch received by Bulloch just before he left Savannah, Mallory to Bulloch, 14 January 1862, *ORN*, II, 2:131. See Chapter 4.

16. Bulloch, *Secret Service*, 1:156.

17. Ibid., pp. 152–54.

18. Russell to Adams, 27 March 1862, enclosed in Adams to Seward, 3 April 1862, no. 140, SDC Despatches Gr. Br., vol. 79. Merli, *Britain and the Confederate Navy*, pp. 68–69, covers these events and cites Russell's letter but does not refer to the last quote. See above, Introduction, n. 11.

19. The documents for this trial are in the PRO, FO, 5/1313 and 5/1314. These documents and others have been used extensively by Frank L. Owsley, Jr., *The C.S.S. Florida Her Building and Operations* (Philadelphia, 1965). See also Merli, *Britain and the Confederate Navy*, pp. 71–72, for a brief account.

20. Bulloch, *Secret Service*, 1:156.

21. Bulloch to Low, 21 March 1862, ibid., pp. 157–59; also in *ORN*, I, 1:755–56.

22. The details of Low's life are based on William Stanley Hoole, *Four years in the Confederate Navy: The Career of Captain John Low on the C.S.S. Fingal, Florida, Alabama, Tuscaloosa, and Ajax* (Athens, Ga., 1964). This work does not stress the family relationships as they relate to Low's naval duties.

23. There were other Southerners with relatives on both sides of the Atlantic: CSN Commander Matthew Fontaine Maury had relatives in both England and France. See Anderson Diary, pp. 32, 141 n. for Hoole's indication of family connections between France and New Orleans.

24. Bulloch, *Secret Service*, 1:154–55.

25. For the *Florida* story in Nassau and on the high seas, see F. L. Owsley, Jr., *C.S.S. Florida*, and Merli, *Britain and the Confederate Navy*, pp. 70–73. The documents are in *ORN*, I, 1:753–70, and in *ORN*, I, 2:639–58.

26. Bulloch to Maffitt, 21 March 1862, *ORN*, I, 1:756, and Bulloch to North, 14 March 1862, ibid., II, 2:166; Bulloch to Mallory, 11 April 1862, ibid., II, 2:184.

27. See Thompson, *Purchasing Operations*, pp. 48–55, and Lester, *Finance and Purchasing*, pp. 3–22.

28. For the impact of Bulloch's reflections on the Confederate navy ironclad procurement policy, see Chapter 4.

29. Bulloch, *Secret Service*, 1:256; Bulloch to Mallory, 19 April 1862, *ORN*, II, 2:185.

30. Bulloch to North, 18 May 1862, *ORN*, II, 2:192–93; for the contract, see ibid., p. 295; for details see Chapter 4.

31. Bulloch, *Secret Service*, 1:230–33.

32. Ibid., p. 232.

33. The intensification of Union information-gathering techniques is reflected in the enclosures mostly from Dudley that Adams sent to Russell, various letters in SDC Despatches Gr. Br., vols. 79 and 80. The British government's increased activity is reflected in the Papers Relating to the *Alabama* in Her Majesty's Custom and Excise Library, London, some copies of which are enclosed in Adams to Seward correspondence in the SDC Despatches Gr. Br., vol. 79. Merli, *Britain and the Confederate Navy*, pp. 90–91, uses these and other sources to summarize these efforts. See also Bulloch, *Secret Service*, 1:238, 229.

34. Bulloch to North, 11 June 1862, *ORN*, II, 2:206; Bulloch, *Secret Service*, 1:233.

35. Semmes to Mallory, Nassau, 15 June 1862, Semmes, *Memoirs*, pp. 351–53; Semmes to North, Nassau, 8 June 1862, *ORN*, I, 1:771; Mallory to North, 2 May 1862, *ORN*, II, 2:188; Mallory to Bulloch, 20 April and 3 May 1862, *ORN*, II, 2:186–187 and 190.

36. Mallory to Bulloch, 29 May 1862, *ORN*, II, 2:205.

37. Semmes to Mallory, 15 June 1862, Semmes, *Memoirs*, p. 353.

38. Bulloch to North, 17 June 1862, *ORN*, II, 2:207.

39. Bulloch to North, 11 June 1862, ibid., p. 206.

40. North to Bulloch, 14 June 1862, ibid., p. 297.

41. Bulloch to North, 17 June 1862, ibid., p. 207; North to Thomson, 18 June 1862, ibid., p. 208.

42. North to Bulloch, Liverpool, 26 June 1862, ibid., p. 209, and Bulloch to North, Liverpool, 27 June 1862, ibid.; Bulloch to Mallory, 4 July 1862, and North to Mallory, 5 July 1862, ibid., pp. 212–13.

43. Bulloch, *Secret Service*, 1:236.

44. Bulloch to North, 8 July 1862, *ORN*, II, 2:213.

45. Bulloch to North, 10 July 1862, ibid., pp. 214–15.

46. Bulloch, *Secret Service*, 1:236–44. There are many secondary accounts of the *Alabama*'s escape and cruise, some scholarly and some overly romanticized. This account is based on the official sources listed in n. 33 above and on the story as told by the participants.

47. Bulloch to Yonge, 28 July 1862, ibid., pp. 249–50.

48. Ibid., p. 253.

49. Bulloch to Mallory, 11 August 1862, *ORN*, II, 2:235–39.

50. Semmes, *Memoirs*, p. 402; Semmes to North, Liverpool, 11 August 1862, *ORN*, II, 2:239.

51. Bulloch to Mallory, 21 July 1862, *ORN*, II, 2:226; Arthur Sinclair, *Two Years on the Alabama* (Boston, 1896), p. 127. Sinclair maintained that the "stack of gold on hand at the end of the cruise was much larger than at the outset, being recruited by the sale of the prize *Sea Bride* and cargo, and also by smaller sums secured from prizes at sundry times." See Sinclair, pp. 153, 165, 251, and

Semmes, *Memoirs*, p. 666, for the *Sea Bride* story. It was the only Confederate prize ever sold. Sinclair's reference to gold is substantiated by the deposition of a sailor who refused at Praya Bay to sign aboard a Confederate cruiser and who then returned to England. He said that "two chests full of money in gold" were transferred from the *Bahama* to the *Alabama* (Deposition of Henry Redden, enclosure no. 2 in Adams to Russell, 4 September 1862, *Parliamentary Papers, Correspondence Respecting the Alabama*, 1863, in IUP Area Studies Series, *The United States*, 17:108).

52. For these officer assignments, see Semmes, *Memoirs*, pp. 416–17. Sinclair (*Two Years*, pp. 343–52) lists all officers and crew and (pp. 297–338) gives a biographical sketch of each officer. See also Semmes to North, Nassau, 8 June 1862, *ORN*, I, 1:771.

53. *Register of Officers*, pp. 180–81.

54. Bulloch to Mallory, 10 September 1862, *ORN*, II, 2:263–64. The *Florida* did not leave Mobile until 17 January 1863.

55. United States, Congress, House, *Papers Relating to the Foreign Relations of the United States*, pt. 2, 42d Cong., 3d sess., exec. doc. 1, pt. 1, *Papers Relating to the Treaty of Washington*, 4 vols., vol. 1, *Geneva Arbitration* (Washington, 1872), p. 14. Hereafter cited as *FRUS, Geneva Arbitration*. A more convenient source is IUP Area Studies, *The United States*, 56:14; the arbitral decision quote is on p. 314. See above, Introduction, n. 11.

56. R. C. Jarvis, "The *Alabama* and the Law," *Transactions of the Historical Society of Lancashire and Cheshire* 3 (1959): 198.

57. Ibid.

58. *FRUS, Geneva Arbitration*, 1:325; also in IUP Area Studies, *The United States*, 56:205–06; see also Jones, *Confederate Rams*, p. 37. It has not been the intention in this chapter to afford "intriguing insights into official thinking at the British Foreign Office and admiralty" (Crook, *Powers*, p. 385) nor to describe the day-to-day activities and decisions of Russell, Adams, the law officers, or Dudley—all of which is basically peripheral to the story of the Confederate navy. Besides, others already have done it (see Merli, *Britain and the Confederate Navy*, pp. 91–92; Jones, *Confederate Rams;* E. D. Adams, *Britain and the Civil War*, 2:119–21; Jenkins, *Britain and the War*, 2:120–23). But no work heretofore has related all the Confederate naval activity to British policy evolution. See Chapter 4.

Chapter 3
The Hope-filled Era: First Ironclad
Construction, July–December 1862

1. See Introduction. George Mercer Brooke, Jr., states that Mallory's orders to Lieutenant North were "the same as those which [Lieutenant John M.] Brooke had proposed to Mallory eleven days earlier" ("John Mercer Brooke, Naval Scientist" [2 vols., Ph.D. diss., University of North Carolina, 1955]).

2. This information is from James Phinney Baxter, 3rd, *The Introduction of the Ironclad Warship* (Cambridge, Mass., 1933), introduction.

3. Ibid., p. 3. The following paragraphs are based extensively on this work, especially pp. 78, 90, 110–11, 112–15, 140–80, 100, 109, 158–59, 185, 188, 192, 327, and 194 respectively. Only direct quotes will be further noted.

4. Ibid., pp. 113, 115.

5. Ibid., pp. 24, 66.

6. For Mallory's expectations, see Mallory to Conrad, 8 May 1861, *ORN*, II, 1:742; for the quotes, see Baxter, *Introduction of the Ironclad*, p. 110 and note.

7. Baxter, *Introduction of the Ironclad*, pp. 285, 181.

8. Bulloch to Mallory, 14 March 1862 and 11 April 1862, *ORN*, II, 2:165 and 183–84.

9. Baxter (*Introduction of the Ironclad*, pp. 315–16, 325) affirms this action but attributes it to the high cost of constructing new ships.

10. Mallory to North, 27 September 1861, *ORN*, II, 2:96. See Baxter (*Introduction of the Ironclad*, pp. 233–35) for the 1861 ironclad building efforts within the Confederacy.

11. Mallory to Bulloch, 20 September 1862, *ORN*, II, 2:271.

12. James H. North was promoted to the rank of commander on 5 May 1862 (Mallory to North, ibid., p. 191) but did not learn of the promotion until the end of August (North to Mallory, 30 August 1862, ibid., p. 255).

13. Semmes to North, 11 August 1862, ibid., p. 239. This note was written apparently at North's request when Semmes had returned to take command of the *Alabama;* it referred to a meeting between the two "last April."

14. North to Thomson, 11 April 1862, ibid., p. 182. The ship plans were completed by 9 May (Thomson to North, 9 May 1862, ibid., p. 193).

15. This paragraph is based on North's explanation of 25 July 1862 to Mallory (ibid., p. 228), written after Semmes had assumed the *Alabama*'s command. North's request for the 200,000 pounds is in ibid., p. 185, 14 April 1862; the date he learned of the real purpose of the funds is inferred from his letter to Bulloch, 26 June 1862, ibid., p. 209. In the 1860s 200,000 pounds were roughly equivalent to 2,000,000 dollars.

16. See Merli, *Britain and the Confederate Navy*, chap. 7, where there is an excellent, illustrated description of the ship on pp. 138–42; also see Merli et al., "The South's Scottish Sea Monster," *American Neptune* 29, no. 1 (1969): 5–29, where the derogatory epithet first was applied to North's ship, and especially pp. 12–14 for the Confederate financial crisis. Nowhere does Merli relate this ship to North's original orders nor does he compare it to the French ships.

17. Bulloch to Mallory, 21 July 1862, *ORN*, II, 2:223. Bulloch had no way of knowing of Dupuy de Lôme's limitation on the *Gloire*'s operating range, but such reservations about the seagoing qualities of iron ships were common among European mariners.

18. Merli, *Britain and the Confederate Navy*, p. 142.

19. Bulloch to North, 28 May 1862, *ORN*, II, 2:192.

20. For Stringer's relationship to Lindsay and Company, see Mallory to Barron, 29 August 1863, ibid., p. 484. For Mason's comment, see his letter to Benjamin, 18 September 1862, ibid., 3:529. For the Lindsay-Roebuck French overtures, see Case and Spencer, *Civil War Diplomacy*, chap. 12, *passim*.

21. Anderson Diary, p. 63.

22. North to Mallory, 11 November 1862, *ORN*, II, 2:295.

23. Bulloch to Mallory, 4 July 1862, ibid., p. 212.

24. North-Thomson contract, ibid., p. 199.

25. For Bulloch's payments, see ibid., pp. 228–29; North to Mallory, 25 July 1862, ibid., pp. 228–29; Bulloch to Mallory, 24 September 1862, ibid., p. 275; Bulloch to North, 28 December 1862, ibid., p. 322. For the financial crisis, see Todd, *Finance*, pp. 175–93; Thompson, *Purchasing Operations*, pp. 50–61; Merli, *Britain and the Confederate Navy*, pp. 143–47; Merli et al., "Scottish Sea Monster," pp. 15–18.

26 North to Mallory, 22 December 1862, *ORN*, II, 2:318. For the criticism of North, see Merli, *Britain and the Confederate Navy*, p. 142.

27. The commanding officer of the French ironclad frigate, *Normandie*, the first ironclad to cross the Atlantic, referred to coal as an armored ship's "first munition of war" (Frank J. Merli and Charles S. Williams, eds. and trans., "The *Normandie* Shows the Way: Report of a Voyage from Cherbourg to Vera Cruz, 4 September 1862," *Mariner's Mirror*, 54, no. 2 [1968]: 160).

28. North to Thomson, 15 August 1862, *ORN*, II, 2:240.

29. Three letters, North to Mallory, 30 August, 19 September, and 22 December 1862, ibid., pp. 255, 269, 318.

30. Two letters, North to Mallory, 30 August and 19 September 1862, ibid., pp. 255, 268–69.

31. Two letters, North to Thomson, 6 and 24 November 1862, ibid., pp. 291, 301.

32. These two letters are in their original chronological order in ibid., pp. 168–69 and 272–73.

33. Mallory to North, 2 October 1862, ibid., pp. 278–79.

34. Mallory to North, 26 October 1862, ibid., pp. 283–84.

35. North to Mallory, 22 December 1862, ibid., pp. 315–19.

36. Bulloch to Mallory, 28 December 1862, ibid., p. 323.

37. Bulloch to North, 18 May 1862, ibid., p. 193.

38. Bulloch, *Secret Service*, 1:383.

39. Baxter, *Introduction of the Ironclad*, pp. 33–35, 179.

40. Bulloch to Mallory, 21 July 1862, *ORN*, II, 2:222–24. Except as otherwise noted, the following material on the contract and on the ships comes from this source.

41. In a cyphered paragraph of a dispatch dated 4 July 1862 (ibid., p. 212), Bulloch reported to Mallory: "Have contracted for three armored ships." This message led to some confusion on Mallory's part because he did not know whether Bulloch had contracted for three ships in addition to North's Number 61.

42. Bulloch, *Secret Service*, 1:386–87.

43. Merli, *Britain and the Confederate Navy*, p. 318. Professor Merli's diligent scholarship uncovered this indefinite description not in a Confederate source but in a second-hand account by a sailor who saw one of the ships launched and whose description is in the British Home Office files at the Public Record Office

(PRO, HO 45/7261, box 2). Oscar Parkes (*British Battleships* [London, 1970], pp. 77–81) in his detailed description of the two ships gives no dimensions of the rams.

44. Mallory to Bulloch, 20 September 1862, *ORN*, II, 2:271; Bulloch to Mallory, 24 September 1862, ibid., p. 277; Bulloch to Mallory, 18 December 1862, ibid., p. 309.

45. Bulloch, *Secret Service*, 1:386–88, and Bulloch to Mallory, 2 December 1862, *ORN*, II, 2:307.

46. Two letters, Bulloch to Mallory, 11 August and 7 November 1862, *ORN*, II, 2:237 and 293; Mallory to Bulloch, 3 October 1862, ibid., p. 279.

47. See Douglas H. Maynard, "The Confederacy's Super *Alabama*," *Civil War History* 5, no. 1 (March 1959): 81. The ship, first named the *Canton*, was referred to secretly as the *Texas* and later renamed the *Pampero* to conceal its Southern connection. Here it will be called the *Canton* throughout.

48. North Diary, 23 March 1861.

49. Anderson Diary, 12 December 1861.

50. Mallory to North, 12 July 1862, *ORN*, II, 2:215. North never received this letter and Mallory rescinded the order after learning of the contract for Number 61 (ibid., p. 229, 29 July 1862). Secretary Mallory, though, would have been no better satisfied with Sinclair than with North; he twice complained to Commodore Barron that he had had no news of Sinclair's ship (Whittle Papers, Kirn Memorial Public Library, Norfolk, Virginia [hereafter cited as Whittle Papers], folder III, nos. 4 and 5, Mallory to Barron, 28 October and 3 December 1863).

51. Bulloch, *Secret Service*, 2:249, 260, 272.

52. The story of private contractors unfolds from *ORN*, II, 2:235, and Bulloch *Secret Service*, 2:245, 250–52.

53. Maury's activities are discussed in Chapter 5.

54. *ORN*, II, 2:220–21, 226–27.

55. For Sanders's relationship to the various Confederate government departments, see the correspondence concerning Sanders, all to Mason, from Secretary of State Benjamin, 28 October 1862; from Secretary of the Treasury C. G. Memminger, 24 October 1862; with enclosures of cotton certificate forms, 25 October 1862; from Secretary of the Navy Mallory, 26 October 1862, all in IUP Area Studies, *The United States*, 17:492–96. These documents were intercepted by the United States and submitted to Lord John Russell by United States Minister Charles Francis Adams; they do not appear in the *ORN* or in any Confederate collection and have not been used by other scholars in relation to the Sinclair contract or to Sanders's mission to England. See Maynard ("Super *Alabama*"), who despite an excellent analysis of Sinclair's contract nowhere mentions the Sanders mission; Lester (*Finance and Purchasing*, pp. 18–19) refers to Sanders as an agent of Mallory only and does not relate him to Sinclair's contract, nor does Merli (*Britain and the Confederate Navy*, pp. 144–46).

56. North to Mallory, 11 November 1862, *ORN*, II, 2:295; Mason to Benjamin and Mason to Mallory, both 18 September 1862, ibid., 3:530–32. Merli (*Britain and the Confederate Navy*, pp. 144–46) in discussing the Confederate navy's financial problems presents a detailed account of North's presumed opportunity

to raise a large amount of money, citing the same *ORN* sources cited here, but he does not identify Stringer as North's contact. Sanders returned to the Confederacy for instructions and was never able to implement his scheme.

57. Lester, *Finance and Purchasing,* pp. 18–19; Merli (*Britain and the Confederate Navy,* pp. 120–21) does not mention Sanders nor does he relate the cotton certificate scheme to Sinclair's financing.

58. Mason to Mallory, 18 November 1862, *ORN,* II, 3:532. Mason explained in one paragraph that Sanders would raise money through the cotton manufacturers, and in the next paragraph he explained that he approved Sinclair's scheme "because it involved a comparatively small expenditure"; he added: "I have therefore advised him that the necessary funds should be raised through William [S.] Lindsay and Company by means of those cotton bonds" (ibid.). Maynard ("Super *Alabama,*" p. 81) explains briefly the role of the Lindsay company in Sinclair's financing and establishes the seven-man combine as the actual owners of the ship, but he does not explain the sale of the certificates directly to the cotton manufacturers; he fails to mention Stringer, Sanders, or North.

59. Bulloch to Mallory, 16 May 1863, *ORN,* II, 2:424. Bulloch was recapping earlier events.

60. Lester (*Finance and Purchasing,* pp. 19–23), in discussing "Cotton as a basis for [Confederate] Credit" and citing British business archives and periodicals, establishes the Sinclair loan as the basis for the Erlanger loan and the appointment of Spence as the sole Confederate agent to handle the cotton certificates. See also Todd, *Finance,* pp. 179–86, and Thompson, *Purchasing Operations,* pp. 51–54.

61. Sinclair to North, 29 January and 2 February 1863, *ORN,* II, 2:347 and 349.

Chapter 4
British Neutrality Tightens: 1863–1864

1. Although scholars identify the turning point of the war with Lee's defeat at Antietam on 17 September 1862, especially as it affected the British cabinet's informal discussion on intervention, the contemporaries in Europe did not at the time fully realize this. Even Lord Palmerston considered that decision only to be postponed (Case and Spencer, *Civil War Diplomacy,* p. 363). For the Confederates in Europe the year 1863 was filled with hope until the autumn.

2. For an evaluation of these diplomatic shifts, see Case and Spencer, ibid., pp. 399–403. For the Austrian view, see ibid., p. 400, n. 6, citing the Austrian archives.

3. Ibid., pp. 400–01.

4. Ibid., pp. 374–81; Owsley, *Cotton Diplomacy,* pp. 146–50.

5. Bulloch, *Secret Service,* 2:22.

6. Olive Anderson, *A Liberal State at War* (London and New York, 1967).

7. Adams's letters and enclosures are in IUP Area Studies, *The United States,* 17:99–113; Russell's letter of 4 October 1862 is in ibid., p. 111. Russell's letter of 22 September 1862 is mangled by IUP editors (pp. 109–10) but is in Great Britain, House of Commons, Sessional Papers, vol. 72 (1863).

8. These events have been thoroughly presented and analyzed in E. D. Adams, *Britain and the Civil War,* 2:33–66, and in Case and Spencer, *Civil War Diplomacy,* pp. 347–73. For the role of the cotton shortage in both the English and French considerations, see especially E. D. Adams, 2:64, and Case and Spencer, pp. 358–59 and 364–66.

9. Adams to Russell, 20 November 1862, IUP Area Studies, *The United States,* 17:113–15, and Russell to Adams, 19 December 1862, enclosed in Adams to Seward, 25 December 1862, no. 281, SDC Despatches Gr. Br., vol. 81. Because neither government was anxious to change its law, this proposal bore no fruit (Russell to Lord Lyons, British minister to the United States, 14 February 1863, quoted in *Hansard,* 3rd series, vol. 170, col. 50).

10. For the problem involved in the privateer exchanges, see E. D. Adams, *Britain and the Civil War,* 2:125–28 and 137–41. E. D. Adams maintained that British fear of Northern privateers led to tighter control over Confederate ship construction in Great Britain. See C. F. Adams on the Confederate cotton certificates, IUP Area Studies, *The United States,* 17:487–504. Both sources contain references to inadequacy in the British Foreign Enlistment Act to which citations are made below.

11. Lyons to Russell, 24 February 1863, PRO, FO, 5/878/180; also cited in E. D. Adams, *Britain and the Civil War,* 2:125–26. Russell to Adams, 25 March 1863, IUP Area Studies, *The United States,* 17:500.

12. Adams to Russell, 14 March 1863, copy enclosed in Adams to Seward, 19 March 1863, no. 352, SDC Despatches Gr. Br., vol. 82, and in IUP Area Studies, *The United States,* 17:501.

13. E. D. Adams (*Britain and the Civil War,* 2:129–30) summarizes this.

14. Russell to Adams, 21 March 1863; Adams on 23 March responded that he was "deeply gratified" as much for Russell's initiative as for the information. Copies of both letters are enclosed in Adams to Seward, 27 March 1863, no. 357, SDC Despatches Gr. Br., vol. 82.

15. Adams to Seward, 27 March 1863, no. 356, ibid. Russell's note of 27 March 1863 is in Palmerston Papers, Historical Manuscripts Commission, National Register of Archives, London (hereafter cited as Palmerston Papers), and also is cited in E. D. Adams, *Britain and the Civil War,* 2:131, and David F. Krein, "Russell's Decision to Detain the Laird Rams," *Civil War History* 22, no. 2 (June 1976): 159. See also Russell to Lyons, 27 March 1863, IUP Area Studies, *The United States,* 17:718–19.

16. This whole debate is in *Hansard,* 3rd series, vol. 170, cols. 33–94. The quotations for each speaker, respectively, are: Forster, col. 38; Palmer, cols. 47, 56; Bright, col. 68; Palmerston, cols. 93, 94. For Forster's pro-North position, see E. D. Adams, *Britain and the Civil War,* 1:58, n. 2. Forster's description of the *Alabama* was a quote from Yonge's deposition, which appears in many of the records, most conveniently in IUP Area Studies, *The United States,* 17:714–23.

17. On the principle that "the obligation of a neutral state to prevent the violation of its neutral soil is independent of all interior or local law" (see above, Introduction, n. 11). Minister for Foreign Affairs Lord John Russell had accepted this principle as early as the *Nashville* and *Florida* cases, yet scholars strangely have ignored it in their studies on British neutrality during the Civil War: see Merli, *Britain and the Confederate Navy,* p. 175; Crook, *Powers,* p. 298; Jarvis, "*Alabama* and the Law," pp. 193–94; E. D. Adams, *Britain and the Civil War,* 2:125–28 and 137–41; Jenkins, *Britain and the War,* vol. 1, especially chaps. 7, 8, and 9 and p. 272, where the Duke of Argyll comments on the relationship between international and domestic law. Cook, *Alabama Claims,* p. 27, refers briefly to the need for changing the 1819 law but makes no mention of the principle behind the need; he does refer to the reason for Palmerston's reluctance to change the law in Parliament.

18. Merli, *Britain and the Confederate Navy,* entitles his chapter on the *Alexandra* "The Curious Case" (chap. 8); see especially p. 173. Merli's interpretation of the case is based in part on a letter Russell wrote to Adams on 2 April (IUP Area Studies, *The United States,* 17:501–02) from which he quotes Russell as saying that the government could not interfere with commercial dealings even if the subject of the dealings were "ships adapted for warlike purposes." But Russell had just cited two decisions of United States courts from which he derived the quoted statement. Indeed, British officials returned to this theme for several more months in an effort to establish grounds for denying any responsibility to pay the United States damages for the *Alabama*'s destruction of American merchantmen; Russell denied such responsibility as late as 1871 (*Hansard,* 3rd series, 206:1823–24 ff.). In the same letter from which the quote is taken, Russell also assured Adams of the government's strict enforcement of the Foreign Enlistment Act and requested United States cooperation in gathering necessary evidence. The total letter even in light of the seizure of the *Alexandra* three days later is not as curious as the single sentence that Merli quotes would imply. Jones (*Confederate Rams,* pp. 42–43) also refers to the *Alexandra* seizure as unusual. Neither scholar had reason within his context to relate the case to the deficiency of the Foreign Enlistment Act in face of the changing naval technology and the government's obligation to enforce its neutrality.

19. Bulloch to Mallory, 17 January 1863, *ORN,* II, 2:331.

20. Adams to Russell, 30 March 1863, PRO, FO, 5/1040, also cited in Merli, *Britain and the Confederate Navy,* p. 164; two letters, Russell to Adams, 3 April 1863, enclosed in Adams to Seward, 9 April 1863, no. 370, SDC Despatches Gr. Br., vol. 82.

21. Russell to Palmerston, 3 April 1863, Palmerston Papers. E. D. Adams (*Britain and the Civil War,* 2:135) quotes this letter as proof that Russell was unimpressed by Palmerston's speech of 27 March; on the contrary, this judicial test of the law was necessitated by that speech.

22. Law Office to Foreign Office, 4 April 1863, PRO, FO, 83/2217, and FO, 5/1084. Merli (*Britain and the Confederate Navy,* p. 165) cites this memorandum as prompting Russell to act on the *Alexandra,* but Russell had decided on the previous day to do so.

23. Russell to Adams, 5 April 1863, and Adams to Russell, 6 April 1863, copies enclosed in Adams to Seward, 9 April 1863, no. 368, SDC Despatches Gr. Br., vol. 82.

24. Just two days later Russell informed Lyons that orders had been given "to watch, and stop when evidence can be procured, vessels *apparently* intended for Confederate service" (Russell to Lyons, 7 April 1863, PRO, FO, 5/869/183; also quoted in E. D. Adams, *Britain and the Civil War,* 2:136).

25. Bulloch to Mallory, 16 May 1863, *ORN,* II, 2:423 (at that same time Bulloch signed the first contract to build ships in France); North to Mallory, 6 June 1863, ibid., p. 434.

26. Jones, *Confederate Rams,* p. 47; see also Merli, *Britain and the Confederate Navy,* pp. 166–67.

27. Merli, *Britain and the Confederate Navy,* pp. 167–72, presents an excellent analysis of the trial and these quotes are taken from his account; see also Jones, *Confederate Rams,* p. 48. See Jenkins, *Britain and the War,* 2:273, for a statement on the government's indictment of the *Alexandra* as an "illusion of strength."

28. The C.S.S. *Georgia* was purchased half-completed in March 1863 by Commander Maury (Lester, *Finance and Purchasing,* p. 97). Crook (*Powers,* p. 324) uses the phrase "an act outside the law" in reference to the British government's action against the Laird rams. Krein ("Russell's Decision," p. 163) states that Russell "was determined to stop the vessels as a matter of policy, law or no law." Because Krein was unaware of the principle of international law behind Russell's decision, he erroneously concluded: "At all events, Russell acted as though bona fide neutrality meant going beyond the requirements of international law." See Jenkins, *Britain and the War,* 2:287, for evidence that the *Alexandra* decision forced the government to act outside the law in the Laird rams case.

29. Adams claimed that Yonge came to him seeking permission to go to the United States and volunteered his statement. Adams turned Yonge over to Dudley "to defray the expenses of his passage to the United States" (Adams to Seward, 3 April 1863, no. 364, SDC Despatches Gr. Br., vol. 82). Yonge's deposition is in IUP Area Studies, *The United States,* 17:714–23.

30. Bulloch to Mallory, 30 June 1863, *ORN,* II, 2:445; Bulloch, *Secret Service,* 1:3.

31. Jones, *Confederate Rams,* p. 49.

32. Lamar, Slidell, and Mason to North, 13 June 1863, *ORN,* II, 2:439; North to Mason, 26 June 1863, ibid., p. 443.

33. The quotes are from the following four letters respectively: Bulloch to Mallory, 30 June 1863, ibid., p. 445; North to Mason, 26 June 1863, ibid., p. 443; Mason to North, 27 June 1863, ibid., North to Thomson, 27 June 1863, ibid.

34. Two dispatches: Bulloch to Mallory, 23 January 1863, ibid., pp. 345–46, and 3 February 1863 (in cypher), ibid., pp. 351–52. Both are partially reproduced in Bulloch, *Secret Service,* 1:394–95.

35. Mallory to Bulloch, [7] January 1863, *ORN,* II, 2:333, and Bulloch to Mallory, 9 March 1863, ibid., p. 373. Internal evidence in Bulloch's letter indicates the *ORN* editors misdated Mallory's letter; it should be sometime immediately after 14 January.

36. This and subsequent quotes in this paragraph are from Bulloch to Mallory, 9 July 1863, ibid., pp. 455–56. The letter is partially reproduced in Bulloch, *Secret Service,* 1:409–10.

37. This plan, although never executed, was accepted by Mallory (Mallory to Bulloch, 29 August 1863, *ORN,* II, 2:484).

38. Bulloch to Mallory, 30 June 1863, ibid., pp. 444–45.

39. J. T. Durkin, *Stephen R. Mallory: Confederate Navy Chief* (Chapel Hill, 1954), pp. 70, 126, 149, 257; *Register of Officers,* p. 10.

40. Two letters, Mallory to Bulloch, 30 August and 17 October 1863, *ORN,* II, 2:485–87 and 507.

41. Diary of William C. Whittle, Jr., Whittle Papers (hereafter cited as Whittle Diary), 1 September 1863. Other quotes in this passage are from this entry and those through 5 September 1863. The details of this trip are important to the story of the Confederate navy in Europe because one of Mallory's chief problems was transporting officer personnel to Europe. No accounts of that activity are more clear than this one. Young Whittle's diary reveals not only the problems Southern officers faced in getting to Europe but also the interests and prejudices of a rather typical Confederate navy officer who served in Europe.

42. Ibid., 9–19 September 1863.

43. Ibid., 19 September–12 October 1863. The phlegmatic Barron recorded this whole trip in nine lines. He does refer to the voyage from Bermuda as "an unpleasant passage" (Diary of Captain S. Barron, C.S. Navy, *ORN,* II, 2:813; hereafter cited as Barron Diary).

44. Whittle Diary, 15–26 October 1863; Barron Diary, 14–23 October 1863, p. 813.

45. The documents of this diplomatic exchange have been published in IUP Area Studies, *The United States,* 17:853–85. Several scholars (Jones, E. D. Adams, Crook) have analyzed them and recounted the sequence and development of events. The most recent and most thorough such account is Merli, *Britain and the Confederate Navy,* pp. 196–202, based on documents in the British Home Office archives as well as the published ones. Since my own research in PRO, FO, and SDC has uncovered no new information, I have depended here on Merli's account for the quotes in this passage. I do have some differences with Merli on interpretation. For instance, I do not agree with his statement (p. 202) that Russell's motivation in seizing the Laird rams "was simply to test the Enlistment Act again." Krein ("Russell's Decision," pp. 159–63) comes much closer to the mark when he refers to Russell's action, "as a matter of policy, law or no law" (see above, n. 28). Krein's fine analysis of the evolution of Russell's thinking from March to September 1863 is based on Russell's correspondence with his undersecretary at the foreign office, A. H. Layard. See also Jenkins, *Britain and the War,* 2:287–91, for the evolution of Russell's thought regarding a neutral's obligation to international law despite the weakness of its domestic law and his decision to retain the rams.

46. Bulloch, *Secret Service,* 1:424.

47. The Bravay contract story is based on several sources: Mallory to Bulloch, 19 March 1863, *ORN,* II, 2:375–76; Mallory to Slidell, 27 March 1863, ibid., pp. 395–96; Bulloch to Mallory, 30 June 1863, ibid., p. 445, all reproduced in part or

in whole in Bulloch, *Secret Service,* 1:397–403. See also Jones, *Confederate Rams,* pp. 66–67, and Merli, *Britain and the Confederate Navy,* p. 193.

48. Bulloch to Mallory, 9 July 1863, *ORN,* II, 2:455; Bulloch, *Secret Service,* 1:422–23.

49. Bulloch to Mallory, 20 October 1863, *ORN,* II, 2:507–11; also in Bulloch, *Secret Service,* 1:416–23.

50. Jenkins, *Britain and the War,* 2:296.

51. For the French diplomatic posture, see Case and Spencer, *Civil War Diplomacy,* pp. 437–38, 440, 443–49, 553–55; for Bulloch's news of the rejection and his reaction, see Bulloch to Mallory, 17 February 1864, *ORN,* II, 2:584, and Bulloch, *Secret Service,* 1:247.

52. Jones, *Confederate Rams,* p. 101; Bulloch to Mallory, 17 February 1864, *ORN,* II, 2:584, and Bulloch to Messrs. A. Bravay and Company, 7 February 1864, *ORN,* II, 2:586.

53. Jones, *Confederate Rams,* p. 108.

54. Palmerston to Russell, two letters, 13 and 22 September 1863, PRO, Russell Papers, 30/22/14; also quoted in Merli, *Britain and the Confederate Navy,* pp. 211, 206, respectively. The italics are mine. For Captain Hoare's overture, see Bulloch, *Secret Service,* 1:418. Thus the British *technique* of purchase as means of fulfilling the *policy* of denying the rams to the South actually was attempted as early as October 1863. See Jenkins, *Britain and the War,* 2:296–97, for other suggestions made in September to buy the rams.

55. Jones, *Confederate Rams,* pp. 93–105 (the quotes are on p. 94). This section is a remarkable piece of research and unfolds a most intriguing story.

56. Merli, *Britain and the Confederate Navy,* p. 211; Jones, *Confederate Rams,* p. 108; Bulloch, *Secret Service,* 1:430–31.

57. Bulloch, *Secret Service,* 1:431, 433, and Bulloch to Mallory, 13 May 1864, *ORN,* II, 2:656. Jones (*Confederate Rams,* p. 105) is mistaken as to this date. See Jones, pp. 109–10, for the final offer to sell.

58. For the terms of the final sale, see Jones, *Confederate Rams,* p. 110, and Merli, *Britain and the Confederate Navy,* p. 211; Bulloch to Mallory, 13 May 1864, *ORN,* II, 2:655.

59. Somerset to Gladstone, 13 June 1864, Gladstone Papers, 44304, quoted in Jones, *Confederate Rams,* pp. 110–11; italics are mine. Lord Somerset was convinced that light-draft turret ironclads were "the best form of vessel . . . for the protection of our coast" (Baxter, *Introduction of the Ironclad,* p. 325), and this belief may have influenced his change of opinion about the rams.

60. Merli, *Britain and the Confederate Navy,* p. 179, and Crook, *Powers,* p. 323.

61. Bulloch to Mallory, 18 December 1862, *ORN,* II, 2:309 (see above, Chapter 3, for the two men's earlier plans for the ship); Bulloch to Mallory, 9 July 1863, ibid., pp. 456–57. All quotes from Bulloch on the ships' use come from this latter letter except as specifically noted. All italics are mine. The quotes concerning the Laird rams versus the monitors are from Bulloch, *Secret Service,* 1:445–46.

62. Baxter, *Introduction of the Ironclad,* p. 304. That the monitors could not keep to the high seas, much less fight on them, is illustrated amply in William Frederick Keeler, *Aboard the USS Monitor: 1862. The Letters of Acting Paymaster*

William Frederick Keeler, U.S. Navy to his Wife, Anna, ed. Robert W. Daley (Annapolis, 1964), especially pp. 27–29, 40.

63. Parkes, *British Battleships,* pp. 69–80.

64. See Chapter 6.

65. *Illustrated London News,* 27 October 1866, cited in Jones, *Confederate Rams,* p. 118; Merli, *Britain and the Confederate Navy,* p. 217; see also Frank J. Merli and Thomas W. Green, "Could the Laird Rams have Lifted the Union Blockade?" *Civil War Times Illustrated* 2 (April 1963): 14–17.

66. Parkes, *British Battleships,* p. 80.

67. Ibid., p. 78.

68. Maynard, "Super *Alabama,*" pp. 91–94, which is a clear and conclusive account based on documents submitted to the Geneva arbitration, on the Dudley Papers, and on United States State Department Correspondence. My own research has revealed no additional material on the *Canton* story itself.

69. This paragraph is based on three letters from North: two letters, 21 November 1863, one to Mason, the other to Barron, *ORN,* II, 2:519; one to Mallory, 14 December 1863, ibid., p. 566.

70. North's memorandum on the meeting, undated, ibid., p. 327. This memo was misplaced by editors: it appears in the section with letters dated in December 1862, yet Barron, who attended the meeting, did not arrive in Europe until October 1863.

71. Merli, *Britain and the Confederate Navy,* pp. 154–59, using *ORN* documents cited below in this chapter, has summarized these difficulties.

72. The records curiously do not reveal the exact amount Thomson paid to North (see *ORN,* II, 2:704, 705, 731, 734, 735, and 737) nor are they precise on the date of the final settlement (ibid., p. 785).

73. The quotes in this paragraph come from various letters: two letters, Barron to North, 12 October 1864 (p. 734) and 2 January 1865 (p. 785); two letters, North to Mallory, 18 February 1864 (pp. 587–88) and 24 October 1864 (pp. 737–38); and M. P. Robertson to North, December 1864 (p. 776), all in ibid.

74. Barron to Mallory, 10 November 1863, ibid., p. 518; Merli, *Britain and the Confederate Navy,* pp. 157, 159, based on extensive and unique research in Denmark.

75. Maynard, "Super *Alabama,*" pp. 90, 95. The compromise settlement was reached in March 1864.

76. Barron to Sinclair, 10 November 1863, *ORN,* II, 2:515; Barron to Mallory, 22 January 1864, ibid., pp. 574–75.

77. Three letters in the Whittle Papers: Barron to Sinclair, 14 June 1864, folder X, no. 9; Bulloch to Barron, 27 August 1864, folder II, no. 18; Bulloch to Barron, 31 August 1864, folder II, no. 19.

78. Barron to Mallory, two letters, 9 and 23 November 1864, *ORN,* II, 2:764, 772.

79. Bulloch to Mallory, 23 January 1863, ibid., p. 345; Bulloch, *Secret Service,* 1:394.

80. In 1864 Sir Roundell Palmer, then attorney general, supported this policy before Parliament: "Can it be said that a neutral Sovereign has not the right to make orders for the preservation of its own neutrality . . . [by] any means which

the neutral Sovereign may see fit to adopt for the assertion of its territorial rights?" (*Hansard*, 3rd series, 174:1595; also in IUP Area Studies, *The United States*, 56:341).

Chapter 5
Matthew Fontaine Maury in England

1. Lester, *Finance and Purchasing*, pp. 24–25, 180–81; Merli, *Britain and the Confederate Navy*, pp. 127–33.

2. *ORN*, II, 2:index.

3. See Frances Leigh Williams, *Matthew Fontaine Maury: Scientist of the Sea* (New Brunswick, N. J., 1963). This book is used exclusively for Maury's prewar career and for his personal life because of all the works on Maury it is the most thorough and the only one based on Maury's private papers and his diary. Chap. 20 is devoted to Maury's wartime activities in England but fails to relate them to the other Confederate navy personnel and activities. Jaquelin Ambler Caskie's *Life and Letters of Matthew Fontaine Maury* (Richmond, 1928) is a highly personalized account and the letters are personal ones that cast little light on Maury's career. Patricia Jahns's *Scientists of the Civil War: Matthew Fontaine Maury & Joseph Henry* (New York, 1961) recounts Maury's clash with Henry but throws no light on his wartime service.

4. Durkin, *Mallory*, pp. 72–77.

5. He was known in Europe simply as "Lieutenant Maury."

6. M. F. Maury to B. Franklin Minor, 11 June 1861, Matthew Fontaine Maury Papers, Library of Congress, Washington, Manuscript Division (hereafter cited as Maury Papers), vol. 14. Also cited in Williams, *Scientist of the Sea*, p. 372.

7. Brooke, "Naval Scientist," 2:822, 833–35.

8. Ibid., pp. 822, 833–35.

9. Williams, *Scientist of the Sea*, pp. 384–85.

10. Ibid., pp. 396–97. See pp. 398–401 for this episode and Maury's orders to Europe. Nowhere does Durkin in his chapter on this investigation (*Mallory*, pp. 224–52) mention Maury.

11. Mallory to Bulloch, 20 September 1862, Confidential, *ORN*, II, 2:270. Williams cites only this dispatch to justify these statements: "Maury carried authorization from Secretary Mallory for Bulloch to be responsible for Maury's travel expenses and pay. Mallory, however, in the official order, made it very clear to Bulloch that Maury had special authorization to carry out certain projects. Maury also had general authority to purchase ships to serve as cruisers" (*Scientist of the Sea*, p. 402). Williams, who had access to all of Maury's papers, does not cite an "official order," nor does Durkin. No such order or reference to one appears in the Maury Papers or Diary.

12. Bulloch, *Secret Service*, 2:260.

13. Bulloch to Mallory, 2 December 1862, *ORN*, II, 2:306.

14. Geoffrey Best, *Mid-Victorian Britain, 1851–1875* (New York, 1972), pp. 9–10. All quotes and all references to the city come from these pages.

15. Williams, *Scientist of the Sea*, p. 404.

16. Mason to Benjamin, 11 December 1862, *ORN*, II, 3:618.

17. Maury to "My Dear Sir.—," 20 January 1863, Maury Papers, vol. 17.

18. M. F. Maury to B. Franklin Minor, 21 January 1863, ibid. Both letters are partially quoted in Williams, *Scientist of the Sea*, p. 404. When Benjamin finally did instruct Mason to withdraw from London, the *Times* of London commented that it had been folly for the Confederacy to seek recognition "before it had won it" (*Times* [London], 23 September 1863, quoted in E. D. Adams, *Britain and the Civil War*, 2:181).

19. Slidell was still optimistic from his interview with Napoleon III in October 1862 and his contacts throughout January and February 1863 to build Confederate ships in France. See Case and Spencer, *Civil War Diplomacy*, chap. 13, *passim*.

20. Letter reprinted in *ORN*, II, 2:335–36.

21. Mallory to M. F. Maury, 7 November 1862, ibid., p. 295. This correspondence is only a cover letter; the original orders do not exist. See also M. F. Maury to R. D. Minor, 21 April 1863, Maury Papers, vol. 18.

22. Bulloch, *Secret Service*, 2:261–63.

23. See for example Philip Van Doren Stern, *When the Guns Roared: World Aspects of the American Civil War* (Garden City, N.Y., 1965), p. 166; Stern wrote that Maury "was like a child compared to Bulloch" in the task of acquiring cruisers, and that "Maury's cruiser turned out to be more of a liability than an asset."

24. M. F. Maury to Marin Jansen, Confidential, 20 December 1862, Maury Papers, vol. 17.

25. M. F. Maury to R. D. Minor, 21 April 1863, ibid., vol. 18. See also Lester (*Finance and Purchasing*, pp. 77–78), who used various depositories of business archives in Great Britain, and Williams, *Scientist of the Sea*, pp. 407–08. None of this material appears in *ORN* or in any memoir accounts by Bulloch or any other Confederate official in Europe. For W. L. Maury's role, see Todd, *Finance*, pp. 182, 185.

26. Various documents on the *Georgia* were submitted by both sides at the Geneva arbitration (IUP Area Studies, *The United States*, 56:230–45 and 393–97; see also *FRUS, Geneva Arbitration*, 1:367). Lester, *Finance and Purchasing*, p. 77, cites the correspondence between Maury and J. H. Schroder and Company. General McRae's financial report (*ORN*, II, 2:522) lists a payment of almost 40,000 pounds to Maury on 24 March 1865 without stating the source or purpose of the funds; they could have been used to buy up the cotton warrants M. F. Maury used as collateral for the bank loan (see Todd, *Finance*, p. 185, n. 50).

27. Jansen to M. F. Maury, 8 November 1863, Maury Papers, vol. 19.

28. M. F. Maury to Jansen, 8 March 1863, ibid., vol. 17.

29. M. F. Maury to R. D. Minor, 21 April 1863, ibid., vol. 18.

30. J. Thomas Scharf, *History of the Confederate States Navy: From Its Organization to the Surrender of Its Last Vessel* (New York, 1887), p. 803, and *Register of Officers*. The other seven were Lieutenant John H. Ingraham and Passed Midshipman John T. Walker of South Carolina, Midshipman James Morris Morgan of Louisiana, Paymaster R. W. Curtis of Arkansas, Surgeon Thomas J.

Wheedon of Maryland, Lieutenant Smith and Chief Engineer Pearson, both otherwise unidentified.

31. M. F. Maury to R. D. Minor, 21 April 1863, Maury Papers, vol. 18.

32. R. J. Dolan, Collector of Customs, Newhaven, to Commissioners of Customs, 6 April 1863, IUP Area Studies, *The United States,* 56:233.

33. Ibid., p. 240.

34. See Lester, *Finance and Purchasing,* p. 79, for the value of the *Georgia*'s victims, and IUP Area Studies, *The United States,* 58:16.

35. The best and most recent accounts are: Williams, *Scientist of the Sea,* pp. 410–11, based on the Maury Papers; Merli, *Britain and the Confederate Navy,* pp. 218–26, based on official United States, Confederate, and British papers; Lester, *Finance and Purchasing,* pp. 71–84, based on other and unusual British sources. For the French story, see Case and Spencer, *Civil War Diplomacy,* pp. 500–10, based on official French, United States, and Confederate sources and on the Whittle Papers.

36. Merli, *Britain and the Confederate Navy,* p. 219, states that Bulloch provided the necessary funds, but uncharacteristically Merli cites no source for the statement.

37. M. F. Maury to Mallory, 6 July 1863, Maury Papers, vol. 18. For Maury's activities in France, see Chapter 7.

38. M. F. Maury to Carter, London, 24 July 1863, *ORN,* II, 2:471.

39. Lester, *Finance and Purchasing,* p. 81. Matthew Fontaine Maury Diary, Library of Congress, Washington, Manuscript Division (hereafter cited as Maury Diary followed by entry dates), 1 October 1863.

40. Maury had been authorized by the secretary to draw funds from the Erlanger loan for a steamer, and he corresponded with James Mason on the subject (8 August 1863, Maury Papers, vol. 19) but there is no evidence that such funds were forthcoming from any source.

41. Lester, *Finance and Operations,* p. 81; Williams, *Scientist of the Sea,* p. 410; Merli, *Britain and the Confederate Navy,* pp. 219–20.

42. Maury Diary, 17 September and 6 October 1863; Williams, *Scientist of the Sea,* p. 410; *ORN,* II, 2:522–23.

43. Lester, *Finance and Purchasing,* p. 87; Merli, *Britain and the Confederate Navy,* p. 220. Maury Diary, 14 August, 17 September, 9 and 31 October, and 23 November 1863; Whittle Papers, folder I, which contains letters from Lieutenant Campbell; Lester, *Finance and Purchasing,* p. 82; see also Maury Diary, 25 and 26 November, 1863.

44. Maury Diary, 26 October 1863; Merli, *Britain and the Confederate Navy,* p. 222; Bulloch, *Secret Service,* 2:266.

45. Maury Diary, 10 December 1863.

46. Case and Spencer, *Civil War Diplomacy,* pp. 503, 509.

47. Merli (*Britain and the Confederate Navy,* pp. 220–21), basing his work on Foreign Office correspondence with other British government departments, has recounted these events. The United States made no claims against Great Britain for the *Rappahannock* affair and thus submitted only a synopsis of it at the Geneva arbitration (IUP Area Studies, *The United States,* 56:365). There are some documents concerning the trial in *FRUS, Geneva Arbitration,* 1:141–59.

48. This section is based on various entries in the Maury Diary and Papers, all cited in Williams, *Scientist of the Sea,* pp. 411–18.

49. Mallory to M. F. Maury, 18 June 1864, Maury Papers, vol. 19; also cited in Williams, *Scientist of the Sea,* p. 415.

50. Milton F. Perry, *Infernal Machines: The Story of Confederate Submarine and Mine Warfare* (Baton Rouge, 1965), p. 175.

51. For background on this peace movement, see E. D. Adams, *Britain and the Civil War,* 2:203–18.

52. The letter is in *ORN,* II, 2:597–601; M. F. Maury to Mallory, 3 February 1864, ibid., p. 597.

53. M. F. Maury's role is revealed in various entries in his diary in May and June 1864 and in several letters to family members in Maury Papers, vol. 19. Williams, *Scientist of the Sea,* pp. 414–15, summarizes the story.

54. This material included an underwater mine known only from its patent application. More sure and more powerful than its Cape Fear River example, it was at once more versatile. Maury had designed it to lie deep in the water to allow passage of friendly vessels and to automatically rise to destroy enemy ones. It even permitted land operators, stationed apart, to communicate with one another through the mine's electrical impulses (Perry, *Infernal Machines,* pp. 191–92). See also Bulloch, *Secret Service,* 2:270.

Chapter 6
Confederate Naval Operations in France

1. Bulloch to Mallory, two letters, 29 January and 3 February 1863, *ORN,* II, 2:346 and 351.

2. For the Slidell–Napoleon III meeting, see "Memorandum of an interview of Mr. Slidell with the Emperor at St. Cloud" on Tuesday, 28 October 1862, ibid., 3:576–77. For Slidell's subsequent efforts to gain the ministers' approval, see Case and Spencer, *Civil War Diplomacy,* pp. 430–32; for Napoleon III's reasons for making the suggestion, see below in this chapter. For Bulloch's immediate reaction, see Bulloch, *Secret Service,* 2:24.

3. Bulloch, *Secret Service,* 2:25–29, and Case and Spencer, *Civil War Diplomacy,* pp. 430–32.

4. For French ministerial correspondence on the subject, see AM, BB⁴/1345/I, especially Chasseloup-Laubat to Arman, Paris, 6 June 1863, for permission to arm the corvettes; for Slidell's approval of the contract, see Slidell to Arman and Voruz, Paris, 6 June 1863, *ORN,* II, 2:432.

5. For details, see Case and Spencer, *Civil War Diplomacy,* pp. 374–81.

6. Maury to French Admiral Charbonnes, 24 October 1863, Maury Papers, vol. 19.

7. Seward to Dayton, 8 July 1863, nos. 399–400, National Archives, Washington, Foreign Office Division, State Department Correspondence, Instructions, France, vol. 16. This letter was written with the knowledge of European events as

of the end of June, prior to Gettysburg and Vicksburg. For the full story of the Roebuck affair, see Case and Spencer, *Civil War Diplomacy,* pp. 398–426 and especially pp. 399–400 for the diplomacy of the Polish Insurrection.

8. For the Union's internal problems, see Wood Gray, *The Hidden Civil War: The Story of the Copperheads* (New York, 1942). The French government was well informed of Lee's preparations because Alfred Paul, French consul in Richmond, reported them along with descriptions of many Confederate problems, such as inflation and low civilian morale, during April, May, and June 1863. See Paul to Drouyn de Lhuys, Richmond, various dates, AMAE, Correspondance Consulaire, vol. 5 (Richmond), beginning with no. 36, and see AMAE, Correspondance Politique Consulaire, beginning with 15:62–72, no. 79. For Dayton's despondency, see his dispatch to Seward, 25 November 1862, no. 231, National Archives, Washington, Foreign Office Division, State Department Correspondence, Despatches, France (hereafter cited as SDC Despatches Fr.), vol. 52. For the details of the French mediatory efforts in October 1862 and January 1863, see Case and Spencer, *Civil War Diplomacy,* pp. 347–73 and 374–97.

9. Mallory to Bulloch, 26 May 1863, *ORN,* II, 2:428, and Bulloch's response, 7 August 1863, ibid., p. 477.

10. This background is from Baxter, *Introduction of the Ironclad,* pp. 96, 103, 104, 113–14.

11. Bulloch expressed this opinion of Arman when the corvettes were about two-thirds completed in a letter to Mallory, 20 July 1863, *ORN,* II, 2:468. In his memoirs, written many years after the war, he was not so kind to the French shipbuilder.

12. Bulloch, *Secret Service,* 2:28; Slidell to Benjamin, 20 April 1863, *ORN,* II, 3:742; Arman to Chasseloup-Laubat, 1 June 1863, AM, BB⁴/1345/I, a translation of which is in John Bigelow, *Retrospections of an Active Life* (2 vols., New York, 1909), 2:61. A superficial description of the corvettes' cabin areas and sails is in *ORN,* I, 3:206–07.

13. Bulloch, *Secret Service,* 2:28.

14. Ibid.

15. Ibid., pp. 28–29, where Bulloch summarizes these arrangements. The roles of Voruz and the other principals also emerge from various documents located in *ORN,* II, 2:437–38, 462–63 ff., 471–72, and Bigelow, *Retrospections,* 2:61. Bigelow in his *France and the Confederate Navy, 1862–1868* (New York, 1888) reproduces these and additional documents in app. A, pp. 200–13.

16. Erlanger to Arman, 9 June 1863, Bigelow, *France and the Confederate Navy,* p. 7; Arman to Voruz, 10 June 1863, *ORN,* II, 2:437; Bulloch to Mallory, 20 July 1863, *ORN,* II, 2:469.

17. The originals are in AM, BB⁴/1345/I; translations are in *ORN,* II, 2:431, 433, and Bigelow, *Retrospections,* 2:61; in *France and the Confederate Navy,* pp. 200–01, Bigelow gives an accurate French version of Arman's request.

18. These figures and facts are taken from a group of letters in a dossier marked: "Voruz et Arman concernant les navires construits à Bordeaux et Nantes," AM, BB⁴/1345/I. This dossier contains all ten letters taken from the files of Voruz, only some of which have been published in *ORN* and Bigelow's two works. Bigelow referred to the collection as the "Trémont Papers" and the

French referred to it as the "Pestermann Papers"; for clarity's sake they will be referred to here as the "Voruz Papers."

19. Bulloch, *Secret Service*, 2:32; Mallory to Bulloch, 6 May 1863, and Bulloch's acknowledgment, 30 June 1863, *ORN*, II, 2:416 and 446.

20. Maury to Jansen, 21 April 1863, Maury Papers, vol. 18.

21. Maury to Jansen, 29 April 1863, ibid. For Mallory's instructions, see Maury Diary, 1 May 1863.

22. Jansen to Maury, 8 November 1863, Maury Papers, vol. 19; Maury Diary, 4 May 1863 (Maury wrote to Mallory: "Send me the funds and I can build six ships as well as one in France" [Maury Diary, 7 May 1863]); Maury Diary, 5 May 1863.

23. Maury Diary, 18, 20, and 21 May 1863.

24. Ibid., 27 May and 4 June 1863.

25. For the commissioners' decision to assume responsibility for dispersion of the Erlanger funds and for Slidell's opinions on France's preoccupation with Mexican and Polish affairs and his views on the Roebuck maneuver, see Slidell to Benjamin, 12 June 1863, *ORN*, II, 3:806–07. For Slidell's knowledge of the Lindsay-Roebuck plans, see Slidell to Mason, 18 June 1863, ibid., p. 808.

26. Maury Diary, 6 June 1863. Italics are mine.

27. The Arman plan is in Arman to Maury, Bordeaux, 12 June 1863, *ORN*, II, 2:438–39. Curiously, the new displacement of the ship was cited as "1,358,000 kilos," which would amount to 1,493 tons, not the 1,358 mentioned by Arman and accepted by Maury. This difference perhaps illustrates the Southerners' problem in dealing in the unfamiliar metric system.

28. Memorandum of an interview with the emperor at the Tuileries, 18 June 1863, ibid., 3:812–14. Italics are mine. Heretofore this interview mistakenly has been related to Bulloch's ironclad building activities in France (see my own work in Case and Spencer, *Civil War Diplomacy*, p. 433, and see Bigelow, *France and the Confederate Navy*, chap. 11, especially p. 137) because Maury's story has never before been told.

29. Maury Diary, entries for 22 and 25 June 1863; Maury Papers, Maury to North, 5 July 1863, vol. 18, and Jansen to Maury, 8 November 1863, vol. 19.

30. Voruz to his son, Paris, 14 July 1863, *ORN*, II, 2:462–63. The contract from which the following description is derived is in ibid., pp. 464–66. See also Bulloch, *Secret Service*, 2:33–34, and compare with Bulloch, 1:384. The displacement for the Arman rams is not mentioned, but it certainly would be less than the 1,850 tons of the larger Laird rams.

31. Bulloch to Mallory, Paris, 20 July 1863, *ORN*, II, 2:468–69. The money expected from Richmond never arrived and Bulloch had to use funds from the sale of the ships in England (Bulloch, *Secret Service*, 2:35).

32. For Arman's pretense of building for Egypt, see Chasseloup-Laubat to Arman, Paris, 8 August 1863, *ORN*, II, 2:478; for the names of the vessels, see the various correspondence between the Bordeaux and Nantes port officials and the minister of marine, AM, BB⁴/1345/I; for Bulloch's despondency, see Bulloch, *Secret Service*, 2:38.

33. For this diplomatic story related to the Confederate navy, see Case and Spencer, *Civil War Diplomacy*, chaps. 13 and 14, especially pp. 497–98. It will be

necessary to repeat some of that material in this narrative. See also Hanna and Hanna, *Napoleon III and Mexico,* pp. 119–20 ff. For the French preoccupation with Mexican affairs during the summer and autumn of 1863, see Hanna and Hanna, pp. 88–95.

34. Maury to Charbonnes, 24 October 1863, Maury Papers, vol. 19. Much of this material is similar to ideas contained in a pamphlet published in 1863 by a close adviser to Napoleon III: Michel Chevalier, *La France, le Mexique et les Etats Confédérés* (Paris, 1863). There is no evidence that Maury had read this pamphlet, nor does Chevalier mention Brigham Young, California, or the role of a Pacific fleet. For an analysis of the Chevalier work, see Hanna and Hanna, *Napoleon III and Mexico,* pp. 58–68.

35. Maury to Maximilian, 8 and 10 October and 25 November 1863, in the Archiv Kaiser Maximillians von Mexiko, cited by Hanna and Hanna, *Napoleon III and Mexico,* p. 119. The 25 November letter is also in the Maury Papers, vol. 19, where there is also a letter of 22 December 1863 to Maximilian acknowledging the archduke's inability to buy the ship because he was not yet emperor of Mexico.

36. The movements of the *Florida* are detailed from the ship's records in *ORN,* I, 2, beginning on p. 639. Bulloch (*Secret Service,* 1:178–84) presents a candid narrative of the *Florida*'s stay at Brest; the diplomatic aspects are in Case and Spencer, *Civil War Diplomacy,* pp. 483–500. The present account is based on all of these sources and therefore, except for direct quotes and new material, no further documentation will be offered.

37. These French decisions are in telegrams exchanged between Vice Admiral Count de Gueyton, Prefect of Marine at Brest, and Chasseloup-Laubat, Minister of the Marine (Paris), 23 August 1863, and the several telegrams exchanged between Chasseloup-Laubat and Drouyn de Lhuys, dated between 23 and 27 August 1863, all in AM, BB⁴/1345/I, dossier marked "Guerre de Sécession, Affaires de la Florida à Brest. Arrivée du Kearsarge. Divers mouvements de ces bâtiments" (hereafter cited as *Florida* dossier). For the reasons behind Drouyn de Lhuys's decision, see Case and Spencer, *Civil War Diplomacy,* pp. 484–88.

38. Bulloch, *Secret Service,* 1:179; Thomas H. Dudley, United States Consul at Liverpool, to Gideon Welles, United States Secretary of the Navy, 18 September 1863, *ORN,* I, 2:460.

39. Prefect of Marine at Brest to Minister of Marine, 23 September 1863, telegram and letter containing Maffitt's affidavits, AM, BB⁴/1345/I, *Florida* dossier. Bulloch, *Secret Service,* 1:180, confirms this.

40. Two letters, Maury to Maffitt, 9 and 11 September 1863, *ORN,* I, 2:660–61; Barron to Barney, 5 January 1864, ibid., p. 661; Barron to Morris, 5 January 1864, ibid., p. 662.

41. Drouyn de Lhuys to Chasseloup-Laubat, 21 October 1863, AM, BB⁴/1345/I, *Florida* dossier; Chasseloup-Laubat to Drouyn de Lhuys, 19 October 1863, Archives Nationales (Ministère de la Marine) (hereafter cited as AN [M]), BB²419. The various legalistic considerations leading to this decision are presented in Case and Spencer, *Civil War Diplomacy,* pp. 489–90.

42. Bulloch, *Secret Service,* 1:82; Slidell to Benjamin, 29 December 1863, *ORN,* II, 3:986; Morris to Barron, 9 February 1864, *ORN,* I, 2:664. It may be that the

Florida's new crew, after all, could speak only broken English because they were mostly Italian, Spanish, and Dutch (*ORN,* I, 3:263).

43. Bulloch, *Secret Service,* 1:179–80; Barron to Mallory, 10 November 1863, *ORN,* II, 2:519, and Morris to Barron, 9 and 18 February 1864, *ORN,* I, 2:664–65.

44. The movements of the *Kearsarge* are in *ORN,* I, 2, beginning on p. 458, including many letters too numerous to cite separately. A translation of the new French rules is in ibid., pp. 607–09. The information concerning their formulation is from AM, BB⁴/1345/I, *Florida* dossier, letters exchanged among Count de Gueyton, Chasseloup-Laubat, and Drouyn de Lhuys dated between 16 January and 19 February 1864, including a French copy of the rules. The rumor that the Confederate vessels would try to converge on the *Kearsarge* was not without foundation: on 31 October, three days after the *Georgia* arrived in Cherbourg, Commander M. F. Maury noted in his diary: "Lewis Maury—set a trap—you and *Florida*—for the *Kearsarge*" (Maury Diary, 31 October 1863).

45. This full story, based on Confederate, Union, French, and British documents, is in Case and Spencer, *Civil War Diplomacy,* pp. 436–66. It will not be repeated here except as it affected Confederate navy activity; inevitably, some of the documents will be cited and some narrative will be repeated. A Captain Pierre from Chasseloup-Laubat's office inspected the corvettes and found them to be "veritable ships of war" by virtue of the special rooms for ammunition, facilities for gun emplacements, and deck hatches too small for cargo (Captain Pierre to Chasseloup-Laubat, 5 May 1864, AM, BB⁴/1345/I, and letters, Chasseloup-Laubat to Drouyn de Lhuys, 13 May 1864, AN [M], BB²426, and to the builders, 20 May 1864, AM, BB⁴/1345/I). The letters to the builders were prepared as early as 1 May 1864 (copy, John Bigelow Papers, New York Public Library, New York City, 1865, France and the Confederate Navy, folder 3); a translation appears in *ORN,* II, 2:692, dated 20 May.

46. Adolphe Jean Baptiste Lacan, *Plaidoirie de M. Lacan pour M. Arman contre les Etats-Unis d'Amerique* (Paris, 1868), p. 93. The two corvettes were delivered to Prussia during an armistice in the war on 3 July and 9 September, the *Cheops* not until April 1865; the *Sphinx* was delivered to Denmark after the war's conclusion, in October 1864 (ibid.). For the emperor's personal orders to sell, see Bulloch to Mallory, 10 June 1864, *ORN,* II, 2:667, and Bulloch to Barron, 9 June 1864, Whittle Papers, folder II, no. 15. Bulloch, *Secret Service,* 2:44–48, reprints his 10 June 1864 letter to Mallory with some elisions. Voruz sold his two corvettes to Peru (Case and Spencer, *Civil War Diplomacy,* p. 464).

47. Drouyn de Lhuys to Chasseloup-Laubat, 18 February 1864, AM, BB⁴/1346/II; for other Drouyn de Lhuys references to Mexico, see his letter to Chasseloup-Laubat, 22 April 1864, AM, BB⁴/1345/I, and Dayton to Seward, 29 January 1864, no. 409, SDC Despatches Fr., vol. 54.

48. See the two reports of the decision to sell the rams: Slidell to Benjamin, 16 February 1864, *ORN,* II, 3:1028–29, and Bulloch to Mallory, 18 February 1864, ibid., 2:588–89.

49. Bulloch to Barron, 9 June 1864, Whittle Papers, folder II, no. 15. For Bulloch's authorization to sell the rams, see his letter to Arman, 8 February 1864, *ORN,* II, 2:590–91, and Arman's response of the same day in Lacan, *Plaidoirie,* pp. 26–27.

50. Bulloch related the full story, starting with the February understanding and including the Paris meetings and Arman's unhappy interview with Napoleon III, in his 10 June 1864 letter to Mallory, *ORN,* II, 2:665–67.

51. Bulloch to Barron, 9 June 1864, Whittle Papers, folder II, no. 15.

52. Bulloch, *Secret Service,* 2:62–63.

53. Bigelow, *Retrospections,* 2:56. Captain Hoare to William Grey, PRO, FO, 27/1496/confidential, no. 1; Case and Spencer, *Civil War Diplomacy,* pp. 449–50.

Chapter 7
Last Desperate Hopes

1. W. L. Maury to Barron, 27 December 1863, *ORN,* I, 2:809; see the various letters exchanged among the officers involved, Whittle Papers, folder I, February and March 1864, and in *ORN,* I, 2, same period.

2. For the officers' failure to get aboard, see *ORN,* I, 2:511; for the diplomatic aspects of the *Rappahannock,* see Case and Spencer, *Civil War Diplomacy,* pp. 500–09.

3. Barron's instructions for the *Rappahannock* are dated 28 January 1864 in *ORN,* I, 2:819; his instructions for the *Georgia* are dated 29 January 1864, ibid., p. 810; he explained the plans to Mallory on 22 January 1864, ibid., II, 2:575. The ship's sailing dates are in Barron to Mallory, 16 February 1864, ibid., II, 2:580.

4. For the French orders to leave port, see Drouyn de Lhuys to Chasseloup-Laubat, 4 February 1864, and Chasseloup-Laubat to Calais Official, 15 February 1864, AM, BB⁴/1346/II; Evans to Barron, 9 February 1864, Whittle Papers, folder X, no. 1; Bulloch to Mallory, 14 April 1864, *ORN,* II, 2:624.

5. Barron to W. L. Maury, 19 January 1864, *ORN,* I, 2:810. W. L. Maury returned to the Confederacy within a week.

6. See Campbell's various letters to Barron, dated between 8 February and 21 March 1864, Whittle Papers, folder I, nos. 1–13. This folder contains thirty-four letters dated between 8 February and 12 August 1864 relative to the *Rappahannock* that supplement the correspondence in *ORN,* I, 2 and 3. For Slidell's comment on Campbell's performance and Mallory's suggestion, see Mallory to Barron, 25 April 1865, *ORN,* II, 2:629–30. Amusingly, Campbell, knowing the ship, rejected Barron's suggestion that he return to the Confederate States on the *Rappahannock* (Whittle Papers, folder I, no. 12, 18 March 1864).

7. Fauntleroy to Barron, 21 March 1864, Whittle Papers, folder I, no. 14, and 22 March 1864, *ORN,* I, 2:820–21.

8. The quotes are in Fauntleroy to Barron, 8 April 1864, Whittle Papers, folder I, no. 17. See also Fauntleroy's two letters of 14 and 24 April 1864 in *ORN,* I, 3:684–85, and Whittle Papers, folder I, no. 18.

9. See the various papers concerning the *Rappahannock, ORN,* II, 3:1037–42, and Slidell to Benjamin, 16 March and 7 April 1864, ibid., pp. 1064 and 1077. The scheme was delayed for over a month after the Georgia's arrival in Bordeaux because Barron and Slidell did not want to complicate matters for that ship. Fauntleroy actually gave notice that on 16 May he would abandon the ship

(Fauntleroy to Commissioner of Marine of the Port of Calais, 1 May 1864, ibid., I, 3:687–88).

10. In order, see Slidell to Benjamin, 15, 12, and 21 May and 2 June 1864, *ORN,* II, 3:1114, 1118–19, 1140; Bulloch to Barron, 29 April 1864, Whittle Papers, folder II, no. 9; Fauntleroy to Barron, 15 May 1864, Whittle Papers, folder I, no. 19, and Barron's curt reply that he, not Fauntleroy, was the responsible one, 16 May 1864, *ORN,* I, 3:691.

11. For the harbor incidents, see Fauntleroy to Barron, 2 May 1864, *ORN,* I, 3:687, and 25 May 1864, Whittle Papers, folder I, no. 22. For the *Nil* affair, see the various documents, *ORN,* I, 3:689–90; the originals are in AM, BB⁴/1346/II.

12. Fauntleroy to Barron, 24 April 1864, Whittle Papers, folder I, no. 18. Barron's letter is not extant, but Fauntleroy's references are to a Barron letter of 23 April.

13. Bulloch to Barron, 16 and 29 April and 3 May 1864, Whittle Papers, folder II, nos. 8, 9, and 10; Evans to Barron, Bordeaux, 22 April 1864, *ORN,* I, 3:682–83, and from Birkenhead Docks, 9 May 1864, Whittle Papers, folder X, no. 4; two letters from the captain of the U.S.S. *Niagara,* off Portugal, 15 August 1864, *ORN,* I, 3:186–87. The United States case against the *Georgia* presented to the Geneva Tribunal of Arbitration contains quotes from documents related to the vessel's arrival in Liverpool and her subsequent sale (IUP Area Studies, *The United States,* 56:395–97).

14. The best accounts remain those by participants and by Bulloch. Captain Semmes rendered an impressionistic report (*ORN,* I, 3:649–51) and an even more subjective account in his *Memoirs* (pp. 751–65); Captain Winslow's reports were matter-of-fact (*ORN,* I, 3:59–82, especially 79–81); Lieutenant Arthur Sinclair of the *Alabama,* writing almost thirty years after Semmes, gave a subjective yet amazingly honest account (Sinclair, *Two Years,* pp. 259–91); Commander Bulloch, writing with the aid of documents including the two captains' reports, presented an analytical and balanced account (*Secret Service,* 1:277–94). For accounts of eyewitnesses, see George T. Sinclair to Barron, Cherbourg, 20 June 1864, Whittle Papers, folder X, no. 9, and William M. Leary, Jr., "The Alabama vs. the Kearsarge," *American Neptune* 29, no. 3 (1969): 167–68 ff. Excellent illustrations are in Norman C. Delaney, "Showdown at Cherbourg," *Civil War Times Illustrated* 15, no. 3 (June 1976): 16–21. Good secondary accounts are: W. Adolphe Roberts, *Semmes of the Alabama* (New York, 1938), pp. 195–211, and Edward Boykin, *Ghost Ship of the Confederacy. The Story of the Alabama and her Captain, Raphael Semmes* (New York, 1957), pp. 344–84. For the diplomacy of the pre- and postbattle days, see Case and Spencer, *Civil War Diplomacy,* pp. 509–15.

15. In order: Sinclair, *Two Years,* p. 274; Bulloch, *Secret Service,* 1:278; Sinclair to Barron, 20 June 1864, Whittle Papers, folder X, no. 9; paraphrase of Semmes, *Memoirs,* p. 752.

16. This and the next six quotes are all from Semmes, *Memoirs,* in order: pp. 763 (italics are mine), 748, 749–50, 750 and 746, 756, 761, 765. For the sword incident, see ibid., p. 773. U.S. Secretary of the Navy Welles later criticized Semmes for failing to surrender his sword to Captain Winslow (ibid.).

17. Winslow to Welles, 30 July 1864, *ORN,* I, 3:80; Semmes, *Memoirs,* pp. 761 and 762. Arthur Sinclair in his narrative implies that the powder was weak and

in a footnote cites a fellow officer as firmly believing it (*Two Years,* p. 259); George T. Sinclair, having visited the *Kearsarge* in the harbor after the battle, reported several unexploded shells (G. T. Sinclair to Barron, Cherbourg, 21 June 1864, Whittle Papers, folder X, no. 10).

18. Bulloch, *Secret Service,* 1:279, 284, 286–87.

19. Semmes to Barron, 21 June 1864, *ORN,* I, 3:650; Semmes to Slidell, 1 July 1864, ibid., p. 663; Semmes, *Memoirs,* pp. 754, 761, 762, 763.

20. Bulloch, *Secret Service,* 1:287; Sinclair, *Two Years,* pp. 261, 269; Semmes to Barron, 21 June 1864, *ORN,* I, 3:650.

21. Surgeon's report, *ORN,* I, 3:69–70.

22. Semmes to Barron, 5 July 1864, ibid., pp. 664–65; Semmes's final *Alabama* payroll roster, Whittle Papers, folder X, nos. 27 and 28; Sinclair to Barron, 21 June 1864, Whittle Papers, folder X, no. 10.

23. Winslow to Welles, 30 July 1864, *ORN,* I, 3:78; Barron to Mallory, 22 June 1865, ibid., p. 655. The story of the *Deerhound* is fully covered by Semmes in his *Memoirs* (pp. 777–88) and need not be repeated here because it does not otherwise bear upon the history of the Confederate navy in Europe.

24. In order: Semmes, *Memoirs,* pp. 763, 751; Sinclair, *Two Years,* pp. 275–76; Semmes, *Memoirs,* p. 763.

25. Barron to Semmes, draft, 14 June 1864, Whittle Papers, folder X, no. 7.

26. *ORN,* I, 3:389. The *Niagara* was a ship of 4,582 tons, compared to the *Kearsarge*'s 1,031 tons. For descriptions of the various United States warships, see United States, Department of the Navy, Naval History Division, *Civil War Naval Chronology: 1861–1865* (Washington, 1971).

27. Fauntleroy to Barron, 11 July 1864, Whittle Papers, folder I, no. 24.

28. Slidell to Benjamin, 11 July 1864, *ORN,* II, 3:1170; Fauntleroy to Barron, 14 July 1864, two letters, Whittle Papers, folder I, nos. 25 and 26, and 22 July 1864, Whittle Papers, folder I, no. 28 with enclosures. Barron inspected the ship on 17 July 1864 and found it to be in "fine, wholesome order," ready to sail; Fauntleroy "seems to expect failure" (Barron Diary, 16 July 1864, p. 815). However, when the decision not to sail was made, Barron justified it in almost the same words Fauntleroy had been writing in July (Barron Diary, 1 and 2 August 1864, pp. 816–17).

29. Slidell to Benjamin, 1 August 1864, *ORN,* II, 3:1182–83. Drouyn de Lhuys's argument was based on expediency; see his "Rapport à l'Empereur sur l'affaire du *Rappahannock,*" 10 July 1864, AM, BB⁴/1346/II, as discussed in Case and Spencer, *Civil War Diplomacy,* pp. 506–07.

30. Fauntleroy to Barron, 1 August 1864, and the response, 2 August 1864, *ORN,* I, 3:700; Fauntleroy to Barron, 3 August 1864, Whittle Papers, folder I, no. 32. The arms Bulloch intended for the *Rappahannock* were those Commander North had bought for his Number 61; they eventually were shipped to the Confederacy (Bulloch to Mallory, 23 September 1864, *ORN,* II, 2:726). The decision to refuse to sail with only thirty-five men was made in conference among Bulloch, Barron, and Fauntleroy (Barron Diary, p. 816).

31. Slidell to Benjamin, 30 June 1864, *ORN,* I, 3:660, and Dayton to Seward, 23 August 1864, no. 527, SDC Despatches Fr., vol. 55.

32. Lester, *Finance and Purchasing*, p. 90. See Lester's app. 8 for a list of British-built blockade-runners.

33. Lester, ibid., p. 109, says these ships "were taken over by the Confederate naval forces." This is obviously a mistake because the Confederate navy did not have the personnel to do so; also, Bulloch never mentions it.

34. See Lester, ibid., p. 110, for percentage of profits. For the navy's use of Confederate agents on the islands, see Bulloch, *Secret Service*, 2:232–33, and Frank E. Vandiver, ed., *Confederate Blockade-Running Through Bermuda, 1861–1865: Letters and Cargo Manifests* (Austin, 1947); Frances Bradlee, *Blockade Running during the Civil War* (Salem, Mass., 1925); James Russell Soley, *The Blockade and the Cruisers* (New York, 1890).

35. The *Coquette* story is in Bulloch, *Secret Service*, 2:233–37, and Bulloch to Mallory, 22 October 1863, *ORN*, II, 2:512.

36. Bulloch to Mallory, 18 February 1864, *ORN*, II, 2:590.

37. Two letters, Mallory to Bulloch, 22 February and 21 March 1864, ibid., pp. 594 and 614.

38. Lester, *Finance and Purchasing*, p. 49, summarizes the 6 February 1864 acts of Congress. Bulloch, *Secret Service*, 2:237–38, describes the agreement with McRae. It was the agreement and not the government ownership that was new; the War Department as early as January 1863 had begun to operate government-owned steamers through the blockade (*ORN*, II, 3:882).

39. Mallory to Bulloch, 19 August 1864, *ORN*, II, 2:707. Lester, *Finance and Purchasing*, pp. 103–07, summarizes the ships' histories, citing the proper sources.

40. Bulloch to Barron, 6 June 1864, Whittle Papers, folder II, no. 14, and Bulloch to Mallory, 15 September 1864, *ORN*, II, 2:720–22; also in Bulloch, *Secret Service*, 2:239–41.

41. As has been the case in so much of the writing of Confederate history, analysis and even truth often are sacrificed to romanticism and eulogy. Stanley F. Horn's *The Gallant Rebel: The Fabulous Cruise of the C.S.S. Shenandoah* (New Brunswick, N.J., 1947) is based, according to the bibliography, on selected documents but treats the *Shenandoah* episode as an entity in itself and concentrates on romantic description and detail. James D. Horan (James I. Waddell, *C.S.S. Shenandoah: The Memoirs of Lieutenant Commanding James I. Waddell*, ed. James D. Horan [New York, 1960] introduction) presents an error-filled, simplistic setting for the episode and fails altogether to analyze Waddell the man. Only in Merli, *Britain and the Confederate Navy*, pp. 226–34, where the futility is noted, is there a competent, accurate account of the ship; Merli's purpose, however, was to examine the ship only insofar as it fit into the British government–Confederate navy story, not to analyze the ship within the whole of the navy's European activities.

42. Bulloch, *Secret Service*, 2:111–12; Bulloch to Mallory, 16 September 1864, *ORN*, II, 2:723.

43. On 1 September 1864 (letters from Bulloch to Mallory, *ORN*, II, 2:717) Bulloch was sure no satisfactory ship with a lifting screw was available; on 16 September, he described the ship in detail (ibid., p. 723), and on 8 October 1864

the ship sailed safely from England (ibid., 20 October 1864, p. 736). See also Bulloch letters to Barron, dated 31 August, 2, 10, and 15 September 1864, Whittle Papers, folder X, nos. 19–22, in which Bulloch obliquely refers to negotiations and asks that Lieutenant Whittle be assigned to him for special service.

44. For Carter's role in suggesting the area of the cruise, see Mallory to Bulloch, 19 August 1864, *ORN*, II, 2:708. For Wright's role, see Bulloch, *Secret Service*, 2:126. Bulloch was worried that the large "number of Youngsters" would leak the whole plot to Federal "spies" (Bulloch to Barron, 11 October 1864, Whittle Papers, folder II, no. 24). The tender was the *Laurel*, whose story is told by Horn (*Gallant Rebel*, pp. 23–26) and by Merli (*Britain and the Confederate Navy*, p. 231).

45. Waddell to Mallory, Melbourne, Australia, 25 January 1865, *ORN*, I, 3:760.

46. Bulloch to Mallory, 29 September 1864, ibid., II, 2:729–30.

47. Waddell, *Memoirs*, pp. 78, 102.

48. *ORN*, I, 3, *Shenandoah*'s log, p. 789, and list and value of prizes, ibid., p. 792. The order book of the *Shenandoah*'s executive officer, Lieutenant W. C. Whittle, Jr., is in the Whittle Papers. It unfortunately has no historical value, covering only the daily housekeeping assignments. Three *Alabama* crew members shipped on the *Shenandoah*, two of whom had previously served on the *Sumter*.

49. Merli, *Britain and the Confederate Navy*, p. 234.

50. Bulloch to Mallory, 24 October 1864, *ORN*, II, 2:740. There are several accounts of the *Stonewall* story. The best is still Bulloch's (*Secret Service*, 2:72–105). Bulloch wrote from the documents faithfully; his memory of events was clear. Lee Kennett's "The Strange Career of the 'Stonewall,' " *United States Naval Institute Proceedings* 94, no. 2 (February 1968): 74–85, is an entertaining and sound account of the ship's experience at sea. Case and Spencer (*Civil War Diplomacy*, pp. 466–80) have analyzed the diplomatic side of the story. The documents are in: AM, BB⁴/1346/II; *ORN*, II, 2, various letters, Bulloch to Mallory; *ORN*, I, 3, various letters exchanged among the officers involved in the episode; Whittle Papers, folders II and X, letters supplemental to those mentioned above.

51. The ship had sailed from Bordeaux on 15 October 1864 under the French flag, with a French master and crew and with Drouyn de Lhuys's approval because the actual fighting had ended (AM, BB⁴/1346/II, dossier marked "The Sphinx-Ster-Kodder-Stonewall Affair"). The Treaty of Vienna (30 October 1864) officially concluded the war.

52. Bulloch, *Secret Service*, 2:79.

53. Bulloch to Mallory, 10 January 1865, *ORN*, I, 3:721–22. I can find no other reference to Hall's rockets. See Bulloch, *Secret Service*, 2:77, 78, 81. The idea of a negotiated settlement to the war was not an idle one. President Lincoln did meet with Confederate commissioners on 3 February 1865 on a ship in Hampton Roads.

54. For the Arnous de Rivière–Bulloch agreement, see *ORN*, I, 3:722–24. For Bulloch's letter to Arman, see Lacan, *Plaidoirie*, pp. 42–43. The Danish government cancelled the contract on 21 December 1864.

55. For Barron's role in assigning the personnel, see Bulloch to Barron, 19 and 21 December 1864, Whittle Papers, folder II, nos. 33 and 34. For Page's and Carter's roles, see Bulloch, *Secret Service*, 2:81–83, and Page to Barron, Copenhagen, 5 January 1865, Whittle Papers, folder X, no. 20. Quiberon Bay is within French territorial waters.

56. Bulloch, *Secret Service*, 2:84–87; letters exchanged between Bulloch and Crenshaw, 18 and 19 December 1864, *ORN*, I, 3:724–26.

57. For Bulloch's short temper (to which he does *not* refer in his memoirs), see Bulloch to Barron, 9 January 1865, Whittle Papers, folder II, no. 36. Davidson to Bulloch, 6 February 1865, *ORN*, I, 3:732–33, is a detailed account of the ships' meeting, transfers, and sailings.

58. See Barron's instructions to Page, 17 December 1864, *ORN*, I, 3:719–20; Bulloch's suggestion is in a letter to Barron, 1 February 1865, Whittle Papers, folder II, no. 38.

59. See Page's two letters to Bulloch, 12 February 1865, in *ORN*, I, 3:737, and Whittle Papers, folder X, no. 24. The quote is from Bulloch to Barron, 10 February 1864, referring to a letter from Page of 8 February, in Whittle Papers, folder II, no. 39. The junior officers' petition is in Whittle Papers, folder II, no. 41; for a more detailed treatment of it, see Case and Spencer, *Civil War Diplomacy*, pp. 471–72; Lieutenant Samuel Barron, Jr., was one of the signers.

60. Various letters exchanged among the officials mentioned, dated from 10 to 16 February 1865, in Whittle Papers, folder II, nos. 39, 40, 41, 42, and folder X, nos. 23 and 25; also those in *ORN*, I, 3:735–41, dated between 9 February and 19 March 1865. Barron's draft response to the junior officers is in Whittle Papers, folder X, no. 23.

61. The quotes are from Page to Bulloch, 25 March 1865, *ORN*, I, 3:741–42; Page also wrote from Lisbon, 27 March 1865, ibid., pp. 743–45. For his voyage across the ocean and his actions in Havana, see Kennett, "The 'Stonewall'," p. 85, and Bulloch, *Secret Service*, 2:101–02. Captain Craven was court-martialed for his failure to engage the *Stonewall*. After the war the *Stonewall* was purchased for the Japanese navy and remained on active duty for thirty years.

62. Both Kennett ("The 'Stonewall'," p. 85) and Spencer (Case and Spencer, *Civil War Diplomacy*, pp. 471–72, 478–79) make these charges.

63. Godon to Welles, 3 June 1865, *ORN*, I, 3:539. Even Godon's opinion must be qualified: he inspected the *Stonewall* when she had been docked for a month after a trans-Atlantic crossing without making repairs.

64. See the dispatches from Belle Isle (31 January), Auray (1 February), and Nantes (2 and 7 February), AM, BB⁴/1346/II; see Case and Spencer, *Civil War Diplomacy*, p. 476, for French diplomatic actions to detain the vessel in Ferrol.

Chapter 8
Evaluations

1. Slidell to Benjamin, 20 April 1863, *ORN*, II, 3:741.

2. Whittle Diary, 19 November 1863.

3. Fauntleroy to Barron, Rome, 17 December 1864, Whittle Papers, folder X, no. 19; Page to Barron, Copenhagen, 5 January 1865, ibid., no. 20.

4. See the conclusions of Merli (*Britain and the Confederate Navy*), of Crook (*Powers*), of E. D. Adams (*Britain and the Civil War*), of Owsley (*Cotton Diplomacy*), and of Case and Spencer (*Civil War Diplomacy*).

5. Dayton to Seward, 30 July 1863, no. 329, SDC Despatches Fr., vol. 53.

6. "To intervene" does not imply military participation on the side of the South. In the case of France, it would have been a recognition of what Count Mercier (French minister to the United States), Thouvenel, and Napoleon III would have considered to be an accomplished fact: the separation of those states forming the Confederate States and their successful establishment of a new sovereign nation. Military intervention was not contemplated as a desirable thing in England even by Palmerston's critics, and certainly not by him or Russell. Also, there were good reasons in both France and England to oppose the separation because both countries saw a value in a stable North America. The studies of Crook and Merli make these points clear. Those studies also indicate that the course of battles influenced specific actions of the British government. Merli maintains that Antietam was significant in Palmerston's thinking, as I have indicated above; Crook maintains that Gettysburg affected the British detention of the Laird rams.

7. See above, Chapter 4.

8. Crook, *Powers*, p. v.

9. Bulloch, *Secret Service*, 2:68–72.

10. "The Decision and Award" of the Geneva Arbitration Tribunal, 14 September 1872, IUP Area Studies, *The United States*, 58:15–17.

Bibliography

Official Archives

France.
  Archives de la Marine. Paris.
    Fonds BB^4 1345, 1346.
  Archives du Ministère des Affaires Etrangères.
    Paris.
      Correspondance Politique.
        Angleterre, 1861–1865.
        Etats-Unis, 1861–1865.
      Correspondance Politique Consulaire.
        Etats-Unis: Richmond, 1861–1865.
      Correspondance Consulaire.
        Etats-Unis: Richmond, 1861–1865.
      Fonds Divers.
        Guerre des Etats-Unis, 1861–1865 (Etats Confédérés; Droit Maritime).
  Archives Nationales. Paris.
    Ministère de la Marine.
      Fonds BB^4 419; GG^2 42.
Great Britain.
  Public Record Office. London.
    Foreign Office Series.
      France. Despatches to and from Lord Cowley, 1861–1865.
      United States. Despatches to and from Lord Lyons, 1861–1865.
    Russell Papers.
United States.
  National Archives. Washington.
    Foreign Office Division. State Department Correspondence.
      France, Despatches, 1861–1865.
      France, Instructions, 1861–1865.
      Great Britain, Despatches, 1861–1865.
      Great Britain, Instructions, 1861–1865.

Private Papers

Bigelow, John. Papers. New York Public Library. New York City.
Maury, Matthew Fontaine. Library of Congress. Washington, Manuscript Division.
  Diary, 1861–1865.
  Papers, vols. 14, 17, 18, 19.
North, James H. Diary. University of North Carolina Library. Southern History Collection #862. Chapel Hill, N.C.
Palmerston, Henry John Temple, Viscount. Papers. Historical Manuscripts Commission. National Register of Archives. London.
Whittle Papers. Kirn Memorial Public Library. Norfolk. Correspondence of Commodore Barron and other Confederate navy officers in Europe, 1863–1865. Diary of William C. Whittle, Jr.
Whittle, William Conway. Papers. University of Virginia Library. Manuscripts Department. No. 3973, MSS ViU 661233.

Published Sources and Memoirs

Anderson, Edward C. *Confederate Foreign Agent: The European Diary of Major Edward C. Anderson.* Edited with a prologue and an epilogue by W. Stanley Hoole. University, Ala.: Confederate Publishing Co., 1976.
Bigelow, John. *Retrospections of an Active Life.* 2 vols. New York: Baker & Taylor Co., 1909.
Bulloch, James D. *The Secret Service of the Confederate States in Europe or How the Confederate Cruisers Were Equipped.* 2 vols. Liverpool, 1883. Reprint with a new introduction by Philip Van Doren Stern. New York and London: Thomas Yoseloff, 1959.
Case, Lynn M., ed. *French Opinion on the United States and Mexico, 1861–1867. Reports of the procureurs généraux.* New York: Appleton-Century, 1936.
Great Britain. *Hansard Parliamentary Debates.* 3rd series. Vols. 170 (27 March–28 May 1863), 174 (15 March–3 May 1864), 203 (11 July–10 August 1870), 206 (2 May–13 June 1871).
————. House of Commons. *Sessional Papers.* Vol. 72 (1863). London, 1863.
————. House of Commons. *Parliamentary Papers.* Irish University Press Area Studies Series, *The United States of America.* Vol. 17, *The American Civil War.* Vols. 56–59, *The Treaty of Washington.* Shannon, Ireland: Irish University Press, 1971.
Keeler, William Frederick. *Aboard the USS Monitor: 1862. The Letters of Acting Paymaster William Frederick Keeler, U.S. Navy to His Wife, Anna.* Edited by Robert W. Daley. Naval Letters Series, vol. 1. Annapolis: United States Naval Institute, 1964.
Kell, John McIntosh. *Recollections of a Naval Life Including the Cruises of the Confederate States Steamers "Sumter" and "Alabama."* Washington: Neale Co., 1900.

Lacan, Adolphe Jean Baptiste. *Plaidoirie de M. Lacan pour M. Arman contre les Etats-Unis d'Amerique.* Paris: Dubisson, 1868.

Publications of the Navy Records Society. Vol. 49. *Documents Relating to Law and Custom of the Sea,* 2 vols. Edited by Reginald G. Marsden. Vol. 1. London, 1915.

Richardson, James D., ed. *A Compilation of Messages and Papers of the Presidents, 1789–1897.* Vol. 7. New York: Bureau of National Literature, 1896–99.

Semmes, Admiral Raphael. *Memoirs of Service Afloat during the War Between the States.* Baltimore: Kelly, Piet & Co., 1869.

Sinclair, Arthur. *Two Years on the Alabama.* Boston: Lee & Shepard, 1896.

United States. Department of the Navy. *Official Records of the Union and Confederate Navies in the War of the Rebellion.* 30 vols. and index. Series I, vols. 1–3; series II, vols. 1–3. Washington, 1894–1927.

————. Department of the Navy. Naval History Division. *Civil War Naval Chronology: 1861–1865.* Washington: Government Printing Office, 1971.

————. Department of the Navy. Office of Naval Records and Library. *Register of Officers of the Confederate States Navy: 1861–1865.* Washington: Government Printing Office, 1931.

————. Congress. House. *Papers Relating to the Foreign Relations of the United States.* Part 2. 42d Cong., 3d sess., Executive Document 1, Part 1. *Papers Relating to the Treaty of Washington.* 4 vols. Vol. 1, *Geneva Arbitration.* Washington: Government Printing Office, 1872.

Waddell, James I. *C.S.S. Shenandoah: The Memoirs of Lieutenant Commanding James I. Waddell.* Edited by James D. Horan. New York: Crown Publishers, 1960.

Secondary Sources

Adams, Charles Francis, Jr. *Lee at Appomattox and Other Papers.* Cambridge, Mass.: Houghton, Mifflin & Co., 1902.

Adams, Ephraim Douglas. *Great Britain and the American Civil War.* 2 vols. New York: Russell & Russell, 1925.

Anderson, Olive. *A Liberal State at War.* London: Macmillan & Co.; and New York: St. Martin's Press, 1967.

Barker, Nancy Nichols. "France, Austria and the Mexican Venture." *French Historical Studies* 3 (1963): 224–45.

Baxter, James Phinney, 3rd. *The Introduction of the Ironclad Warship.* Cambridge, Mass.: Harvard University Press, 1933.

Beaman, Charles C., Jr. *The National and Private "Alabama Claims" and Their "Final and Amicable Settlement."* Washington: W. H. Moore, 1871.

Bernath, Stuart L. *Squall Across the Atlantic.* Berkeley and Los Angeles: University of California Press, 1970.

Best, Geoffrey. *Mid-Victorian Britain, 1851–1875.* New York: Schocken Books, 1972.

Bigelow, John. *France and the Confederate Navy, 1862–1868.* New York: Harper & Brothers, 1888.

Blumenthal, Henry. *France and the United States: Their Diplomatic Relations, 1789–1914.* New York: W. W. Norton & Co., 1970.

Bourne, Kenneth. *Britain and the Balance of Power in North America 1815–1908*. Berkeley and Los Angeles: University of California Press, 1967.

Boykin, Edward. *Ghost Ship of the Confederacy. The Story of the Alabama and her Captain, Raphael Semmes*. New York: Funk & Wagnalls Co., 1957.

Bradlee, Francis. *Blockade Running during the Civil War*. Reprinted from the historical collection of the Essex Institute, vols. 60 and 61. Salem, Mass.: Essex Institute, 1925.

Brooke, George Mercer, Jr. "John Mercer Brooke Naval Scientist." 2 vols. Ph.D. dissertation, University of North Carolina, 1955.

Carroll, Daniel B. *Henri Mercier and the American Civil War*. Princeton: Princeton University Press, 1971.

Case, Lynn M. *Edouard Thouvenel et la Diplomatie du Second Empire*. French translation by Guillaume de Bertier de Sauvigny. Paris: A Pedone, 1976.

———. *French Opinion on War and Peace During the Second Empire*. Philadelphia: University of Pennsylvania Press, 1954.

Case, Lynn M., and Warren F. Spencer. *The United States and France: Civil War Diplomacy*. Philadelphia: University of Pennsylvania Press, 1970.

Caskie, Jaquelin Ambler. *Life and Letters of Matthew Fontaine Maury*. Richmond: Richmond Press, 1928.

Chevalier, Michel. *La France, le Mexique et les Etats Confédérés*. Paris, 1863.

Cook, Adrian. *The Alabama Claims. American Politics and Anglo-American Relations, 1865–1872*. Ithaca: Cornell University Press, 1975.

Crook, David Paul. *The North, the South, and the Powers 1861–1865*. New York, London, Sydney, and Toronto: Wiley, 1974.

Davis, Charles S. *Colin J. McRae: Confederate Financial Agent*. Tuscaloosa: Confederate Publishing Co., 1961.

Delaney, Norman C. "Showdown at Cherbourg." *Civil War Times Illustrated* 15, no. 3 (June 1976): 16–21.

Dunham, Arthur L. *The Anglo-French Treaty of Commerce of 1860 and the Progress of the Industrial Revolution in France*. Ann Arbor: University of Michigan Press, 1930.

Durkin, J. T. *Stephen R. Mallory: Confederate Navy Chief*. Chapel Hill: University of North Carolina Press, 1954.

Ferris, Norman B. *Desperate Diplomacy: William H. Seward's Foreign Policy, 1861*. Knoxville: University of Tennessee Press, 1976.

———. *The Trent Affair: A Diplomatic Crisis*. Knoxville: University of Tennessee Press, 1977.

Fohlen, Claude. *L'industrie textile au temps du Second Empire*. Paris: Plon, 1956.

Gentry, Judith Fenner. "A Confederate Success in Europe: The Erlanger Loan." *Journal of Southern History* 36, no. 2 (May 1970): 157–88.

Gray, Wood. *The Hidden Civil War: The Story of the Copperheads*. New York: Viking Press, 1942.

Hanna, Alfred Jackson, and Kathryn Abbey Hanna. *Napoleon III and Mexico*. Chapel Hill: University of North Carolina Press, 1971.

Henderson, William O. *The Lancashire Cotton Famine, 1860–1865*. Manchester: Victoria University of Manchester, Publications, 1934.

Hoole, William Stanley. *Four Years in the Confederate Navy: The Career of Captain John Low on the C.S.S. Fingal, Florida, Alabama, Tuscaloosa, and Ajax*. Athens:

University of Georgia Press, 1964.

Horn, Stanley F. *The Gallant Rebel: The Fabulous Cruise of the C.S.S. Shenandoah.* New Brunswick: Rutgers University Press, 1947.

Huse, Caleb. *Supplies for the Confederate Army, How They Were Obtained in Europe and How Paid For. Personal Reminiscences and Unpublished History.* Boston: Press of T. R. Marvin & Son, 1904.

Jahns, Patricia. *Scientists of the Civil War: Matthew Fontaine Maury & Joseph Henry.* New York: Hastings House, 1961.

Jarvis, R. C. "The *Alabama* and the Law." *Transactions of the Historical Society of Lancashire and Cheshire* 3 (1959): 181–98.

Jenkins, Brian. *Britain and the War for the Union.* 2 vols. Vol. 1, Montreal and London: McGill-Queens University Press, 1974; Vol. 2, Montreal: McGill-Queens University Press, 1980.

Jessup, Philip C., and Francis Deák. *Neutrality: Its History, Economics and Law.* 4 vols. Vol. 1, New York: Columbia University Press, 1935.

Jones, Wilbur Devereux. *The Confederate Rams at Birkenhead: A Chapter in Anglo-American Relations.* Tuscaloosa: Confederate Publishing Co., 1961.

Kennett, Lee. "The Strange Career of the 'Stonewall.'" *United States Naval Institute Proceedings* 94, no. 2 (February 1968): 74–85.

Krein, David F. "Russell's Decision to Detain the Laird Rams." *Civil War History* 22, no. 2 (June 1976): 158–63.

Leary, William M., Jr. "The Alabama vs. the Kearsarge." *American Neptune* 29, no. 3 (1969): 167–73.

Lester, Richard I. *Confederate Finance and Purchasing in Great Britain.* Charlottesville: University Press of Virginia, 1975.

Maynard, Douglas H. "The Confederacy's Super *Alabama*." *Civil War History* 5, no. 1 (March 1959): 80–95.

Merli, Frank J. *Great Britain and the Confederate Navy 1861–1865.* Bloomington: Indiana University Press, 1970.

————. "Crown Versus Cruiser: The Curious Case of the Alexandra." *Civil War History* 9, no. 2 (June 1963): 167–77.

Merli, Frank J., William E. Geoghegan, Thomas W. Green, Captain R. Steen Steenson, R. D. N. "The South's Scottish Sea Monster." *American Neptune* 29, no. 1 (1969): 5–29.

Merli, Frank J., and Thomas W. Green. "Could the Laird Rams have Lifted the Union Blockade?" *Civil War Times Illustrated* 2 (April 1963): 14–17.

Merli, Frank J. and Charles S. Williams, eds. and trans. "The *Normandie* Shows the Way: Report of a Voyage from Cherbourg to Vera Cruz, 4 September 1862." *Mariner's Mirror* 54, no. 2 (1968): 153–62.

Midwinter, Eric. *Victorian Social Reform.* New York and London: Longmans, 1968.

Nevins, Allan. *The War for the Union.* Vol. 2, New York: Charles Scribner's Sons, 1960.

Owsley, Frank L. *King Cotton Diplomacy.* 2nd ed. Chicago: University of Chicago Press, 1959.

Owsley, Frank L., Jr. *The C.S.S. Florida Her Building and Operations.* Philadelphia: University of Pennsylvania Press, 1965.

Parkes, Oscar. *British Battleships.* London: Seeley Service & Co., 1970.

Perry, Milton F. *Infernal Machines: The Story of Confederate Submarine and Mine Warfare.* Baton Rouge: Louisiana State University Press, 1965.

Phillimore, Robert. *Commentaries upon International Law.* 3rd ed. Vol. 1, Philadelphia: I. & J. W. Johnson, 1854.

Prest, John M. *Lord John Russell.* London: Macmillan & Co.; and Columbia, S.C.: University of South Carolina Press, 1972.

Ridley, Jasper. *Lord Palmerston.* London: Constable, 1970.

Roberts, W. Adolphe. *Semmes of the Alabama.* New York: Bobbs-Merrill Co., 1938.

Scharf, J. Thomas. *History of the Confederate States Navy: From Its Organization to the Surrender of Its Last Vessel.* New York: Rogers & Sherwood, 1887.

Smith, Goldwin. *The Treaty of Washington 1871.* Ithaca: Cornell University Press, 1941.

Soley, James Russell. *The Blockade and the Cruisers.* New York: Jack Brussel, 1890.

Southgate, Donald. *"The Most English Minister . . . " The Policy and Politics of Palmerston.* New York: St. Martin's Press, 1966.

Stern, Philip Van Doren. *When the Guns Roared: World Aspects of the American Civil War.* Garden City, N. Y.: Doubleday & Co., 1965.

Summersell, Charles Grayson. *The Cruise of the C.S.S. Sumter.* Tuscaloosa: Confederate Publishing Co., 1965.

Thompson, Samuel Bernard. *Confederate Purchasing Operations Abroad.* Chapel Hill: University of North Carolina Press, 1935.

Tilby, A. Wyatt. *Lord John Russell: A Study in Civil and Religious Liberty.* London: Cassell & Co., 1930; and New York, 1931.

Todd, Richard Cecil. *Confederate Finance.* Athens: University of Georgia Press, 1954.

Vandiver, Frank E., ed. *Confederate Blockade-Running Through Bermuda, 1861–1865: Letters and Cargo Manifests.* Austin: University of Texas Press, 1947.

Walpole, Spencer. *Life of Lord John Russell.* 2 vols. New York: Longmans, Green & Co., 1889.

West, Warren R. *Contemporary French Opinion on the American Civil War.* Baltimore: Johns Hopkins Press, 1924.

Williams, Frances Leigh. *Matthew Fontaine Maury: Scientist of the Sea.* New Brunswick: Rutgers University Press, 1963.

Wood, W. Birkbeck, and Sir James E. Edmonds. *Military History of the Civil War: With Special Reference to the Campaigns of 1864 and 1865.* New York: G. P. Putnam's Sons, 1937.

Index